W9-BTD-679

BLACKS IN THE NEW WORLD
August Meier, Series Editor

A list of books in the series Blacks in the New World
appears at the end of this book.

Other Books by August Meier and Elliott Rudwick

BY AUGUST MEIER

Negro Thought in America, 1880-1915 (1963)
Negro Protest Thought in the Twentieth Century (1965)
(Co-edited with Francis L. Broderick)
Black Leaders of the Twentieth Century (1982)
(Co-edited with John Hope Franklin)

BY ELLIOTT RUDWICK

W. E. B. Du Bois: A Study in Minority Group Leadership (1960)
Race Riot at East St. Louis, July 2, 1917 (1964)

BY AUGUST MEIER AND ELLIOTT RUDWICK

From Plantation to Ghetto (1966; third edition, 1976)
CORE: A Study in the Civil Rights Movement, 1942-1968 (1973)
Along the Color Line (1976)
Black Detroit and the Rise of the UAW (1979)
Black Nationalism in America (1970)
(Co-edited with John H. Bracey, Jr.)
Black Protest Thought in the Twentieth Century (1971)
(Co-edited with Francis L. Broderick)

Black History and
the Historical Profession,
1915-1980

BLACK HISTORY
AND THE
HISTORICAL PROFESSION,
1915-1980

August Meier and Elliott Rudwick

UNIVERSITY OF ILLINOIS PRESS

Urbana and Chicago

© 1986 by the Board of Trustees of the University of Illinois
Manufactured in the United States of America
1 2 3 4 5 C P 5 4 3 2 1

This book is printed on acid-free paper.

Library of Congress Cataloging-in-Publication Data

Meier, August, 1923-
　Black history and the historical profession, 1915-1980.

　(Blacks in the New World)
　Bibliography: p.
　Includes index.
　1. Afro-Americans — Historiography — Addresses,
essays, lectures.　2. Afro-American historians —
History — 20th century — Addresses, essays, lectures.
3. Afro-Americans — Study and teaching (Higher) — United
States — History — 20th century — Addresses, essays,
lectures.　I. Rudwick, Elliott M.　II. Title.
III. Series.
E184.65.M45　　1986　　973'.0496073'072　　85-16817
ISBN 0-252-01269-0 (cloth; alk. paper)
ISBN 0-252-01274-7 (paper; alk. paper)

For Richard L. Wentworth
A.M.

For Helen and Stanford Gregory, Jr.
E.R.

CONTENTS

PREFACE

This book consists of five essays on selected aspects of the development of Afro-American history as a scholarly specialty since Carter G. Woodson founded the Association for the Study of Negro Life and History and the *Journal of Negro History* in 1915-16. Our original intention was to write a traditional kind of historiographical monograph examining the major scholarly contributions and on the basis of these to describe the principal changes in interpretation that have taken place in the field over the years. In the course of research the scope of our inquiry shifted. We grew less interested in analyzing specific works than in understanding the interrelations between the trajectory of a scholarly specialty and developments in the changing social milieu and in the profession at large. Moreover, except for certain aspects of slavery historiography, we have not given a systematic or detailed treatment to the various subspecialties in the field of Afro-American history. Or to state the matter somewhat differently, we have been chiefly interested in explaining the ways in which historians came to do their scholarly work in the history of American blacks. And accordingly we have focused on the historians' intellectual careers rather than on the monographs that they produced. Thus, this volume is not a standard historiography, but an examination of several topics that illuminate the rise and the transformation of black history as a research field.

We sought to find out what motivated individual scholars to do their research in black history, how their intellectual perspectives shaped their work, and how the motivations and perspectives of historians undertaking studies in the field changed over time. In this connection we were interested furthermore in understanding the relationship between historians' values and ideologies and the nature of their scholarly monographs. We have also explored the ways in which the actions of philanthropists, book publishers, history departments, and the major professional organizations affected the field over time. Finally we were interested in studying the nature of intellectual interaction among scholars and the extent to which such specific interaction, operating within a changing intellectual milieu, shaped the course of shifting historical interpretation. All of these involved assessing the impact of broad social changes in American race relations upon the nature of scholarly inquiry and brought us to the generational analysis that is at the heart of this book. Although it was not the question we started out with, the principal theme that emerged from our researches was the analysis of the process by which black history, originally a Jim Crow specialty ignored by nearly the entire profession, became legitimated into one of the liveliest and most active fields of study in American history.

Central to our research strategy were the interviews we conducted with over 175 scholars. By utilizing an oral history approach, we sought to examine with as much specificity as possible the dynamics behind the generational changes and to elucidate the nature of interaction among scholars in the field. We are aware of the problems inherent in all oral history, but our interviews provided us with data and illumination that the surviving printed and written sources by themselves could not begin to offer. A useful supplement to the interviews has been the manuscript collections that some historians have placed in depositories, where they are open to scholars. In a different context the archives of the philanthropic foundations also provided valuable information.

Our treatment has not been exhaustive. We have not been able to interview or treat every scholar who has made a contribution to the field, nor have we treated systematically the published corpus of the historians we have chosen to discuss. The essays themselves are on selected questions, and our use of monographic, manuscript, and oral data has been shaped accordingly.

A word as to the criteria employed in choosing individual historians for analysis and/or interview. The selection cannot, of course, be a statistically representative sample. Our focus is on the professionally trained historians, the products of the system of university graduate education that matured by the beginning of the twentieth century. We have also generally limited ourselves to individuals with Ph.D.s and a record of significant publication. Within these parameters our focus has been on students of the history of the black experience and race relations within the United States. In some instances, however, we have interviewed and discussed individuals who fall outside these categories because their particular experience and perspectives added to our understanding of the developments that we describe. We have discussed in our study virtually all of the scholars associated with Carter G. Woodson and all of the historians beginning with W. E. B. Du Bois who are generally regarded as having made major contributions to the field. Beyond that we have attempted to treat and interview a wide range of historians of many different experiences and viewpoints and have consciously included both well-established and younger, less well-known people.

ACKNOWLEDGMENTS

Our first debt is to our friend, David L. Lewis, who insisted that a historiographical study was in order and that we should do it (even though in the end our monograph turned out to be something very different from what he had in mind).

Most of all we want to thank our numerous colleagues in the field who agreed to be interviewed for this book. (A complete list of the scholars interviewed will be found in the "Essay on Sources.") Only four of the individuals we contacted refused to be interviewed, and we think that the overwhelmingly cooperative response, even from people whose work we have reviewed critically, speaks volumes for the profession. Although space considerations have prevented us from treating individually some of the scholars we interviewed, the information so generously supplied by all of them informs the generalizations and interpretations offered in this book. We hope that we have been true to the spirit of the information we obtained from our colleagues and that their trust in us is justified by the pages that follow.

Numerous librarians have greatly facilitated our work. We can name here only those who were the most helpful. Susan B. Barnard, Greg W. Byerly, Michael R. Cole, Martha L. Goold, and Ruth C. Main of the reference and interlibrary loan departments at the Kent State University Library were, as always, most cooperative. The personnel at the manuscript divisions at Tuskegee Institute's Library, Fisk University, Morgan State University, the Rockefeller Research Center, the University of California Los Angeles Research Library, the Library of Congress, the Schomburg Collection of the New York Public Library, and the Moorland-Spingarn Research Center at Howard University greatly aided our research when we visited those institutions. Linda K. Harvey at Tuskegee was most cooperative, and Esme Bhan of Howard was unstinting in searching out recondite information for us and in straightening out discrepancies in our data. Librarians at the State Historical Society of Wisconsin, the University of Mississippi, Harvard University, Columbia University, the Chicago Historical Society, the University of Massachusetts at Amherst, the University of North Carolina, and the Carnegie Corporation of New York enormously facilitated our work by photocopying portions of relevant manuscript collections in their possession. Kenneth Fones-Wolf of the University of

Massachusetts, Linda Evans of the Chicago Historical Society, Harold Miller at Wisconsin, and Patricia Haynes of the Carnegie Corporation were especially prompt and thorough in this regard. Registrars, alumni officers, and reference librarians at a score of colleges and universities were helpful in running down biographical data and confirming titles and dates of dissertations and especially master's theses. G. T. Robinson, reference librarian at the D. B. Weldon Library of the University of Western Ontario, was especially diligent in supplying us with sources and information about the Canadian historians who contributed to Woodson's publication program during the 1920s. Clifton H. Johnson, director of the Amistad Research Center in New Orleans, was helpful on a number of occasions in supplying copies of relevant materials in the center's holdings, including lending us microfilms of the Rosenwald Fund Archives. Our friends David Wigdor and Sandye Wigdor of the Library of Congress Manuscript Division and the National Academy of Sciences, respectively, more than once ferreted out important materials in the holdings of their respective institutions. Staff members of the American Historical Association and the Organization of American Historians kindly provided us with photocopies of relevant materials in their files. Morton Sosna, formerly with the National Endowment for the Humanities, supplied us with useful data on NEH fellowships awarded to individuals researching in black history. Arthur Schlesinger, Jr., kindly granted us permission to consult relevant documents in his father's papers.

Lorenzo J. Greene, Stanley Elkins, Kenneth Stampp, Bertram Wyatt-Brown, and David Brion Davis each shared with us important relevant documents in their possession. Lucious Edwards, archivist at Virginia State University Library, provided us with a copy of an unpublished paper he had written on Luther Porter Jackson. Jacqueline Goggin, Darlene Clark Hine, and Robert L. Harris, Jr., shared with us copies of as yet unpublished articles that provided us with important data; Goggin and Hine pointed us to certain manuscript collections; and with Harris we have had several highly stimulating dialogues. We are especially indebted to Harris for letting us see the original manuscript of his essay on the Committee on Negro Studies of the American Council of Learned Societies.* We are also indebted to Robert L. Zangrando, Otey Scruggs, Alfred Moss, Ronald L. Lewis, and Mary F. Berry for the insights and formulations that they offered in the course of our interviews with them.

A. Gilbert Belles was most helpful in supplying information that supplemented his dissertation on the Julius Rosenwald Fund. John Ricks of

---

* This was published as "Segregation and Scholarship: The American Council of Learned Societies Committee on Negro Studies, 1941-1950," *Journal of Black Studies* 12 (Mar. 1982).

Valdosta State College, who is writing a book on the Albany (Georgia) Movement of the early 1960s, fleshed out our information on Vincent Harding's role. Linda O. McMurry helped us unravel certain aspects of the career of Monroe N. Work. And we are thankful to Leroy Davis of Morehouse College for searching the catalogues of that institution for information on the introduction of a course in Negro history there.

We are particularly grateful for the support that this project received from the Kent State University Office of Research and Sponsored Programs, directed by Dean Eugene P. Wenninger, and for a grant-in-aid from the Rockefeller Research Center.

We thank the *American Historical Review* for permission to reprint material from August Meier and Elliott Rudwick, "J. Franklin Jameson, Carter G. Woodson, and the Foundations of Black Historiography," *American Historical Review* 89 (Oct. 1984).

Finally, we are deeply indebted to John H. Bracey, Jr., Carl N. Degler, Louis R. Harlan, William S. McFeely, Edward Pessen, and Benjamin Quarles for their careful reading of the entire manuscript and their numerous helpful suggestions. In addition, John Bracey was unfailingly helpful on numerous occasions as we were writing this book.

ABBREVIATIONS USED IN TEXT AND NOTES

ACLS   American Council of Learned Societies
AHA   American Historical Association
AHR   *American Historical Review*
ASNLH   Association for the Study of Negro Life and History
GEB   General Education Board
JAH   *Journal of American History*
JNH   *Journal of Negro History*
JSH   *Journal of Southern History*
LSRM   Laura Spelman Rockefeller Memorial
MVHA   Mississippi Valley Historical Association
MVHR   *Mississippi Valley Historical Review*
NAACP   National Association for the Advancement of Colored People
NHB   *Negro History Bulletin*
OAH   Organization of American Historians
SHA   Southern Historical Association
SSRC   Social Science Research Council

Carter G. Woodson as Entrepreneur: Laying the Foundation of a Historical Specialty

THE CAREER OF CARTER GODWIN WOODSON* (1875-1950), W. E. B. Du Bois observed just after the founder of the Association for the Study of Negro Life and History (ASNLH) had died in 1950, "illustrates what race prejudice can do to a human soul and also what it is powerless to prevent."[1] Woodson, the son of ex-slaves, was born in poverty, worked as a youth in a West Virginia coal mine, and was not able to begin high school until he was twenty. Yet he went on to become the second black American (after Du Bois) to receive a doctorate in history, and with his drive and vision was virtually single-handedly responsible for establishing Afro-American history as a historical specialty. Seeking to preserve and to publicize among both blacks and whites the historical record of the race, he created the ASNLH, established a learned journal, sponsored pioneering research, and had an influential role in encouraging the development of a whole generation of black scholars. On the other hand, while Woodson thus laid the foundations, he did not live to see Afro-American history either recognized by the mainstream of white historians as anything more than a marginal specialty or to be embraced by Negroes themselves with the enthusiasm that he had envisioned. These things did not come to pass until nearly two decades after his death.

It was his training at the turn of the century at the interracial Berea College, founded by the Kentucky abolitionist John G. Fee, that provided

---

* For other perspectives on Woodson's career, in addition to those discussed in this chapter, see especially Patricia W. Romero, "Carter G. Woodson: A Biography" (Ph.D. diss., Ohio State University, 1971), and Jacqueline A. Goggin, "Carter G. Woodson and the Movement to Promote Black History" (Ph.D. diss., University of Rochester, 1984).

Woodson with a path for upward mobility into a professional career. Then for a half dozen years he interspersed public-school teaching in Huntington, West Virginia, and the Philippine Islands with advanced study at the Sorbonne and at the University of Chicago, where he received his M.A. in 1908 with a thesis in European diplomatic history. Twelve months later he had completed his doctoral coursework at Harvard. For the next decade Woodson worked in the Washington, D.C., high schools, meanwhile completing his Ph.D. in 1912 under Edward Channing, with a dissertation on West Virginia's secession from the Old Dominion.[2] Even though his graduate research had not dealt with the black experience, Woodson personally had long been interested in the subject. Originally, in fact, he had planned to do his master's thesis on the history of the Negro church but dropped the idea, evidently because he found that adequate sources were inaccessible.[3] Once he had obtained his Ph.D., Woodson immediately embarked on the study of the Afro-American past, with his first monograph, *The Education of the Negro Prior to 1861*, appearing in 1915. Soon after, during the autumn and winter of 1915-16, when Woodson was forty years old, he established the ASNLH and inaugurated the *Journal of Negro History (JNH)*.

Coming to intellectual maturity amid the tide of disfranchisement, sharecropping, Jim Crow, and mob violence that marked what Rayford W. Logan has termed the "nadir" in the fortunes of American blacks during the post–Civil War era, Woodson sought to build and popularize a serious interest in Negro history at the apogee of popular and scientific racism in Western thought. In pursuing this task he represented the convergence of two distinct streams of historical publication: the long tradition of writing on the black past on the part of black intellectuals and polemicists, on the one hand, and the professionalization of American historical study and the triumph of "scientific" history, on the other.

Blacks had been writing about their experience in Africa and America since the antebellum period. Their books and pamphlets, largely informed by biblical arguments and celebrating both black contributions to ancient civilizations and more recent individual accomplishments, had been infused with the purposes of stimulating racial self-esteem and pride among blacks and of educating whites regarding Negro achievements and contributions. Through the first decade of the twentieth century nearly all of this work—like the bulk of the books on American history produced prior to the hegemony of the new graduate departments—came from the pens of popularizers rather than scholars. There had been, however, one important exception prior to the work of Du Bois and Woodson: in 1882 G. P. Putnam's Sons published George Washington Williams's *History of the*

Negro Race in America from 1619 to 1880. A minister and politician, Williams (1849-91) wrote in the tradition of self-trained American historians like George Bancroft and Francis Parkman; his two-volume book, the product of considerable digging in primary sources, was the first scholarly account of the history of black Americans.[4]

By the turn of the century growing numbers of the black intelligentsia, anxious to counter the pseudoscientific racism then reaching its crest, were urging the study of black history as a key to the development of racial pride and self-respect. Interest in studying and publicizing the race's history was being championed by black spokesmen ranging across the ideological spectrum of the period—from southern conservatives like the accommodating Alabama educators W. H. Councill and Booker T. Washington[5] to leaders of the radical wing of Negro thought, most notably Du Bois. Perhaps partly influenced by the example of the ethnic historical societies proliferating at the time, enthusiastic Negro bibliophiles in Philadelphia and the New York City area established, respectively, the American Negro Historical Society in 1897 and the Negro Society for Historical Research in 1911. These organizations can be regarded as foreshadowing Woodson's subsequent activities. In fact, when the *JNH* appeared in 1916, Arthur A. Schomburg, the secretary of the Negro Society for Historical Research, adjudged it as "a very creditable" effort that was "stealing our thunder."[6]

Meanwhile, the professionalization of historical scholarship—involving the development of graduate departments emphasizing "scientific" method and the rise of the American Historical Association and the Mississippi Valley Historical Association—happened to coincide with the peaking of racist thinking among American intellectuals. Early historical studies of slavery were centered at Johns Hopkins University, where they were largely executed within the institutional framework of Herbert Baxter Adams, a man who "thought it difficult for black and white men to live peaceably together with equal civil rights."[7] Studies of Reconstruction were an area of concentration under the more blatantly racist John W. Burgess and William Archibald Dunning at Columbia University. Nor did the so-called Progressive historians concern themselves with the question of racial justice. Neither Frederick Jackson Turner's interest in the American democratic ethos nor Charles A. Beard's materialist analysis of the economic motivations underlying the Constitution and the nineteenth-century sectional conflict included any concern about race as a moral issue. Turner, who ignored the subject, was himself a racist; the Beardian perspective, by relegating slavery to a purely economic matter over which contending economic interest groups fought and by discounting the moral motivations involved in the Civil War and Reconstruction, lent itself to a pro-southern interpretation. (Charles and Mary Beard themselves once wrote that "at no time during the long gathering of the storm did Garrison's abolition creed rise to the dignity of a first rate political issue in the North. Nobody but agitators, beneath the contempt of the towering statesmen of the age, ever dared to advocate it. No great political organization even gave it the most casual indorsement.")[8]

Representing an especially important amalgam of influences from both the late nineteenth-century scientific school and some of the early twentieth-century Progressive historians was U. B. Phillips, whose name would become virtually synonymous with slavery historiography with the appearance of *American Negro Slavery* in 1918, just three years after Woodson founded the ASNLH. A native Georgian, Phillips took his doctorate at Columbia under Dunning in 1902, but his approach to history was more decisively shaped by the inspiration of Turner and by the racist labor economist John R. Commons, both of whom were Phillips's colleagues at the University of Wisconsin (1902-8), where he composed his earliest articles on the plantation system and prepared his noted documentary *Plantation and Frontier Documents, 1649-1863.*[9] The gap between what most white historians were saying in the first half of the twentieth century and the perspective of the black historians is indicated by Woodson's apt observation about Phillips's *American Negro Slavery:* "In just the same way as a writer of the history of New England in describing the fisheries of that section would have little to say about the species figuring conspicuously in that industry, so has the author treated the negro in his work."[10]

On the other hand, the very fact that Woodson was asked to write this evaluation of Phillips's magnum opus for the *MVHR* indicates that there was always a degree of pluralism within the profession. There were indeed a few white historians — ambiguous though their own racial attitudes sometimes were — who perceived the significance of the blacks' role and of race as a moral issue in American history and who were supportive of study in this area. To the extent that Negro history elicited a sympathetic interest among white historians, it came principally from a small group of distinguished scholars with antislavery antecedents, people like Albert Bushnell Hart of Harvard and a president of the AHA; J. Franklin Jameson, for many years editor of the *AHR* and head of the Department of Historical Research at the Carnegie Institution of Washington; and Clarence W. Alvord, editor of the *MVHR*.[11] Jameson would come to play an important role in support of Woodson's operations. Both he and especially Hart encouraged Du Bois in the latter's historical research. Alvord exhibited what was, for that period, an unusual sensitivity in inviting Woodson to write occasional reviews for the *MVHR*. Another individual of strong antislavery antecedents, Frederic Bancroft, belonged to the same generation and would eventually make an important monographic contribution to Negro history in his *Slave Trading in the Old South* (1931). Finally, interestingly enough, even the native southerner William E. Dodd, possessing a relatively liberal view on race by the standards of his region, also provided a modest supportive role during his tenure as professor of southern history at the University of Chicago.

In this context there emerged the earliest handful of black intellectuals who, products of the graduate training available at leading universities, made pioneering scholarly contributions to the writing of black history: W. E. B. Du Bois, Richard R. Wright, Jr., and Benjamin Brawley.

The most distinguished of the group was, of course, Du Bois (1868-1963), who in 1895 was both the first black to receive a doctorate from Harvard and the first to earn a Ph.D. in history, writing his dissertation on *The Suppression of the African Slave Trade to the United States of America, 1638-1870*. It was his advisor, Hart, who suggested the topic and then arranged "with delicate compliment" for its publication the following year as the first volume in the Harvard Historical Studies series.[12] Hart personally was not an unalloyed racial egalitarian; he believed in the Teutonic origins of American democracy and thought that "the average of the Negro race is much below that of the white race."[13] On the other hand, he was a serious student of the abolitionist movement, served as a longtime trustee of Howard University, and was an early member of the *JNH* editorial board and ASNLH Council. Personally he sympathized with Washington's approach. Yet Hart also assured Du Bois of both his "friendship and the warmest interest in the cause for which you are so strongly battling." He once confided to his former student that although the latter had "sometimes preached strong and unpalatable doctrine," as "an extremist" in the tradition of William Lloyd Garrison he had "done a great work for your race—and for all races in the United States."[14] Du Bois himself enjoyed a warm relationship with his doctoral advisor. He recalled, "I became one of Hart's favorite pupils," and in fact he was a frequent visitor to his professor's home and also maintained a friendly relationship with Mrs. Hart.[15] Du Bois's own evaluation of Hart's writings was that the latter "has done much for the Negro in America."[16] Undoubtedly it was Hart who arranged for Du Bois to appear as a participant at the AHA convention in 1891 and again in 1909, when as AHA president the Harvard professor personally presided at "the general session" on which Du Bois presented his noted paper "On the Benefits of Reconstruction," which some months later appeared in the *AHR*. (In the discussion from the floor that followed Du Bois's presentation, Hart tactfully called upon Phillips "to speak extemporaneously," and the southerner equally tactfully confined himself to discussing the importance of studying black labor in the South since the Civil War.)[17]

Du Bois's appearances at AHA conventions and in the pages of the *AHR* established precedents that would have no sequels for decades. But they symbolized the importance of the role of this black scholar in the emergence of Negro history as a research specialty. Also indicative of Du Bois's role was the publication of his succinct survey of the black past in both Africa and America, *The Negro*, which appeared in 1915. The most widely learned Negro scholar of that era, Du Bois brought to bear in this volume not only the historical knowledge then available, but also the latest anthropological studies, including the work of Franz Boas; the volume was notable for its extensive, sophisticated discussion of the history and cultures of Africa south of the Sahara. Although it was never widely used as a textbook either in high schools or colleges, *The Negro*, appearing as it did in the year that Woodson founded the ASNLH, similarly attested to the crystallization of black history as a research specialty.

A second black to produce a doctoral dissertation on a historical topic was the African Methodist Episcopal (AME) minister Richard R. Wright, Jr. (1878-1967). Actually Wright took his degree at the University of Pennsylvania in 1911 in sociology; but it was a period when boundary lines between disciplines were less sharply defined than they are now— and, in fact, Du Bois at Harvard had pursued as much work in what today would be called sociology as he did in history. Wright's interest in history had likely been stimulated by his father, R. R. Wright, Sr. (1855?-1947), president of the Georgia State Industrial College at Savannah, and known for his pioneering research at the turn of the century on the role of blacks in the discovery and exploration of the New World. Wright Jr.'s own historical monograph was rooted in his personal involvement in social settlement work to improve the economic conditions of black migrants to northern cities, his earlier 1901 bachelor of divinity thesis at the University of Chicago having been on "The Industrial Condition of Negroes in Chicago." His dissertation, published in 1912 as *The Negro in Pennsylvania: A Study in Economic History*, was his final contribution to scholarship, for he decided to carve out a career not in academe but as an editor and a bishop of the AME church.[18]

Benjamin Brawley (1882-1939), a professor at Morehouse and later at Howard University, was a Baptist minister and English teacher who never received the doctorate, but during his period of postgraduate study at the University of Chicago worked under William E. Dodd. Dodd, a Wilsonian Progressive who can scarcely be classed as unprejudiced, nevertheless encouraged Brawley in the writing of his *Short History of the American Negro* (1913), a widely used survey. Dodd's interest impressed Brawley so much in that era of the "nadir" that he once wrote the Chicago professor: "This whole thing [racial oppression in the South] has been troubling you for years. What I am wondering is, with your great sincerity, how much farther you are going to be able to go without becoming—an abolitionist." Half a dozen years after his *Short History* appeared, Brawley confided: "I can never forget how you helped with the work at first."[19]

The surveys by both Brawley and Du Bois were published at a significant crossroads in the teaching and writing of Afro-American history. Appearing on the eve of the launching of the ASNLH, they had been written amid a rising agitation for the inclusion of courses on black history in the curricula of Negro schools and colleges. The impetus for the introduction of such courses appeared in two forms. On the one hand, there were pleas directed chiefly at incorporating into public school curricula materials that would inculcate black youth with a sense of racial pride and solidarity. At the same time there were efforts to introduce Negro history in the black colleges as part of a more analytical approach to the study of racial problems.

Popularizers like Arthur A. Schomburg and C. V. Roman—a Nashville physician known for his accommodating strategy toward southern racism and for his advocacy of separate "parallel civilizations"—argued with a decidedly nationalist fervor for the study of black history in public schools. Roman's pamphlet, *A Knowledge of History Is Conducive to Racial Solidarity* (1911), urged that an awareness of the "glorious deeds of Negro men and women" would "furnish an atmosphere of mutual cooperation and helpfulness that will change the winter of our discontent into the glorious summer of racial solidarity, that magic alembic in which most of our racial difficulties will disappear." Schomburg was of a similar turn of mind. In one speech he urged his black listeners to learn Arabic "because much of our life is undoubtedly wrapped up" in Africa's traditions and history; proposed to stimulate racial patriotism by the study of Negro books; and called for the inclusion of Negro history in the curriculum, since "it is the season for us to devote our time to kindling the torches that will inspire us to racial integrity." On the other hand, a highly assimilationist spokesman like Harry C. Smith, editor of the Cleveland *Gazette*, also insisted that "every Afro-American school ought for obvious reasons to compel its students to study Williams' *History of the Negro Race in America.*"[20]

More significant from the point of view of the long-range development of professional scholarship in the field was the inauguration of the first courses in black history at Negro colleges. In 1911-12 George Edmund Haynes, another member of the tiny new elite of black doctorates,* trained

---

* In all fields as of 1914 a total of only fourteen blacks had earned Ph.D. degrees.[21]

in sociology and economics at Columbia University (where in 1912 he was the first Negro to earn a Ph.D.), introduced a course in Negro history at Fisk University. (Required of all students in the junior class, the course would inspire two major scholars in the field—Charles H. Wesley and Luther Porter Jackson.) Lacking a suitable textbook Haynes at first assigned readings in Du Bois's *Suppression of the African Slave Trade,* Williams's *History of the Negro Race in America,* Washington's *Up From Slavery,* and Hart's *Slavery and Abolition.*[22] The following academic year Brawley started such a course at Atlanta Baptist College (later Morehouse), using his own just published *Short History* as a text.[23]

At Howard University Kelly Miller, professor of sociology and dean of the College of Arts and Sciences, and Alain Locke, professor of philosophy, led the faculty's agitation for the introduction of Negro studies. But the board of trustees was skeptical, even though Jesse E. Moorland, the most influential black trustee, would have liked to see Howard become a major center of research on black life and history.[24] Indeed, it was exactly with this end in mind that Moorland, persuaded by Miller, in 1914 had donated his extensive collection of a thousand books on the black experience to the university.[25] At that very time, beginning with the academic year 1913-14, materials on black history were being introduced into the curriculum of the university's Teachers College, but cloaked under the rubric of a course on the history of Negro education. (It is perhaps not entirely a coincidence that Woodson's first book, on *The Education of the Negro Prior to 1861,* was published in 1915 soon after this course began.) In 1917-18 this was expanded into a two-semester sequence in Negro history for students preparing to become teachers, taught by the future historian of Howard University, Walter Dyson. But such a course would not be offered in the university's College of Arts and Sciences until Woodson introduced it when he came to Howard in 1919.[26]

Woodson thus stood at the confluence of the rising interest in the race's past among the black intelligentsia that would flower during the New Negro movement of the 1920s and the appearance of that small cohort of blacks numbered in the ranks of the newly professionalized scientific historians. Woodson himself, in his passionate desire to save and make known the record of the race's accomplishments, and in his dedication to the spirit of the dry-as-dust turn-of-the-century empiricism that saw itself as arriving at historical truth, was thus heir to both a well-rooted black tradition of history-writing and also to the scientific methodology in which the new crop of doctorates was steeped. History for Woodson was a scientific search for the truth. Historical truth, knowledge of the past as it really was, would flow from a scientific investigation and presentation of the facts of the black experience in Africa and the Americas.

Woodson's justification for his work is best summed up in the oft-repeated phraseology that he was interested in preserving and publishing the records of the Negro, so that the race "may not become a negligible factor in the thought of the world." Thus, looking back on the ASNLH's acomplishments some ten years after its founding, he declared that his efforts to produce "scientific research" had "set forth with objectivity the story of this despised people that they may not become a negligible factor in the thought of the world."[27] In Woodson's view, dissemination of the scientific truth would, besides building self-esteem among blacks, help eliminate prejudice among whites. He aimed both "to inculcate in the mind of the youth of African blood an appreciation of what their race has thought and felt and done" and to publicize the facts of the black past among whites, so that the Negro "may enjoy a larger share of the privileges of democracy as a result of the recognition of his worth."[28]

Woodson tirelessly preached that as a race of people with a distinguished and heroic past, blacks could proudly claim "a great inheritance." As he put it in a speech at Hampton Institute in 1921:

We have a wonderful history behind us. . . . If you are unable to demonstrate to the world that you have this record, the world will say to you, "You are not worthy to enjoy the blessings of democracy or anything else." They will say to you, "Who are you, anyway? Your ancestors have never controlled empires or kingdoms and most of your race have contributed little or nothing to science and philosophy and mathematics." So far as you know, they have not; but if you will read the history of Africa, the history of your ancestors—people of whom you should feel proud—you will realize that they have a history that is worth while. They have traditions . . . of which you can boast and upon which you can base a claim for a right to a share in the blessings of democracy.

Let us, then, study . . . this history . . . with the understanding that we are not, after all, an inferior people. . . . We are going back to that beautiful history and it is going to inspire us to greater achievements. It is not going to be long before we can so sing the story to the outside world as to convince it of the value of our history . . . and we are going to be recognized as men.

In a more typical presentation at an ASNLH meeting in 1923 Woodson "sketched in brief the record of the Negro from time immemorial, mentioning the important contributions of the race to civilization and the necessity for the study of this record to inspire the race with a hope of greater achievement and to disabuse the mind of the white man of the idea of racial superiority." Negro History Week, inaugurated in 1926, was celebrated principally in black schools, but through it Woodson also aimed to attract white interest. In his efforts to universalize the celebration Woodson declared: "It is not so much a Negro History Week as it is History Week. We should emphasize not Negro History, but the Negro in history. What we need is not a history of selected races or nations, but the history of the world void of national bias, race hate and religious prejudice."[29]

In pursuit of these twin goals of building black pride and eroding white prejudice, Woodson in much of his writing placed his emphasis on black achievers and their contributions, on what Brawley called "Builders and Heroes."[30] More recent generations of historians have criticized Woodson for this. But he was thoroughly within both the nineteenth-century tradition of black historical writing that sought to build self-esteem and to mitigate the racism of the majority population and also the genre of the early immigrant histories being spawned in this era. Both he and the defenders of the hyphenated-Americans—and for very similar reasons—sought pride through exploring their group's past and, on the basis of what they discovered, argued for its acceptance into the mainstream of American society.

Woodson thus dedicated his life to advancing the race through the promotion of Negro history. Propagandizing for the black past functioned as his form of social activism. Yet it is not at all clear how Woodson's profound beliefs in the value and importance of black history were articulated with a broader perspective for elevating the race. Actually Woodson's worldview is something of a puzzle. Nowhere did he set forth a coherent racial philosophy in the way that Washington, Du Bois, and other spokesmen did. The fragmentary evidence available on this aspect of Woodson's thought is often so contradictory that one is even unsure whether the views expounded at one time or another were expressions of a genuine belief or were articulated for particular tactical reasons. His utterances indicate that he was wedded to a petit-bourgeois philosophy of individual and business striving. A longtime hostile critic of trade unions, he retained considerable skepticism about the labor movement even after the rise of the CIO. Woodson did follow the swing in black political opinion from Republican to Democrat in the 1930s, and Franklin D. Roosevelt seems to have been virtually the only white politician he admired. Yet in the editorials on contemporary events that he penned for the *Negro History Bulletin* during the 1940s he exhibited a skeptical—even cynical—stance about people and events and embraced no political or social program.[31]

Du Bois, ordinarily an astute observer of where his contemporaries stood ideologicaly, contended after Woodson's death that "he was not a follower of the school of Booker T. Washington." Yet Woodson certainly was no follower of Du Bois, and, in fact, was actually a life-long admirer of the Tuskegean. The first issue of the *JNH* carried a laudatory notice of the recently deceased Washington, labeling him a "man of vision" and without question one of the "greatest figures" in all of history. Woodson's text, *The Negro in Our History* (1922), accorded Du Bois brief, even-handed treatment. Woodson recognized that the Tuskegean, with all his power, "dictated the rise and fall of all Negroes occupying positions subject to the will of whites," yet the volume heaped encomiums upon the man who "as an educator . . . stands out as the greatest of all Americans . . . Washington's long silence as to the rights of the Negro . . . did not necessarily mean that he was in favor of the oppression of the race. He was aware of the fact that mere agitation for political rights could not at that time be of much benefit to the race, and that their [*sic*] economic improvement, a thing fundamental in real progress, could easily be promoted without incurring the disapproval of the . . . South." "Washington never advocated," he said elsewhere, "the abandonment of the struggle for the rights of his race. No man living at that time raised or spent more than he did to contest laws in the courts." Woodson once waxed eloquently: "No president of a republic, no king of a country, no emperor of a universal domain of that day approached anywhere near doing as much for the uplift of humanity as did Booker T. Washington."[32]

Though Woodson's disinclination to express a coherent philosophy of racial advancement confused an observer like Du Bois, it may have been quite conscious. After Woodson's death A. A. Taylor, one of the historians who had worked most closely with him, recalled that Woodson "divorced scholarship from leadership *per se*, refusing to function either primarily or specifically as a race leader."[33] On certain occasions Woodson could be quite outspoken about the evils of racial oppression, and he could even in a southern setting express his admiration for a rebel like Nat Turner.[34] Yet he consistently maintained that in his work he eschewed "controversial literature which beclouds, rather than clarifies, the vision." Promotional materials he sent out announcing the *JNH*'s inaugural issue assured the public that its purpose was not to debate ways of settling "the Negro problem," but simply "to exhibit the facts of Negro history," and a decade later Negro History Week was established "not to play up their grievances but to demonstrate what Negroes have actually achieved in spite of their handicaps." Publicizing the annual observance in 1935, Woodson explained: "The method employed by the Association . . . is not spectacular propaganda or fire-eating agitation. Nothing can be accomplished in such fashion. . . . The aim of this organization is to set forth facts in scientific form, for facts properly set forth will tell their own story. No advantage can be gained by merely inflaming the Negro's mind against his traducers. . . . The Association for the Study of Negro Life and History has no special brand [sic] for the solution of the race problem except to learn to think."³⁵ In the last years of his life, during the post–World War II era when black militance was reaching new heights, Woodson on occasion gave favorable notice to those who had led the struggle for reform — referring, for example, to the "great achievements of the NAACP" under the leadership of Walter White, whom he called "one of the most daring and effective men" of the century.³⁶ Yet he continued to distance himself and his work from that of organizations like the NAACP. "The work of the Association for the Study of Negro Life and History is educational and scientific," he declared a year before he died, and "the organization decries any effort to divert it from this channel. . . . The Negro History Week celebration has usually been kept clear of indignation meetings, protesting bodies, and agitation efforts. The Association does not object to such endeavors, but its approach to the solution of the problem confronting the Negro is through the channels of scientific research and education."³⁷

Woodson's disavowal of any radical bent, and the way in which he deliberately distanced himself from anything smacking of agitation, consciously or unconsciously functioned to advance the legitimacy of his work among important groups, both black and white, that were in a position to help his cause. His efforts appealed to associates of Washington and other conservative blacks and their white philanthropic friends. *The Education of the Negro Prior to 1861* sufficiently impressed Washington by its attention to early industrial education efforts, to black endeavors to support schooling on their own behalf, and to evidence of southern white help for black schooling that shortly before he died the Tuskegee principal invited Woodson to address his faculty. Washington's successor, Robert Russa Moton, was much interested in the black historian's program and became the most substantial Negro financial supporter during the ASNLH's early years.³⁸ Both educators consistently advocated study of the Negro's past as essential to creating racial self-esteem. Nothing that Woodson said about his aims was likely to antagonize such individuals or their white friends. Indeed anyone, even southern public school officials, who claimed to be interested in the blacks' advancement, could only support a nonagitational program that sought to instill racial pride. In reporting on the favorable reception accorded the second observance of Negro History Week, Woodson noted that "in parts of the South . . . the whites have been favorably impressed. They concede that in the education of Negroes some attention must be given to their own past in order that the race may have proper aspirations." A decade later a close associate of Woodson could even report that "the majority of the state superintendents in the South, as well as many local city and county superintendents, support and promote the celebration of Negro History Week and the other offerings of the Association."[39]

Woodson's own predilections led to friendships with Negro conservatives of the era. It is perhaps significant that in launching his enterprise he appealed to a person like Moton[40] for funds but not to Du Bois. Indeed, there never was any close relationship between the two pioneering Harvard Ph.D.s, Du Bois and Woodson. As one of Woodson's longtime associates put it, Woodson was a great admirer of Washington, but his relationship with Du Bois was "coldly distant." Although in 1923 Woodson invited Du Bois to speak at the ASNLH meetings and although Du Bois did make a single appearance in 1930,[41] the two never worked together, and on certain occasions they even clashed violently. How much this distance between them was based on ideology or social outlook is not entirely clear. Certainly personal incompatibility was a big part of the problem. Both men had highly sensitive egos, making it difficult for either to work easily with others. Additionally, Woodson may have envied the recognition accorded Du Bois's early work.

For his part Du Bois was always scrupulously fair in dealing with Woodson, whose contribution he greatly admired. When the ASNLH founder became the second black to earn a history Ph.D., the *Crisis* recounted his rise from coal miner to Harvard graduate. When the *JNH* completed its first year, Du Bois exclaimed in the *Crisis,* "Dr. Carter G. Woodson and his associates have a right to feel proud." It was Du Bois who was responsible for Woodson's receiving the NAACP's coveted Spingarn Award in 1926. As the *Crisis* editor put it in making this nomination, "He has done the most striking piece of scientific work for the Negro race in the last ten years of any man that I know."[42] Nevertheless, of the black scholars engaged in the study of Afro-American history before World War II, only Du Bois was not a member of Woodson's circle. Du Bois, the innovator and prophet, thus stood outside the mainstream of scholarship in the field of Negro history, dominated as it was by Woodson and his associates until nearly the middle of the century.

Naturally Du Bois was not among those consulted in the founding of the ASNLH. Rather Woodson, as he matured his plans for an organization that would collect and publish materials on Negro history, maintain a bureau of research, and sponsor a journal, turned to a group of Tuskegee supporters, whose connections were with the YMCA and the National Urban League rather than the NAACP. In laying the groundwork Woodson sought to enlist Jesse E. Moorland, senior secretary of the national YMCA's

Colored Department, whom he had come to know in Washington; A. L. Jackson, who had developed a friendship with Woodson while working at the black YMCA branch in the nation's capital and who was now in charge of Chicago's new Wabash Avenue YMCA; Jackson's friend, Dr. George Cleveland Hall, the Chicago surgeon and formerly personal physician to Washington; Monroe N. Work, since 1908 director of records and research at Tuskegee Institute;* and Robert E. Park, the University of Chicago sociologist and acquaintance of Hall and Jackson who had earlier spent a decade working with Washington at Tuskegee.[43] With the exception of Moorland, all of these individuals encouraged Woodson in his plans. Moorland's reservations did not of course stem from any skepticism about the importance of what the historian wanted to do, and in fact he described Woodson as "probably the best fitted man we could lay hands on anywhere in the country to do the work he is doing." But Moorland had wanted Woodson to carry out his program under the sponsorship of Howard University, as part of a plan to build that institution into a serious academic and graduate research center, akin to that at Johns Hopkins. "If such a thing could be done," he once wrote Woodson, "I would be able to realize my fondest hope and make the contribution to the race . . . which it has been my ambition to make through life."[44]

Woodson, engaging in research at the University of Chicago during the summer of 1915, secured Dr. Hall's assent to serve as president of the ASNLH and prevailed upon the reluctant Moorland to accept the position of secretary-treasurer. Finally, with a few of his black friends in Chicago Woodson organized the ASNLH at a meeting in the Wabash Avenue YMCA on September 9, 1915.[45] Woodson (who assumed the duties of editor and director of research), Hall, and Moorland were named executive officers. The council also included individuals like Garnet C. Wilkinson, principal of Washington's Dunbar High School; Robert E. Park and another white who taught at the University of Chicago, the prominent social worker Sophonisba P. Breckinridge. The list of associate editors of the *JNH* launched a few months later included Walter Dyson, Monroe Work, Benjamin Brawley, George Edmund Haynes, and Kelly Miller.

The configuration of officers and editorial board members is significant. Nearly all were black moderates and conservatives. A high proportion had been personally friendly with Washington; none was identified with the

---

* Earlier, however, Work, holder of an M.A. in sociology from the University of Chicago (1903), for a few years had been associated with Du Bois. The relationship grew out of their mutual interest in sociological research, Work providing Du Bois with materials for the 1903 and 1904 *Atlanta University Publications*. Then in 1905 Work attended the founding meeting of the Niagara Movement, but beginning in 1906 he became increasingly conservative in his outlook.

anti-Tuskegee radicals or (except for Miller, an ideological moderate well known for his efforts to "straddle" between the camps of Du Bois and the Washingtonians) with the NAACP. On the other hand, a substantial number were deeply involved with the moderate Urban League. Haynes, who had started his career as a YMCA worker, was at this time nearing the end of his service as the first executive secretary of the National Urban League. Park, early in 1917, had been elected the first president of the local Chicago affiliate. Similarly Jackson, Breckinridge, and Hall had also all been actively connected with the formation of the Chicago League; Breckinridge was also a board member of the national organization; and Hall, who succeeded Park as head of the Chicago unit, was a national vice-president by 1920.[46]

The most prominent among the circle of blacks active in the early work of the ASNLH was Jesse E. Moorland, who had agreed to become secretary-treasurer only because "Woodson insisted that I serve." As Woodson well knew, Moorland, given his credentials and connections, was an incomparable asset. As the Association's founder confided to the YMCA official: "Your interest in this cause and the confidence the people have in you, make you the most valuable man for the position." Among other things Moorland had developed vital contacts with important philanthropists. Heading YMCA work among urban blacks, beginning in 1910 he played the central role in raising funds for the erection of up-to-date brick buildings for black Y branches in fourteen cities across the country over the next decade. Moorland, a man of conservative leanings, was a racial diplomat who had been elected to the Howard University board of trustees along with Washington in 1907. Although Moorland aimed for the development of a distinguished liberal arts institution, critics at the time saw the choice of these two men as a plot to industrialize the university.[47]

The significance of Woodson's associating himself with Moorland and the others in this Tuskegee–YMCA–Urban League network was not lost on people in influential places. Hampton Institute's *Southern Workman* enthused that Hall, Moorland, "and the other names associated with them on the executive council and on the board of associate editors, guarantee an earnestness of purpose and a literary ability which will doubtless be able to maintain the high standard set in the first issue" of the *JNH*. In appealing to Moton for money, Woodson did not hesitate to state: "Dr. Moorland has a very exalted opinion of you and a very keen appreciation of your interest in all things pertaining to the uplift of the colored people."[48] More to the point Moorland and his colleagues on the council and editorial board had the respect of those philanthropists interested in Negro causes, most notably Julius Rosenwald and the Rockefeller family boards.

Thus Moorland's first successful fund-raising for the YMCA—his superlative efforts for the 12th Street Y in Washington—were greatly aided by a large donation from John D. Rockefeller, Jr. Fresh from this drive, Moorland at the end of 1910 turned his attention to Chicago, where he met the Jewish mail-order magnate Julius Rosenwald, who was then beginning his justly known philanthropies for Negro causes. Rosenwald had already pledged $25,000 for the black Chicago Y and was so impressed with Moorland that he volunteered to give an equal amount toward a YMCA building in any city where Moorland and the local citizens raised $75,000. Actually Rosenwald's first involvement in Negro philanthropy had begun with the fledgling National Urban League in 1910, and next to Rockefeller, he was the largest contributor to that organization during its early years. Soon after meeting Moorland, Rosenwald came to know Washington, who prevailed upon him to pour millions into erecting school buildings in southern rural areas.[49] It was not long before Rosenwald joined other supporters of Washington on the boards of the Rockefeller philanthropies, which were to play such an important role in encouraging the early work of the ASNLH.

The Rockefeller foundations were at the center of the network of philanthropies interested in Negro advancement, although only a tiny proportion of their monies went to black causes. In particular the General Education Board, founded in 1902, and the Laura Spelman Rockefeller Memorial, created in 1918 in memory of John D. Rockefeller Sr.'s wife, whose own concern about race relations stemmed from her abolitionist background, played important roles in the development of black education and scholarship. The Rockefeller boards sustained close relationships with persons connected with other charitable foundations established to aid black education, and who would, like the Rockefeller agencies, be involved in the history of Woodson's ASNLH. The network connections of James Hardy Dillard, whose many years of service on Woodson's ASNLH Council proved helpful for legitimizing the Association with white philanthropy, were a case in point. It was the GEB's president, Wallace Buttrick, who having consulted Washington, prevailed upon Dillard—then a Tulane University professor—to direct the work of two major philanthropies supporting black education in the South, heading the Anna T. Jeanes Fund in 1907 and later taking over Buttrick's own part-time work as general agent of the John F. Slater Fund in 1911.[50] Dillard, who was named a trustee of the GEB in 1917, was an unusually enlightened southerner for his time; although a tactful gradualist, this prominent leader in the southern interracial movement was greatly admired by both black conservatives and radicals such as Du Bois. For his part John D. Rockefeller, Jr., was personally devoted to Dillard.[51] Profoundly interested in the spirit that Dillard represented, the Rockefellers did much to encourage that frail postwar effort at southern interracial understanding, the Commission on Interracial Cooperation (CIC), several of whose leaders would be drawn into support of Woodson's work.[52] In fact, the CIC, established in 1919, benefited from substantial amounts of Rockefeller money, first channeled through the War Work Council of the YMCA and during the 1920s donated directly by the Laura Spelman Rockefeller Memorial.* Rosenwald, in a natural extension of his efforts to secure interracial cooperation through the YMCA, also contributed substantial sums to CIC.[54]

Also supporting the southern interracial movement, although disliked by the black radicals, was another philanthropy in which Dillard was active, and which would figure prominently in Woodson's affairs. This was the Phelps-Stokes Fund, established in 1911 in close collaboration with Washington and devoted primarily to fostering industrial education for blacks on both sides of the Atlantic.[55] Its president was Anson Phelps Stokes, secretary of Yale University, a trustee of the GEB and later of the Rockefeller Foundation; its chief executive was the Welsh-born Columbia University–trained sociologist, Thomas Jesse Jones. Earlier, as director of the Hampton Institute research department, Jones had recommended Monroe Work to Washington for the post he held at Tuskegee and had sought diligently but unsuccessfully to co-opt Du Bois for Hampton's research program. Joining the Phelps-Stokes Fund in 1913, Jones had become widely known for his critical examination, co-sponsored by the U.S. Bureau of Education, of black educational institutions.[56] From its inception the fund had encouraged the incipient southern interracial movement. Jones himself, firmly wedded to the brand of "interracial cooperation" fostered by Hampton and Tuskegee, was one of the cadre of people instrumental in establishing the CIC. Although the establishment of this body owed more to the dynamic drive of Will W. Alexander, the young Methodist minister and wartime YMCA worker among Negroes, Jones and his good friend Moton are credited with conceiving the idea when the two men were in France just after World War I ended, working together to allay the unrest among the black soldiers there.[57]

Stokes, in his capacity as secretary of Yale University, came to know another person who would lend significant support to Woodson's work: Edwin R. Embree, a descendent of the Tennessee emancipationist Elihu Embree and grandson of the founder of Berea College, where Embree attended the academy at the time that Woodson was pursuing his undergraduate degree there. After graduating from Yale, Embree worked on Stokes's staff, which brought him into contact with people like the pres-

---

* On the other hand, the officials at the cautious Rockefeller philanthropies were skeptical about contributing to the work of the NAACP, regarding that organization as overly "aggressive" in much of its activity.[53]

ident of the University of Minnesota, George E. Vincent, who, when he became president of the Rockefeller Foundation, arranged for Embree to join him as that philanthropy's secretary in 1917. In time Embree became a vice-president of the foundation. In these capacities he became well acquainted with the Rockefeller Foundation trustee Julius Rosenwald, and in 1928 moved over to become the Rosenwald Fund's president.[58]

How conscious Woodson was of the full extent of this network is unknown, although Du Bois was vividly impressed by it, charging that the GEB "by a system of interlocking directorates bids fair to dominate philanthropy toward the Negro." Certainly the ASNLH founder was aware of the highly publicized assistance that Rosenwald had lent Woodson's friends in the YMCA. And obviously substantial amounts of outside money were essential for the ASNLH: even in financing the *JNH*, donations were needed to supplement subscriptions, and more substantial philanthropy was imperative if a significant research program were to be implemented. Early efforts to raise substantial amounts of money from well-to-do blacks were unsuccessful. Once, in the course of a campaign to obtain $2,000 through individual contributions Woodson advised Moton: "You may be surprised to learn that every penny of the $1200.00 thus already pledged has come from white persons." Not until the 1930s would Woodson learn how to support even the non-research functions of his organization with money drawn primarily from the black community. Meanwhile, given the state of mind of both individual donors and organized philanthropy, Woodson would almost certainly have to attract funding from sources friendly to Tuskegee, Hampton, the YMCA, and the Urban League. As we have seen, the membership on his council and editorial board was eminently suited to appeal to just this sort of agency. Woodson himself once put the matter succinctly when he informed Moorland frankly, "The important duty of a member of an executive board is either to raise money or give money."[59]

Complicating Woodson's efforts to raise funds and carry out his program were certain personal characteristics. The qualities that were responsible for his achievement — the single-minded vision, the jealous guarding of his autonomy, the virtually dictatorial control he exercised over the Association — also posed serious difficulties when he sought support for ASNLH activities. He was consistently leery of linking his work with another black institution like a college or university that might have helped subsidize his operations. At the same time he insisted on retaining full personal control over the organization, leaving his other officers and council members without a significant voice in the managment of affairs. By all reports, in fact, Woodson was a passionately dedicated, authoritarian individual, determined to run the ASNLH and the *JNH* in his own way. All of those who worked with him agree that he made every decision; that he was, for example, the sole judge of articles submitted to the *JNH;* that he was "arrogant," "cantankerous," and "domineering." Moorland found that though pleasant in face-to-face contacts, "he can write the most insulting letters of any man I have ever had anything to do with," and that "he could put more acid and sting in a letter than any man I ever knew." Lorenzo J. Greene, one of those who worked closely with Woodson and among his most warmest admirers, once observed: "Enemies he makes in profusion. . . . But he doesn't care. . . . He belongs to that group of mortals who, unloving and unloved, are prized because they possess some unique attribute which the world desires."[60]

Du Bois put the matter concisely when in nominating Woodson for the NAACP's Spingarn Award he wrote, "Woodson is not a popular man." This was more than a matter of temperament and personal style. For beyond his cantankerous and dictatorial behavior lay a fierce desire for absolute independence in carrying forward the work as he saw fit. The historian Charles H. Wesley, who worked closely with Woodson for longer than anyone else, noted delicately: he was a "rugged individualist" possessed of "a type of intolerance and self-opinion" who, devoting himself to the cause with "an amazing self-denial . . . believed that it was necessary to work one's plans alone." Du Bois recalled that Woodson's own friends "concluded that he must be left to carry on his great work without interference in any way from others." As another associate of the ASNLH founder, L. D. Reddick, wrote Du Bois shortly after Woodson's death, "As you know, the Association has been really one man."[61]

All these qualities would create difficulties and controversies with both the black intelligentsia and with the white philanthropists and would place serious obstacles in the way of fulfilling his goals. Woodson's achievement in the face of such problems is a tribute to his vision, his determination, and his perseverance.

Woodson's style of operation was evident from the start, and dissatisfaction quickly developed among his friends on the ASNLH Council because he failed to consult them about financial and other matters. He himself once pointedly informed Rosenwald's secretary, William C. Graves, "You readily understand that the offices of President and Secretary-Treasurer are largely cooperative. These functionaries are not sufficiently active to determine the policy of the Association. The Executive of the Association, the chief factor in shaping its destiny, is the Director, who, in this case, is the man who founded the Association almost seven years ago and sacrificed all his means and the most promising period of his life to establish it." Moorland attempted to get Woodson to be more businesslike, but Hall became so disgusted that he refused to serve more than one term, and Moorland himself concluded that Woodson "is not temperamentally adapted to working harmoniously with other people and he needs a job where he can be trustee, president of the faculty and janitor all at once."[62]

Anxious to begin operations as soon as the Association was launched, Woodson secured pledges for support of the *JNH* from Park, Jackson, and Hall and was prepared to pay the office expenses at first himself. Indeed, during the early years the Association's routine expenditures were met from his own pocket, Woodson donating up to half his salary to absorb the annual deficit.[63] The first issue appeared only four months after the Association's founding, Woodson having written all four articles himself, signing the names of friends to three of them, and borrowing on his life insurance to pay the printer.[64] Breckinridge found this behavior so irregular that she promptly resigned from the council. But Woodson would later proudly recount the incident: " 'A white woman who was a member of the Board of Directors, became indignant, asked me in a letter how dare I plunge the Association some $350 in debt and sent in her resignation. But the *Journal* and the Association are very much alive today.' "[65]

The *Journal*'s inaugural number was well received. J. Franklin Jameson, editor of the *AHR,* gave it a "cordial welcome," describing it as "an excellent beginning" and pronouncing the Association's objectives "admirable." Edward Channing wrote, "How much I liked the looks of the publication . . . and how good the matter of this first number seemed to me to be." Even the less sympathetic Frederick Jackson Turner informed Woodson, "It is a credit to its editors and contributors and I hope it may continue to preserve high standards and to prosper." Du Bois also wrote, proclaiming, "Your Journal is excellent."[66] Woodson at once sent 200 copies to "philanthropists and scholars" and embarked upon a campaign to find "an interested philanthropist" ready to provide a large subsidy for the publication. Such publicity brought subscriptions from historians and university libraries, but no large donations. The nearest Woodson came to realizing his goal was when Hall persuaded Rosenwald to pledge $100 per quarter for the *JNH.*[67] With this offer in hand Woodson promptly approached the GEB. But although Rockefeller, Jr., was personally interested, the board rejected the request because the ASNLH was "too small an operation."[68] Accordingly for the next five years Rosenwald's subsidy would remain the Association's largest single source of outside revenue.

By the spring of 1917 Woodson, discouraged over the accumulated debts and unhappy with his friends' efforts to make him accountable to the council, talked of resigning. However, the founder spurned Park's attempt to have him and the *Journal* go to Howard University.[69] At this juncture, Du Bois, aware of the ASNLH's fiscal problems and perhaps having learned of the internal wrangling, proposed that Woodson bring the *Journal* under the sponsorship and partial subsidy of the NAACP. Woodson was so desperate by then that he actually considered that idea. But given the incompatibility between the personalities of the two men, the basically conservative leanings of both Woodson and Moorland, and most of all Woodson's need for complete autonomy, it was undoubtedly inevitable that the proposal would founder.

In any event Du Bois's offer to incorporate the *JNH* into the NAACP's Department of Publications and Research, "with promise of as much autonomy as was allowed me," was a serious one and had the support of other top NAACP officials. On a fund-raising trip to Boston, Woodson found that NAACP President Moorfield Storey was sufficiently interested to purchase an ASNLH life membership, and in complete agreement with Du Bois "that the N.A.A.C.P. should do something to save the Journal." Moorland was probably negative to the idea, and besides, Woodson's notion of cooperation with the NAACP precluded a satisfactory arrangement. As Du Bois recalled, "He considered, but refused, unless an entirely separate department was set up for him. This the Board refused to consider as I knew it would."[70]*

Having rejected the NAACP overture, Woodson was worried. For with Hall irritated and wishing to step aside as ASNLH president, Rosenwald's continued support was doubtful. Park feared "that if Hall goes, Rosenwald will lose interest." Woodson hoped to shore things up by securing Moton for the council and, reminding Moorland that the latter had promised to help find alternative funding if Woodson turned down the Du Bois offer, pleaded with the Y secretary to raise money to pay pressing bills. Moorland proved as good as his word, taking the initiative of writing Rosenwald an enthusiastic letter about Woodson's "splendid progress." Woodson also adopted the strategy of revamping the council to make it more palatable to white philanthropy. He and Moorland agreed that Park would make an ideal president and that the new council should be mostly white.[72] Although the approaches to Moton failed,[73] the three black members of the reconstituted body were all individuals of decidedly conservative leanings: besides A. L. Jackson, the others were John R. Hawkins, a Wash-

---

* Moorland and Du Bois had a distant relationship but always kept the lines of communication open. The *Crisis* gave a fair amount of attention to black YMCA work. Privately Moorland could take the initiative in defending Du Bois from gross misinterpretation, even though he did not personally agree with the latter's position. On one occasion, at a time of serious strain in his relations with Moton, Moorland wrote the Tuskegee principal: "I join with you, as I have always done, in fighting the common enemy, and not fighting among ourselves. I have been accused, for this reason of being friendly to both yourself and Dr. Du Bois. I stand guilty of the charge."[71]

ington, D.C., banker, Republican party stalwart, and financial secretary of the AME church, and Robert E. Jones, the highly accommodationist editor of the Methodist church's New Orleans *Southwestern Christian Advocate,* who would soon become the first black bishop in the Methodist Episcopal church.[74] While the carefully selected group of six whites included the NAACP's Storey, more significantly all the others were individuals in the network of philanthropies—James Hardy Dillard, Thomas Jesse Jones, Urban League board chairman L. Hollingsworth Wood, and philanthropists Julius Rosenwald and George Foster Peabody. Peabody, a prominent investment banker and Progressive Era reformer, Hampton and Tuskegee trustee, and former treasurer of the GEB, had been the one to inaugurate the Negro YMCA building program with a gift toward one in his native Columbus, Georgia, in 1907; he also served as chairman of the advisory committee to the Colored Men's Department of the YMCA.[75] Rosenwald was pleased "to serve on the Executive Council with Dr. Dillard, Mr. Wood, Mr. Storey, and Dr. T. J. Jones."[76]

The invitation to Thomas Jesse Jones was extended just about the time that his survey on Negro education appeared in print. With Du Bois having sounded the alarm in the January 1917 *Crisis,* Woodson was certainly aware of the reports circulating even before the study's publication concerning its highly negative assessment of the black colleges. Indeed, the two volumes when they appeared confirmed the worst, and Du Bois denounced them as "dangerous" both in their overall analysis and in their specific evaluations of individual institutions, charging that the Phelps-Stokes executive "again and again" insisted that academic and higher education among blacks "should be restricted" in favor of industrial and agricultural training. Moreover, the *Crisis* editor pointed out that the Jones study, in its plea for greater cooperation with the white South and for more unity among the interested boards and foundations (or what Du Bois called "the ring of rich philanthropists represented by the General Education Board" who "sneered" at the black liberal arts colleges and who "long ago surrendered to the white South"), meant "that the Negro must be trained according to the will of the white South and not as the Negro desires."[77] Woodson, however, responded quite differently. He commented quite favorably in the *JNH* on a recent conference where black and white educators used it as a basis for proposing "a more extensive cooperation of all agencies in the uplift of the Negro"—exactly the kind of monolithic unity that Du Bois feared. Woodson also arranged to have Jones's good friend, Monroe Work, review the study in the *Journal.* For its part, the Phelps-Stokes Fund, responding to Jones's appointment to the ASNLH Council, doubled its previous modest annual $100 contribution.[78]

The fruits of Woodson's strategy were evident at the ASNLH's first biennial convention, held in the autumn of 1917. At his invitation four leaders from the philanthropies—Peabody, Dillard, Jones, and Rosenwald himself—and four black YMCA officers—Moorland, Moorland's assistant for youth work, Channing H. Tobias, Jackson, and John W. Davis, secretary of Washington's 12th Street Y—turned up for the meeting. Woodson used the opportunity to advance his plans to broaden the work of the ASNLH. Although he was still digging deeply into his own salary to keep the organization afloat,[79] Woodson's concern at this point was less mere financial solvency than in obtaining funds that would enable him to embark upon his research program. After both Dillard and Jones, speaking at this convention, endorsed his hopes for trained investigators to undertake the work immediately,[80] Woodson promptly applied to both Rosenwald and the GEB for appropriate funding.

Couching his requests in the vocabulary of "social adjustment" used by the southern interracialists and their philanthropic allies, Woodson explained that "only through ethnological and historical investigation can men understand their beginnings, their achievements and their possibilities . . . the Negro of today . . . exhibits social phenomena which require scientific investigation to determine how the various elements of society may best cooperate with the [black] race for the greatest good." In Rosenwald's case Woodson even went so far as to ask for $100,000 to endow a "Rosenwald Foundation for the Study of the Negro."[81] Turned down by both philanthropies, he temporarily abandoned the quest for research money, but within weeks returned to the same sources requesting operating expenses for the ASNLH. Utilizing the good offices of one of his new council members, Woodson was able to prevail upon Peabody to contact both Rosenwald and the GEB. Simultaneously, undoubtedly prodded by Moorland, Rosenwald's secretary urged his employer to help out in paying off the ASNLH's obligations. The GEB's Buttrick, who consulted Dillard on the matter, was impressed: "It would seem that with that splendid Executive Council it ought to be possible to secure the small sum of money that is necessary to secure the permanence of this valuable Journal."[82] But again both sources denied the request.[83]

By the end of 1918 Woodson's situation was, if anything, more precarious than ever. Moton had personally interceded with Peabody to see if something further might be done to raise money among the latter's friends, but without avail. Woodson addressed a fund-raising appeal to a select group of prominent blacks, but, as he well knew, few of them were in a position to make large contributions, and the most he could hope for were only "small sums."[84] With Rosenwald indicating that the maintenance of his $100 quarterly contributions to the *Journal* was contingent on securing matching funds from others, Woodson prevailed upon Storey and the YMCA's 1918 national president, the mining fortune heir Cleveland H. Dodge, to pledge $400 annually.[85] Woodson also made a systematic approach to individual trustees of Tuskegee Institute and as a result obtained commitments from people like Frank Trumbull, chairman of the board of directors of the Chesapeake and Ohio Railroad, and William G. Willcox, the New York insurance underwriter who chaired the school's trustee board.[86] Given both the postwar inflation and an actual decline in *Journal* subscriptions, these donations were vital to the ASNLH; and Woodson wanted his readers to know that it had been "persons of means" who provided "sufficient relief to keep the work going."[87]

Meanwhile, in the spring of 1919 steps were once again taken to reorganize the council's membership, this time with an equal number of prominent names from both races. Dodge declined to serve, but Willcox accepted, "glad to be associated with Mr. Rosenwald, Mr. Peabody, Mr. Dillard, and others of your Board." So also did another prominent personage with Tuskegee credentials: Emmett J. Scott, Washington's devoted private secretary, who had just become secretary-treasurer of Howard University. Woodson promptly enlisted Scott's help in the continuing campaign to raise money from wealthy whites. Scott also appeared on the program of the second biennial ASNLH convention in June 1919, along with Work, Dillard, Haynes, Moorland, Davis, and Howard University's white president, J. Stanley Durkee. There was much discussion at this meeting by Durkee, Dillard, and others of the pedagogical and identity-building values of black history.[88]

The participation of Scott and Durkee in the proceedings was scarcely coincidental, since Woodson would join the Howard faculty that autumn. This was certainly the result of Moorland's intervention,[89] done with the aim of solving the Association's chronic financial problems and promoting the study of black history at the university. But it turned out to be a stormy year, and in the end Woodson left Howard in a bitter row with Durkee. Given both Woodson's personality and Durkee's serious limitations, the president was unwise in assigning many other responsibilities to the man he had originally employed to be publications director. Woodson taught black history to advanced students, but spent most of his time as dean of the School of Arts and Sciences.[90]

Woodson's first brush with Durkee came in December 1919, when the American Negro Academy, an organization of black intellectuals founded in 1897 by Alexander Crummell, invited the radical socialist A. Philip Randolph to speak at its annual conference. In the days of the Red Scare and the Palmer raids, this was a bold and controversial act, the militant editor of the *Messenger* magazine being highly suspect at the Department of Justice. Nevertheless, although Moorland objected, the academy's executive committee, at the high point of postwar black militance, unanimously favored inviting the fiery Marxist. Randolph's address and his eloquent denunciation of racist, capitalist society provoked a spirited debate from the audience. Woodson just six months earlier had praised Dillard's southern University Commission on Race Relations on the grounds that its efforts for interracial understanding were needed to prevent socialist and Bolshevik doctrines from spreading among blacks. But now, stirred by the charismatic Randolph's "splendid" oration, and mirroring the audience's enthusiasm, Woodson took the floor and to "deafening" and extended applause declared "Mr. Randolph is a prophet."[91]

Within days, Republican Senator Reed Smoot rose in Congress to denounce the presence of Bolshevik literature in the Howard University library, and Durkee promptly removed the single offending book. Woodson later recalled that when he protested to Durkee against this infringement of academic freedom, the Howard University president "countered by pulling from his files a letter from A. Mitchell Palmer's Department of Justice . . . that I had communistic tendencies. . . . I was branded as a red because I publicly commended the stand of a Negro who advocated justice and equality in the administration of the affairs of the government." Thereupon Woodson promptly backpedaled and sent the senator an innocuous request for financial help that pictured the ASNLH as an effort "to apply science to the solution of the race problem. . . . . The method employed is to interpret the Negro to the white man by inculcating an appreciation of the achievements of the despised race rather than leave this task to the hot-headed radicals who are interested in self-aggrandizement through agitation and politics." Someone leaked the document to the unfriendly Washington *Bee*, which archly commented: "no doubt its contents will be surprising to the radical he [Woodson] loudly and eloquently applauded a few weeks ago."[92]

While this controversy simmered down, internal administrative problems, arising from Durkee's petty and autocratic style, rankled Woodson.[93] Scott personally intervened to prevent his summary dismissal, and Moorland urged Woodson to adopt a less uncompromising attitude, but the determined historian submitted his resignation, together with an outspoken letter to Durkee.[94] At the same time the independent-minded Woodson insulted Moorland, his warmest supporter among the trustees, impugning his race loyalty: "You have a weakness for good-for-nothing white people because of your broken down theory that in the Negro schools the best of the two races may be uplifted." Woodson added that because the quality of whites working in black schools had deteriorated sharply since the idealistic heyday of Reconstruction, "I feel that the time has come for all Negro schools to be turned over to Negroes . . . you and every other Negro in a position of leadership must decide to question whether he will stand by the race or those who are exploiting the race. In bringing Dr. Durkee to Howard University you took a stand with the latter." Moorland defended himself and observed quietly: "It is futile to carry on an extended correspondence over the good of cooperation, so long as most organizations have no hesitancy in approaching white people for support. I am quite sure the support you are receiving from substantial white friends is very strong evidence that the program of cooperation has not by any means broken down." Moreover, even after Woodson's resignation, both Moorland and Scott tried to patch things up, prevailing upon Howard's trustees to reappoint the historian if he made a satisfactory apology to Durkee, as the latter demanded. Woodson regarded the trustees' resolution as an "insult" but, responding to his friends' entreaties, submitted the apologetic letter. But Durkee would not be placated, and Moorland sadly concluded that Woodson had been too intemperate for his own good: "I told Dr. Woodson he was capable of writing history, but I had doubts about his ability to make history."[95]

Meanwhile, once his position at Howard had become jeopardized, Woodson renewed his efforts to obtain better financing for the ASNLH, making another futile appeal to the GEB. In discouragement he confided to Scott: "Raising money for an enterprise like this is a hard task. . . . The average philanthropist is not interested in the study of Negro life and history for the reason that he does not believe it is worthwhile and, even if it is of value, he seriously doubts that Negroes are qualified to do the work scientifically."[96] Finally, in desperation he took the initiative in reviving the idea of an NAACP connection. He did this even though eighteen months earlier he and the *Crisis* editor had been at odds over Du Bois's attempt to merge the plans being made independently by himself, Woodson, and Scott to write the history of black troops during World War I. Not only was it hardly conceivable that Washington's closest aide would have consented to work with Du Bois, but cooperation between the two Harvard-trained historians almost inevitably foundered because each wanted primary responsibility and control. Woodson, fearful that Du Bois would dominate the project, had gone so far as to demand over half the budget for his own salary.[97]* But now in May 1920, a few days after submitting his resignation from Howard University, he requested that the NAACP

* In the end only Scott's *Official History of the American Negro in the World War* (1919) appeared.

"maintain" the *JNH* by subsidizing his salary as editor. As he explained to Moorland, financial necessity dictated that "some organization must take it over."[98]

The NAACP, always hard-pressed for funds, treated Woodson's appeal coolly. As he himself realized, a serious obstacle lay in his insistence on operating the *Journal* as a completely autonomous department within the organization. In addition, the NAACP Board judged that Woodson's work was "so unrelated to our main objects and appeals . . . to so different a public, that it seems to us wise" for the *Journal* to go its own way.[99] The NAACP was, of course, quite correct in its assessment that by and large the two organizations appealed to different supporters, Woodson having deliberately cultivated the very sort of people, black and white, who were skeptical of the NAACP and its methods. In fact, in the long run, identification with the NAACP would likely have discouraged much, if not all, of the help Woodson ultimately did obtain from the philanthropies, and it certainly would have made it exceedingly difficult to promote black history and Negro History Week in the public schools of the South, where most blacks still lived and where most of the adoptions of his text, *The Negro in Our History,* were made. As already noted, Woodson, for his part, consistently made a virtue of the fact that his work was unconnected with the kind of agitation and social action that was the hallmark of the NAACP.

At this juncture John W. Davis came to the rescue. Having just assumed the presidency of West Virginia Collegiate Institute, he invited his friend to help him organize the college department. For the historian this was a stopgap measure while he sought to obtain adequate funding for his life work. He remained at West Virginia for two years (1920-22), continuing to support the ASNLH and the *JNH* with his own salary and private contributions from the donors with whom he had made previous contacts. The fiscal problem, however, remained serious; in late 1920, for example, unpaid printing bills amounted to $2,400.[100] Fortunately, at this point circumstances finally enabled the Association's founder to enlist the help of both the Carnegie and the Rockefeller philanthropies.

The individual who finally unlocked for Woodson the virtually closed doors of philanthropy was J. Franklin Jameson (1859-1937), at the time both editor of the *AHR* and director of the Department of Historical Research at the Carnegie Institution of Washington. The influential Jameson was not a man of passionate social or political convictions, and when he died Woodson described him as one who "had none of the abolition spirit in him. It is doubtful that he ever attended a meeting called in behalf of the Negro race."[101] Actually Jameson was proud of his abolitionist background,[102] and although he was temperamentally a judicious "middle-of-the-roader,"[103] his racial views when compared with most historians of his generation would have been considered unusually liberal. Thus for many years he employed a black American, Ruth Anna Fisher, who had graduated from Oberlin College and studied at the London School of Economics, as resident agent in England for the Carnegie Institution and later for the Manuscript Division of the Library of Congress, searching out documents at the British Museum and Public Record Office. He thought very highly of this "very clever . . . learned, accurate, businesslike" woman, "who knows the American materials in the Public Record Office better than anyone else does, or ever has, except [the distinguished colonialist] Charles Andrews." He deeply regretted that his wife's attitude prevented him from having Fisher as a guest in his home. For her part Fisher had only the highest admiration for "the giant Dr. Jameson," "my beloved Chief."[104] Moreover, Jameson, as a pioneering social historian, grasped the need to study the history and role of blacks because they constituted a significant segment of the American people. As he once wrote to Julius Rosenwald's secretary: "I believe that it is important, indeed, that it is an imperative duty, that we should make a far more thorough study of negro history than has hitherto been made. The negro constitutes something like a tenth of our population, and is, like the rest of us, a product of historical development, yet how much less effort we have expended on learning the actual facts respecting his past than on the history of our other elements."[105]

Jameson had long exhibited an interest in black history. As far back as the 1880s, the early Johns Hopkins University monographs on Negroes undoubtedly owed much to him. Jeffrey R. Brackett, who produced the most numerous publications on the black past that appeared in the Hopkins studies, was particularly close to Jameson.[106] The continuity of his interest can be seen in the fact that in 1913, when invited to present a series of lectures at the University of Wisconsin, he chose to speak on slavery (including a paper on slave revolts).[107] A dozen years later appeared his well-known *The American Revolution Considered as a Social Movement* (1926), which devoted considerable attention to a discussion of its impact on the prohibition of the transatlantic slave trade and the emancipation of slaves in the North. Throughout Jameson maintained a healthy skepticism about Phillips's roseate perspective on the peculiar institution. It is true that unlike Clarence Alvord, who selected Woodson to review Phillips's *American Negro Slavery* in the *MVHR*, and unlike Harvard professor W. B. Munro, who invited Du Bois to undertake the same task for the *American Political Science Review*,[108] the more cautious Jameson deliberately recruited a southern white paternalist interested in the study of blacks.* Privately, however, Jameson agreed with Du Bois's assessment "that Phillips whitewashes the whole institution of slavery."[113]

Jameson, during his tenure at the Carnegie Institution, conceived and initiated two major multivolume documentary research projects on slavery: Elizabeth Donnan's *Documents Illustrative of the History of the Slave Trade to America* (1930-35), and Helen T. Catterall's *Judicial Cases Concerning American Slavery and the Negro* (1926-37). However, back in 1905 at the time he first joined the staff of that agency, other investigations had taken first priority. Indeed when in 1907 the enterprising Du Bois, then at Atlanta University and desirous of doing "some more work and work on a larger scale in the history of the Negro people," inquired of Jameson "if there is any chance to do this under your department of the Carnegie Institution," the latter replied: "I am interested in your letter . . . having read with pleasure your book on the suppression of the African slave trade. I do not, however, see any opportunity for doing the sort of work you mention." Three years later Jameson did arrange to publish Du Bois's 1909 AHA convention paper, making him the first black to write for the *AHR*.[114]† Moreover, the idea of collecting and printing documentary ma-

* Jameson first approached the Mississippi cotton planter, Alfred Holt Stone, who had earlier been in charge of the Division of Negro Economics in the now-defunct Department of Economics and Sociology in the Carnegie Institution. The *AHR* editor finally turned to Theodore Jervey, a Charleston lawyer who had appeared on the same session as Du Bois at the 1909 AHA convention.[109] Jameson's actions in this instance are probably best understood in the context of certain previous research supported by the Carnegie Institution. Its Department of Economics and Sociology had provided subventions for much of Phillips's early work,[110] and in 1906 laid plans for an ambitious investigation of "The Negro in Slavery and Freedom" under Stone's direction. Stone's activities were suspended in 1909 when boll-weevil depradations forced him to return to Mississippi to manage his plantation, but the Carnegie Institution continued for several years to hope for the resumption of his project.[111] As part of this research into the blacks' economic role and condition, modest amounts had been awarded in 1907 to both R. R. Wright, Jr., for work on blacks in Philadelphia, and to Du Bois for his study of "Economic Co-Operation among Negro Americans." As these grants suggest, Stone had a way of presenting himself as an objective, even sympathetic student of Negro progress. Jameson had considerable respect for his knowledge and published an article by him in the *AHR*.[112]

† Some of the circumstances surrounding the publication of this essay are fairly well known, since Jameson, following what was pretty standard orthography at the time, turned down Du Bois's request to capitalize the "N" in Negro. Actually, the principal significance of this incident has been obscured, for it was Jameson himself who invited Du Bois to submit this paper for publication, and it remained the only article by a black to appear in the *AHR* until John Hope Franklin's 1979 AHA presidential address. Neither Du Bois's nor Jameson's papers nor the selections from them that have been published contain any hint of Jameson's initiative, which is to be found in Du Bois to Jameson, Jan. 5, 1910, in the AHA Archives, box 275.

terial relating to slavery was long on Jameson's mind, for he believed that "we shall continue to have merely one man's opinion against another's on what slavery was really like until we bring out a body of evidence that is unimpeachable as representative of the sum total." Finally, by the end of 1915 he had secured appropriations for this project.[115] Although the resulting research was only a small part of all that Jameson hoped to do in documenting the history of American slavery, he saw it as representing his very real commitment to the study of the black experience: "My own strong feeling as to the importance of a fuller pursuit of negro history in the United States," he once wrote, "may be seen from the large place which I have given to it in the programme of my own department."[116]

The Carnegie Institution's slavery investigations were inaugurated virtually simultaneously with the establishment of the ASNLH and the *JNH*. In fact, Jameson and Woodson, although they both lived and worked in Washington, first met in the spring of 1916. Certainly they had much in common, sharing not only an interest in black history but a mutual passion for collecting documents dealing with the Afro-American past. Jameson was quite aware of what Woodson was doing; not only had the *AHR* extended a cordial welcome to the *Journal*'s inaugural issue, but Jameson had arranged for his former student, Marcus W. Jernegan, to review Woodson's first published monograph, *The Education of the Negro Prior to 1861*. It was, however, Woodson who just after he had received such favorable notice, and undoubtedly having learned of the slavery project that Jameson was undertaking, made the initial contact, seeking an opportunity to discuss his own research plans. Jameson responded: "I am warmly interested in the work you are doing and, if at any time you happen to be in this neighborhood, [I] should be glad to have the opportunity to talk with you about it. I . . . am glad to enclose a small personal contribution toward the work of your Association."[117]

The two men did confer shortly afterward. Woodson was anxious both for some financial support and for a mutually satisfactory delineation of their respective areas of research. Years later he recalled that they had even discussed the possibilities of Woodson joining Jameson's staff. But that idea fell through, partly because the latter "did not have the courage" to arrange this in the nation's Jim Crow capital, and partly because both men "believed . . . much more could be achieved by maintaining the work of the Association as an independent enterprise." Woodson added that Jameson himself felt that after "the white man has written all he can about the Negro, there will still remain certain neglected aspects which only the Negro himself can develop." The fragmentary contemporary evidence indicates that what Woodson really hoped for was a subsidy from the Carnegie Institution to enable him to employ research investigators of his own. But Jameson explained that while he was "distinctly appreciative of the need of more work upon the history of the negro in America," it was against Carnegie Institution policy to subsidize others for research related to projects already being undertaken by its own departments. Jameson thought the avoidance of overlapping research posed no problem, given the large and untapped fields requiring investigation. Moreover, he definitely felt that "you can do some things which I cannot do." Both agreed that Woodson's operation was ideally suited for transcribing manuscripts and documents in the hands of private individuals, black and white. And with Jameson projecting what became Catterall's volumes on judicial cases in state and federal courts, he also urged Woodson to research "papers relating to slavery and the negro in county courthouses and other local archives."[118] In the long run the solution to the question of a division of labor between the two organizations proved obvious enough, with Woodson, once he obtained funding, focusing the Association's research mainly on antebellum free Negroes and the post-Emancipation experience. And it was at the suggestion of Jameson—who possessed an avant-garde awareness of the potential in the manuscript census for social history—that Woodson personally turned to exploiting unpublished census data for his own studies of free black heads of families and owners of slaves.[119]

Although Jameson, quite aware of Woodson's efforts to obtain philanthropic funding, was skeptical of the kind of "grandiose scheme" that had been presented to Rosenwald for an endowment of $100,000,[120] the *AHR* editor thought highly of what Woodson was doing. In 1920 when his good friend James Rowland Angell, a former colleague at the University of Chicago and the future president of Yale University, became president of the Carnegie Corporation of New York, Jameson personally orchestrated with Woodson the ASNLH's application to this sister philanthropy. Jameson informed Angell of Woodson's application in advance and explained, "I thoroughly believe in the worth and utility of what he [Woodson] is trying to do, and am confident that it . . . will be well done." Woodson, he added, was "a well-educated colored man" with "excellent methods of work, and . . . excellent judgement." Woodson's own publications had been "work of real scientific research"; the *Journal* articles had "uniformly been of respectable quality, and in many cases of great value"; and Woodson's plans constituted "a very intelligent programme." A few days later Woodson sent his own letter of application for a subvention that would erase the deficit and enable the ASNLH to become self-sustaining. He pointed to support not only from Jameson but from Albert Bushnell Hart, who had just accepted a place on the ASNLH Council.[121] A flurry of endorsements followed from Hart and other leading scholars, including Woodson's doctoral advisor Edward Channing and William E. Dodd.

Angell was impressed by all these "reassuring letters from several influential persons," and by the fact that another old friend and colleague of his at the University of Chicago, the sociologist Robert E. Park, was the ASNLH's president.[122]

Woodson was highly optimistic. But almost at once difficulties arose for his proposal because others in the network of race advancement agencies with which he was connected had submitted to the Carnegie Corporation applications for funding. Both Tuskegee Institute and the National Urban League, also becoming aware of Angell's willingness to underwrite research on black Americans, requested financial support for their own investigations on current social and economic conditions. Tuskegee wished to secure more funding for the activities of Monroe Work, while the Urban League was about to hire Charles S. Johnson, one of Park's favorite students, for its newly created post of director of research.[123] When Angell proposed that Tuskegee and the ASNLH carry out their studies under a cooperative arrangement, Woodson became furious with Work and Moton. In his mind these erstwhile warm supporters had now become "unprincipled men . . . who, seeing that I was about to succeed in getting a handsome sum for research, endeavored either to swing it to Tuskegee or prevent me from obtaining it." But he "refused absolutely to have anything to do" with "the scavengers of Tuskegee" who "came to me to let them in on it, implying that if I did not do so, they would offer arguments to block it."[124]*

Actually the problem appears to have been not whether the Carnegie Corporation would allocate money to the ASNLH, but the skepticism among Angell's key trustees over making such a grant to a new and untried organization like Woodson's without imposing some sort of supervision. The chairman of the Board of Trustees, Elihu Root, a former secretary of war, particularly raised objections, and Angell therefore proposed an arrangement by which Tuskegee would have general oversight over the disbursements for Woodson's historical investigations.[126] But Woodson, whose research interests were very different from those of Tuskegee and the Urban League and who feared any dilution of his autonomy, adamantly opposed any such plan, placing the blame upon Moton and Work, who "by putting their powerful machine at work . . . have made an impression on Dr. Angell and have probably made it impossible for me to secure the appropriation except on the condition that they shall administer the fund to be granted."[127]

---

* On the other hand, Moorland was convinced that Moton was acting in good faith. Moton for his part informed Angell that when Tuskegee first discussed the matter of a research grant with him it had no knowledge that Woodson had applied.[125]

Characteristically Woodson had failed to consult with his council or even with secretary-treasurer Moorland. As Woodson himself put it, he had kept the subject "a secret for the reason that I did not want my nominal members of the Executive Council, who have done nothing to promote the cause, to step in at this hour and impede its progress."[128] It was Moton, concerned over Angell's postponement of a decision on all three applications, who brought the news to Moorland, hoping that the latter could iron things out. The Tuskegee principal explained that he had offered to withdraw his institution's application, but the Carnegie Corporation was insistent on its plan.[129] Moorland, now working out of New York, was disturbed. As in the initial stages of the Association's history, he had a decided view that the council was being bypassed, and indeed, on this ground he had recently declined to make further financial contributions, thus incurring Woodson's ire. Because he felt that Woodson was jeopardizing the Carnegie grant, he informed Park, "I believe in Woodson and I love him. We must support him. Sometimes a man's best support is not that of money but that of . . . strong steadying counsel." Accordingly it was imperative for the council to demonstrate exactly how its members felt. "Executive bodies have functions and sometimes it is necessary for them to act. I will serve on no board or Council without maintaining the right to so use my official power as to safeguard my own self-respect and the respect of those who depend upon me."[130]

Woodson of course did not look favorably on such intervention. When Moorland, acting on Moton's request,[131] contacted the ASNLH director, he was scolded for "dickering" with Moton and Work: "I would not have any connection with such jackasses . . . even if I had to go back to the coal mines for my living." He directed his secretary-treasurer to "say to all inquiries that you are not in a position to speak for the Association or for the *Journal,* since your connection with it is merely nominal." Moorland, however, fearing that the founder's precipitous actions would doom the Carnegie application with disastrous consequences for the ASNLH, wrote Park: "I think as an Executive Council we must make up our minds to bear responsibility if we allow this matter to fail . . . I do not see how we could make a case to our present donors if we let this proferred offer get away from us." Worried that Moorland was prepared to enter negotiations with Angell himself, Woodson warned, "Such action would be an expensive mistake. I am the Director of the Association and all matters of this sort must pass through this office. . . . Furthermore," he continued, "I am not by myself in feeling that your race leadership is unsound because of your slavish attachment to the incompetent poor whites who are exploiting the Negro race under the pretext that the time has not yet come when the Negro can dispense with these ignorant traducers. . . . You see then how uncomfortable I would feel to have you representing me or my cause behind closed doors." Planning to renew his appeal to the Carnegie Corporation, Woodson insisted: "You must not, therefore, say or do anything which will embarrass me in carrying on my program."[132]

Moorland chose to ignore these remarks and agreed to do nothing for the time being. With the Y official's attempts to convince Woodson having failed, Moton resumed negotiations with Angell, informing him that "we have made earnest efforts to secure the co-operation of Dr. Carter G. Woodson, but without success." To Park, Angell confessed to being "a little disturbed" by Woodson's attitude. "I fear a greatly disadvantageous effect of presenting to my Board three . . . similar enterprises under quite different auspices." To Jameson he expressed his irritation in even stronger terms: "I am not in the least sympathetic to Dr. Woodson's indisposition to cooperate with that department of the Tuskegee School which deals with the collation of current information about the negro. I do not at all appreciate the temper in which apparently he has dealt with perfectly proper overtures on this matter. I can quite understand that he desires to differentiate rather sharply the scholarly level on which he is trying to do his work from that which is necessarily characteristic of the work done in some of the Tuskegee offices. . . . Suffice it to say that it has left a slightly unpleasant impression on my mind as to Dr. Woodson's willingness and ability to accommodate himself to circumstances."[133]

Nevertheless, Angell finally resigned himself to accommodating Woodson. Though the contemporary record is silent, Jameson almost certainly had played an important role in this decision. It was undoubtedly in this period that, as Woodson later recalled appreciatively, Jameson had even traveled outside of Washington at his own expense, "trying to convince others of the necessity for the prosecution of the study of the Negro scientifically." Moreover, there may have been something about Woodson's single-mindedness that moved Angell. As he put it to Jameson, "We want to help him, and he has been cordially endorsed, not only by you but by other scholars in whose judgment I have confidence." In any event, the solution to this impasse that Angell proposed rested on Jameson. In effect, the ASNLH founder could have both the Carnegie money and his autonomy if Jameson would agree to "stand sponsor for the proper expenditures of funds to support Dr. Carter G. Woodson's work." Actually, Woodson himself had also broached with Jameson such an arrangement. The latter agreed, and Woodson preserved his independence. The Carnegie Corporation executive committee promptly authorized the funding of all three agencies.[134]*

* Among other projects, the Carnegie grant to Tuskegee enormously facilitated the preparation of Work's path-breaking A Bibliography of the Negro in Africa and America (1928).

Thus Woodson's persistence and Jameson's warm support had ultimately brought results. The Carnegie Corporation pledged $25,000 over the next five years to pay off the Association's debt and cover current operating expenses so that Woodson could give up teaching and spend full time with the ASNLH. Since the Association's income at the time was only about $6,000 annually, the Carnegie money constituted a substantial infusion of funds.[135]

More important, as Jameson and Woodson intended, this award provided the ASNLH with the leverage to obtain direct financial support for scholarly investigations from other sources. A letter from Woodson announcing the grant revived Rosenwald's flagging interest in helping the *JNH*. More significantly, the Association's founder soon applied once again to the Rockefeller philanthropies, this time for an amount equal to the Carnegie donation. Personally journeying to New York to discuss his plans, Woodson impressed the Rockefeller staff not only with the superlative recommendations that he had received, but also with the fact "that this Association is not in any way a propagandist one; simply endeavoring to determine facts of interest both to whites and negroes . . . it is easy to see that much good may result where now there is misunderstanding." Soon afterward Wallace Buttrick personally presented the matter to Rockefeller, Jr.[136] In February 1922 the LSRM made an award of $25,000 to finance five years of research. The grant came just in time for a grateful Woodson to insert in the forthcoming *The Negro in Our History* a flattering discussion of the Rockefeller philanthropies, together with a full page photograph of John D. Rockefeller, Sr. and Jr.[137]

It was this Rockefeller award, made possible by the earlier Carnegie grant, that provided the resources for the important and pioneering work concerning both antebellum free Negroes and the freedmen during Reconstruction upon which the Association immediately embarked. Indeed, Rockefeller money was the foundation upon which the entire research program of the ASNLH was built over the next decade. The contribution of Jameson to this development is hard to overestimate. Woodson, who was rarely given to lavish encomiums in obituary notices that he wrote for the *Journal*, recalled upon Jameson's death that although this man was "cold [and] reserved," those whom he thought had "sufficient merit to warrant his assistance found him a great helper and a faithful friend." In Woodson's estimate, "he [Jameson] takes rank as one of the greatest promoters of the study of the Negro."[138]

Meanwhile, the ASNLH director had taken seriously Angell's recommendation that he use money from the Carnegie award to "popularize the work among Negroes," so that when the grant expired the Association could be a self-sufficient organization funded principally by blacks themselves. Reviving his efforts among the black elite, during the winter of 1920-21 Woodson had obtained $25 pledges from over sixty Negroes, including Bishop Robert E. Jones who supervised the southern black congregations of the Methodist Episcopal church, North, Bishop John Hurst of the African Methodist Episcopal church, and college presidents John W. Davis and R. C. Woods of the Baptist-affiliated Virginia Theological Seminary and College in Lynchburg. At the same time, sparked mainly by women, clubs in a number of cities had agreed to contribute $100 each. Meanwhile, Woodson also sought to broaden his constituency in the black community by changes in the composition of his executive council. Bishop Hurst had been elected in 1920, and, with the addition of Bishop R. E. Carter of the Colored Methodist Episcopal church in 1921, all black Methodist groups except the African Methodist Episcopal Zion connection were represented. In the latter year the new council members also included college presidents Woods, Davis, and Clement Richardson of Lincoln Institute in Missouri, and the wealthy businessman R. R. Church of Memphis, while two Washington, D.C., entrepreneurs, John R. Hawkins and S. W. Rutherford, became the president and secretary-treasurer, respectively. Rutherford, Woodson's "close friend," was founder and president of one of the largest black business enterprises, the National Benefit Life Insurance Company. Both he and Hawkins were active in movements for racial advancement in the nation's capital, Rutherford, for example, having for years "been the mainspring in the machinery of the local Young Men's Christian Association, taking the leading part in their drives and often raising the largest amount of money."[139]

In the following years Woodson intensified his campaign with the black churches. In 1922, for example, he secured modest contributions from the general conference of the CME church and from Woods's associates in the Virginia Baptist State Convention. Two years later he addressed the quadrennial general conferences of both the AME and AME Zion churches and made appearances "before ministers and bishops representing hundreds of thousands of Negroes" that provided him "with an unusual opportunity to bring the work of the Association nearer to the rank and file of the race." Moreover, ASNLH conventions in this period were seldom lacking at least one session "devoted to the consideration of the Negro Church" at which prominent clerics spoke of the black denominations' contributions to race progress.[140] Unfortunately, the fruits of this outreach to the black community did not live up to Woodson's hopes.[141] This situation would lead him into a futile appeal for renewal of the Carnegie grant in 1926.

The effort to broaden the Association's base among blacks was only one aspect of the extensive changes made in the organization's officers in 1921. Among the old circle Dillard, Rosenwald, and A. L. Jackson still remained, as did the more recent appointees, Storey, Peabody, and Hart. But in the aftermath of the bitterness over the application to the Carnegie Corporation, Park had stepped down, while Moorland, Scott, and Thomas Jesse Jones had been summarily dropped from their posts.

Park, who had served as ASNLH president rather reluctantly in the first place and who was much closer to both Tuskegee and the Urban League than he was to Woodson, expressed a sense of ineffectiveness that was undoubtedly connected with his impotence in the face of the Tuskegee-ASNLH conflict. He tendered his resignation in May 1921.[142] Moorland's removal, rooted fundamentally in an unwillingness to permit himself and the council to function as rubber stamps, was also precipitated by the controversy surrounding the Carnegie application. To Rosenwald's personal secretary, Woodson claimed that Moorland's interference and "misrepresentation" had made it "almost a miracle" that the grant had finally been made. Moreover, the ASNLH founder disingenuously added, Moorland himself had twice volunteered his resignation. Indeed in 1919, upon moving from Washington to New York, the YMCA executive had thought it best to give up the secretary-treasurer post, but decided to remain because of "the Doctor's warm protest." But at this point it was Woodson, now arguing that Moorland's distant location away from Washington was an impediment to the effective functioning of the ASNLH, who forced the latter's hand. Moorland had replied guardedly to the founder's strong suggestion that he step down, simply observing that the council should "feel free to do whatever they feel is the best thing for the good of the Association."[143] This provided Woodson with all he needed to discard the YMCA secretary, who was deeply hurt because throughout he had served at the historian's insistence, giving "the best service I could." Emmett Scott, who had been slated by Woodson to succeed Park as president, was removed after he spoke up in support of Moorland, objecting to the dismissal of one who had worked so unselfishly for the cause.[144]

The changes among the ASNLH's black officers had been made without public commotion, but the dropping of Jones was an entirely different matter. At the time the Phelps-Stokes executive was embroiled in a controversy that made him anathema to virtually all sections of black opinion. Woodson, though he consciously eschewed agitation, joined the uproar of protest, penning a passage that he hastily inserted as his new book, *The History of the Negro Church,* went to press in late 1921, excoriating the activities of this white official, whom Du Bois had called "that evil genius of the Negro race."[145]

Actually many black leaders had long resented Jones as an empire builder who sought considerable influence for himself and the Phelps-Stokes Fund over many aspects of black advancement efforts. Thoroughly wedded as he was to the Tuskegee-Hampton strategy, Jones displayed a tendency to pigeonhole black leaders as either Washingtonians or Du Boisians and then to declare that those in the latter category "cannot undertake to minister to the needs of the race." Du Bois, not surprisingly, charged Jones with calculated plans "to displace Negro leaders" and arrogate to himself "the position of arbiter and patron of the Negro race." But the way Jones employed his influence also became disturbing to black YMCA leaders, when during and directly after World War I high-level white YMCA executives were following Jones's counsel on various matters, even to placing him in virtual control over which black Y secretaries would be permitted to serve with the troops in Europe.[146] Under these circumstances things naturally reached the point where Jones tangled with the tactful and circumspect Moorland, and temporary strains even arose between Moorland and Moton, who was helping to advise the Phelps-Stokes official on appointments to Y posts both abroad and in the South.[147] Jones first sought to discredit Moorland by accusing him of making disloyal speeches and of sending abroad "radical" YMCA workers (who were filing protests against the flagrant mistreatment of black troops). Moorland's superiors acquitted him of these charges. Jones's subsequent ploy to secure Moorland's dismissal on the grounds that he lacked any real program was defeated only by the threat of mass resignation on the part of Moorland's black co-workers.[148]

Jones's actions would have caused resentment at any time, but at this juncture they collided with the growing sense of self-reliance and assertiveness among the Negro Y secretaries, which the Phelps-Stokes official and his white friends on the Y staff interpreted as radical Du Boisian tendencies. This outlook of the black Y workers was rooted in several factors: in the self-help philosophy that was so widely articulated by Washington and his contemporaries; in the rising black militance of the war and postwar period; and in the very success of the new black YMCA branches. As Du Bois put it: it was true that the separate Negro department amounted to "color caste in Christian work," but the arrangement "did at least give the colored people a voice in their own government." College-educated black YMCA secretaries, with their vision expanded by the building program that Rosenwald helped to finance, struggled for autonomy and decision-making powers in their own sphere. At their insistence the 1919 national YMCA convention appointed a special interracial committee, which recommended that steps be taken to give them greater authority. Yet this by no means resolved the problem. A. L. Jackson, who had served on the committee, penned a sharp letter to Moorland's superior, attacking the "narrow-minded attitude" toward Negro branch work shown by the general secretaries in many local associations. For example, the general secretary of the Kansas City, Missouri, YMCA complained that the recently fired Negro branch secretary had exhibited disloyalty by giving blacks the impression that he was not responsible to the white officials. After the black man was fired on grounds that he "sought to use the department as a propagator of Du Bois' doctrines," the white executive reported that he soon turned up on the national office staff of the Colored Department, where "he and Dr. Moorland have used the Kansas City Association as a 'horrible example' in gatherings of colored Association workers."[149]

These matters had been fought quietly behind the scenes. But Jones's interference became widely publicized in 1921 when he advised the government of South Africa to withdraw permission for the YMCA to send its magnetic and dedicated young black secretary, Max Yergan, to work there under the auspices of British missionary organizations. This invitation was particularly significant in view of the suspicion that the European authorities in Africa entertained toward American blacks in this era of Garveyism and Du Bois's Pan-African Movement and the imperialists' desire to sharply limit—even virtually exclude—American Negro missionaries. During World War I Yergan had performed brilliantly, and under great hardships, in East Africa. Now with the invitation to South Africa rescinded because Jones had expressed reservations about him, Yergan angrily circulated a letter among his friends charging that the Phelps-Stokes executive had informed South Africans that he was "doubtful about colored American Association leadership. . . . I might add here," continued Yergan, "that it appears that Dr. Jones is attempting to do in Africa what he did in America," barring all whom he considered to have Du Boisian leanings from responsible positions of leadership. Jones's action, observed Yergan, was virtually tantamount to excluding all American blacks from serving as missionaries in Africa.[150]

The Yergan episode was deeply resented across the whole spectrum of black thinking. Thus Tuskegee students expressed "great concern" in a communication to the YMCA. Although Yergan would become a leading black Communist during the 1930s, at this time he was no radical; in his African missionary work he had lectured "the natives" on Washington's contributions, and during the 1920s he merited consummate praise from Moton as well as financial support from Rockefeller, Jr. John W. Davis, upon hearing from Yergan, concluded that "Du Bois after all is correct relative to Thomas Jesse Jones," and added, "The immediate program of the Young Men's Christian Association as well as every thinking Negro is to dethrone Thomas Jesse Jones from his hold on so-called Negro leadership." Du Bois, supplied with documentation from Yergan, published an exposé of Jones's activities in the October *Crisis* in an essay that evoked favorable responses from widely divergent quarters. One of Woodson's supporters, James E. Shepard, the highly accommodating president of the National Training School in Durham (later North Carolina College for Negroes), privately wrote the *Crisis* editor: "That was a very fine article on Thomas Jesse Jones. I think all the people appreciated your full and frank analysis." Finally, in the wake of the black outcry Yergan was permitted to return to Africa.[151]

Woodson, who dropped Jones from his council just as Du Bois was preparing his *Crisis* article, thus reflected the broad groundswell of black resentment. As the ASNLH director later explained to Rosenwald's secretary: "Dr. Jones is detested by 95% of all Negroes who are seriously concerned with the uplift of the race." Back in 1919, however, in the midst of Moorland's difficulties with the Phelps-Stokes official, Woodson had not hesitated to reappoint Jones to the council. In the meantime Woodson had undoubtedly become privy to the views of Davis, who had in his possession copies of the incriminating documents that Yergan had supplied. Now, in 1921, resonating to the widespread indignation over the matter, Woodson incorporated into his new survey volume of black church history a bitter denunciation of both Jones and the Phelps-Stokes Fund (which he sarcastically labeled a " 'Christian' organization financed by 'philanthropists.' ") Since the capitalist colonial powers feared the kind of gospel that American Negroes might preach in Africa, "the missionary movement must bow to mammon." The "meddler" Jones had "ingratiated himself into the favor of the capitalistic government" of South Africa and torpedoed the invitation to Yergan. Having "made himself the dictator of the appointments" of the Negro YMCA, he was now in the "business . . . of furnishing the world with 'hand-picked' Negro leaders to damn even the natives" of Africa. "In other words, the principles of the humble Nazarene must be crushed out to make money and perpetuate caste."[152]

Jones counterattacked vigorously against Woodson, and what looked like a well-orchestrated campaign was soon evident. A couple years later Woodson publicly charged that "on learning that I had published this matter, Thomas Jesse Jones began to use every possible means to lop off the supporters of the Association for the Study of Negro Life and History. . . . I interviewed rich white people to whom he has written. Some of them have taken letters from their files and have shown them to me." Indeed the Phelps-Stokes Fund did admit that in view of Woodson's "vicious" attack, inquiries received about the reputability of the ASNLH had brought the response that the Association "is not to be supported." At the time, shortly after the appearance of Woodson's book, both Peabody and Hart—influenced by Jones—condemned the "utterly unwarranted" attack, especially in view of Jones's "important work for the whole Negro question and of his earlier support at the critical period of Dr. Woodson." Moton wrote the ASNLH founder along similar lines. But Peabody and Hart went even further. They questioned Woodson about a report that he was illicitly drawing a salary from the LSRM as well as the Carnegie grant. Not surprisingly they found his explanation unsatisfactory and re-signed from the council, promptly informing Rosenwald of that fact.[153*] Queried by Rosenwald's secretary, Jones artfully explained that the ASNLH founder had moved "from the scientific attitude . . . to that of propagandist with a distinct antipathy to movements for racial cooperation," as dem-onstrated by the departure of Park and Moorland, and Woodson's current "speaking quite vehemently against Dr. Moton."[155]

With Rosenwald distinctly worried about these charges and about in-timations "from other sources that Woodson has alienated other former associates and friends . . . and that his inclinations are toward the radical side," the philanthropist also solicited the opinions of Moton, Scott, and Moorland. Although Moton had previously been a warm supporter of Woodson's activities, this single steadfast ally of Jones among the black leadership was now prepared to damage the ASNLH, tersely replying: "I am of the opinion that Dr. Woodson's attitude should undergo considerable change before large sums of money are invested in his work. His present tendencies seem rather to tear down than to build up."[156] In contrast, both Scott and Moorland, although hurt that Woodson had removed them from their ASNLH positions so cavalierly, rose to defend him for his unrivaled contribution to the black history movement—and exonerated him of the charges of radicalism. Thus Scott explained that it was "difficult" for him to evaluate Woodson, "for the reason that he is a man of eccentric mood. I have studied him very carefully during the past few years, and hardly feel that I am even now fully acquainted with his idiosyncrasies." However, while Woodson had indeed "alienated former associates," the charges of radicalism were unwarranted. "It so happens nowadays," Scott explained, "that if any colored man protests against injustices in the matter of his fundamental rights, he is immediately criticized as being a radi-cal . . . many persons condemn a [black] man for protesting against injus-tices which white men would not stand for one fraction of a moment. . . . I have seen nothing that Dr. Woodson has written that would lead me to

___

* The complaint was obviously based on feelers that Woodson was extending to the LSRM, inquiring if he might draw an annual stipend from the Rockefeller money since much of his salary under the Carnegie grant had to be used for general expenses; the staff explained that he could use the funds only to reimburse direct costs.[154]

think that he is radical in the communistic or anarchistic sense. He is radical . . . [simply] in his strong condemnation on several occasions recently of the injustices which the Colored people of this country are at this time the chief victims."[157]

Woodson, learning of the charges, provided Rosenwald with convincing rebuttals of his own while simultaneously inserting into the next issue of the *Journal* a flattering discussion of the Rosenwald rural schools. Dismissing Jones's complaints about the treatment of Moorland as characteristically hypocritical, he explained that Hart, having attended only one meeting, was ignorant of the Association's affairs, and except for Peabody no one else took the false charges about the salary matter seriously. As far as the imputation of radicalism was concerned, Woodson wrote: "I am surprised indeed that Dr. Jones by his propaganda can make anything of me as radical or even socialistically inclined. My father was a dyed in the wool Republican and I have never voted any other ticket." Thus to charge him with having categorized Jones as "a tool of capitalism" was to misread the book; as Woodson explained, "I have never believed . . . that capital is a danger to society . . . every man with common sense realizes that the development of the modern world through capital has laid the foundation for the present progress of mankind." The ASNLH executive also pointed out that most of the reviewers of *The History of the Negro Church* "refer to the author as a conservative historian," an evaluation that he supported by quoting extensive passages in the very chapter that contained the denunciation of Jones. There, defending the "patience" and conservatism of black churches, Woodson had written, "The Negro has learned not to avenge his own wrongs, believing that God will adjust matters in the end. . . . At heart the Negro is a conservative Christian and looks forward to that favorable turn in the affairs of men when the wrongs of the oppressed shall be righted without the shedding of blood." It was "fortunate that providence" had made the Negro church "a conservative force . . . [that] has known how far it can safely instruct its people to go in righting their own wrongs, and this conservatism has saved the Negro from the fate of other oppressed groups who have suffered extermination because of their failure to handle their case more diplomatically."[158]

Woodson's own assessment of the essentially conservative nature of his strategy for racial advancement was confirmed by the investigative agency that Rosenwald employed to check into the ASNLH founder's ideological leanings. The report concluded that the Association's activities constituted not "propaganda but a scientific effort"; Woodson's "unique record as a scholar" made him highly regarded by the officers of the "standard negro organizations"; while he was "a man of decided viewpoints and somewhat difficult to work with," "he has succeeded in retaining the confidence of nearly all factions working with . . . negro programs and is, for the most part, considered unbiased in his presentation of facts."[159]

Accordingly, while the rupture with the Phelps-Stokes Fund remained permanent, neither the controversy over Yergan nor Woodson's treatment of influential supporters like Scott and Moorland had any significant impact on the course of the ASNLH's history or on the funding of its activities. In later years Woodson would perceive Jones's implacable hostility as causing the loss of philanthropic support for his work in the 1930s. Yet, although the Phelps-Stokes Fund cut off its small annual contribution and although Jones was able to discourage some individual donors, Woodson retained the respect and support of other agencies in the Rockefeller Foundation–Tuskegee network. Hampton's *Southern Workman* expressed only mild regrets about the offending passage in *The History of the Negro Church* and continued to accord Woodson's work good coverage.[160] Even Moton personally arranged for the director to speak at Tuskegee the following year.[161] Stokes himself vainly attempted to keep open lines of communication with Woodson.[162] The Rockefeller boards continued to give money to Woodson for a decade, Rosenwald also continued to make donations, and both he and the Phelps-Stokes Fund vice-president, James Hardy Dillard, served on the ASNLH Council until their deaths in the early 1930s.

An important reason for Woodson's ability to retain the support of the philanthropists was the way in which he continued to court their approval. In this connection he adopted a two-pronged strategy. On the one hand, he carefully replaced the white council members with whom he had quarreled with an impressive group of prestigious white scholars. On the other hand, he took steps to identify himself more closely with the conservative wing of Negro leadership and with some of those, white and black, who were associated with the southern "interracial cooperation" movement endorsed by the hated Thomas Jesse Jones.

As Moorland had indicated to the ASNLH director during the latter's fight with the paternalistic white president of Howard University, in the context of the times a course of "interracial cooperation" was advisable. Indeed, given the support accorded by the Rockefeller philanthropies to the Commission on Interracial Cooperation, Woodson considered it necessary to endorse the concept of "interracial cooperation" and to cultivate some of its supporters. Of course, "interracial cooperation" was one of those elastic phrases open to a considerable range of meaning. For Jones it implied white domination in the work for Negro advancement; for Moton and Dillard, who were both close to Jones, and for the CIC's prime mover, Will W. Alexander, it betokened a genuine cooperation of both races in a movement of gradual amelioration. Still, it did not escape the attention of someone like Du Bois that whites who projected such accommodating Negro leaders as CIC members Moton and Bishop Jones were scarcely encouraging much social change. The *Crisis* editor admired a handful of individuals identified with the CIC, like Morehouse College president John Hope and Dillard, but editorially he was highly critical of "interracial cooperation," categorizing most of the whites involved as "enemies of the Negro race" who sought "an excuse for inaction" while exploiting the organization's subservient blacks whom Du Bois labeled "catspaws," "pussy-footers," and "white-folks' niggers."[163] In contrast Woodson now turned to emphasizing "interracial cooperation" as one of the ASNLH's goals and to securing the participation on Association programs of individuals prominently connected with the southern interracial movement. His actions in this connection were, of course, similar to those of many leaders in black advancement organizations of that era even in the North. Moreover, to eschew the blacks prominent in the CIC would have cut Woodson off from just about every important black leader in the South.

Woodson later recalled that the creation of interracial harmony was one of his original aims in founding the ASNLH.[164]* More to the point, at an ASNLH conference held in New York in April 1922, Woodson, with the controversy over the Negro church history book exploding around him, arranged to devote a session to the subject of interracial cooperation. Papers were presented by Bishop Carter and by one of the most sought after speakers on the subject, George Edmund Haynes, who dwelt on "the bright prospects for the cooperation of the races in the country."[166] Over the next two years the theme achieved real salience at ASNLH meetings. In publicizing the 1923 convention at Atlanta, where CIC headquarters were located, Woodson announced that "harmony between the races by interpreting the one to the other is to be the keynote of the annual meeting." He had, he explained, "enlisted the support of many thinkers of the North and South, who believe that a scientific presentation of the claims of both races will do more for the re-adjustment of their differences than all the firebrands who have been or will be hurled from either side of the controversy." Convention sessions featured black speakers who delivered talks on interracial topics, and an address by one of the CIC's

* The extant records on the establishment of the ASNLH do not lend explicit support for this claim. The only reference to such a purpose before 1922 is in an application for funding that Woodson submitted to the Rockefeller philanthropies at the time CIC was being set up in 1919, where he listed as one of his aims the encouragement of harmony between the races by interpreting one to the other.[165]

white founders, Emory University's divinity professor Plato T. Durham. Several months later at the 1924 spring conference, Woodson reported that "representatives . . . of the Inter-Racial Movement regularly attended the sessions," and Haynes spoke once again on the history and methods of the interracial movement. The proceedings of the fall 1924 annual convention held in Richmond included addresses by the principal of Hampton Institute and by Jackson Davis, the white Virginian who was generally responsible for handling the GEB's work among southern blacks and who had high praise for the ASNLH. Dillard, who attended the Association's conventions quite regularly, was also present, and Woodson astutely asked him to speak informally on his recent educational mission to Africa with Thomas Jesse Jones.[167]

In subsequent years Woodson maintained his practice of cultivating Rockefeller and Rosenwald with flattering references to their work. Thus he composed a highly laudatory study of Rosenwald's unselfish and "most statesmanlike" role in fostering interracial cooperation through his encouragement of Negro rural schools. (Rosenwald declined Woodson's request to subsidize publication of this worshipful book-length manuscript; the study later appeared as part of *The Rural Negro*.)[168] Woodson also continued to sustain close ties with blacks active in the CIC: the conservative Bishop Jones; President John M. Gandy of Virginia Normal and Collegiate Institute; Du Bois's old friend, John Hope, who joined the ASNLH Council in 1926 and who, after Woodson had a tiff with Hawkins,[169] became ASNLH's president in 1931; and Mary McLeod Bethune, president of Bethune-Cookman College, who succeeded Hope as head of the ASNLH in 1936. Moton, it is true, still declined to serve on the council but continued to endorse Woodson's activities; for example, attending the 1929 ASNLH convention he pledged a life membership from Tuskegee Institute. Slightly over a decade later, when this long-time friend of the Association died, Woodson would compose a highly favorable obituary for the *Journal*.[170]

Woodson also continued to cultivate the support of white scholars who would carry weight with the philanthropists. Hart and Peabody were quickly replaced on the council with distinguished academicians: the anthropologists Franz Boas of Columbia and E. A. Hooton of Harvard, and the historians Carl Russell Fish of Wisconsin (a former student of Jameson) and William E. Dodd. They remained on the council for the next decade until removed by either death or resignation in the early 1930s. At that point, Woodson named Evarts B. Greene of Columbia and Arthur Schlesinger, Sr., of Harvard. These scholars all had a high regard for what Woodson was doing. Boas, for example, who found it impossible to implement a cooperative program of training blacks in advanced work in anthropology due to Woodson's personality, nevertheless "always considered his work of sufficient importance . . . to join his executive council." Schlesinger, though he virtually ignored the black experience in his books and in his teaching at Harvard, was proud of his connection with the ASNLH and expressed himself as having "great confidence in Dr. Woodson's accurate scholarship. . . . [H]is work ranks high in comparison with the work produced by the better white historians."[171] On the other hand by 1934, when it became clear that further subventions from the foundations would not be awarded, Woodson discontinued the practice of reserving a few council seats for whites. After Greene died in 1947, Schlesinger remained as the lone white member of the council.

In helping Woodson legitimize the scientific and scholarly nature of his enterprise, these and other prominent academicians had been invaluable. Thus in applying to the LSRM for a grant renewal in 1926, Woodson secured endorsements from a veritable galaxy of scholars: Yale professor and former AHA president Charles M. Andrews; Greene and Boas of Columbia; Hooton, William B. Munro, and Edward Channing, all of Harvard. On this occasion Channing, effectively discounting the negative reports emanating from his colleague A. B. Hart, wrote to the foundation: "The Association has certainly made good use of the opportunities that your benefaction made possible. . . . Dr. Woodson is one of my former students and I have a great deal of respect for him. . . . Naturally, there has been some harsh criticism . . . but I think they [Woodson and the ASNLH] have distinctly made good." On other occasions, Dodd, queried by the Rosenwald and Rockefeller people, came through handsomely: "At the beginning I was doubtful of the value of his undertaking, but every year of his work has shown that he has both ability and judgment and his output has been extraordinary. . . . In my judgment, the money which has been appropriated to this purpose has been better spent than any other money I know . . . in similar fields. . . . I need not, therefore, say that I most heartily endorse the allowance which you have it in mind to grant. Somehow I wish they might have a great deal more."[172]

Such evaluations reflected the importance of the pioneering and productive record of research and publication made possible by the Carnegie award and, more directly, by the Rockefeller grant. The latter had provided the resources for the important and path-breaking work on antebellum free Negroes and on blacks during Reconstruction that the ASNLH produced during the 1920s—the finest corpus of scholarship that the Association would sponsor. The most important had been the studies by Woodson and by Alrutheus A. Taylor, whom he hired as his principal investigator.[173] In addition, Woodson did not entirely ignore slavery studies. He provided a grant-in-aid to professor James Hugo Johnston of the Virginia Normal and Collegiate Institute for research in black-Indian relationships in colonial and antebellum Virginia.[174] Moreover, Woodson employed on a part-time basis both Ruth Anna Fisher and another woman who was also extracting material for Jameson from European archives, Irene A. Wright, working in the Archives of the Indies in Seville.[175]

It is worthy of emphasis that this first floresence of scholarship among black historians associated with the ASNLH had its counterpart in the outlook of the "New Negro" of the 1920s and the Harlem Renaissance that flourished in the middle of the decade. Part of the spirit of race pride articulated by the black intelligentsia of the period, this point of view was epitomized by a frequently cited essay in Alain Locke's 1925 anthology, *The New Negro* — Arthur A. Schomburg's aptly titled piece, "The Negro Digs Up His Past."

Woodson was proud both of "the scientific order" of the research and of the fact that "the work has been prosecuted economically."[176] Indeed, the record of productivity, the esteem that it engendered among prominent scholars, and Woodson's success at cultivating the southern interracialists all would have seemed to have augured well for the future. Unfortunately, however, he ran athwart of the changing policies of the foundations. As a result, Woodson was first diverted from historical studies to sponsoring policy-oriented social research, and then in the early 1930s came to a complete rupture with the philanthropists.

With his first two awards about to expire, Woodson applied in 1925-26 for a renewal of both the Rockefeller and Carnegie grants. While still dreaming of building an endowment of as much as $500,000,[177] realistically he recognized that his only viable options were to hope for renewals of these more modest awards. His application to Frederick P. Keppel, the new president of the Carnegie Corporation, was orchestrated with simultaneous lobbying by Jameson and Jameson's good friend, Waldo G. Leland, executive secretary of the ACLS and former secretary of the AHA. But even though Jameson personally appealed to Keppel, the board of trustees voted against continuing assistance to the three black agencies to which it had made awards in 1921. (In 1926, however, the Carnegie Corporation donated $10,000 to the New York Public Library for the purchase of Arthur A. Schomburg's library of books and pamphlets, which became the nucleus of the important collection that bears the black bibliophile's name.[178]) Because the ASNLH no longer had Carnegie support, Leland and Jameson looked for another way of impressing the Rockefeller people and commissioned an "impartial" investigation of the Association's activities, which was forwarded the following year to the LSRM, along with the references from leading historians and anthropologists. Significantly, in his supporting letter Leland stressed Woodson's "conservative" character. The report that he enclosed recognized the autocratic way in which Woodson ran his organization, but emphasized how the ASNLH and the *JNH* told "the truth . . . free from the controversial spirit in which heretofore the subject had almost uniformly been handled," and how Woodson aimed to "promote harmony between the races."[179]

Woodson was aware that his prospects for a renewal from the LSRM would be contingent upon the fact that the Rockefeller philanthropies were really interested in applied research into current social problems, which they hoped to ameliorate, and not in historical studies. This was the view underlying the generous support that they afforded to sociological investigations into race relations under the southern liberal Howard W. Odum at the University of North Carolina and under Charles S. Johnson, first at the National Urban League and then, beginning in 1928, at Fisk University. By the mid-1920s, when the LSRM had sorted out priorities and established a coherent policy, it decided that it was interested in "scientific research [not] as an end in itself" but as subsidiary to the practical assistance it gave the CIC and to developing black leadership.[180] The spirit of the LSRM's activities was reflected in the views of Leonard Outhwaite, an anthropologist who served as its race relations program officer. To Outhwaite, it appeared that since "we are dealing with a group of people . . . handicapped in many respects . . . [o]ur objective . . . is to bring them as nearly as possible to a state where they can develop their own leadership, and . . . finance their own welfare." Echoing this rationale in his application for money from the LSRM that subsidized the creation of Fisk's Social Science Department beginning in the late 1920s, the university president, Thomas Elsa Jones, stated that its main purposes would be not only to train scholars and encourage investigation of "social and economic problems," but to "develop Negro leaders who will more fully understand the social background, problems and possibilities of their race in America" and to "provide the kind of instruction that will help prepare Negroes to enter the fields of business, law, [and] social science."[181]

This wish to encourage educated and knowledgeable black leadership underlay the changing nature of the philanthropic leaders' long-range plans for Negro education, which in turn would have momentous impact both on the course of Woodson's relationships with the philanthropists and on the course of black historical scholarship. At the heart of the change was a shift from focusing on industrial and rural elementary schools to improving facilities at the black colleges and universities in the South. These institutions would not only provide educated leaders, but would also function as centers of research on blacks in America. By the end of the

1920s the GEB, with the enthusiastic support of Embree and the Rosenwald Fund, had embarked upon the development of four major centers of black higher education: in New Orleans, where they encouraged the merger of long-established Congregationalist and Methodist colleges to form a new university named in honor of James Hardy Dillard; in Washington, where GEB contributions supplemented increased funding for Howard University from the federal government; in Atlanta, where under the leadership of John Hope a federation of the half-dozen black colleges was created and Atlanta University was transformed into a graduate and professional school; and in Nashville, at Fisk University, where GEB contributions enhanced the undergraduate teaching and money from both the Rockefeller boards and the Rosenwald Fund provided the base for Charles S. Johnson's operations.[182] Three of these institutions—Fisk, Howard, and Atlanta—became the leading centers of black scholarship in the country.

In addition to such direct financing of selected institutions, both foundations also sponsored fellowship programs to improve the quality of these and other black colleges. The Rosenwald Fellowships, inaugurated in 1928, became justly celebrated; less publicized but at least as important, was the GEB's own fellowship program, inaugurated in 1924, to assist teachers in southern schools, both black and white, in obtaining their doctorates. As the GEB's historian stated, the list of black recipients read like a "Who's Who among Negro American Educators."[183]

Thus from the 1920s through the 1940s, these two foundations were of incalculable importance in encouraging black higher education and scholarship. In fostering the development of a well-trained leadership class they had quite unconsciously adopted Du Bois's strategy of the "Talented Tenth." And even this formerly caustic critic of the GEB as early as 1930 observed: "Notwithstanding all of its past mistakes in attitude and personnel, there can be no doubt but that, in the lamentable failure of democracy in the South and the persistent enmity of the white worker, the General Education Board in later years has been the salvation of education among Negroes."[184]

The encouragement of Afro-American historical scholarship was scarcely a major consideration in the minds of those who projected this program. Still the professional preparation of nearly all of the black historians who received their advanced training between the mid-1920s and the close of World War II was facilitated—and often actually made possible—by fellowships from either the GEB, the Rosenwald Fund, or both. As for Woodson, the philanthropists not only wanted him to supervise research projects on the current economic and social status of the Negro, but they also hoped that he would enhance their efforts on behalf of higher education by transferring his operations to one of the black universities.

Woodson certainly did not have the consummate respect from Embree and the Rockefeller boards enjoyed by Charles S. Johnson, whom the GEB's Jackson Davis once described as "scholarly, judicial and objective in his attitude. Utterly unselfish, widely known and respected by both races, North and South."[185] Still the staff of the Rockefeller philanthropies undoubtedly envisaged for Woodson a role similar to, though considerably more modest than, the one played by Johnson in developing the Social Science Department at Fisk.

When as early as 1925 the LSRM had suggested to Woodson the desirability of connecting his work with one of the black universities,[186] it is scarcely likely that the philanthropists' thinking on the future of Woodson's activities had fully crystallized or that the ASNLH founder was aware of its full import. Still, in applying at this time for a second grant from the LSRM, Woodson tailored his research proposals to satisfy its ideas. Outhwaite recommended to his superiors "that Carter Woodson's organization might be utilized as a medium through which studies could be made in . . . contemporary Negro life. . . . It also seems that Woodson's Journal loses a good deal of its popular appeal and also of its value as a social service in confining itself strictly to documentary history."[187] Outhwaite desired to promote studies that would illuminate the economic status of Negroes, and when Woodson introduced him to the delegates at the ASNLH's 1925 spring conference, Outhwaite's remarks dwelt on the importance of Negro business development.[188] Soon afterward Woodson modified the direction of his research program and announced that he was preparing to do a survey of Negro business. In his application for the grant renewal he explained: "In the future the Association will not prosecute any further the study of the Negro prior to the Civil War," but will confine its efforts "largely to a study of the social and economic conditions since their emancipation." Personally he was still deeply interested in strictly historical research, but the exigencies of foundation funding pushed him away from what both he and Jameson had envisaged. As he would later say in applying for a third Rockefeller grant in 1929: "I should make it clear . . . that this program of studying the social and economic conditions of Negroes in the United States since the Civil War is not exactly our program. It was suggested to us by the representative of the Memorial. That board was very much interested in such studies, and believed that the Association should pay more attention to matters of this sort. We agreed to do so. The Memorial gave us the money for the purpose, and we spent it as suggested. You will remember that our special interest is in history rather than things purely social or economic."[189]

Impressed by the evidences of Woodson's conservatism and satisfied with the new direction of his research program, the LSRM in 1926 made an award that Woodson described as "decidedly the most substantial uplift the Association has so far received"—a total of $30,000 for research over three years and $15,000 as a revolving fund for publishing studies resulting from the ASNLH's investigations.[190] Employing Lorenzo J. Greene, the future historian of New England slavery, and several part-time investigators, Woodson used the bulk of the new research monies to undertake occupational studies of black businessmen, wage earners, and professional men.[191] With a $16,000 grant from another agency, the Institute of Social and Religious Research (ironically headed by John R. Mott, who earlier as Moorland's boss at the YMCA had followed the advice of Thomas Jesse Jones), the ASNLH also began a study of the contemporary Negro church. As with the other investigations, Woodson offered assurances that "it is not the intention of the staff to make a study of the Negro church from the historical point of view."[192]*

When the second LSRM grant was about to expire in 1929, Woodson applied to the Rockefeller philanthropies for an even larger sum to continue the social and economic investigations. About the same time he asked the Rosenwald Fund, now headed by Embree, to underwrite a subject closer to his heart, antebellum free Negroes and their distinguished descendants. But he found both foundations, whose operations relative to black scholarship and education were now closely integrated, exhibiting considerable reluctance. Flattering letters to the aging Rosenwald notwithstanding, the historian was not only denied a grant, but the philanthropist also reduced sharply his personal annual contribution in support of the *Journal*.[194] On the other hand, the personnel of the Rockefeller philanthropies, though ambivalent and evidently divided in their counsels, did finally make a modest one-year award.

Woodson's application for this second renewal of the LSRM grant had arrived early in 1929 soon after the Rockefeller Foundation had absorbed the Memorial. The staff was in fact scrutinizing Woodson's operations and expressed skepticism on several grounds. Perhaps the fundamental consideration was the view that Woodson's work would best be connected with one of the black colleges. Believing that the ASNLH "can[not] be indefinitely sustained as an individual organization," "opinion among the officers . . . was that the research program of the Association might well be tied up to some negro university." A degree of unhappiness was also expressed because the small volume of sales for the books he published

---

* Woodson was able to appropriate modest amounts for purely historical topics to Ruth Anna Fisher and Alain Locke for studies of the slave trade and the African background and to James Hugo Johnston for further research into the relations between blacks and Indians. Zora Neale Hurston also received assistance for her investigation into Afro-American folklore in Florida.[193]

had forced Woodson to treat as an outright subsidy the revolving fund that had been granted in 1926.[195] Certain of the staff even entertained doubts about the quality of the Association's published historical works. One official alleged to Woodson that the foundation had secured negative assessments from prominent historians, which led to the conclusion that during the first grant he had attempted far too much and that both his and Taylor's monographs were repetitive and unnecessarily detailed. The Rockefeller staff had even obtained the opinion of four white southern historians, whose evaluations they assumed might be unfavorable. Yet of the assessments elicited by this fishing expedition, only Phillips, calling the publications of Woodson and Taylor hasty and "amateurish," was unequivocally negative. Dodd had high praise, and although Dunningites Walter L. Fleming and J. G. de Roulhac Hamilton expressed some reservations, both found the Woodson and Taylor volumes "very worth while," containing "very useful sources," and distinctly valuable because of "the new and fresh point of view."[196] Learning that such views were being solicited, Woodson promptly rounded up friendly historians to write on his behalf. For example, Jameson, now chief of the Manuscript Division of the Library of Congress, came through with his usual enthusiasm, "thoroughly believing [as he did] in the excellence and value" of the Association's "judiciously planned and well executed program."[197]* Accordingly, the Rockefeller Foundation reluctantly granted $10,000 for the year 1929-30 but informed Woodson that he could not expect much support in the future.[199]

At the same time the Rockefeller Foundation, renewing the suggestion first broached with Woodson in 1925, indicated that it would be open to further requests for funding if he would conduct his research program under the auspices of one of the black universities. At the Rosenwald Fund Embree agreed and informed Woodson that both foundations were "committed to the general idea of building up research under strong universities." Naturally the man who from the first had been reluctant to develop his program under the auspices of Howard University and who subsequently bridled at the very thought of a cooperative relationship with Tuskegee was hardly likely to respond favorably to this kind of proposal. And he presented several arguments against any such plans. Unlike Charles S. Johnson, he did not consider the black colleges to be places where serious scholarship was viable. Since "the very best [Negro] colleges . . . are

---

* Jameson, as chief of the division, also vigorously supported Woodson's efforts to collect manuscripts to be deposited at the Library of Congress. Although Woodson received initial funding from the SSRC in 1928, subsequent efforts to obtain money from various philanthropies failed.[198] The fruits of this endeavor are to be seen in the Woodson Papers at the Library of Congress.

not yet doing accredited college work equivalent to two years . . . at Harvard or Yale," establishing any link between the ASNLH and "such undeveloped institutions . . . [is] out of the question." He explained that his own experiences teaching at black colleges had shown that neither the students, who were aiming for professional careers in law, medicine, and teaching, nor (with rare exceptions) the professors, who "were concerned only with salaries," had any interest in scholarship. "There is no such thing," he observed, "as a Negro university in the sense of a circle of teachers addressing themselves to the advanced phases of their work"; and "in all these years . . . none of the so-called Negro universities have carried out a research program . . . appraised as scientifically valuable." In a thinly veiled slap at what had been accomplished at Tuskegee under the Carnegie award to Work and the more recent Rockefeller and Rosenwald funding of Johnson at Fisk, he added that large sums granted to black educational institutions for research were unproductive: "I know of one case of such an appropriation of $50,000," yet the recipient produced nothing. "Another institution is now receiving a large sum . . . but we cannot tell as yet whether these funds will be profitably used. The Director of these studies has only a few well prepared teachers to cooperate with him, and one of the men connected with his staff was dismissed here by the Association because of inefficiency. The others get the money, and the Association does the work." In his view, therefore, the ASNLH could best continue to make its contribution as an independent organization, training research scholars for the black colleges. He argued that if the Association lost its independent status, it would result in impeding the organizing of branches, obtaining adoptions of his textbook in the public schools, and the fund-raising among black teachers.[200]

The philanthropies had not quite closed the door, and Woodson, undaunted by the very clear signals they were sending, in March 1930 once more applied to both the Rosenwald Fund and the GEB. Pressed yet again to affiliate with one of the black universities, he reiterated the view that "the Association has developed so far beyond the capacity of the social science department of any Negro institution that it would be impracticable thus to reduce its status." At first the Rosenwald Fund and the GEB stood firm. Yet certain people on the staff of the Rockefeller boards realized that Woodson's arguments had considerable merit and recognized that his work was too valuable to be jettisoned. In the end the GEB pledged $7,500 annually for three more years of research and publication, provided that the ASNLH succeeded in raising matching funds from other sources. Sydnor H. Walker of the Rockefeller philanthropies, who had been handling the negotiations with Woodson, explained to a surprised Embree that although the GEB had made clear its unswerving commitment to the idea of a university affiliation for the ASNLH director, nonetheless Woodson had presented "a pretty good case for the independent existence of the research program for a limited period. If Mr. Woodson were a different type of man it would seem simpler to work out an affiliation . . . ., but every one appears to agree that neither Howard nor Fisk nor Atlanta is carrying graduate work which would enrich the program of the Association. Mr. Woodson is not the individual to subordinate his interests to those of a university"; but he "is doing a valuable piece of work" that would be terminated without foundation support.[201]

In the course of the next three years Woodson strove successfully to raise the matching funds[202] for what turned out to be his final assistance from the Rockefeller and Rosenwald philanthropies. His first thought was to turn to other foundations, and he appealed at once to Embree. The Rosenwald Fund was restricting itself to helping build the new educational centers, but Embree recognized, as did the Rockefeller people, that Woodson "is an important man in the Negro field and apparently cannot work with a university group" and offered to ask Julius Rosenwald himself to give the ASNLH $1,000 annually for the life of the GEB grant. Woodson, unhappy with the fund's position, replied tartly: "I regret very much that the Fund does not see its way to make an appropriation . . . I am sure that you will live long enough to regret it also. . . . We shall be glad to have you take up with Mr. Rosenwald the matter of a personal contribution."[203] Embree ignored the insult, and soon afterward Rosenwald guaranteed $1,000 for the first year—more than any of his previous annual gifts. Later when Rosenwald decided against continuing this arrangement, Embree felt constrained to help Woodson himself and arranged to have the fund appropriate $2,500.[204] A request for similar assistance from the Carnegie Corporation proved fruitless. Accordingly in order to meet the GEB's matching requirement, Woodson turned to raising the remainder in small amounts, chiefly from individuals, schools, and churches in the black community.[205]

This activity prefigured the future. Woodson's efforts were now focused more on seeking donations than on supervising research, and productivity declined. His investigators did bring to a close the occupational studies begun in the late 1920s, but the projected books on the black religious and fraternal organizations were never completed,[206] and thereafter research ground to a halt. On the other hand, building partly on this fund-raising experience Woodson by the mid-1930s would learn how to finance the Association's operating expenses—though not any research program—by pitching his appeals to the black community. By then Woodson's flair for controversy had embroiled him in a fight with much of the black leadership establishment, and his relationships with both them and the philanthropists ended in extraordinary bitterness and a public row.

In a stream of press releases during 1931 and 1932 Woodson publicly aired his hostility toward the black liberal arts colleges and universities. Printed in a number of the black newspapers, his sweeping indictment of these institutions and the Negro college–educated elite caused quite a stir. The director reported an unprecedented number of speaking engagements as a result; at Du Bois's invitation, Woodson summarized his views in the Crisis;[207] and in 1933 much of the material was published in book form as The Mis-Education of the Negro.

As Horace Mann Bond, then a professor at Fisk, pointed out, Woodson's broad-gauged attack was marred by numerous inconsistencies and contradictions.[208] But its central message was clear: that the black institutions of higher education, by imitating the curriculum of white liberal arts colleges instead of gearing their curricula to the practical needs, innate talents, and indigenous culture of the blacks themselves, failed to prepare their students for racial leadership. As he observed apropos of GEB–Rosenwald Fund plans for Fisk, Dillard, Atlanta, and Howard: "I believe that the establishment of these four centres . . . can be carried out as to mark an epoch in the development of the Negro race. On the other hand, there is just as much possibility for a colossal failure of the whole scheme. If these institutions are to be the replica of universities like Harvard, Yale, Columbia and Chicago . . . the money thus invested will be just as profitably spent if it is used to buy peanuts to throw at the animals in a circus." At times, in fact, this Harvard Ph.D. sounded like an extreme version of Booker T. Washington in his emphasis upon the practical trades. Nearly all "successful Negroes in this country," he averred, had "entered upon their life's work without formal education. The large majority of the Negroes who have put on the finishing touches of our best colleges, however, are all but worthless in the uplift of their people."[209]

Some of Woodson's arguments reflected views about blacks' inborn artistic genius that had been widely current during the Harlem Renaissance of the 1920s. According to his statements, the problem with the black liberal arts colleges and universities was largely rooted in the fact that in seeking to have their students conform to white standards "and thus remove the pretext for the barriers between the races," they ignored the "unusual gifts of the race" and decried the idea of such expressions as "Negro literature," "African art," or "thinking black." "In their own as well as in mixed schools, Negroes are taught to admire the Hebrew, the Greek, the Latin and the Teuton and to despise the African." The " 'highly educated' Negroes" failed to see that it was the whites who forced this position upon them and compelled them to ignore the fact "that each race has certain gifts which the others do not possess." For blacks, the greatest opportunity lay in the cultivation of the arts, an area for which the Negro was particularly talented. Only "the ignorant and the biased" regarded such differences as indicating "inferiority or superiority"; as a matter of fact "only in the development of a race from within can we appreciate its differences and discover the particular thing which one race can do better than any other." Thus, for example, the " 'highly educated' Negro ministers . . . know practically nothing of the religious background of their parishioners, do not appreciate their philosophy of life, and do not understand their spiritual development as influenced by African survivals in America and the peculiar development of the Negro church. The result, therefore, is that while the illiterate minister . . . preaches to the masses, the 'highly educated' Negro minister talks to benches."[210]

Suffusing this critique was the view that the black liberal arts colleges ignored the study of black history and the observance of Negro History Week. In fact, Woodson's opening broadside against the black liberal arts institutions came in connection with the publicity he disseminated concerning Negro History Week in 1931.[211] The ASNLH director informed the readers of the Crisis: "Looking over the recent catalogues of the leading Negro colleges, I find their courses drawn up without much thought about the Negro. Invariably these institutions give courses in ancient, medieval, and modern Europe, but they do not offer courses in ancient, medieval, and modern Africa. Yet Africa, according to recent discoveries, has contributed about as much to the progress of mankind as Europe." As he said apropos of the ASNLH's twentieth anniversary observance in 1935, at a time when he was particularly bitter against Du Bois and the whole black higher education establishment, "The thought of basing the education of the Negro primarily upon his own culture, upon his own history and status, is so distasteful to the majority of our colleges and universities that they wish that Carter G. Woodson were dead and his work buried with him. . . . From our 'higher' institutions from which we should naturally expect most help we get practically none at all." In contrast he extolled the land-grant colleges, which he said offered training in useful occupations rather than the literature of the ancient Greeks; "determined to make the most of segregation," they had built fine institutions even in the South's most backward states and had done much to ease the hostility of the white South at the same time as they instilled race pride. "In these schools in control of the Negro race you do not find any agitation of the race question, but you see favorable beginnings here and there in the scientific study of the Negro. They are taking up Negro history, Negro literature, Negro art and Negro life." In short, the public school systems and the lesser black colleges were far ahead of the Negro universities who gave "little thought . . . to the celebration of Negro History Week or to the work of the Association for the Study of Negro Life and History."[212]

There was a certain amount of irony about Woodson's critique. This liberally educated scholar was decrying the aspirations of the liberal arts colleges at the very time that he was complaining to the philanthropists that these institutions were not enough like Harvard or Chicago to warrant carrying out his work under their auspices. Although he was probably correct that black history courses were more commonly taught in the land-grant colleges, nevertheless at the time courses in the field were being offered in the best black institutions of higher education. At Howard University William Leo Hansberry and Benjamin Brawley were teaching African and Afro-American history, respectively; at Atlanta (perhaps in response to Woodson's criticism) a special professorship was created in 1933 for the teaching of Negro history to students at the four under-graduate colleges there.[213] Moreover in the autumn of 1931, when the stir over his attacks was at its peak, Woodson prevailed upon Atlanta University's John Hope to serve as the ASNLH president. For all the vehemence of his denunciation, Woodson realized that this leading spokesman for black higher education and a favorite of the GEB provided exactly the kind of prestigious symbol that he hoped would impress the philanthropists.

Meanwhile, Woodson had become involved in a battle with nearly the entire black intellectual establishment — ranging from Charles S. Johnson through John Hope and Benjamin Brawley to W. E. B. Du Bois — over a proposal made by Anson Phelps Stokes for an Encyclopedia of the Negro. At an exploratory conference hosted by the Phelps-Stokes Fund at Howard University in November 1931, it was painfully clear to the blacks present (including men like Johnson, Brawley, Kelly Miller, Walter White of the NAACP, Monroe Work, and John Hope) that the individuals who probably had the most expertise for such a project were conspicuous by their absence: neither Du Bois nor Alain Locke nor Woodson had been invited. At the insistence of the black conferees invitations were extended to these three men to attend the next meeting.[214]

The two historians, however, were both skeptical about the new en-terprise. They were unhappy with the seeming domination of the project by people like Thomas Jesse Jones and the Univeristy of North Carolina sociologist, T. J. Woofter (who early in his career had worked for the Phelps-Stokes Fund and assisted Jones on the 1917 Negro education survey). Woodson maintained that Jones, having made himself "the dictator of the program of the social uplift of the Negro," was now hoping "to do the same with research." Both Du Bois and the ASNLH director were emphatic in their belief that a publication such as this, if not "in the main edited and written by Negroes would be as inconceivable as a Catholic Encyclopedia projected by Protestants."[215] Yet their responses to the invitation were very different. Du Bois, long known for his interest in editing an *Encyclopedia Africana*,[216] regarded the omission from the original invitation list as insulting. Nevertheless, he concluded that because "it is a great project," "I have no right to let my personal feeling stand between me and the best accomplishment of this work." After securing reassurances from Dillard, Du Bois decided to accept. Woodson, however, refused to attend. Although neither Du Bois nor anyone connected with the Phelps-Stokes meeting had ever heard of it, the ASNLH director claimed to have been engaged for a long time on his own encyclopedia project.[218] Communications from Dillard and a conciliatory one from Stokes himself failed to move him, and he went public with charges that the Phelps-Stokes Fund had concocted the encyclopedia enterprise "to duplicate and, if possible, to destroy the work of the Association. . . . If they can secure the cooperation of the outstanding Negroes, who have been invited to participate . . . they may do much in reaching this end just as Thomas Jesse Jones did in the production of his report of Negro education which," Woodson now believed, "set back the wheels of progress . . . for almost a generation." At the same time, in a financial appeal to a supporter of the ASNLH and critic of the black leadership establishment, the young Howard University Professor Ralph J. Bunche, Woodson explained: "Instead of being assisted the Association is being systematically opposed by certain 'friends of the race' like Anson Phelps Stokes and Thomas Jesse Jones and thoughtless Negroes who cooperate with them to dictate the program for the Negro in America."[219]

At the second conference, held in January 1932, the question of what to do about Woodson became the first order of business. ASNLH President John Hope, who had met personally with him, reported that Woodson adamantly refused to have anything to do with the Phelps-Stokes encyclopedia. Du Bois was not inclined to give up, however, and was added to the committee to negotiate with Woodson. At the same time the conferees went a considerable way toward resolving the question of black control of the project. In the compromise that was reached, Du Bois and Park were named as joint editors-in-chief, with Du Bois serving as chairman of the editorial staff, while Jones and Woofter were excluded from any participation on the editorial board that would be composed of equal numbers of whites and blacks.[220]

The arrangements, with Du Bois moving into de facto leadership of the project, could scarcely have placated Woodson, who would never have tolerated playing a subordinate role to the *Crisis* editor. Trying to break through to Woodson, Du Bois urged him "to remember . . . that the enemy has the money and they are going to use it. Our choice then is not how that money could be used best from our point of view, but how far without great sacrifice of principle, we can keep it from being misused. . . . If you do not accept . . . that will leave us so much the weaker." Almost predictably, Woodson curtly replied, "I never accept the gifts of Greeks." Besides, he added, his own encyclopedia on the Negro would soon be coming out. Then he proceeded to take pot-shots at the Phelps-Stokes project in his press releases. In one he raked over the old misdeeds of Thomas Jesse Jones. In another he even charged that both Kelly Miller and Du Bois had originally been negative about the prospects for inaugurating the *JNH*: "Kelly Miller's prediction of failure, supported by that of W. E. B. Du Bois" had "not come to pass" because "a small number . . . have stood by this work."[221]

Woodson accused the leaders of the Phelps-Stokes enterprise of misrepresentation when they claimed he had not been engaged in his own encyclopedia venture.[222] Du Bois, like others, thought that the ASNLH director was bluffing. Having carefully searched the public record to no avail, the *Crisis* editor sought from Woodson some verification of the ASNLH's original decision to undertake such a project. He received a peremptory reply: "I must say frankly that you take yourself too seriously. You are no judge presiding in a court into which we have been called to prove something. You write like a child. Why should we send you anything? . . . We shall go along with our work as we have been, and you and your coworkers may do the same." The situation ended in acrimony, with the *Crisis* editor deeply pained over reports that Woodson was circulating a press release, charging that the Phelps-Stokes Fund had in effect bribed Du Bois "to give up my principles."[223] By then the Great Depression, whose impact seriously hurt the Rosenwald Fund and other donors whom Stokes had hoped to attract, forced a postponement of further active consideration of the encyclopedia. Yet as far as Woodson was concerned, Du Bois remained "perfectly willing to do anything possible to secure his cooperation."[224]

Woodson's attacks on black higher education and his opposition to the encyclopedists could scarcely have impressed the philanthropic boards favorably. Moreover, so little research was being done under his latest grant that after 1930 the ASNLH was not even submitting reports to the GEB; and, of course, it took "no steps . . . in the direction of university affiliation."[225] Amid the mild uproar he was causing, Woodson nevertheless continued to press for further funding, and both the GEB and old friends like John Hope were still willing to help him if only he would connect himself with one of the university centers. Twice—once in 1932 when

Woodson applied to the GEB for still another three-year grant and again the following year when he sought $5,000 to sustain the heavily indebted *Journal*—Jackson Davis journeyed to Washington to try to convince Woodson that despite the board's high regard for his work, additional financial help would be forthcoming only if "some plan can be worked out by which the *Journal of Negro History* can be brought under the aegis of the Negro universities."[226] Woodson, in rallying his supporters to press the GEB, unburdened himself to Arthur Schlesinger: the GEB was wrong to think that any of these institutions had as yet achieved the atmosphere and resources necessary for serious scholarship. Even at the highly touted Fisk University, the publications flowing from Johnson's "inadequate effort," he believed, "support my contention that it is money merely thrown away."[227]

Finally in early 1934 John Hope once again fruitlessly conferred with Woodson, offering him a position at Atlanta University that would pay his salary and defray the *Journal*'s publication costs. But Hope "could do nothing" to convince the historian, who adamantly maintained that to go to Atlanta would mean the ASNLH's "disestablishment."[228] Very likely the fact that Du Bois had recently returned to teaching at Atlanta, where he would presumably direct the production of the encyclopedia, only reinforced Woodson's resolve. In any event, upon further consideration he began to browbeat Hope, denouncing those associated with the encyclopedia as "traducing whites and hired Negroes." Hope, having received the treatment accorded Moorland a decade and half earlier, was deeply hurt, being "perfectly innocent of any desire to do Mr. Woodson anything but good." The Atlanta University president decided to break off this "painful correspondence that will not be of any service," thus bringing to an end both the effort to locate Woodson at a black university and all possibilities of subvention from the foundations that, as one of Woodson's close associates put it, had provided "the bulk of the support for the Association" into the early 1930s.[229]

Woodson's refusal to fit into the foundations' long-range plans for Negro higher education led him to look to the black community to finance his program. In fact, his final rejection of a philanthropy-sponsored connection with a Negro university was symbolized by his recruitment of the presidents of land-grant and lesser collegiate institutions for his council. Actually during the 1920s, one or two representatives of this kind of institution had usually been on the council. Between 1930 and 1933 John Hope was the sole member with any connection to college-level education. But in 1933, with the termination of the GEB and Rosenwald Fund grants, a striking shift occurred, and for the next decade there were always between four and six people on the council like J. M. Gandy of Virginia State; H. Councill Trenholm of Alabama State College; W. R. Banks of Prairie View State College in Texas; and the future New Deal bureaucrat, Mary McLeod Bethune of Bethune-Cookman College in Florida.

This kind of image-building was simply one aspect of Woodson's long-range and growing dependence on the black community, especially on a state college and public school constituency. In the long run the attempt to reach blacks through the churches had not proved fruitful; while for a decade there had been three clergymen on the council, beginning in 1933 the number was reduced to one. Yet as early as the mid-1920s Woodson reported that the *JNH* subscribers had shifted from an originally white to a black majority, while well over half of the life members were also blacks.[230] More important was the fund-raising that became associated with the Negro History Week celebrations inaugurated in 1926. Although thinking at first that he would need philanthropic assistance to prepare educational materials for the observances,[231] Woodson quickly found that enthusiasm among blacks provided a new source of income, stimulating subscriptions and life memberships from clubs and prominent individuals in addition to the "penny collections" at Negro History Week meetings. These observances attracted support from people including the eminent businessman C. C. Spaulding and the conservative educator J. E. Shepard, both of Durham; Susie Quander of the Order of the Eastern Star; and public school administrators, most notably in Washington and Baltimore. The public school officials, like the state college presidents, proved pivotal because through these two groups Woodson reached the city and state teachers organizations with their thousands of members. The local ASNLH branches, which Woodson developed beginning in the late 1920s, generally dominated by public school people (in many instances led by women teachers), and which regularly sponsored the Negro History Week cele-brations, reinforced this kind of fund-raising at the same time as they fulfilled their primary purpose of awakening an interest in Negro history among Negroes. Teachers appeared prominently on the sessions of ASNLH conventions, and in 1937 Woodson established a second journal, the *Negro History Bulletin*, designed specifically as an organ for this public school constituency.[232]

Thus even before Woodson had lost foundation assistance, he had created a valuable base for future financing. The Depression accentuated the fiscal problems stemming from the end of the foundation money, forcing him to develop further his appeals to the black community if he was to keep the Association and the *JNH* operating. The twentieth an-niversary of the ASNLH in 1935 witnessed the maturation of this effort. Woodson had made a fruitless stab at approaching white philanthropy for contributions toward a $30,000 Anniversary Fund.[233] Then, pushed by Charles H. Wesley and others, he laid plans during the anniversary celebration in Chicago for "a more organized effort to obtain small amounts of money from a larger number of people." The "Nation-Wide Sustaining Membership Campaign" was built around one-dollar annual memberships. Wesley served as chairman and Quander as secretary of the national committee.[234] Over the following years the success of this enterprise was based chiefly on the activity of a group of educators and a few businessmen. Noteworthy support came from people like Shepard, John W. Davis, Trenholm, and Roscoe Dunjee, publisher of the *Oklahoma Black Dispatch*.[235] Woodson's associates, A. A. Taylor of Fisk and Lorenzo J. Greene of Lincoln University in Missouri, headed the campaigns in their respective states. Over the years the most fruitful efforts were carried out among teachers and pupils by the Washington public school administrators Roscoe Conkling Bruce and Garnet Wilkinson and by Professor Luther P. Jackson of Virginia State College. Annually the largest amount came from the relatively well-paid Washington teachers. But Jackson's work, encouraged by his president, council member John Gandy, and built upon a painstakingly organized campaign first mounted in connection with Negro History Week in early 1935, was especially impressive. Through his contacts in the Virginia Teachers Association he developed a wide network among personnel at the state department of education, urban school principals, and county rural school supervisors. County supervisors were asked for 15 cents; city teachers 25 cents, and college professors 50 cents, while public school pupils and college students were urged to give a penny and a nickel, respectively. Woodson regarded Jackson's fund-raising as "the outstanding example of how an appeal can be made."[236]

These campaigns could not provide funding for research, but they did sustain the ASNLH and the *JNH* through the Depression. As Woodson put it a few years after World War II: "The Negroes of the country proved equal to the occasion and kept the Association above pecuniary embarrassment. Its income comes now almost altogether from Negroes, and it is very rare that the management seeks any sort of assistance from the members of the oppressing race."[237]

The Association thus entered its third decade with growing financial support in the black community. But at the same time Woodson was estranged not only from the white philanthropists but also from important elements in the black leadership elite. He had gathered about him a loyal band of historians, but otherwise he had largely alienated himself from leading Negro intellectuals. Rebuffed and angry, he lashed out at the foundations, at the black encyclopedists, and at the black participants in the southern interracial movement that he had once so assiduously courted. Actually as late as 1935, although the situation was quite unfavorable, there were still indications of interest in Woodson on the part of both Embree and those associated with the encyclopedia project. Thus when Woodson, with the support of George Arthur, secretary of the Wabash Avenue YMCA, appealed to the Rosenwald Family Association for a $750 subvention to help defray the expenses of the twentieth anniversary meeting, Embree behind the scenes was instrumental in securing it. Consulted by the reluctant administrators of this foundation, he wrote: "I warmly recommend the contribution." Embree added that while both he and the recently deceased Julius Rosenwald "had reservations . . . , he even more than I believed in Dr. Woodson."[238] About the same time another feeler came from the encyclopedists. Although Stokes had been unable to obtain funding from the GEB or the Carnegie Corporation, at Du Bois's prodding he arranged a meeting of the executive committee in April.[239] Not only was it decided that Du Bois should draw up a preliminary outline of the topics to be included, but the conferees also assigned Hope and Dillard to make a final approach to Woodson, in the belief that if he could be persuaded of the project's importance he might set aside personal differences. But the ASNLH director's response was distinctly negative.[240]

Simultaneously with this revival of activity concerning the encyclopedia came the appearance that spring of Du Bois's *Black Reconstruction*. Facilitated as the monograph had been by three years of fellowships from the Rosenwald Fund (1931, 1933, 1934) and lesser grants from the Carnegie Corporation,[241] the book could scarcely have mollified the ASNLH director. In any event Woodson warmed to the fray. In announcing his plans for the Association's twentieth anniversary celebration, he issued a press release headlined " 'Race Leaders' Barred from History Conference/Ablest Scholars Have Been Poor Thinkers," in which he excoriated Du Bois and others as "miseducated Negroes" dependent on the philanthropy of white oppressors. Du Bois—who had recently turned to a separatist program— was cited as the leading Afro-American scholar, who as "the idol of the Miseducated Negro" was a prime "disaster" for the race. Having "from the beginning of his career even into advanced age relied upon empty protest rather than work to solve the race problem, [Du Bois] now confesses himself a failure and advances as the proper remedy segregation which, carried to its logical conclusions, means inevitably the extermination of his race." In general, "The Negro leaders are not Negro thinkers. Their minds have been Caucasianized by their traducers that they may never depart from the groove into which they have been directed. At the [Association's] celebration in Chicago . . . , then, there will be no race leaders, and only a few of our so-called educators . . . certainly not many of those who have had 'the best in our accredited institutions.' The Association expects the opposition of this class and the oppressors who control and direct their downsitting and uprising."[242]

The following year Woodson engaged in insulting exchanges with both Embree and the black encyclopedists. Appealing to the Rosenwald Family Association for another gift, he simultaneously wrote the Rosenwald Fund president: "You believe in helping the Negro to do what he is told to do or what you want him to do. I am trying to help the Negro to help himself. The verdict of history is with me and against you. You may live long enough to see the error of your way." A weary Embree replied that the fund's purpose was to provide blacks with opportunities to "accomplish in their own way their full potentialities," and he advised the Family Association to deny the request, since "such research and publication should be in association with similar work at a strong university center." Embree then resigned from the ASNLH Council, and Woodson penned a characteristic farewell to his onetime fellow-student at Berea: "We had hoped that in your position you would render some valuable service in doing the work we have demonstrated . . . that we can do efficiently. In this we feel very much disappointed."[243]*

At the same time, with Stokes having released some money so that Du Bois could prepare his preliminary outline, Woodson lashed out again at the Atlanta University professor and his associates on the encyclopedia. In an interview with a reporter for the *Afro-American* newspapers he charged that "anyone who carries out a project led by Anson Phelps Stokes and Thomas Jesse Jones . . . is a traitor to his race." The only purpose that he could see for the encyclopedia enterprise was the white opposition's insidious determination "to supplant me and my work." Those like Hope and Brawley who had attended the original planning conference were "a group of politicians" chosen because they "would say 'Yes, this is a fine thing.'" Brawley was dismissed as nothing more than "an English teacher who has dabbled in history." And Stokes's alleged claim that Hope as the ASNLH president represented the organization was nonsense. Hope was awarded the presidency only because he was expected to be "purely

---

* A few months later, Woodson, seeking to counter the position of people such as Du Bois and Brawley, reached out to a younger intellectual Ralph J. Bunche, who accepted a position on the *JNH*'s editorial board. Extending the invitation, Woodson wrote: "We are seeking qualified men of independent thought and action. . . . We do not want anyone who has joined or will join the staff of the Anson Phelps Stokes–Thomas Jesse Jones–Benjamin Brawley–William Edward Burghardt Du Bois *Encyclopedia for the Negro*." Bunche replied, "I wish you to know that I am in full sympathy with your position relating to The Negro Encyclopedia." On the other hand, both earlier and later Bunche expressed to Du Bois his enthusiasm for the project and his willingness to contribute articles to it.[244]

cooperative" and ratify Woodson's viewpoints. The ASNLH director claimed that of all these blacks, not one could survive independently of white people's money. It was only Woodson who possessed the incorruptibility to spurn foundation funds: "What in the devil is [their] money to me, when I'm tied up in the hands of some man who's been oppressing my race for three centuries?" This explosion was followed a week later by an open letter to the *Afro* singling out Du Bois again for an ad hominem attack: not only was this to be an encyclopedia "financed with the white man's money and written according to his will," but also Du Bois "had gone over to his former enemy's camp," the person whom he had once termed " 'that evil genius of the Negro race.' "[245]

In the face of all this, Du Bois chose to remain silent—but not Brawley. Originally when the planning for the encyclopedia was getting underway, Brawley and Woodson had remained on cordial terms. The two scholars had projected a series of black biographies, to be edited by the Howard University English professor and printed through Woodson's Associated Publishers. But in 1934 Brawley's complaint that Woodson was not going "to protect the rights of the authors" had led to the abandonment of the series.[246] Now Brawley was incensed about the ASNLH director's accusations over the encyclopedia. How, he demanded, could there be any possibility of white domination on an editorial board equally divided between blacks and whites and chaired by Du Bois, in whom even detractors recognized a life devoted to racial service? Brawley also asked where was the justice of Woodson's "amazing" assault on John Hope, the tirelessly helpful, recently deceased ASNLH president: "Now that he is gone, however, and can no longer assist, Dr. Woodson names him first among a group of so-called politicians" whose yearning for the white philanthropists' approval had motivated their support for the encyclopedia. "Ingratitude could hardly go further." Then reacting to those Woodson barbs directed at him personally, Brawley pointed to factual inaccuracies in the ASNLH director's own research. He also contrasted Woodson's books, which had been mostly issued by the in-house Associated Publishers, and his own volumes, which had appeared under the imprint of Macmillan and other prestigious firms that submitted all manuscripts to "the most searching criticism." This rebuttal elicited a vitriolic response from Woodson. True scholarship consisted of fresh contributions to knowledge, and if Brawley were to present his summaries of well-known information to the history faculties at Harvard and Yale, "they would laugh him to scorn." Further Brawley's claim about his publishers' prominence "may be an argument against him, for these firms will publish anything to make money, and they refuse, as a rule, to bring out what is favorable to the Negro because it will not sell well."[247]

In the end neither encyclopedia ever appeared. Despite approaches to the GEB and the Carnegie Corporation, the Phelps-Stokes enterprise was never able to obtain funding for anything more than a single preliminary volume. Although both Embree and influential GEB staff members became convinced of the project's value and of the appropriateness of having Du Bois direct it, among other leaders at the foundations negative judgments concerning Du Bois remained. In any event the Carnegie Corporation — whose cooperation the Rockefeller people deemed essential — beginning in 1937 was sponsoring its own investigation of American race relations under the direction of Gunnar Myrdal.[248] Nor was Woodson, who could no longer finance any research, able to put together his encyclopedia, although virtually until he died the ASNLH director reported making considerable progress.[249]

Embittered about the foundations, Woodson blamed his problems partly on his insistence upon independence, but believed them to be mainly the product of an unending vendetta mounted by Thomas Jesse Jones. Originally, of course, Woodson had courted the network of blacks and whites connected with the southern interracialists and their philanthropic supporters, presenting himself as a scientific historian eschewing any agitation on the race question. For a period he had even consciously shaped the Association's research to the sort of inquiry that the foundations had specified. But he now saw himself as a consistently fearless, uncompromising seeker after scientific truth being punished for resisting the white philanthropists in their determined drive to dominate his work and even to use subservient black leaders as tools to destroy the ASNLH. Woodson's position had crystallized by the time of the Association's twentieth anniversary in 1935. In his annual report that year he averred that the ASNLH "could have a larger income if it formed some of the attachments which boards and foundations often exact to control agencies. . . . The Director has always taken the position that to do the work of this organization with scientific objectivity . . . the management must continue to be untrammelled. To swerve from this course might bring the Association to the position of producing history to order."[250]

Actually, for several years Woodson made futile attempts to secure further donations from the GEB, but the Rockefeller philanthropies had become increasingly negative about him. Across one such appeal a staff member scrawled: "D [E. E. Day] says Woodson is a pest and that everyone had sent [sic] him 'no.' "[251] And after his final exchange with Embree, Woodson wrote off the Rosenwald Fund entirely. Although he himself knew and on occasion correctly reported having received a total of about $6,000 from Rosenwald personally and $2,500 from the Rosenwald Fund, some years later he would assert: "The Fund . . . never gave any assistance to this only systematic effort to save and publicize the records of the Race." Julius Rosenwald himself, he added, "never gave the work of the Association any large sum."[252]

The ASNLH director, however, reserved his most vigorous denunciations for the Phelps-Stokes Fund and the "narrow minded, spying and hamstringing Thomas Jesse Jones," whom he excoriated for "lopping off all support of the Association from boards and foundations." Jones's 1917 report was now characterized as "a biased survey" "calculated to deal a terrible blow to the education of the Negro and [to] serve as an all but insuperable obstacle to the progress of the race." It had made him "immediately successful as the most advanced agent of Negro control," utilizing the Phelps-Stokes Fund as "a dreadful machine to finance the espionage." Because Woodson had criticized their scheming in the Yergan affair, Jones and Stokes, "assuming the authority to dictate the leadership of the Negro race ... became most vicious" in their attacks; and their "clandestine" efforts "finally ... had the effect of depriving the Association of the assistance of all foundations and the rich people who had formerly assisted the undertaking."[253] In fact, so firmly convinced was Woodson that Jones had successfully conspired to turn the philanthropies against the ASNLH that the accusation became an accepted truth firmly embedded in the oral traditions of the organization.[254]

Needless to say Woodson took a highly negative view of the foundation-sponsored research of the 1930s and 1940s. Virtually nothing passed muster with him: not the work subsidized by Rockefeller and Rosenwald money at the University of North Carolina[255] and Fisk University, nor the Carnegie Corporation's Gunnar Myrdal study, nor the preliminary volume that finally appeared as the result of the Phelps-Stokes encyclopedia project. Myrdal, for example, was a Swede of such limited contact with black Americans that he "could see only through a glass darkly. ... It is doubtful then, that in this expensive survey we have made a long step in the direction of understanding the Negro, or in acquainting the unwilling and indifferent world of his plight." (Of the other specialized volumes published as an outgrowth of the Carnegie-Myrdal project, only Melville J. Herskovits's *Myth of the Negro Past* could be regarded as "mainly scientific.")[256] Another example was Charles S. Johnson. In earlier years the Fisk sociologist had several times graced ASNLH programs, but now this special favorite of the foundations that were ignoring Woodson came in for particularly severe criticisms. In writing a book review of Johnson's *The Negro College Graduate* (1938)—a product of the same philanthropic concern that had led to Woodson's *The Negro Professional Man*—the ASNLH director not only called attention to many factual errors but also described the volume as having been produced at the bidding of the GEB, which wanted a defense of its decision to develop the new university centers: "Large sums were placed by this agency at his disposal. He collected what was wanted, tabulated the data, and published the work in the spirit of 'Your order has been obeyed.' " Johnson's contribution to the Carnegie-Myrdal project, *Patterns of Negro Segregation* (1943), was treated with Woodson's most acid prose: It "contains practically nothing that a sixteen-year-old Southern Negro does not know, although such a Negro would not be able thus to becloud the obvious in such beautiful phrases."[257]

Du Bois received similar treatment. His autobiography *Dusk of Dawn* (1940) was greeted tepidly, and other works of his received withering commentary. *Black Folk Then and Now* (1939), the updated and expanded treatment of the black past in Africa and the New World, which had first been issued in 1915 as *The Negro,* was criticized for a lack of balance and a failure to consult certain monographs on Africa. The preparatory volume on the encyclopedia, which finally appeared in 1945, was evaluated sarcastically. The editors had "not done themselves much credit" because the list of proposed articles revealed that they were not compiled by people familiar with Negro history, while important topics were conspicuous by their absence. Although the encyclopedia staff was to be congratulated for their honesty in making numerous citations to works published under ASNLH auspices, "intelligent readers" would hardly be satisfied with a volume so "inadequate and undocumented." Du Bois's "reputation as a race leader" was no assurance of quality, and impressive as the encyclopedia's editorial board appeared on paper, scientific objectivity required that the staff "be strengthened with scholars who know something about the Negro."[258] In particular Woodson singled out for attack associate editor Guy B. Johnson, the University of North Carolina sociologist who had replaced Park on the project. Du Bois himself had accepted Johnson only reluctantly: the latter was a gradualist on desegregation and not the outspoken kind of southern liberal like his colleague Arthur Raper, whom Du Bois would have much preferred. Moreover Johnson was known for his tortured thesis that black culture was derived from archaic English sources. But Stokes, in anxiously trying to attract Rockefeller money, had wanted to balance Du Bois's editorship with a southern scholar of Johnson's connections and moderate reputation. Du Bois, ardently hoping to see the project get under way and making every effort to be reasonable, had finally acquiesced. Therefore it must have been especially painful to him when Woodson articulated the reservations he himself held about Johnson and added: "Why the crew took this biased mariner on board is not clear unless the captain of the ship [Du Bois] believed that he can cooperate with Anson Phelps Stokes in finding an angel to pay the freight."[259]

Woodson's critique of the two Johnsons — Guy B. and Charles S. — was symptomatic of his complete estrangement from the kind of southern interracialists and their philanthropic supporters whom he had cultivated so carefully earlier in his career. Indeed at the very time that he was penning his scorching comments about the work of these two sociologists, he was also engaged in denouncing the creation of the Southern Regional Council, the largely Rosenwald- and Rockefeller-funded organization that in 1944 superseded the CIC.* The CIC itself, amid the growing black militance of the later New Deal and World War II years, had lost its earlier credibility. Moderate southern black leaders underwent a shift in their expectations and at the same time became increasingly sensitive to the rising criticism of their gradualist strategy being leveled by northern Negro leadership. Yet they also believed it essential to retain support among the more sympathetic elements of the white elite that had been represented in the CIC and to maneuver them to a more progressive course. At the initiative of three distinguished Virginia Negroes—P. B. Young, publisher of the Norfolk *Journal and Guide,* Gordon Blaine Hancock of Virginia Union University, and Woodson's close associate, Luther Porter Jackson— southern black leaders conferred in Durham in late 1942 and issued a public report that was for most of them unprecedentedly outspoken on matters of discrimination. While this compromise "Durham Statement," crafted chiefly by Will W. Alexander's old friend, Charles S. Johnson, was obviously gradualist in enunciating a short-range strategy, it did spell out in unmistakable terms the southern blacks' long-range insistence on what had virtually been a taboo subject—an end to segregation. Hailed by NAACP leaders and others as a turning point, marking a new spirit of southern black assertiveness, the document nevertheless was disparaged in some quarters as essentially the same old kind of accommodation to the limited vision of most southern white "liberals."[261]

Woodson, who had always avoided expressing himself on matters of broad racial strategy, took the unprecedented step of publicly aligning himself with a small segment of black spokesmen who criticized these developments. Editorializing in the *NHB,* he pictured the Durham Conference and the Southern Regional Council as a plot concocted by southern "white exponents of interracial politics" and "unprincipled [Negro] politicians" to undermine the northern black militant demands for the end of segregation everywhere. "The protest of the Negro . . . was weakened by the divide-and-rule policy of their enemies. Southern 'liberals' urged the Uncle Tom leaders of the Negroes to secede from the leadership of the militant Negroes demanding the abolition of all segregation, and the

* Since 1928 when the LSRM was winding up its affairs, the Rosenwald Fund had assumed the role formerly played by the Rockefeller philanthropies in helping fund the CIC.[260]

'boys' thus controlled . . . work[ed] out a program in opposition to such aggressive action." The southern black leaders, he averred, "offered no program toward liberty and freedom," but had actually "placed themselves in the position of defending segregation." From Virginia an indignant and pained Luther Porter Jackson informed Woodson that the initiative for the Durham Statement and the Southern Regional Council had come entirely from the Negroes, who had financed the Durham Conference themselves. "We your so-called 'Uncle Tom' leaders were urged by nobody to do what we have done. . . . For the first time a group of Southern Negroes got together and laid down to Southern whites a program which we want them to follow." As he explained, they were playing a delicate "double role": encouraging northern militant blacks to bring pressure on the South while simultaneously "trying to reach a basis of understanding and cooperation with our Southern white friends."[262] Of course the ASNLH director was intending his blast not for Jackson but for those whom he despised—people like Charles S. Johnson and Howard W. Odum, who were so prominently involved in the proceedings leading to the Southern Regional Council, and the philanthropists who supported them. Thus the ASNLH director's editorial denunciations can best be viewed in the context of his sweeping attack on everyone—from the southern white interracialists to the black encyclopedists—who looked for aid to the philanthropies that had one time played a pivotal role in encouraging Woodson's work.

In his obituary notice of Woodson, Du Bois pronounced a restrained epitaph on the ASNLH director's relations with the philanthropists: "Woodson did not prove the ideal recipient of philanthropy. . . . His independence of thought and action was exaggerated; he went out to meet opposition before it arose, and he was fiercely determined to be master of his own enterprises and final judge of what he wanted to do and say. He pretty soon got the reputation of not being the kind of 'trustworthy' Negro to whom help should be given. . . . After a while it became the settled policy of philanthropic foundations and of academic circles to intimate that Carter Woodson was altogether too self-centered and self-assertive to receive any great encouragement. . . . There was just enough truth in this accusation to make the criticism stick."[263]

Throughout their careers, these first two pioneering Harvard-trained black historians had each gone his own separate way, and indeed each had a different influence on the course of Afro-American historiography. Du Bois functioned in his day as an isolated scholar, quite outside the organized Negro history movement. His standing and influence, however, stemmed directly from his scholarly work. *Suppression of the African Slave*

Trade still stands as a piece of model historical scholarship for the era in which it was written; *The Philadelphia Negro* has been admired and found useful by sociologists and historians alike; *Black Reconstruction,* despite its controversial interpretive framework, has been a seminal work and source of inspiration for many of the more recent generations of scholars, black and white. Unlike Du Bois, Woodson did not function as an influential historian through his own monographs; outside the group of historians he gathered about him in the 1920s and 1930s he has not functioned as an inspirational figure in the profession. Rather like Charles S. Johnson, whom he detested, and J. Franklin Jameson, whom he admired, Woodson was the entrepreneur.

The suave Johnson was, of course, far more successful than Woodson in attracting philanthropy. As a result he succeeded in creating at Fisk a machine that not only almost came to dominate black sociology, but — by virtue of the esteem in which he was held by the philanthropic boards — made this latter-day Booker T. Washington perhaps the most powerful Negro in the country during the 1940s and early 1950s.[264] Yet curiously enough it was Woodson, not Johnson, who inspired the development of a band of scholars that made distinguished contributions to the study of the black experience.

Woodson, unlike Du Bois, did not produce monographs that are read and admired to this day. Instead he established an association and created a journal that launched Afro-American history on its way as a viable historical specialty; he sponsored important pioneering research; and through the *JNH* he provided a major avenue of publication for those, black and white, doing research in the field. Many of his personality traits notwithstanding, Woodson was able to inspire a small band of black intellectuals who, as we shall see in the next chapter, produced the leading books in Afro-American history during the 1920s and 1930s and remained deeply loyal to both him and the ASNLH. In short, Du Bois composed his influential monographs in scholarly isolation, while Woodson created the black history movement.

CHAPTER 2

Generational Change and the Shaping of a Scholarly Specialty

PART I, 1915-60

D URING THE NEARLY THREE-QUARTERS of a century since Carter G. Woodson founded the Association for the Study of Negro Life and History, there has been a transformation in the way that Afro-American history has been treated by the historical profession. In this and the next chapter we will explore the changes in the kinds of historians who have made scholarly contributions to the field, the varied paths by which they came to the study of the black past, and the shifting perspectives with which they approached their work. In the course of our discussion we will also be examining the process by which Afro-American history achieved legitimacy as a subject central to research into the American past.

In discussing the generational changes that have occurred, it must be kept in mind that any periodization is of necessity somewhat arbitrary. Nevertheless, upon analyzing our data, it appeared reasonable to divide the history of Afro-American historiography into five periods of unequal length: (1) from the ASNLH's founding into the 1930s; (2) the Roosevelt era of the New Deal and World War II; (3) the decade and a half between the war's end and the opening of the "Civil Rights Revolution" of the 1960s; (4) the brief half-dozen years marked by the apogee of the direct-action phase of the black protest movement; and (5) the climax of scholarship that followed, 1967-80. In each of the periods we have found distinct patterns of socialization that shaped the outlook of the historians who entered the field.

A word about the criterion adopted for choosing the particular period in which we have discussed an individual scholar and how he or she came to do research in black history. After considerable thought it seemed most suitable to use the date when an individual's first written work in black history appeared—whether this was a dissertation, an article, or a book. This procedure seemed to produce the most satisfactory understanding of the dynamics underlying the changes in the field over the years.

In this chapter we will deal first—and at some length—with Woodson's contemporaries. We will then take up changes that were occurring by the time he died in 1950, focusing especially on the nature of the growing interest in black history between World War II and the end of the 1950s. In the next chapter we will discuss developments of the 1960s and 1970s when Afro-American history finally achieved legitimacy and, in fact, became for a time probably the most active specialty among historians studying the American experience.

By the end of the 1920s Woodson and the ASNLH had made the study of the Afro-American past a viable enterprise. The publication of *The Negro in Our History* in 1922 at the time that he received the first awards from the foundations and the inauguration of Negro History Week four years later had done much to encourage the interest in black history in the black community. Meanwhile, the assist from the philanthropies gave Woodson leverage that he used to gather around him a group of productive black scholars who virtually dominated the field until World War II. At the same time a small number of whites, although their output was far less significant, also found in the *JNH* and in Woodson's Associated Publishers company, outlets for the publication of their essays and monographs.

During the first dozen years of the ASNLH's history Woodson attracted to his orbit seven black scholars: Alrutheus A. Taylor, a specialist in the Reconstruction period; Charles H. Wesley, best known for his contributions to the history of the black worker and of Negroes in the abolitionist movement; Lorenzo J. Greene, the authority on blacks in colonial New England; W. Sherman Savage, the historian of blacks on the western frontier; James Hugo Johnston, who researched early miscegenation and relations among blacks, whites, and Indians; Luther Porter Jackson, the student of free Negroes in antebellum Virginia; and Rayford W. Logan, whose most noted monographs were on Haitian-American diplomatic relations and on the rising tide of American racism at the turn of the century.

All seven were born in the 1890s, and except for Greene, who hailed from Connecticut, all started life in the upper South or border states. They came from a wide range of socioeconomic backgrounds, but all seven had done their undergraduate work either at the finest black schools (Howard, Fisk, and Virginia Union) or at superior northern institutions (Williams College and the University of Michigan). Belonging to the small band of blacks who were able to obtain doctorates during the 1920s and 1930s, all but one had secured their Ph.D.s at some of the most prestigious graduate history departments (Harvard, Columbia, Chicago). For five, preparation for the doctorate was financed in part by foundation money — some of it from grants made to Woodson, but mostly in the form of Rosenwald Fund and especially GEB fellowships. All produced important published monographs, some of which have not yet been superseded. The seven were all intensely loyal to Woodson and the Negro history movement, even though most of them had their problems with the domineering director. As Wesley put it after Woodson's death, "It was more in his tradition than not, to witness the development of either divisions of opinion, a break in relationships, or an indifference . . . that only the stouthearted would deign to carry on with him."[1]

Of this generation of black historians, Alrutheus Ambush Taylor (1893-1954) was along with Greene the one whose entry into the field was most directly influenced by Woodson. He was also the one whose monographic research was fully subsidized by grants that the ASNLH director had obtained from the LSRM.[2] Born in poverty in the District of Columbia, Woodson's first staff investigator was educated in the local public schools and on a scholarship at the University of Michigan, where he obtained his M.A. in mathematics in 1916. He then entered the network of social service that attracted some of the ablest and best-educated black college graduates of that era. After two years of working for the National and New York Urban Leagues, Taylor returned in 1919 to Washington as membership and social secretary of the 12th Street YMCA, where he directed the lecture series at which Woodson made frequent appearances. Branch secretary John W. Davis brought Taylor with him when he became president of the West Virginia Collegiate Institute that autumn, and after Woodson joined the faculty a year later Taylor and he became very friendly. With $500 that Woodson supplied from the LSRM grant, Taylor went to Harvard in 1922, taking his M.A. degree a year later under Edward Channing with a thesis on "The Social Conditions and Treatment of Negroes in South Carolina, 1865-1880." Woodson, having secured favorable assessments of Taylor's work from the latter's Harvard professors, employed him full time to continue the study of the Reconstruction period. Taylor's South Carolina monograph, expanded to include the political story, appeared in 1924 as *The Negro in South Carolina during the Reconstruction,* and two years afterward, *The Negro in the Reconstruction of Virginia* was published. The two men parted amicably when Taylor accepted a professorship at Fisk in 1926. Ten years later, having been aided by a special grant from the LSRM,[3] he received his doctorate from Harvard. As academic dean at Fisk, Taylor remained active in the ASNLH, annually leading the local fund-raising drives and Negro History Week observances. Elected to the ASNLH's Council in 1936, unlike some others he never had any serious argument with Woodson, who described him as a "faithful friend." When Woodson pointedly warned him against contributing articles to the Phelps-Stokes encyclopedia, the Fisk historian assured him that "my loyalty and support are pledged . . . to this program of the Association."[4]

Taylor's contribution to Reconstruction historiography was in two areas: his refutation of the biased accounts of the blacks' role that were standard in the literature, and his exploration of social and economic history. His first foray into the subject had been a rehabilitation of the black Congressmen based on the printed congressional records.[5] While this revisionist perspective on how blacks functioned politically was also an important aspect of his two state monographs, the attention to social and economic subjects in these volumes was unprecedented, making his work a timely parallel to the contemporary vogue of the "New History." Although this emphasis in Taylor's books undoubtedly owed much to the J. Franklin Jameson–Woodson interest in social history, in two respects it also reflected Taylor's response to the racist views prevalent in the profession. On the one hand, an examination of economic striving, educational efforts, and the building of religious institutions refuted the biased portrayal of black laziness, vagabondage, and social disorganization to be found in the writings of the Dunning school.[6] On the other hand, it seems that Channing, feeling that the Dunning studies had preempted the political story, advised Taylor to avoid dealing with it.[7]

Taylor's monographs were written with a style notable for their restraint and detachment. Carl Russell Fish in reviewing the South Carolina volume wrote that "while Mr. Taylor's comments and adjectives fully indicate his sympathies . . . he cannot be accused of unfairness in the selection and presentation of his . . . material." John Hope Franklin, in evaluating the corpus of Taylor's work, has written of the Fisk historian's "determination not to engage in the polemical writing that had filled the pages of the historical works he undertook to refute. Invariably he was governed by the maxim, 'Let the facts speak for themselves.' He adhered to the view that truth needed no rhetorical flourishes, didactic digressions, or picturesque metaphors. Thus, his books and numerous articles are straightforward, logical, and unemotional." Nevertheless, although Taylor's research obviously informed Francis Butler Simkins and Robert H. Woody's *South Carolina during Reconstruction* (1932), his scholarship was pretty much ignored over the years by white historians of the Reconstruction. It was Samuel Denny Smith's dim view of *The Negro in Congress* (1940), not Taylor's more favorable assessment, that prevailed in the profession. As Woodson sarcastically observed in the introduction he penned anonymously for Taylor's second book, white historians "really believe that the history of Reconstruction has been written. Any statement to the contrary is regarded as heresy."[8]

Charles Harris Wesley (b. 1891), who had known Woodson even earlier than Taylor did, came from a middle-class Louisville family and received his B.A. from Fisk University at the age of nineteen.[9] There he had been introduced to Negro history by George Edmund Haynes. Securing a fellowship to Yale, he took his M.A. in 1913, presenting seminar papers on the Haitian and Liberian struggles to gain diplomatic recognition that became the basis of his first scholarly publication. Accepting a position on the faculty of the Teachers College at Howard University, in his American history survey he quickly introduced "special lectures [that] will consider the contributions of the Negro to American Civilization." Wesley thus shared important mutual interests with Woodson, whom he must have met soon after coming to Washington to teach. Although he was not involved in the establishment of the ASNLH, Wesley was prominently identified with the group of Howard University faculty who were pressing for courses on the black experience, and, like Woodson, was anxious to end the neglect under which Negro history suffered. As he said in an article written for the *AME Church Review* soon after the ASNLH was founded, it was time to overcome the lack of racial pride and "dearth" of historical investigation: "An interest should be awakened among Colored America in its history, and encouragement should be given to its general reading, study and investigation."[10]

In residence for a doctorate at Harvard, 1919-21, with a fellowship awarded by the university, Wesley became particularly close friends with his fellow student Merle Curti (whose writings were to reveal an avant-garde interest in the black past), and by coincidence pursued his Ph.D. under Woodson's advisor, Channing. Having developed an interest in Civil War history as far back as his period of study at Yale,[11] and intrigued by discussions at the time concerning the loss of morale as a cause of Germany's defeat in World War I, Wesley wanted to write a doctoral dissertation on "The Collapse of the Confederacy." But Channing, as he did in the case of Taylor's M.A. thesis, vetoed the proposal, this time because Albert Bushnell Hart, who would have to be one of the readers, had already concluded that the Confederacy's defeat was due to the superior strength of the North. Years later when Wesley finally published a book on this topic, Woodson offered a different explanation for Wesley's change of subject, indicating that the racist attitudes of white academicians were the cause of his decision. In a veiled reference aimed at former council member Hart, rather than Channing, Woodson observed: "Dr. Wesley has upset a tradition. Negroes are supposed to talk and write about the affairs which are peculiarly their own history. While the history of the Confederacy is history influenced by the Negro, white men, we are told, can handle that satisfactorily. . . . In the graduate schools of the North, Negroes working for advanced degrees are often confronted with this attitude. Dr. Wesley had to deal with it himself." In any event, Wesley took up instead a topic suggested by his advisor, a history of blacks in the industrial labor force since the Civil War. Channing, who was interested in uncovering evidence that would refute current shibboleths about the inefficiency of black labor, had thus, as in Taylor's case, encouraged the investigation of an important phase of black social and economic history. The resulting 1925 dissertation was an avant-garde and pioneering monograph published as *Negro Labor in the United States, 1850-1925* (1927).[12]

Woodson appointed Wesley in 1927 as a part-time investigator and the following year selected him to direct the survey of the Negro church funded by the Institute of Social and Religious Research. Within several months, however, the ASNLH founder angrily and abruptly cancelled the project, alleging that the data collection was proceeding too slowly. But the causes actually lay elsewhere. Woodson had ambivalent feelings toward the able and magnetic Wesley; people who knew both men well considered that Woodson was at least a little jealous of the Howard University professor. From the project's start there had been some misgivings on Woodson's part, ostensibly because of the fear that Wesley as a practicing AME minister might lack the necessary objectivity for research on the black church. Subsequently when Wesley accepted the additional position of presiding elder for the Washington District, Woodson became so infuriated that he telegraphed the funding agency announcing the termination of the project. The rupture between the two lasted for about one year, Wesley reconciling with Woodson because, as he has always maintained, "The cause is greater than the man." In 1935 there appeared under the auspices of Woodson's Associated Publishers Wesley's *Richard Allen, Apostle of Freedom*, the only volume to be published in the aborted Benjamin Brawley biography series.[13]

Wesley's heavy teaching and pastoral duties notwithstanding, he remained a productive scholar. The first black historian to be awarded a Guggenheim Fellowship, he spent 1930-31 in England investigating the history of emancipation in the British empire; this in turn led to his seminal studies on the role of blacks in the American antislavery movement. At a time when the important new literature on the abolitionist movement in the publications of U. B. Phillips's students Dwight L. Dumond and Gilbert H. Barnes was devoted exclusively to revisionist views of the activities of white abolitionists, Wesley was demonstrating that "Negroes worked to improve their own status and to advance the cause of emancipation.... In the light of ... historical facts no one may say... that the Negroes ... did nothing for the emancipation of themselves and the group to which they belonged."[14]

Through the years Wesley appeared frequently at ASNLH conventions and fulfilled numerous other speaking engagements. A superb orator, he played a major role in fund-raising, giving speeches all over the country for the ASNLH and regularly accepting the task of making the financial appeal at the conventions. Even after he turned to university administration, Wesley remained active in ASNLH affairs, and after Woodson died would become its president (1950-65) and then its executive director (1965-72). Ever the tireless campaigner for the Negro history movement, Wesley reflected the spirit of the 1920s cultural pluralism explicated in the writings of Horace Kallen and of that sensitive interpreter of the New Negro, his Howard University colleague Alain Locke. Wesley viewed the activity of the ASNLH as part of the broadening of historical perspective being carried out by the ethnic historical societies, which had flourished since the turn of the century. Historians, he noted, had minimized the contributions of non-Anglo-Saxon peoples to the richness and diversity of culture in this "nation of nations"; the ASNLH, like the ethnic historical societies, developed out of "the dominance of group pride, the need for defense against persistent adverse racial opinions and the desire to sponsor truthful estimates of ... past achievements." Thus for him, "Our Association ... has expanded the field of history so as to include the Negro," revealing "the truth concerning this race ... so that all who read may learn." In the end one could envision a time when all racial and ethnic groups "shall join hands in the making of a new America," but for this to transpire each of them needed "first ... to be proud of [itself]. ... Ours then is that first step, to write, to publish, to read and to believe in ourselves and our capacities. To this first task, may we devote ourselves confident of success, for pride in self has been the touchstone of destiny for nations and races in all the past." Only by cultivating a belief in their own powers and capacities through a study of their past would blacks be able to "link themselves to the future of American democracy."[15]

It was Wesley who introduced Lorenzo J. Greene to Woodson. Greene (b. 1899), the son of a teamster, grew up relatively well integrated into the white world of a small industrial town, Ansonia, Connecticut. Even though it was the inspiration provided by his professors, especially the dynamic Wesley, that led Greene to major in history as an undergraduate at Howard (B.A., 1924), he went on to Columbia University for advanced work without having the faintest interest in Negro history. His first contact with the subject came in a seminar with Dixon Ryan Fox, who urged him to do a research paper on the antislavery movement in New England. This investigation resulted in Greene's first published essay and paved the way for his later scholarly specialty. Financial exigencies interrupted his studies at Columbia; unable to secure employment in New York, he appealed to Wesley, who turned to Woodson and the latter arranged for him to assist in the church research project. For several months, beginning in March 1928, Greene was responsible for most of the fieldwork on this study, but when Woodson abruptly terminated the investigation, he retained the young researcher to help on the study of Negro occupations being carried out with the second LSRM grant. For Greene, the move to Washington proved decisive: the experience of working with Woodson gave him a life-long commitment to the study of black history.[16]

Greene's relationship with Woodson proved to be a highly ambivalent one, as admiration warred with resentment. For two years he was busy researching and writing what became *The Negro Wage Earner* (1930). Like Rayford W. Logan after him (and undoubtedly like Taylor before him), Greene was also involved with Woodson in the routine chores of the ASNLH and the *JNH,* committed to a "grueling schedule, stimulated partly by the long hours and selfless devotion to the cause of Dr. Woodson." Greene's diary entries at the time reflect his awe and deep admiration for his employer: "Left Woodson wrapping books. His capacity for work is certainly astounding. Eighteen hours a day seems to be routine for him. He does everything from writing books, editing the *Journal,* wrapping books, mailing letters and parcels. Nor is he above acting as janitor. . . . Truly a remarkable man." He marveled at the way in which Woodson organized the arrangements for the 1930 Negro History Week celebration, going out on a limb to schedule a banquet featuring Representative Oscar DePriest and the three black surviving former congressmen, despite considerable skepticism from some associates. After one planning session, Greene wrote: "If it fails, Woodson will be the loser. He already has given his personal check for $100 as a down payment on the auditorium. I constantly marvel at him. The secret of his success is that he has the courage to plan and confidence that . . . the project will ultimately succeed. Asked . . . where the money will come from should the subscriptions fail, Woodson answered: 'I am not worrying about that; it will go over. I just start things and never worry whence the money will come. I started the *Journal of Negro History* that way.' " Thrilled with Woodson's style, Greene observed to himself: "I for one am firmly dedicated to this movement. It has captivated me. Negro history is the greatest inspirer of race pride. Thank God for Woodson."[17]

Here were a faith and a commitment that would sustain Greene when Woodson acted capriciously and unfairly. Serious problems began in May 1930 when Woodson abruptly sent him a letter of dismissal. The following day when Greene went to the office to clear out his desk, the ASNLH director explained that there was no money to continue his services and then proceeded to air the difficulties the ASNLH had in selling its books. Though deeply pained, Greene subsequently volunteered to go on a tour promoting the volumes in schools and churches and among black business and professional people.[18] His travels through the South, Midwest, and Northeast over the following months proved quite successful, but the otherwise stimulating experience was marred by serious conflicts with Woodson over both the book sales and the publication of *The Negro Wage Earner.*

On one occasion Woodson wrote sarcastically, complaining how the sales were being handled and on another accused Greene of failing to remit some of the monies. More shocking was Woodson's unilateral decision to list himself as co-author of *The Negro Wage Earner.* As late as July 1930 advertisements in the *JNH* announced Greene as the sole author. When the book appeared with Woodson as co-author, a greatly disillusioned and angry Greene—finding himself losing the full credit to which he was entitled—wrote a stinging letter to Woodson and privately he continued to fume about what he regarded as an infamous fabrication. Woodson, he jotted down in his diary, had taken credit for everything in the book except the collection of the data. But actually there was "not an idea of Woodson's in the entire book." Greene, in his frustration and anger, assessed Woodson as not only dictatorial and temperamental but as a man whose honor he now questioned. In this dark moment the younger scholar was reminded of how Woodson had treated Wesley. As he pondered his predicament, he observed that Woodson did not care about the many enemies he had made; he was one of those people with thousands of admirers but no true friends and valued only because they have some unique gift which the world wants.[19]

Yet in the midst of these problems Greene could still find Woodson inspiring. Recording his impressions of Woodson's speech at the ASNLH 1930 convention banquet in Cleveland, he wrote: "The great treat of the evening . . . came from Dr. Woodson. In this setting of nearly . . . 200 people, half of whom were white, spurred on by the many attestations of interest and pride in the work he was doing . . . Woodson delivered [what Greene thought must have been] the greatest effort of his career. . . . Beginning in his usual sarcastic manner, he ran through the necessity of studying Negro history, told of the efforts of some to look up their own past . . . ; recounted others who don't want to hear about it, because they are ashamed of their color, then narrated the disabilities . . . under which the Negro lives here; showed how it was interwoven with the ignorance of his past; passed over briefly the achievements of the Negro in Africa and America, then ended in a stirring, eloquent, and thrilling plea for justice to the Negro in all spheres, because of his rich heritage and his ability to do the same things as the white man." Both whites and blacks in the audience "hung on his every word, and the acclamation with which his speech was received ought to have been full compensation to him. I was thrilled." Although on several occasions Greene thought seriously about breaking with Woodson, on reflection he realized that despite the man's mercurial personality, "I owed whatever success I have earned to my association with him." After all, Woodson had provided him with the opportunity to write *The Negro Wage Earner*. When a wealthy physician in Philadelphia sought to persuade Greene to remain in that city since in Washington he might become a threat to Woodson and thereby incur his jealousy, Greene replied: "I am interested in the Association and the *cause* is *bigger* than the *man.* . . . I am interested in Negro history, my life is dedicated to it. . . . My life's purpose is to *further the Negro's appreciation of himself,*" and Woodson's pettiness would not deter him.[20]

In any event Greene returned to Washington to assist in the study of Negro employment in the capital, and later while continuing his graduate work, he, like Logan had done in the interim, would do fieldwork for what became Woodson's *The Negro Professional Man and the Community* (1934). Meanwhile, Woodson, evidently drawing on the final LSRM grant, had provided Greene with a fellowship for a further year of residence at Columbia University. Taking a teaching post at Lincoln University, Missouri (for which Woodson had recommended him), in the autumn of 1933, Greene continued working on his doctoral dissertation with the help of fellowships from the Rosenwald Fund and the GEB. His degree was awarded in 1942 with his dissertation on *The Negro in Colonial New England, 1620-1776,* published as one of the Columbia University Studies in History, Economics and Public Law. But even this achievement produced a confrontation with Woodson, who had refused to read the manuscript, throwing it on the floor and declaring it worthless. This row was also mended, with Woodson personally penning a highly laudatory review for the *Journal.* Although the two men continued to have a "rocky relationship," Greene remained active in ASNLH activities and regularly headed the sustaining membership drives in Missouri. Special GEB grants enabled him to embark upon a study of the New England antislavery movement, but a heavy teaching schedule and the lack of additional funding prevented its completion. At the same time this highly activist historian became immersed in editing the *Midwest Journal* and in the valuable service he rendered the civil rights struggle through the Missouri Council on Social Welfare.[21]

For Greene, as he has said apropos of Woodson, the Negro history movement had functioned almost as a kind of civil rights movement. To both men, black history was a vehicle for social change, a movement to which they were unreservedly and unstintingly committed. Like his close friend Wesley, Greene remained loyal on the ground that "the cause was more important than the man." As an almost penniless Greene expressed it to himself at the lowest point in his relations with the ASNLH director: "I am sick of eternally speaking for nothing. . . . But it is *the cause*. I presume it is my destiny to give unstintingly to this work. And why should one enter any field if he is not willing to give his all?"[22] Greene had warmed to Woodson's crusade for building racial pride and self-esteem, to fill in the gaps in the fabric of American history caused by the prejudices of white historians, to celebrate how much blacks had achieved in the face of terrible obstacles.[23] Yet the published work of the two men differed considerably. Strongly committed to the craft of scholarship, Greene's work was more thorough than Woodson's and, like Taylor's, a model of detachment and "objectivity." His publications lacked the didactic quality so characteristic of Woodson's. Moreover, Greene's writing is cast in a more universalistic and less parochial framework; moving beyond the inspiration he found in black achievements under adversity, he wrote from the perspective that there is only one history—human history—and that what was important was to study the black experience as part of that human history. It was these qualities that have made *The Negro in Colonial New England* a classic that has not been superseded to this day.

The career of Greene's colleague at Lincoln for nearly thirty years, W. Sherman Savage (1890-1981), displayed a very different trajectory, for his research interests were shaped long before he came into Woodson's orbit in the late 1920s.[24] Born in poverty on Virginia's Eastern Shore, he was over twenty before he was able to complete his elementary education and twenty-seven when he obtained his B.A. from Howard University. Joining the Lincoln faculty in 1921, he took graduate courses at the University of Kansas and then, attracted by the low tuition, pursued his M.A. at the University of Oregon. Professors at these institutions encouraged his interest in black history and called his attention to the research possibilities in studying the abolitionist movement and the role of blacks on the western frontier. Both of these topics were the subjects of his earliest historical writings, which appeared in published form in the *Journal* in 1928.[25] A half-pay arrangement enabled Savage to use leaves of absence to attend Ohio State for a Ph.D. By the time he received his degree in 1934 with a full-scale study of *The Controversy over the Distribution of Abolitionist Literature, 1830-1860,* published in book form by Woodson in 1938, Savage was concentrating his research efforts on a life-long investigation of blacks on the western frontier. The fruits of much of his research on the West originally appeared in the pages of the *JNH*. Yet, although he had voiced "a deep sense of gratitude" to Woodson for help in getting his dissertation published,[26] Savage expressed no indebtedness to the ASNLH director when in 1976, a few years before he died, he published *Blacks in the West,* the final distillation of his frontier researches. While Woodson numbered Savage among his "boys," the Lincoln University historian was not as close to the founder as were others and never quarreled with him.

Two of Woodson's associates — James Hugo Johnston and Luther Porter Jackson — were University of Chicago Ph.D.s who taught at Virginia State College in Petersburg, Virginia. This was the land-grant school that under President John M. Gandy provided more support for the ASNLH than any other black college. Originally established on a collegiate level, it had been reduced by the state legislature to a purely secondary and industrial school early in the century. The presence of teachers like Jackson and Johnston, with their scholarly aspirations, was closely related to Gandy's successful efforts during the late 1920s to restore the college program.[27]

Johnston (1891-1970), the son of the man who had been forced to preside over the downgrading of the institution, devoted his career to teaching and administration there.[28] Having received his undergraduate training at one of the finest Negro colleges of the period, Virginia Union University (A.B., 1913), he began advanced work at Chicago in 1924-25 on one of the earliest GEB fellowships. His M.A. thesis (1925), under William E. Dodd, was an investigation of "The Social Significance of the Intermixture of Races in the Colonial and National Period." Subsequently assisted by funds that Woodson provided from the LSRM money,[29] Johnston continued his prodigious work on slavery and race relations, finding in the Virginia State Archives startling evidence of extensive miscegenation among blacks, whites, and Indians.

Problems arose with Woodson when Johnston sought a subsidy for publication of his lengthy manuscript. Because Woodson lacked the funds and urged him to request help from some other agency, Johnston turned to persons in the network of the Rockefeller philanthropies — Jackson Davis, and to Will Alexander and Charles S. Johnson, both of whom served on the Advisory Committee on Interracial Relations of the Rockefeller-funded SSRC. Involving Johnson in this way upset Woodson, and "a fight" ensued between him and Johnston. The latter attempted to mollify the irate director: "I appreciate the cooperation you have given my efforts. . . . I believe that with your aid, I may be able to do something that will prove of value and that in a small way will reflect on the Association for the Study of Negro Life and History." Woodson, though disgruntled, nevertheless maintained a proprietary interest in the material, and having lost the manuscript, demanded that Charles S. Johnson turn over the author's only other copy. At this point J. Hugo Johnston had no wish to continue negotiations with Woodson, and the Fisk sociologist accordingly rejected Woodson's request: "Your enjoinment . . . seems to be about as irrelevant as it is sudden and incomprehensible. . . . With best wishes and a hope that my next letter from you will mediate [*sic*] less choler."[30]

Still an SSRC subvention did not materialize either, and Johnston, having revised the manuscript while pursuing further graduate work at the University of Chicago on a second GEB fellowship, in the spring of 1932 decided once more to turn to Woodson for help in publication. In doing this he rejected advice to look elsewhere because he still felt obligated to the ASNLH director for his earlier contribution toward financing the research. Moreover, his ties to Woodson were undoubtedly strengthened by the fact that four articles of his had appeared in the *JNH*.[31] But Woodson wanted to publish only the section of the monograph dealing with miscegenation, and Johnston, partly out of prudence, demurred. Undoubtedly he was aware that just a few years earlier, pressures from whites had forced E. Franklin Frazier's resignation from his position as dean of the Atlanta University School of Social Work after publication of an outspoken article on interracial sexual contacts. Johnston explained to Woodson: "I feel that telling the truth about miscegenation may be dangerous to me personally, and I hope that by publishing the whole thing my point of view may appear in a better way before certain of my friends. You see, I now have a job by means of which I am able to support my family, and I must always be able to take care of my wife and boy." But Woodson replied tartly that only the material on race mixture would do—"the other parts are of no particular value."[32]

Johnston periodically continued to negotiate with Woodson, but even after the material had been accepted in dissertation form in 1937, the crusty ASNLH director was still wedded to publishing only the section on miscegenation.[33] Accordingly the monograph, *Race Relations in Virginia and Miscegenation in the South, 1776-1860,* completed under Avery Craven, was not published until 1970, when interest in the black experience had become greatly heightened in the profession. Written in the spirit of the books of most of Woodson's other colleagues, the work treated an explosive and emotionally laden topic with restraint and detachment. Winthrop Jordan in his foreword observed: "Some readers today will find his discussion . . . too gentle, and lacking in appropriate moral outrage. . . . It is precisely the attention to and respect for the 'facts' which give this study its special value."[34]

Luther Porter Jackson (1892-1950), whose father was a Kentucky dairy farmer and mother a schoolteacher, received his B.A. in 1914 from Fisk University, where George Edmund Haynes awakened his interest in Negro history.[35] Committed to a teaching career, he took his M.A. at Columbia University Teachers College in 1922, with a thesis on "The Educational Activities of the Freedmen's Bureau and Freedmen's Aid Societies in South Carolina, 1862-1872." He at once joined the faculty of Gandy's school in Petersburg, where he remained until his death, leading an unusually productive career as teacher, scholar, and civic activist. He became widely known among the state's blacks for his outstanding leadership in voter-registration work; his support of the NAACP's teacher-salary equalization litigation; his role in the formation of the Southern Regional Council; and his fund-raising for the ASNLH. This network of activities was based on his connection with the Virginia Teachers Association, itself "virtually the child of the Virginia State College under the brilliant leadership of . . . John M. Gandy."[36] Jackson not only promoted the voter education work by doubling as president of the Virginia Voters League and secretary of the Office of Civic Education in the teachers' association, but, as indicated in the preceding chapter, he employed his contacts in the educational organization as the foundation for his annual ASNLH financial appeals.

Jackson seems to have first met Woodson shortly after moving to Petersburg, and over the next quarter century (beginning with the publication of his master's thesis that winter) proved to be a prolific contributor to *JNH*. Starting with an essay on blacks in Petersburg in 1927, he made the history of blacks in Virginia his life-long specialty.[37] Following in Johnston's footsteps, by the end of the 1920s he had begun doctoral work (financed through the help of GEB fellowships and an SSRC grant) with Craven at the University of Chicago. Differences in perspective notwithstanding, like most of Craven's black graduate students, Jackson enjoyed cordial relations with this apologist for the Old South, feeling indebted to him for "an awakening to the possibilities of the 1830-1860 period in Virginia history in one of your classes in the Spring quarter of 1928-29." It is perhaps no coincidence that Craven gave a paper at the ASNLH convention the following autumn. As Jackson explained to Woodson: "He is a man who whitewashes . . . some of the sordid features of slavery and who in other ways arises to the defense of the South. In perfect fairness to Mr. Craven, however, I think it should be said that he entertains the very best wishes with respect to the Negro of today and conducts himself with Negro students at Chicago accordingly. I have never received better personal treatment from a northern professor than I have [from] this man. . . . I have fought it out with Mr. Craven in his office with respect to his defense of southern institutions, but at the same time I respect him as one of the most stimulating professors I have ever had."[38]

Jackson obtained his Ph.D. in 1937 with a dissertation on *Free Negro Labor and Propertyholding in Virginia, 1830-1860* (published in 1942).

The industrious and diplomatic Jackson had put in an enormous amount of research in the state archives and county courthouses. Given the hostile attitudes toward black scholars among state archivists, county officials, and even university librarians across the South, this was no small accomplishment. Indeed, to Jackson, his book "represents an effort in race relations. . . . Throughout my long years of study in Virginia archives, state and local, I have had nothing but constant encouragement and cooperation from white officials and libraries."[39] Craven found the dissertation "an excellent piece of research and well presented." It was so outstanding that not only Craven but also Woodson urged him to submit the manuscript for the AHA's Beveridge Award, rather than turn it over to the ASNLH for publication.[40] On Jackson's behalf not only Craven but Charles Sydnor of Duke University, known for his work on blacks in antebellum Mississippi, wrote John D. Hicks, the noted historian of the Populist movement, who was administering this prize.[41] Although the study did not win and even though a coolness developed between Jackson and Craven, Hicks arranged for Jackson to receive a joint publication grant from the AHA's Carnegie Revolving Fund and the ACLS.[42]

For the next eight years until his premature death in 1950, Jackson sought to continue his scholarly research while he engaged in an exhausting program of civic activism. He received a special GEB grant for a second book on Virginia Negroes. But like Greene, he found that the demands of a heavy teaching load, the lack of sustained outside funding that would permit leaves of absence, and the call of civic duty all discouraged the production of another major monograph. Jackson's dedication to a wide range of race advancement activities, helpful though it was in enabling him to promote the work of the ASNLH among Negroes, also led to collisions with Woodson. The latter "frequently cast aspersions upon my not staying in a cloister and mingling with the people instead."[43] When Woodson penned his withering words about the allegedly Uncle Tom blacks associated with the Durham Manifesto and the Southern Regional Council, Jackson vigorously wrote in self-defense. He was proud to have been the co-author of the manifesto's political section, which "reads exactly like any pronouncement which the NAACP or any Northern militant organization might make. . . . I speak in it as the same Jackson who has been a leader in the movement to arouse the voting consciousness of Negroes in Virginia; who has been a leader in the State Conference of the NAACP . . . and the moving spirit in the Petersburg branch of this organization." His work with the ASNLH had been integral in these efforts: "Through essaying the role of the scholar . . . I have been motivated by the idea of trying to advance the Negro race." Two years later Woodson pounced on the omissions in Jackson's booklet *Negro Office-Holders in*

Virginia, 1865-1895 (1945) as "the unfinished product of a race leader. . . . Why jump from one task to another? Why not finish something?" The booklet had been widely distributed among the schoolteachers and pupils, but Woodson thought that such shoddy scholarship was not justified by Jackson's wish "to give the teachers of the state 'something for their money contributed to the cause.' " Jackson, deeply pained by the "unmerciful" criticism, informed Woodson, "Your strictures lead me to classify you as a most immoderate person." The booklet's limitations notwithstanding, it had attracted praise from scholars at Harvard, Chicago, and the University of Virginia and was "easily the most popular work I have ever done." "Yes," he continued, "I am affiliated with a large number of welfare organizations and I lead some of them. . . . Ultimately my success with my booklet stems back to my long association with people. . . . [T]he Association for the Study of Negro Life and History is far better off for my producing *Negro Officeholders in Virginia.* From it will flow larger revenue for the organization . . . and most of all a greater appreciation for Negro history by the thousands who are now reading and studying a small volume in the schools."[44]

Yet, hurt though he was, Jackson remained loyal to Woodson and the ASNLH: "You stabbed me more than once in your memorable letter," Jackson informed Woodson on this occasion, "yet I am trying to recover and do for you and the race all that my training has provided for me to do. I shall be both a scholar and a worker among the people." As this dedicated supporter of the ASNLH informed Taylor a few months before he died, "I have shown this interest over the years partly because I want this work to continue after Woodson shall have passed. . . . Like everybody else I have had my 'run-ins' with him, but I have submerged instances of unpleasantness for the sake of the welfare of the organization."[45]

Like Woodson, Jackson was not only a scholar but also a popularizer. Yet in contrast to Woodson, Jackson—like Lorenzo Greene and Rayford Logan—combined his scholarly interests with a vigorous social activism. Resembling Greene also, his monograph was the fruit of meticulous research, written in objective language. Nevertheless, as he described it to Woodson, the manuscript was underlain with emotion and didactic purpose: "My general argument runs that although the 1830-1860 period was a dark one for the free Negro in so far as the statutes and their frequent enforcement is concerned, yet from the scientific angle this was the very period in which he made his greatest advancement. . . . Chapter VI tells the beautiful story of slaves securing their freedom chiefly through their own initiative, and then becoming owners of property and valuable citizens." Greene expressed similar sentiments; when Jackson warmly congratulated him on the information concerning the wide variety of occupations in which Negroes were engaged in *The Negro in Colonial New England*, Greene replied: "I am particularly glad that you liked the chapter on 'Slave Occupations.' In it I tried to overthrow the time-honored, but erroneous impression that the New England slave was limited either by environment, Yankee economy, or by his own mental make-up from becoming an integral part of the section's labor supply."[46]

Rayford W. Logan (1897-1982) was unique among the scholars who moved in Woodson's circle, for he alone was also close to W. E. B. Du Bois.[47] His intellectual outlook was shaped as profoundly by the *Crisis* editor, in whom he found a kindred spirit, as by the founder of the ASNLH.

The son of a butler who worked for a prominent Washington family, Logan first met Woodson when as a high-school senior he took Woodson's course in French literature. Assisted by scholarship aid, Logan worked his way through Williams College, graduating Phi Beta Kappa in 1917, just after the United States had entered World War I. Enlisting in the army, he rose to the rank of lieutenant and saw service in the Argonne Forest, but angered by the humiliating treatment that the army brass meted out to black troops, he elected to remain in France, a decision that had an enormous impact on the course of his future research.

It was during these postwar years in Paris that Logan came to know Du Bois. "In those days," he recollected, "Du Bois was for me, as for many other young Negro Americans . . . an intellectual idol."[48] So the young man was delighted when the *Crisis* literary editor, Jessie Fauset, another of his high-school French teachers, asked him to assist Du Bois when Du Bois came to Paris for the Second Pan-African Congress in 1921. Logan not only became intimately involved in the subsequent meetings of the Pan-African movement, but also during those years became acquainted with the Haitian minister to France and delegate to the League of Nations, Dantes Bellegarde, who was eloquent in denouncing the American occupation of his country. These exposures left an indelible imprint on the work of Logan, who would come to define himself as a specialist in the "World History of the Negro."[49]

Returning to the United States, he spent the latter half of the 1920s teaching at Virginia Union University. There he initiated voter registration efforts among Richmond blacks; made outspoken attacks on school segregation and other evils; criticized the common practice of having white men serve as presidents of Virginia Union and other black colleges supported by white philanthropy; openly clashed with his cautious colleague, the prominent CIC leader Gordon Blaine Hancock, on these issues and, as a result, in 1930 found himself forced to resign. Meanwhile, inspired by what he had absorbed from Du Bois and Bellegarde, Logan wrote prolifically on the situation in Africa and the Caribbean. His most out-standing work in this connection was a personal investigation of conditions in Haiti that resulted in the 1927 exposé in the *Nation* entitled "The Haze in Haiti."[50] At the same time, Logan was also coming under the intellectual influence of Woodson, whose writings on black accomplish-ments he found very impressive. Logan's participation in the ASNLH blossomed, his papers appearing regularly in the *JNH* and on ASNLH programs.

A GEB fellowship, followed by a year of financial assistance from Wood-son,[51] enabled Logan to spend the academic years 1930-32 at Harvard. Harvard and Boston provided another exposure that left an indelible imprint, for this period witnessed a merging of his activist impulses with a growing concern for the canons of advanced scholarship. He was known for his militant speeches—one in Boston in 1932 was entitled "The Ballot or the Bullet." There was also the stream of articles appearing in *Crisis, Opportunity, Southern Workman, JNH,* and *Journal of Negro Education* dealing with the evils of imperialism abroad and, with increasing frequency, with the black past in the United States. An essay in the Urban League's magazine *Opportunity,* celebrating the centennial anniversary of Nat Turn-er's death, was a highly evocative statement cast in moral and heroic terms. Whites, he noted, rejoiced in the annual observance on November 11 of the armistice that ended World War I; for blacks November 11 also "should be a day of pride—for on that day one hundred years ago a black man kept his 'Rendezvous with Death' rather than live a bondsman. His simple courage surpassed the comprehension of his executioners as did that of the Man of Galilee."[52]

On the other hand, Logan also recalled that his Harvard years liberated him from the kind of "uncritical evaluation" of Negro history that marked Woodson's publications. As a graduate student he received considerable encouragement from his advisor and fellow Williams College alumnus, James Phinney Baxter III, with whom he had a warm social relationship (akin to that of Du Bois and Hart forty years earlier). Previously Logan had agreed with Woodson that the purpose of Negro history should be to glorify blacks' achievements. At Harvard Baxter and Arthur Schlesinger, Sr., encouraged him to take a more detached attitude toward history. For several years, he recollected, these influences were "warring within me." Logan originally wanted to do a dissertation on the American military occupation of Haiti (1915-34), but at Baxter's suggestion he worked on a less charged topic—the earlier history of the diplomatic relations between the two countries. When Logan went to Haiti again for research in 1934, after the inauguration of the Good Neighbor Policy, the U.S. minister, Norman Armour, interceded to have the Haitian archives opened to him.

By the time he completed the dissertation in 1936, Logan concluded that the purpose of Negro history should be the same as that of the history of any people—to find out the facts and present them as "objectively" as possible. *The Diplomatic Relations of the United States with Haiti 1776-1891* (published in 1941) was this kind of book. What had originated in a passionate denunciation of twentieth-century American imperialism had resulted in a judicious discussion of events in the preceding century.

The Diplomatic Relations of the United States with Haiti represented the fusion of the several strands that had gone into Logan's intellectual development. His first inspiration came from Du Bois and the Pan-African movement, and Bellegarde had sparked his specific interest in Haiti. Then there had been the inspiration from the "very stimulating" Woodson and the Negro history movement in the United States. Finally in graduate school he developed a pride in the craft of scholarship that transcended the instrumentalism of his earlier approach to the study of the past.

Meanwhile, during the Depression years Logan worked first for Woodson and then for Du Bois. For fifteen months after completing his coursework at Harvard, he was Woodson's "alter-ego in all aspects" of the ASNLH's activities. As assistant to the director he helped with the *JNH,* processed book orders for the Associated Publishers, organized Negro History Week observances, and filled many speaking engagements. He also did much of the research and writing for Woodson's *The Negro Professional Man and the Community* (1934) and nearly all the work for Woodson's *The African Background Outlined, or Handbook for the Study of the Negro* (1936). Woodson also intended for him to assist on the encyclopedia project, but in the summer of 1933 John Hope prevailed upon Logan to join the faculty at Atlanta University. Here, in addition to his teaching and writing, he also assumed the leadership of the NAACP's highly effective voter registration program, which at times had striking effects in special and general elections in which blacks were allowed to vote.[53]

At the time Du Bois, Logan's colleague at Atlanta, was bringing out *Black Reconstruction* and working on the preliminary plans for the Phelps-Stokes encyclopedia. Logan was not uncritical of *Black Reconstruction*—he thought Woodson had already pointed out the positive side of the blacks' role, and he found the Marxist interpretation stimulating but dubious.[54] Yet in 1936 Logan accepted a position as assistant editor of Du Bois's encyclopedia project. When Woodson learned about this, "his anger knew no bounds," and he denounced his erstwhile colleague as a "traitor to the race." Alleging that Logan had taken with him from the ASNLH the inside knowledge of the plans and materials that had been developed for his own encyclopedia, Woodson dismissed the young scholar from his position as an assistant editor on the *JNH,* "and for more than ten years put him on the black-list." Logan for his part wrote Taylor and others close to Woodson, attacking the latter's dictatorial methods. One student of Woodson's career writes that "the breach between the two men was so deep and Woodson so volatile in expressing his displeasure that the other workers of the Association were concerned that the organization would be crippled through internal dissension." Logan himself, like others, remained loyal to the cause and "continued quietly to support Dr. Woodson." Ultimately things were patched up, and as early as 1941 the *JNH* carried a favorable review of Logan's monograph on Haiti.[55]

By then Logan, recruited by Wesley in 1938, had joined the Howard University faculty. In 1950-51, after Woodson's death, Logan served briefly as editor and director, but the ASNLH's internal politics eliminated him thereafter as an influential voice in the organization. During his long tenure at Howard his publications continued to exhibit his wide range of interests on blacks in Africa and the Americas, although increasingly he came to focus on the United States. He published books on the African Mandate question and the Caribbean; edited an anthology of essays by black leaders on *What the Negro Wants* (1944), neatly timed to coincide with the Durham Manifesto and the formation of the Southern Regional Council; composed a survey of Afro-American history;[56] and published his final monograph, *Howard University: The First Hundred Years* in 1969. His most influential book, informed by the researches of the M.A. students at Howard, was *The Negro in American Life and Thought: The Nadir, 1877-1901* (1954), reissued in expanded form as *The Betrayal of the Negro from Rutherford B. Hayes to Woodrow Wilson* (1965). The history of Howard was a model of dispassionate description, notable in view of Logan's own personal involvement in many of the institution's internal conflicts. But the two more important volumes, as their titles suggest, were infused with a fervent kind of moral condemnation that in the end set Logan's work apart from the other major monographs produced by Woodson's associates. Like his colleagues, Logan had acquired in graduate school a commitment to objective scholarship. Yet his published writings, dealing largely in one way or another with the historical impact of white racism, were more likely to exhibit explicitly the moral passion implicitly underlying all the work of the Woodson group.

Although drawn to Woodson, the group of scholars whose careers we have reviewed cannot be properly regarded as his disciples and cannot, except perhaps loosely, be described as a school of historians. Indeed, only Taylor and Greene can be said to have owed their enthusiasm for the study of Afro-American history to Woodson's inspiration. Moreover, the spirit of their books and articles tended to diverge considerably from that articulated by the ASNLH's founder.

Woodson, as we have seen, in his program of preserving and disseminating a historical record that would inspire pride among blacks and modify the racial views of whites, had, like the ethnic historians of American immigrant groups, focused on individual accomplishments. But in facilitating the work of his colleagues what he encouraged was the production of scholarship of a rather different sort. Where Woodson's works so often today read like archaic pedantry, theirs survive as coherent and systematic syntheses of topics in social history. Where Woodson stressed individual achievements, their works displayed a decided interest in the collective experience of black Americans, and in this regard they adumbrated the interests of our day. They too were inspired by the evidence of Afro-American progress and achievements in a hostile environment, but in their major published writings this was effaced by their commitment to the scholarly canons of objective history. Thus where Woodson, his strictures about scientific history notwithstanding, leaned quite openly toward propaganda, his colleagues (except to some extent for certain of Logan's volumes) wrote in a tone of detachment that contrasted not only with Woodson, but even more with the blatant bias in the writings of nearly all white historians who had anything to say on the role of Negroes in the American past.

Perhaps this dispassionate stance was partly a matter of strategy. A tone of special pleading would have alienated the white historians who might be convinced by a restrained and careful marshalling of the data, by letting the facts speak for themselves. As the evidence indicates, these detached studies of the black past were undergirded by intense convictions identical with Woodson's: a searing awareness of the contradiction between the democratic creed and American racial practices, and a hope—if not a vision—that the study of Negro history would be an instrument that would itself help change the course of history, creating modifications in the thinking of both whites and blacks that would carry America forward to the fulfillment of its fundamental moral values. Indeed, as Lawrence D. Reddick, who would join Woodson's circle in the 1930s, once wrote about his predecessors, their work had been "built upon a faith." Negro history, he observed, "has the generalized objective which it shares with all scholarship of seeking the advancement of knowledge plus the specific design as a lever of what might be termed 'racial progress.' . . . The faith now and then expressed, [and] always implied, is that the part played by Negroid stock has been important and positive in terms of human achievement."[57]

So profound was their commitment to the study of the black past, so deep their emotional involvement in what virtually functioned as a social movement, that even though the majority of Woodson's associates were victims of what they all agreed was his autocratic, arbitrary, and "domineering" personality, they were all deeply loyal to the man whom they admired for his vision and contribution, and to the movement for which he stood. As Wesley, recalling the bitter separations that had occurred with a number of Woodson's associates, observed, "Yet, this apparent weakness was at the time his tower of strength," and his friends realized that "his spirit, crusading . . . questing and unafraid had to find its own way." The result was that as Logan put it, like himself, "Many other supporters have felt his [Woodson's] iron hand . . . and have nonetheless continued to support him and his work."[58]

Neither Du Bois nor Brawley, who had established themselves as historians of the black experience prior to the creation of the ASNLH, felt he had to support Woodson regardless of how he acted. But the other men possessed a commitment to the man and his organization so profound that it transcended Woodson's idiosyncrasies and arbitrariness and militated against any permanent break. They all described their actions as stemming from "loyalty to the cause"; in effect, they tolerated Woodson's acts because of their own deep interest in developing the field and their respect for his drive and role in this effort. For some there was, of course, the sense of personal obligation arising out of the financial support he had been able to provide for their research and advanced training. One suspects also that in an era when the ASNLH represented the institutionalization of black history and in one way or another sponsored the publication of most of the work being done in the field, to be identified with black history was to be identified with the Association — to appear at its meetings and to be published in its *Journal* and by Woodson's Associated Publishers. This was true even for those, both whites and blacks, who came later. For until well after mid-century — when the mainstream journals began to recognize the significance of the black past — the ASNLH and the *JNH* were the preeminent outlets for scholarly expression and institutionally personified the field.

By the early 1930s Woodson had thus gathered about him a highly productive band of black scholars. Of the fourteen Negroes who were awarded Ph.D.s in history and the history of education before 1940, eight were in the ASNLH circle. Among these black doctorates, nine had done significant publishing by the end of the 1930s; two-thirds of these were in the Woodson group.* In short, it was this first generation of professionally trained black doctorates associated with Woodson who were

* The six from the Woodson group were Woodson himself, Wesley, Taylor, Savage, Jackson, and Logan. The three others were Du Bois, Horace Mann Bond, and Joseph C. Carroll (the latter two to be discussed below). Greene had authored a book in the 1930s, but his dissertation was not completed until the 1940s.

chiefly responsible for laying the foundation for the study of Afro-American history as a genuine scholarly specialty.

Down to the latter part of the 1930s contributions to the field by white scholars were — with one exception — distinctly peripheral. Nevertheless, some whites found in the ASNLH's program outlets for their research into the Afro-American past. Although in Woodson's view it was vitally important that blacks themselves set the direction and do most of the research and publication, he regularly scheduled whites on ASNLH convention programs and published articles and monographs by white historians.* Thus, for example, the 1929 convention program included the Harvard anthropologist and ASNLH Council member E. A. Hooton and the young historians Avery Craven and Samuel Flagg Bemis.[59] In addition to Craven, Fred Shannon, the southern historian Francis Butler Simkins, the Latin Americanist J. Fred Rippy, and ASNLH Council member Evarts B. Greene were among those who appeared in the pages of the *JNH*.[60]

During the first decade and a half of the ASNLH's existence, the whites who most regularly found in Woodson's enterprise an outlet for their research were two Canadians and an American who was a specialist in the history of British philanthropy. Neither Ontario Supreme Court Justice William Renwick Riddell (1852-1945) nor the journalist and university administrator Fred Landon (1880-1969) held a doctorate, but both were highly respected among their generation of Canadian historians, and both had had their interests in blacks and antislavery whetted by their acquaintance with the early Negro settlements of Canada West. Riddell was especially prolific — his articles appeared almost annually in the *Journal* between 1919 and 1932 and Woodson also published his *The Slave in Canada* (1920). Actually neither Riddell nor Landon was close to Woodson or associated with Negroes. Riddell's research on Canadian blacks was a minor part of his numerous interests; Landon was a good friend and warm admirer of U. B. Phillips, under whom he studied at Michigan in 1923.[61]

The American was the UCLA professor Frank J. Klingberg (1883-1968). Born into a prosperous Kansas farming family, he had secured his doctorate at Yale (1911) with a dissertation on *The Anti-Slavery Movement in England: A Study in English Humanitarianism,* published in 1926. Klingberg was an old-fashioned Gladstone sort of liberal, his interest in reform stemming from the high sense of moral values instilled by his parents and reinforced by his Quaker-pacifist wife with her socialist sympathies. He himself ex-

---

* In addition to the books by W. R. Riddell and Frank Klingberg discussed below, early volumes by whites, published under Woodson's auspices, included Ivan E. McDougle's *Slavery in Kentucky 1792-1865* (1918) and George F. Zook's *The Company of Royal Adventurers Trading into Africa* (1919).

hibited sustained interests in anticolonialism and the women's rights and peace movements. Klingberg also had a network of friends in the local black community; Woodson was a visitor in his home on several occasions, and his warm admiration for the ASNLH director was evident in his "Salute to Carter G. Woodson" delivered at the ASNLH 1955 meeting.[62] The ASNLH published two of his books, *A Side-Light on Anglo-American Relations, 1839-1858: Furnished by the Correspondence of Lewis Tappan* . . . (with A. H. Abel, 1927), and *An Appraisal of the Negro in Colonial South Carolina* (1941), based upon the records of the English benevolent organization, the Society for the Propagation of the Gospel.

However, easily the most important single contribution by a white scholar to the field of black history during the first two decades of the ASNLH's existence was Frederic Bancroft's *Slave Trading in the Old South* (1931). Bancroft was never a supporter of Woodson in the way that Jameson or even Schlesinger and William E. Dodd were. He like Du Bois never used the *JNH* or the ASNLH as avenues of publication, but composed his classic quite independently of what Woodson was doing. Raised in a center of antislavery agitation (Galesburg, Illinois), Bancroft (1860-1945) came from a family with strong abolitionist sympathies, and his early heroes were William Lloyd Garrison, Wendell Phillips, Charles Sumner, and John Brown. Pursuing graduate work at Columbia, where he developed a life-long friendship with his fellow student, W. A. Dunning, he came under the influence of the revisionist critic of Radical Reconstruction, John W. Burgess. His dissertation, *A Sketch of the Negro in Politics* (1885), reflected both his professor's view on southern politics and his own Mugwump reformism, with its distaste for the corruption that was allegedly the hallmark of Black Reconstruction. On the other hand, he was always very critical of slavery and later reversed his views on Reconstruction, his negative assessment some twenty years later of Walter L. Fleming's *Civil War and Reconstruction in Alabama* (1905) revealing the distance he had traveled. By 1902 Bancroft had begun research for the ambitious history of slavery that he was projecting but was never able to finish. Although his specialized opus on the slave trade would not appear for many years, he was already working on it at about the time that Jameson was inaugurating his documentary projects at the Carnegie Institution. As Bancroft wrote Du Bois in 1918: "I have been too busy working on my *Domestic Slave-Trade* to do or even to think of much else, except of course, the war."[63]

Bancroft was not personally close to blacks or to black historians, but for his day he displayed unusual sensitivities. In his research on slavery this pioneer practitioner of oral history was interested in what blacks had to tell him about the institution. His biographer has written that "while

Bancroft often visited prominent southerners, no interviews more satisfied and pleased him than those with former slaves, for they gladly gave him information on the buying and selling of slaves . . . life on the plantations, and slave discipline." Moreover he was in touch with black historians at a fairly early date. Woodson recalled that Bancroft had written, welcoming the appearance of the *JNH*. Bancroft thought well of Du Bois's restrained indictment of Phillips's opus and he informed the *Crisis* editor, "The review was read with much pleasure. Naturally, I had hoped you would damage him more, for he is very vulnerable; but all things considered, probably it was best for you to hold the mirror to him." Although Bancroft and Woodson corresponded occasionally, he never appeared on an ASNLH program. His one contribution to the work of the ASNLH was the establishment in 1932 of annual prizes for the best article and book review published in the *Journal*.[64]

Black historians greatly admired Bancroft's volume. On Bancroft's death Woodson wrote, "Humanity suffered a great loss in the passing of such a servant of the truth." Nevertheless, its scholarly virtues notwithstanding, *Slave-Trading in the Old South* had little impact on the profession at large until utilized by Kenneth Stampp in his influential study of slavery in the 1950s. The fact was that whites who, like Bancroft and Jameson, were seriously interested in studying the black experience were few and far between.

The milieu in which Woodson and his associates were operating during the 1920s and 1930s was epitomized by the way in which these early black historians functioned—or failed to function—in the major learned historical societies: the American Historical Association and the Mississippi Valley Historical Association. It is true that Phillips and Dunning did not completely dominate the views of all white historians. Nevertheless, despite the influential role that more enlightened individuals like Jameson and Clarence W. Alvord played in these organizations into the 1920s, Negro participation was always miniscule, whether measured by appearances at convention sessions, articles published in the two *Reviews,* or even book reviews published in these journals.

At the AHA Du Bois had been a lonely first on all three counts. As we have seen he presented papers at the AHA meetings in both 1891 and 1909, and the latter essay appeared in the *AHR* the following year; in addition he had been the only black to write a book review for that journal. Jameson naturally arranged to have the monographs of Du Bois and the Woodson group reviewed. In fact, when Woodson in 1927 sent him a personal copy of the fourth edition of *The Negro in Our History,* the meticulous editor, finding that the first edition of the text had not received a review, arranged to have one written and also asked Woodson, for the first time, to review a book. After Jameson's departure from the *AHR* in 1928, only one other review by a black appeared before 1939.[65] Meanwhile the only black to participate on an AHA program in the three decades after Du Bois's 1909 presentation was Monroe Work, who spoke at the 1929 convention.[66]

The record of black participation at the MVHA was even sparser. The most dynamic figure in the organization's early years and the first managing editor of the *MVHR* (1914-24) was Alvord, the son of a Massachusetts abolitionist lawyer and a distant cousin of the Freedmen's Bureau superintendent of education John W. Alvord.[67] Yet blacks appeared neither on convention sessions nor as contributors of essays to the *Review*. Nor did Alvord himself deal with blacks in his own historical research. His leanings were evident, however, in the book review pages, Alvord assigning certain monographs to Woodson. In the context of the time, it was undoubtedly a rather bold step to turn to the ASNLH founder for an evaluation of Phillips's *American Negro Slavery*, and for his part Woodson caustically listed the book's shortcomings: Phillips's disproportionate dependence on the records of the more benevolent plantation owners, his discounting of the prevalence of slave insurrections, "his inability to fathom the negro [*sic*] mind . . . and a tendency to argue to the contrary when the facts seem to be unfavorable to the slaveholders."[68] But after Alvord departed as managing editor, black reviewers were not found in the *MVHR*'s pages until 1940.

The decline during the late 1920s and 1930s of what had never been more than a very limited black presence in the activities of the professional organizations undoubtedly reflects the retirement of influential white historians with New England and abolitionist backgrounds. This situation only reinforced the ascendancy of the racism represented by the regnant historiography in the fields of both slavery and Reconstruction. Yet beyond this one must also note that the paucity of black representation in the conventions and journals of the learned societies was rooted in another product of the pervasive racism in American society: the rarity in the number of black doctorates.[69]

By 1935, four decades after Du Bois had obtained his degree at Harvard, of the nearly 2,000 doctorates that had been awarded in history, only six went to blacks. Five years later the total number of Negroes who had earned Ph.D.s in history at universities in the United States since 1895 had tripled to the modest figure of eighteen.* On the other hand, though

---

* Of these, two were Ph.D.s in the history of education. In addition, two American blacks earned doctorates in history at European universities during the 1930s.

few in number, these individuals had been unusually productive — far more so than the general run of white historians — in large part due to the encouragement of research and publication provided by the ASNLH.

This early group of Negroes pursuing a Ph.D. in history was largely concentrated at Harvard (six) and Chicago (four). Over half of the blacks earning their doctorates in American universities through 1940, and, except for Savage, all of those producing important monographs came from these two institutions. Originally Harvard had stood preeminent: the first three blacks who obtained Ph.D.s in history had been trained there. (The fourth, Rufus Clement [1900-1967], received his at Northwestern in 1930, with a dissertation on the history of black education in North Carolina; scion of a leading AME Zion church family, he achieved prominence not as a scholar but as John Hope's successor in the presidency of Atlanta University.) Then in the late 1930s the University of Chicago temporarily eclipsed Harvard as a source of black doctorates in history. Meanwhile, a scattering of blacks were receiving their degrees from other institutions; in 1940, for example, Wisconsin and Columbia both awarded their first Ph.D.s to a black historian (Benjamin Quarles and Marion Thompson Wright, respectively).

This rise in the number of black doctorates, small though it was both in absolute and relative terms, was part of the general expansion of doctoral programs during the 1930s. At the same time, it is clear that this increase in the number of Negroes acquiring the Ph.D. was indebted considerably to the GEB fellowship program that had begun in 1924 and to a lesser extent to the Rosenwald fellowships that had been inaugurated in 1928.[70] (The Rosenwald Fund awarded few fellowships to historians, and a considerable portion of this assistance went to postdoctoral research rather than to facilitating the earning of advanced degrees.) Of the fifteen Negroes who obtained doctorates in history from the time the GEB program was inaugurated until 1940, nine were the beneficiaries of awards from these programs. Or looking at those who were part of the wave of doctorates coming out of American universities starting in the late 1930s, two-thirds of the blacks earning Ph.D.s in history between 1936 and 1943 — and nearly all in this group who achieved significant publication records — received grants for doctoral training from one or both of these two foundations.

Facilitated by foundation fellowships, the scholarship of the Woodson circle flowered in the late 1930s and early 1940s, with the acquisition of degrees by Taylor and Logan at Harvard, Johnston, Jackson, and Reddick at Chicago, and Greene at Columbia, followed by the publication in 1941 and 1942 of the Logan, Jackson, and Greene dissertations. Of these six men all except Taylor, who had been helped by LSRM funding, were recipients of GEB and/or Rosenwald awards. It seems that this final florescence in the work of the ASNLH group would scarcely have occurred without this financial encouragement. There was a certain irony in this situation, since the fellowships were designed to complement the plans to strengthen the faculties of Fisk, Dillard, Howard, Atlanta, and other black institutions of higher education—the foundation program that had produced the collision between Woodson and the philanthropies.

The status of Negro history as a scholarly endeavor on the eve of World War II was paradoxical. Despite early support from a few white historians, Afro-American history still existed on the peripheries of the profession, and Woodson and his circle remained a small fringe group. Their books were duly reviewed in the learned journals, but in other respects their work was mostly ignored. On the other hand, as a result of his inspiration, assistance from foundations, and their own drive and dedication, Woodson and his colleagues had produced a corpus of solid research and placed black history on a firm scholarly foundation. Moreover, just at this point various forces were operating to expand the circle of historians, black and white, who were making contributions to the field but who stood outside the Woodson group and who would ultimately undermine the ASNLH's preeminence.

Woodson and his associates, though dominating the field for more than two decades, had never been quite alone. But during the late 1930s and early 1940s, as their productivity reached its zenith, there was a quickening of interest in Negro history both among a broader group of black scholars and a small though growing number of whites.

For both blacks and whites this growth of scholarship was in part a function of the considerable expansion in the number of individuals earning doctorates in the period. Yet in other respects the roots of this development appear to have been quite different for the whites and blacks involved. For Negroes, both inside and outside Woodson's circle, the growth flowed from the fact that the Rockefeller and Rosenwald fellowships created unprecedented opportunity for creative scholarship. The growth in scholarship produced by whites was rooted principally in the liberal and radical sensibilities that became so prevalent among intellectuals in the Franklin D. Roosevelt era. The Depression and World War II engendered an awareness of both the sufferings of the nation's dispossessed and of the enormity of the Nazi crimes committed in the name of racial superiority. Equalitarian sentiments, stemming from the social crises of the Depression and its aftermath, converged with the findings of modern anthropology and environmental psychology to help undermine the prevailing white belief in racial inequality. The New Deal period witnessed the appearance of two new sources of white scholars who would be important for the future:

the vanguard of Jewish intellectuals who would enter academe in large numbers during the postwar years, and the first handful of sympathetic native white southerners.

In other ways as well the Roosevelt era witnessed important new directions in Afro-American historiography. Scholars, both black and white, inaugurated and published in-depth studies of slave resistance and the black abolitionists. Economic interpretations, both Marxist and Beardian, had their day, though given the overriding nature of the moral issue for the writing of black history, neither kind of economic analysis became central to the field. Most important in the long run was the trend toward a kind of universalism, apparent not only in the growing number of white scholars sensitive to the importance of the Afro-American experience in American history but also in the point of view expressed by the most prominent among the new generation of black scholars who would be emerging during the World War II years, and who consciously strove to make black history a really integral part of American history. Such developments, while shifting the emphasis and orientation of the study of the black past, were nevertheless heir to the Woodson tradition, utilizing and expanding the foundations that the ASNLH scholars had laid to make Afro-American history an increasingly legitimate field in the eyes of the profession.

Among the works produced during the Depression decade by black scholars outside Woodson's circle, the most readily apparent new departures were to be seen in studies cast in the framework of an economic interpretation and in important contributions to the history of Negro education. In education, two case studies stand out — Marion M. Thompson Wright's volume on New Jersey and Horace Mann Bond's on Alabama. Bond's monograph was also one of the two significant studies by black historians that were infused with an economic interpretation of history; Du Bois's *Black Reconstruction* was the other.

From one perspective *Black Reconstruction* (1935) can be regarded as the lineal descendant of Du Bois's 1909 AHA paper. Synthesizing all of the previous scholarly work on Negroes in the postwar South, he distilled from the mostly racist secondary literature then available the story of the blacks' role and contributions. To this material Du Bois, whose longtime sympathies toward socialism and Marxism were accentuated by the economic crisis of the 1930s, added his own quite individualist use of the Marxist historical model. The volume was influential, however, not because of its application of Marxist theory, but because of its eloquent and compelling illumination of the Negroes' constructive part in Reconstruction. Thus people in Woodson's circle agreed with the rehabilitation of the black man's role but took issue with or virtually ignored Du Bois's economic-and-class interpretation. Not only did Logan, as we have seen, express his reservations in print, but Wesley, who welcomed the book as "a new interpretation of old facts," gave the Marxist thesis only passing reference; Taylor, who considered the book "a significant and substantial contribution," "convincing in its main thesis," found it "hardly persuasive" in applying the concepts of a general strike or a dictatorship of labor.[71]

Black intellectuals in northern cities like New York, Chicago, Detroit, and Los Angeles were often intrigued by Marxism and Communism during the depths of the Depression and the heyday of the Popular Front,[72] but outside of those at Howard University, Negro academicians were nearly all employed at southern colleges and moved in a conservative social milieu that inhibited flirtation with radical ideologies.* It was for different reasons, however, that only one historical monograph by a black scholar, Bond's *Negro Education in Alabama: A Study in Cotton and Steel*, utilized the Beardian approach then in the ascendancy in the profession. The problem with Beard's analysis, as we have indicated in Chapter 1, was that its theoretically amoral perspectives — stripping the Civil War and Radical Reconstruction of moral motivation — in effect condoned the actions of the white South and discredited the efforts of the abolitionists and Radical Republicans. It is true that a different moral temper would infuse the work of Beardians Roger W. Shugg and C. Vann Woodward in the latter part of the 1930s, but at the time they were a distinctly youthful minority; and Howard K. Beale's "On Rewriting Reconstruction History," which fused his Beardianism with a sensitivity to the role of blacks, would not appear until 1940.[73]

Bond, scion of an elite southern family, while pursuing his graduate training (with the assistance of two Rosenwald fellowships) at the University of Chicago Department of Education, formed a close association with Edwin R. Embree. Embree arranged for Bond to go to Fisk as research assistant for Embree's intimate friend, Charles S. Johnson, and it was at Embree's urging that Bond, upon receiving his Ph.D. in 1936, embarked upon his long and distinguished career as a college administrator.[74] His *Negro Education in Alabama*, published in 1939 (five years after his first book, the influential analysis of *The Education of the Negro in the American Social Order*), was not widely reviewed but became something of a classic among interested historians.[75] Bond, who had developed his ties to Johnson and Embree at the time that Woodson's relations with Embree were

* At Howard there had been since the 1920s an important contingent of socialist-oriented professors, including economist Abram L. Harris, political scientist Ralph J. Bunche, and sociologist E. Franklin Frazier.

dissolving, operated in a sphere of academic influence that was mostly quite distinct from Woodson's. Moreover, given his expertise in education, it is not surprising that Bond established a warm relationship with another old friend of Johnson's, the Howard University professor and editor of the newly founded (1932) *Journal of Negro Education,* Charles H. Thompson. It was for Thompson's journal that Bond penned his devastating analysis of Woodson's *Mis-Education of the Negro,* dissecting its inconsistencies and twitting the ASNLH's founder: "One wonders if it is true that Negro Ph.D.s as a rule lose touch with the common people. . . . Of course Dr. Woodson is one admitted exception. . . . Where among those 'of less formal education' is the one who has done more creative work than . . . Du Bois or Woodson himself?"[76] On the other hand, Woodson and Bond each had something to offer the other—the ASNLH director a medium of publication, and Bond a prize-winning dissertation that would enhance Woodson's list—and by the end of the 1930s they had developed a symbiotic relationship. Bond, unable to secure publication with the University of Chicago Press for his specialized monograph on Alabama, turned to Woodson, who issued the volume with a subsidy obtained from the Rosenwald Fund.[77] The two men remained on cordial terms, Bond appearing at least twice thereafter on ASNLH convention programs.[78]

There was, it is true, one close associate of Woodson who displayed a warm enthusiasm for economic interpretations, although it did not find expression in a published monograph—L. D. Reddick (b. 1910). Originally trained at Fisk, where he studied with both Johnson and Bond, this youngest member of the Woodson circle took his doctorate at Chicago. Working at Dillard in the latter part of the 1930s, Reddick exploited the materials gathered by the WPA Writers' Project on the Negro in Louisiana and wrote his 1939 dissertation under Craven on "The Negro in the New Orleans Press, 1850-1860: A Study in Attitudes and Propaganda." In contrast to the situation that obtained with Craven's other black students, the relations between the two men were not friendly, Reddick regarding Craven as a "menace" to Negro scholars.[79] For his part Craven believed that Reddick was "trying to damage me at every opportunity because I did not give him the grades he wanted in my courses." Directly after Reddick received his Ph.D., the *JNH* carried a scathing attack on Craven's latest book, *The Repressible Conflict.* The reviewer, "E. R. Thomas," described Craven as an unmitigated southern fire-eater, and Craven, believing that the critic was his former student, appealed to Luther Porter Jackson to protest to Woodson. (For their part Jackson and his colleague James Hugo Johnston were ambivalent about the review—they "rejoiced over the fact that someone has called Craven to task for his pro-Southern views," but regretted "the personal reference to him which would lead a reader to conclude that he is a fire-eater. He is not a person of that stamp."[80]*

Even before writing his dissertation, Reddick had advocated an avant-garde approach to black history, seeking to bring the field abreast of the historiographical perspectives achieving ascendancy during the Depression crisis. His paper at the 1936 ASNLH convention criticized "the social philosophy of the Negro historians" as essentially the "Emersonian gospel of self-reliance, simple optimism and patient regard for destiny," and "sadly lacking in a grasp of the dynamic forces." Instead he advocated a redefinition of subject matter and a larger focus. Praising the historical monographs of the socialist economist Abram L. Harris (author of *The Negro as Capitalist* and *The Black Worker*) and the works of Bond and Du Bois, Reddick uged taking into account the economic interests shaping American history, while treating developments in Negro life "in connection with those of the general pattern of other racial, minority and laboring groups."[82]†

It is an interesting coincidence that, like Bond, Marion M. Thompson Wright (1904-62), the first black woman historian to make a contribution to the field of Afro-American history, did her dissertation in the history of education and was similarly identified with Charles H. Thompson.[83] A native of New Jersey, Wright was a product of Howard University and Columbia University's Teachers College, returned to Howard to teach, and served as an assistant editor of the *Journal of Negro Education*. Although her 1940 dissertation on *The Education of Negroes in New Jersey* was published the following year in the Teachers College series, the ASNLH also provided Wright with a medium of publication, her two important articles on the history of New Jersey blacks appearing in the pages of the *JNH*.[84] All of these works were the product of painstaking research in scattered sources. In her combination of thorough scholarship and faith in the potential of a democratic society, Wright exemplified the perspective of those engaged in the finest work being done in Afro-American history at the time. The final chapter of her book, "Implications for Education,"

---

* We have been unable to identify "E. R. Thomas." Reddick disclaims any knowledge about the reviewer's identity, but was known for his exceedingly negative feelings about Craven. Moreover, in April 1939 Reddick confided to Wesley and Bond that he had prepared an exposé of Craven's blatant anti-Negro bias, which he would publish after receiving his doctorate—about the time that Craven's new book was scheduled to appear.[81]

† Another important economic interpretation was offered by a West Indian Marxist scholar who for some years studied and taught in the United States. Eric Williams's 1938 doctoral dissertation at Oxford, "Economic Aspects of the Abolition of the British West Indian Slave Trade and Slavery," published by the University of North Carolina Press as *Capitalism and Slavery* (1944), was an influential work in slave trade historiography.

fused the moral view underlying the work of black historians with the instrumentalism of Columbia Teachers College's John Dewey: if, as Dewey maintained, education should prepare youth for participation in a democratic society, elimination of the discriminatory practices in the American educational system was imperative.

Thompson suggested the topic of Wright's dissertation, but she considered that her greatest intellectual debt was to her Teachers College advisor, Merle Curti.[85] Curti represented the vanguard of the slowly growing number of white scholars who would give attention to the Afro-American experience during the coming decades. Though not part of Woodson's circle, most of the whites who were making contributions to the field during the late 1930s and early 1940s either cultivated personal ties with Woodson, published in the *JNH*, or both. But they differed in an important respect from the whites who earlier in the twentieth century had shown an interest in Du Bois's scholarship and Woodson's activities. Unlike the older generation who had been of conventional political sympathies, these men, emerging during the era of Roosevelt, were characterized by distinctly radical and liberal social perspectives.

Merle E. Curti (b. 1897) was himself a pacifist and socialist, who had wide-ranging social concerns, including women's rights and the plight of the average working man, as well as race discrimination. He was not only a good friend of Wesley when the two were graduate students at Harvard in the early 1920s, but subsequently as a professor at Smith College he arranged for the NAACP's Du Bois and Walter White to come to Northampton for lectures.[86] Although this distinguished intellectual and social historian made no fundamental research contributions to the field, during the 1930s he would journey periodically to Washington to meet with Woodson, and he was the first in the guild to seek seriously to integrate the history of blacks into his monographs on the American past. Curti's *Social Ideas of American Educators* (1935) was unprecedented in that it devoted a chapter to a leading black educator, Booker T. Washington. And in the Pulitzer Prize–winning *Growth of American Thought* (1943), Curti, drawing heavily upon the researches published by the ASNLH, gave substantial attention to antebellum black thought, integrating it successfully with his broader analysis of American intellectual history. This approach underlay his views on the study of the black past. He once wrote Du Bois: "I am personally very anxious to have scholars explore race questions as they explore other questions—that is, I should like to have an increasing number of able, sympathetic young white scholars study Negro history, just as I hope many young Negro scholars will study along with the history of the Negro, historical problems chiefly concerned with whites."[87] Curti's pioneering effort to integrate black history into the mainstream of American history has been forgotten, but his recognition of the field's importance and the universalist framework he employed were indicative of trends that would become prominent in the postwar era.

Curti's slightly younger contemporary, Kenneth Wiggins Porter (1905-81), who also took his doctorate at Harvard (1936) and also had socialist sympathies, was establishing himself as a historian of blacks on the frontier at about the time that W. Sherman Savage was developing his reputation in the same area. Porter's reformist concerns were rooted in his family background. His father had been a Populist, his maternal grandfather an abolitionist. His mother, growing up near Nicodemus, Kansas, had been friendly with some of the Exodusters, and Porter, himself raised in a small Kansas town, knew blacks in the local community.[88] Although Porter's reform interests were less wide-ranging than Curti's, he consistently voted the Socialist ticket, and in 1948 confided to the Wisconsin historian that if he had voted that year he would have cast his ballot for Henry Wallace of the Progressive party "solely because of their stand against segregation." Back in the 1920s as an undergraduate at Sterling College, Porter had taken the lead in fighting the discrimination practiced by the administration against black students in this Kansas institution sponsored by the erstwhile abolitionist United Presbyterian church.[89]

From his first articles in the early 1930s,[90] Porter's researches into the black past took two directions. Aware since a youth of the evidence of Indian ancestry among the blacks he knew, Porter probed the relationships between blacks and the Seminole Indians. He also made pioneering investigations of black participation in aspects of the frontier economy, such as the fur trade and the cattle industry. In treating these economic topics, his underlying perspective was akin to that expressed by Lorenzo Greene and Luther Porter Jackson in regard to their own findings about the diversity and range of black occupations. Porter hoped to undermine widely held stereotypes and refute the idea that the Negro "was 'by nature' not qualified for the role of frontiersman and that on the contrary, despite handicaps, he frequently demonstrated the capacity to recognize his own interests and act decisively and intelligently on their own behalf."[91] For years Porter indefatigably pursued his investigations despite limited time and fellowship opportunities.[92] There were numerous articles in the *JNH* and in minor scholarly media, as he delved ever more deeply into his subject. It was indicative of attitudes in the profession that wider recognition for Porter did not come before the 1960s, with the appearance of his mature analysis of Negroes and the Seminole War in the *Journal of Southern History* in 1964 and his collected essays in book form in 1971.[93]

The views of Curti and Porter, representing a Protestant midwestern strain of reform, had crystallized by the early 1920s. More influential in shaping the course of Afro-American historiography, however, were liberal and radical impulses stemming from small numbers of native white southern historians and northern Jewish intellectuals, who were socialized during the Depression era. The former focused their research on the black experience and race relations in the South during the Civil War and postwar years; the later concentrated on studies of opposition to slavery.

Indeed, in a noteworthy convergence, the late 1930s witnessed a flowering of research and publication on the part of both black and white scholars on opposition to the slave system. There were three in-depth investigations of slave revolts, the first fruits of which appeared virtually simultaneously in 1937 and 1938, with publications by Joseph C. Carroll, Harvey Wish, and Herbert Aptheker. Moreover about the same time, Wesley and Aptheker were publishing the results of their research into the role that blacks played in the abolitionist movement, and Philip Foner and Benjamin Quarles were embarking upon their biographies of Frederick Douglass.

Carroll (1886-1951), the second black to receive a doctorate from Ohio State University's history department (1937), was an Indianapolis high-school teacher whose dissertation, *Slave Insurrections in the United States, 1800-1865,* published in 1938, though based on considerable research, had virtually no impact. Perhaps this was because the volume was more a listing than a detailed description, or because his conclusions that the revolts taught the lesson of the "futility of armed resistance"[94] ran counter to the heroic mold in which these black freedom fighters were cast by others seriously interested in the black experience. Moreover, Carroll lacked the standing that would have come with a college professorship, and his work appeared under the imprint of a minor publisher, in contrast to the auspices under which that of Wish and Aptheker were published — Wish's essays appearing in Woodson's own *JNH* and Aptheker's mature statement on the topic in Columbia University's prestigious series in History, Economics and Public Law.

Both Wish and Aptheker were the sons of small businessmen of eastern European Jewish descent. From his family's economic reverses during the Depression and a consciousness of his own minority background, the distinguished social historian Harvey Wish (1909-68) developed a profound feeling for the oppressed and frequently referred to the parallels in the black and Jewish experiences.[95] Wish's researches as a graduate student at Northwestern revealed his reform sympathies: Illinois Governor John Peter Altgeld was the subject of his 1936 dissertation, while his *JNH* essays on slave revolts were done in the seminar of the anthropologist and

Africanist Melville J. Herskovits.[96]* Although as Wish himself pointed out, the essays were far from exhaustive, he pulled together material from scattered sources, and the evidence enabled him to conclude that "no doubt many Negroes made the required adjustments to slavery, but the romantic picture of careless abandon and contentment fails to be convincing. The struggle of the Negro for his liberty, beginning with those dark days on the slaveship, was far from sporadic in nature, but an ever-recurrent battle waged everywhere with desperate courage against the bonds of his master."[98]

Wish was a Chicago liberal whose interest in black history stemmed from his underlying reform concerns. For Aptheker (b. 1915) the dynamics were reversed. A New York Communist, his radicalism was actually an outgrowth of his discovery of racial injustice. As a high-school student he was seared by the bigotry and poverty that he witnessed while accompanying his father on a business trip to Alabama. Later, struck by the blatant racism of the books on slavery that he read as a Columbia University undergraduate, he made Nat Turner the subject of his M.A. thesis in 1937. His first published survey of slave revolts appeared that year in the Communist-oriented periodical, *Science and Society,* and like Wish, he concluded that the evidence of history demonstrated that blacks had consistently sought to break their chains and had played a vital role in the struggle for their freedom. International Publishers brought out his pamphlet, *Negro Slave Revolts, 1526-1860,* about the time that Aptheker joined the Communist party in 1939. That same year his first *JNH* essay, on maroon settlements, appeared. In 1941 both the *Journal* and International Publishers printed the findings of his researches on another dimension of black leadership in the antislavery struggle — the activities of the black abolitionists.[99] Meanwhile, Aptheker had developed a cordial personal relationship with Woodson, from time to time journeying to Washington where, like Curti, he and the ASNLH director would dine at the Union Station restaurant, the only public restaurant outside the ghetto where blacks and whites could eat together. Moreover, by the 1940s this radical activist had embarked upon his tireless efforts as a publicist for the study of Negro history.[100]

Aptheker's dissertation, *American Negro Slave Revolts,* published in 1943, was regarded as a sharp departure from the standard interpretation found in American history books. As would be expected, prominent south-

---

* Herskovits, adumbrating writers of the 1970s, was especially interested in evidence of slave resistance, since he saw it as revealing the existence of a distinct cultural identity rooted in the African background. The often-cited essay by two anthropologists, Raymond Bauer and Alice Bauer, "Day to Day Resistance to Slavery," was also a product of Herskovits's seminar.[97]

ern historians assessed it negatively, while black historians welcomed the refutation of slave docility as a "splendid volume . . . [that] overthrow[s] completely the fiction that the Negro tamely submitted to enslavement."[101] The young Kenneth Stampp summed up the situation in his enthusiastic review in Dwight McDonald's radical journal *Politics;* he was delighted to find that "thus it appears that many not-so-docile 'Old Black Joes' tucked numerous exploiting 'massas' in the cold, cold ground." He judged Aptheker's book would be "as refreshing to the minority of dissenters as it will be disconcerting to the upholders of the Southern legend."[102]

Aptheker's monograph only hinted at the Marxist outlook of its author, and enthusiasm for it among blacks and white sympathizers lay in its "heretical" assertion of black humanity. It and Aptheker's subsequent publications were pioneering works, running athwart of the mainstream of white American scholarship and uncovering previously untapped veins of material. Woodson hailed Aptheker's 1945 *Essays in the History of the American Negro* as a welcome contrast to the dominant pro-southern view; John Hope Franklin writing for the *AHR* similarly praised his 1948 collection, *To Be Free: Studies in American Negro History* for fresh research in unexploited sources on topics neglected or distorted by most historians.[103] And to a later generation of radical black historians like Sterling Stuckey and John Bracey, Aptheker's work—especially *American Negro Slave Revolts* and his *A Documentary History of the Negro People in the United States* (1951)—would be "indispensable."

Philip Foner (b. 1910), known for his work on Frederick Douglass and the history of black labor, was also from a New York Jewish background and moved in Communist circles. Foner, his radicalism shaped by the Depression and exposure to Marxist ideas, became a "fellow-traveler" exceedingly active in Communist-front organizations while studying for his B.A. at the City College of New York. At the same time, disturbingly aware of how history books defamed blacks, he familiarized himself with the works of Du Bois and Woodson. Although his graduate research consisted of applying Marxist analysis to the sectional conflict, as a CCNY faculty member during the 1930s he introduced a good measure of black history materials into his courses and engaged in the agitation that brought about the introduction of what was probably the first formal black history course in the curriculum of a predominantly white college. (The course, introduced in 1937, was taught by Max Yergan. Embittered by his fifteen years as a YMCA secretary in South Africa, Yergan had recently become "a leading Communist spokesman in Harlem" and was the first black to teach at City College.)[104] Meanwhile Foner's interest in the Reconstruction labor movement resulted in his first paper at an ASNLH convention, a 1938 discussion of the Colored National Labor Union, which in turn led quite naturally to Foner's research on that organization's president, Frederick Douglass.

Among southern whites, the first stirrings of sympathetic scholarly interest in the history of blacks and race relations can be seen as largely representing a fusion of the kind of social consciousness engendered by the Depression with the older, moderate stream of southern Christian interracialism associated with the YMCA and the Commission on Interracial Cooperation. They were also related to the flowering of the Univeristy of North Carolina as a relatively liberal outpost of southern intellectual life. Yet the author of the first relevant monograph, Bell Irvin Wiley, defies easy classification.

Wiley (1908-80), U. B. Phillips's last graduate student, was not a product of the 1930s, but he was raised in poverty, in a large family in western Tennessee.[105] It was this background that provided the basis for his lifelong scholarly interest in "plain folks," a category that for him included blacks as well as whites. His dissertation completed at Yale in 1933 and published in 1938 as *Southern Negroes, 1861-1865*, was replete with words like "darkies" and "pickaninnies." It was, in fact, sufficiently southern in facade to have its publication subsidized by the United Daughters of the Confederacy. Yet the evidence presented in this serious effort to study southern blacks during the Civil War undermined the myth of black acquiescence and loyalty to the plantation regime—a conclusion that coincidentally converged with the seminal works on slave revolts that were being published virtually simultaneously. To reviewers, southern white and black alike, this was the book's most significant point. Francis Butler Simkins (himself the co-author of the first Reconstruction state study that made some effort to treat blacks seriously)[106] observed: "Mr. Wiley . . . proves that the whites were whistling in the dark when they professed to believe that they did not fear their slaves." Both Woodson and Wesley took exception to Wiley's "crude epithets," yet praised the remarkably objective treatment that in Wesley's words put the volume "in the front rank of the studies which are presenting the neglected aspects of the history of the Negro in American life."[107] That the perspective of this careful southern white historian was not the same as that of the black historians and their northern white sympathizers, however, seems evident from Wiley's critique of a Benjamin Brawley volume on distinguished blacks, where the reviewer objected to including "such pillaging and murdering insurrectionists as Cato and Turner" among "Negro Builders and Heroes."[108] On the other hand, black historians at the Atlanta University system[109] had a high regard for this Emory University professor.

More influential in the development of historical writing on race and the black experience in the South were two men who earned doctorates during the 1930s at the University of North Carolina: C. Vann Woodward, whose 1937 dissertation *Tom Watson: Agrarian Rebel* appeared the following year, and Vernon Lane Wharton, whose *The Negro in Mississippi, 1865-1890,* though not published until 1947, was finished in 1939. Both Wharton and Woodward came from solidly Methodist families where religion was taken seriously. Yet they took quite different paths to their commitment to race equality and their related historical concerns. Wharton, from a conventional small-town mercantile family, was influenced by the relatively emancipated views to be found in the southern college Christian movement; Woodward, exposed early to relatively liberal influences, moved leftward on a more radical path.

Wharton (1907-64) belonged to the small nucleus of socially concerned students and teachers that existed even on certain southern campuses in the interwar period.[110] As a student at Methodist Millsaps College in Jackson, Mississippi, during the 1920s, he came under the influence of professors of religion who had imbibed social gospel views from their theological training at Emory University. Subsequently, during his residence at Chapel Hill (1929-32), University of North Carolina president Frank Graham's social consciousness (itself rooted in profound religious convictions and his close connections with the more liberal wing of the southern YMCA movement)[111] reinforced Wharton's leanings. Returning to Millsaps to teach in the mid-1930s, Wharton was active in both the campus peace movement and the interracial Inter-Collegiate Council of Mississippi. He completed his dissertation, with financial help from Howard W. Odum's Bureau of Social Research, under the supervision of the relatively open-minded Fletcher Green.

Woodward (b.1908) as a youth had been influenced by the racially liberal views of both his uncle Comer, a Methodist minister and Emory University sociology professor, and also by his childhood neighbor, the liberal sociologist and student of sharecropping, Rupert Vance. As an Emory undergraduate and then while an instructor at the Georgia Institute of Technology in 1930-31, Woodward moved to the left, met black leaders, and was deeply impressed by the Scottsboro case. He took his M.A. at Columbia University the following year during the depths of the Depression on a SSRC fellowship obtained with the assistance of his friend, Will Alexander. There he had a good exposure to the rising tide of student radicalism, met a number of Communists, became acquainted with Langston Hughes and other black intellectuals, interviewed Du Bois, and ended the year with a visit to the Soviet Union. Returning to the Georgia Institute of Technology, he lost his job after becoming deeply involved in the local committee organized for the defense of the black Communist, Angelo Herndon. Doctoral work at the University of North Carolina during the mid-1930s followed, financed largely by GEB fellowships secured with the help of another family friend, Howard Odum. Actually, however, Woodward was impatient with the kind of gradualism that Odum represented, and at Chapel Hill the young man continued to travel in radical circles, associating with "the town Communist" and others whom Odum regarded as "the wrong crowd."[112]

During these years of doctoral study Woodward's views crystallized: he became a left-wing New Dealer, fusing his moral concern about economic and racial inequalities with a Beardian (rather than a Marxist) analysis. At the same time he retained his high respect for the work of the Marxist Du Bois. While Woodward does not appear to have had any contact with Woodson, he sent Du Bois a copy of his pioneering 1938 *JSH* article, "Tom Watson and the Negro in Agrarian Politics," informing the Atlanta University professor: "It is written in a spirit that I hope you will approve, whether you can agree with my conclusion or not. I have followed your work with interest and profit for a number of years. I should like especially to acknowledge my indebtedness for the insight which your admirable book, *Black Reconstruction* provided me."[113]

In many respects Woodward's views conformed to those of the segment of northern New Deal intellectuals who were also seriously concerned with both the causes and moral evil of racist oppression. It is therefore scarcely a coincidence that his outlook converged with that of his doctoral advisor Howard K. Beale (1899-1959), whose own intellectual trajectory suggests something of the changes in racial attitudes beginning to take place in academic circles.[114] Beale's *The Critical Year: A Study of Andrew Johnson and Reconstruction* (1930) had been sympathetic in its treatment of President Andrew Johnson and cynical about the Radicals, placing its Beardian analysis within the framework of the regnant racist scholarship on Reconstruction, though with a literary flair that went beyond anything Dunning, Fleming, or James G. de Roulhac Hamilton had ever written. Soon, however, the youthful critic of capitalist hegemony would also become one of the most outspoken advocates of racial equality and Negro rights in the historical profession. By the early 1930s this pacifist reformer was corresponding with Du Bois, eagerly awaiting the forthcoming *Black Reconstruction*, and consulting the *Crisis* editor in connection with the chapter on Negro educational institutions in *The History of Freedom of Teaching in American Schools* that Beale was writing for the AHA.[115] Moreover, residing in Washington while carrying out this study, he helped pioneer the attack on hotel segregation in the nation's capital, being a member of a local committee that prevailed upon a few major places like the Mayflower (where the AHA regularly met) to serve meals to interracial groups in their private dining rooms.[116] This quiet campaign proved to be the first battle in the long and often acrimonious struggle that would take place in the profession over holding conventions at hotels that discriminated against Negroes. Thus Beale's racial views had crystallized by the time he arrived at Chapel Hill and met Woodward in 1935. The Yankee professor included materials on Negro history in his courses, assigned Du Bois's magnum opus to his class on Reconstruction, and found the students surprisingly open on the race issue.[117]

The reversal of Beale's views on Reconstruction history was dramatized in his 1939 SHA paper, "On Rewriting Reconstruction History," the delivery of which was accompanied by a caustic personal criticism of his Dunningite colleague, de Roulhac Hamilton. This influential essay, appearing in the *AHR* in revised form the following year, fused his Beardian emphasis on economic classes and interest group politics with a call for a fair account of the Negroes' role in Reconstruction. In Beale's analysis the Bourbon-Radical conflict was a struggle between the wealthy whites and the poor of both races.[118] Woodward held similar views about the Bourbons and in his own search for a southern tradition that would sustain his hope for an alliance of downtrodden blacks and whites, as is well known, found it in the Populist movement's brief moment of interracial cooperation.

One indication of this growth in the ranks of sympathetic white scholars was the session on "The Negro in the History of the United States" that Curti and Beale arranged for the AHA convention in 1940; it was the first time since Du Bois's paper in 1909 that black historians had appeared on the convention program of a major professional historical organization. Beale and Curti, both Beardians who were liberal on the race question and friends since their student days at Harvard, were rising influentials in the guild; Beale was also chair of the nominating committee, and Curti was a member of the AHA's executive committee at the time. They were thus in a position to provide a slight measure of correction for the omission of blacks from AHA activities. Indeed, Curti, as program committee chair, chose a "congenial" group, consisting of Beale and others, and they deliberately sought to include sessions on "the common man" and "to give women and Negroes . . . a chance to be on the program."[119] Though the old guard regarded them as rebels for doing so, the committee members arranged a session chaired by Du Bois, with papers by Wesley, Logan, and Beale's former student, Wharton, and with comments by Bond and two southern whites who were products of the University of North Carolina. Blacks were pleased. John Hope Franklin, though unable to make the session, reported, "I didn't get there for the Wesley and Logan papers but understand they were first-rate and very well received." Marion M. Thompson Wright, who did attend, wrote her former professor, "It was a splendid meeting and I appreciate so very much the part you played in making it possible." Curti himself was very pleased with the outcome. Years later when Curti was elected AHA president, he proudly recollected how "we ... had the first session at which Negro and white historians took part in a discussion of interracial history."[120]

Blacks would remain a rarity on mainstream history convention programs until after mid-century. Indeed when the question of permitting Negro membership was raised at the time of the establishment of the Southern Historical Association in 1935, "it was decided that to accept their dues was legitimate because in a Southern association they would be Negroes who would know that they were not expected to attend."[121] By 1941, however, when the SHA met in Atlanta, blacks were developing different expectations. Inquiry elicited from SHA president B. B. Hendrick of North Carolina Women's College the view that Negroes in the organization had all the privileges of membership, and the Biltmore Hotel's owners at the time would have permitted black members to use the hotel's facilities except the public restaurants. But the local arrangements committee "begged that Negroes would not seek to attend luncheon and dinner meetings," lest professors at the Georgia state institutions "become liable to dismissal" at the hands of the racist demagogue, Governor Eugene Talmadge; its views prevailed.[122] Hearing this, an incensed Beale invited Du Bois to breakfast in his room at the Biltmore; instead, Du Bois had Beale to tea at his own apartment: accompanied by Wharton, Beale enjoyed a delightful visit.[123] In the aftermath Du Bois resigned from the SHA. For its part, the SHA executive council discussed but took no action on the question of Negro members attending the conventions, it being "the general sense of the Council that this matter must be left to each local arrangements committee."[124]

Incidents such as the session at the AHA and the faint signs of debate within the SHA over the rights of black members were straws in the wind. So also were the subvention provided for Luther Porter Jackson's book from the AHA revolving fund and a slight flurry of book reviews by blacks in the major professional journals at the turn of the decade.* Woodson himself was aware of the rising interest among whites and in his annual report for 1941, for example, pointed with pleasure to the fact that the *JNH* had carried essays by graduate students working under Eric Goldman of Johns Hopkins and Herskovits at Northwestern.[126] Woodson was even able to secure William Best Hesseltine, a Beardian specialist in southern

---

* The first reviews written by blacks since 1931 appeared in the *AHR* in 1939: one by Woodson and another by Wesley. In 1940 the *JSH* carried its first review by a black, L. D. Reddick; the next review by a Negro would not appear until 1949. The *MVHR* carried four reviews by blacks between 1940 and 1944, two each by Lewis K. McMillan of Wilberforce University and by Robert D. Reid of Tuskegee Institute.[125]

history, to appear at the ASNLH's 1940 convention, with a commendatory review of "A Quarter-Century of the Association for the Study of Negro Life and History."[127]

Moreover, it is probably not entirely coincidental that these actions among historians occurred in a broader context of quickening scholarly interest in race relations and the black experience. In 1937 the Carnegie Corporation of New York inaugurated the comprehensive study directed by the Swedish social scientist Gunnar Myrdal. Three years later Waldo Leland launched the ACLS's Committee on Negro Studies, chaired by Herskovits, to encourage cross-cultural and interdisciplinary studies of blacks in Africa and the New World.[128] Although Leland and Herskovits were never able to implement their ambitious avant-garde ideas, the appearance of Myrdal's *An American Dilemma* in 1944 would prove to be an intellectual milestone in scholarship on American race relations, helping set the stage for a new postwar generation of researchers in Afro-American history.

Simultaneously with the growing attention from white historians there was emerging by the early 1940s a new generation of black historians who stood outside Woodson's orbit. Benjamin Quarles and John Hope Franklin, who received their doctorates at the turn of the decade, would by mid-century establish themselves as the leading scholars in the field of Negro history. From one perspective they can be viewed as the final fruit of the philanthropic encouragement of black historical scholarship, which began with the grants to the ASNLH and continued through the Depression with the GEB and Rosenwald fellowship program, and also as the culmination of the work in which Woodson and his colleagues had pioneered. Indeed, both Quarles and Franklin fairly early established a cordial relationship with the ASNLH. Yet from another perspective they marked a decidedly new departure.

Benjamin Quarles (b. 1904), the son of a Boston subway porter, did not enter college until he was twenty-three.[129] It was as a sophomore at Shaw University in Raleigh, North Carolina, that he was introduced to black history by an inspiring woman teacher, Florence Walter. Subsequently he was able to pursue graduate work at the University of Wisconsin through an SSRC fellowship program financed by the Rosenwald Fund[130] and later on a regular Rosenwald fellowship. Quarles's experience epitomized the role that a philanthropic foundation could play in making it possible for an impecunious but able person to establish himself as a scholar.

Wisconsin in the 1930s was hardly a likely place for nurturing a major historian of the black experience. Quarles's years of residence there occurred during the decade prior to the arrival of Curti and Beale. Not only was the kind of Beardianism associated with a cynical view of the motivations of the northern antislavery forces ensconced at Wisconsin, but when Quarles first went there he found that even a scholar of the older generation, the ASNLH Council member Carl Russell Fish, was reluctant to permit a black graduate student to do research in Negro history, for he regarded it as unlikely that a Negro would write objectively about his past.

On the other hand, William B. Hesseltine, though scarcely a liberal on racial issues, made "an exception" in Quarles's case, permitting him to write his 1940 doctoral dissertation on the career of Frederick Douglass.* Quarles, unlike his advisor and fellow graduate students, was untouched by the Beardian framework and unaffected by Hesseltine's skepticism about the motivations of antislavery and other reformers. Rooted in a black tradition of history-writing and inspired by Douglass's career, he — like the great abolitionist — took a moral view of American history and American destiny and optimistically believed that the country would ultimately bring its racial practices into line with its democratic ethos. This was the perspective that underlay the dissertation, published in revised form as *Frederick Douglass* (1948), and that Quarles would retain throughout his long career. For him, the treatment of the Negro was the central theme of American history.

John Hope Franklin's route into the study of the black past was more circuitous than Quarles's, and he has always considered himself as a specialist in southern rather than Afro-American history.[131] For Franklin (b. 1915), the son of an Oklahoma lawyer, the undergraduate experience at Fisk was crucial. There he assisted Alrutheus A. Taylor in the annual ASNLH sustaining membership drive,[132] but the person who provided the inspiration which led Franklin into a career in history was a white professor,

---

* Both Hesseltine and Fish, each in his own way, reveal much about the ambiguity in racial attitudes that black graduate students found among the professors under whom they worked. Fish, then in his last year of life, was completing a decade on the ASNLH Council when he supervised Quarles's M.A. thesis on the Massachusetts Republican politician, George Boutwell. Actually Quarles had an unusually close relationship with this "liberal professor," who entertained his black graduate student at home and was very supportive in other respects. In Quarles's recollection, Fish's advice, offered in a manner that was in no sense hostile, reflected a degree of ambivalence. The Wisconsin professor willingly lent his name to help Woodson and the ASNLH, and the objectivity factor aside, he also seemed to have felt that the available sources in Negro history were too limited and that the field itself was too marginal. Hesseltine, on the other hand, was a native Virginian and sometime socialist sympathizer, whose position on race, as Kenneth Stampp recalls, was never clear (during World War II this isolationist intellectual became anti-Semitic). Possessed of a crusty and insulting style, he did not hesitate to employ racist epithets in class. Yet certain of his black graduate students enjoyed a fair degree of rapport with him.

Theodore Currier, who ironically never believed that there was such a field as Negro history. Franklin's graduate work at Harvard during the Depression was largely financed first by a loan from Currier and subsequently by two Rosenwald fellowships. At Harvard Franklin faced not a curmudgeon like Hesseltine, but rather the encouraging Arthur Schlesinger, Sr. Nor did the Harvard department, the source of several of the early black Ph.D.s, frown on Negroes researching in Afro-American history. Rather Franklin himself had from the start universalistic goals about his identity as a historian. As he recalled in the mid-1950s, "Very early, I think it was in my graduate years, I had decided that I was going to be an historian without regard to race, and that I was going to remove the tag of Negro from any consideration of my work, whether teaching or writing."[133] Only quite late in his graduate studies did Franklin "back into" his dissertation topic on free blacks in North Carolina. This 1941 dissertation, supervised at Schlesinger's suggestion by the highly pro-southern author of *The Road to Reunion,* Paul Buck (with whom he developed a friendly personal relationship), placed Franklin in the field of southern history. In fact, he next turned to researching what would become *The Militant South,* and only reluctantly was he persuaded to write as his second book the volume that established him as a preeminent scholar in Negro history: *From Slavery to Freedom* (1947).

The idea for this project, which came from Roger W. Shugg, history editor for Alfred A. Knopf, provides an excellent illustration of how an action taken in the publishing industry intersecting with a changing intellectual milieu can help shape the course of a historical specialty. Shugg's own monograph on the *Origins of the Class Struggle in Louisiana* (1939) revealed his interest in the history of the oppressed, though it only hinted at the author's concern about blacks as well as poor whites. On the other hand, his 1937 paper at the SHA convention dealt with an example of interracial working-class solidarity, the New Orleans General Strike of 1892.[134] Shortly before World War II ended, Shugg urged Knopf to commission a black history survey, believing that such a book would appeal to a broad audience; he found the publisher dubious and secured approval only by arguing that black colleges would adopt it as a text. He then wrote, among others, Woodson and Charles S. Johnson for names of "competent Negro scholars" who might do a text "oriented to the needs and interests of Negro students." On the basis of his inquiries Shugg first negotiated with a scholar in Woodson's circle, who submitted material that appeared old-fashioned. Shugg then consulted Schlesinger, who promptly recommended his former student. But Franklin, anxious to complete his southern history manuscript, demurred, so Shugg—placing high priority on the project—personally journeyed to Durham (where Franklin was teaching at North Carolina State College). The young historian, impressed with Shugg's interest and the standing of Knopf in the publishing world, finally agreed.[135]

Franklin produced a synthesis that fulfilled his and Shugg's desire for a survey that would appeal to both black and white audiences. Although most of the early sales consisted of classroom adoptions in black colleges, *From Slavery to Freedom* was everywhere favorably received. The reviewers, even those who felt that there was a degree of special pleading, emphasized the volume's unemotional, balanced tone. Black intellectuals welcomed the impressive scholarship and absence of "chauvinism."[136] Prominent white historians of the South and the sectional crisis, scarcely known for their support of black rights, were also impressed. Hesseltine, favorably comparing the volume to earlier surveys, observed: "With a minimum of emotion-charged words, he brings together the conclusions of the best studies. . . . The volume is restrained in diction, lucid in exposition. It is, indeed, a highly intelligent piece of overemphasis on the Negro's role in American history."[137]

Although Franklin and Quarles both came to scholarly maturity quite autonomously of Woodson, they were represented in the pages of the *Journal* and at the meetings of the ASNLH. Quarles only met the editor in 1940, after receiving his doctorate, but his first two scholarly articles had previously appeared in the *JNH*.[138] Subsequently, discouraged by a rejection from the first trade publisher he approached, Quarles turned to Woodson for the publication of his Douglass biography. Franklin's initial appearance in the *Journal*—just before publication of his first book—was an enthusiastic review of Luther Porter Jackson's *Free Negro Labor and Propertyholding in Virginia, 1830-1860,* and some months later Woodson personally reviewed Franklin's North Carolina monograph.[139] Woodson did express some reservations about the book, but Franklin quickly became friendly with Jackson, who had reviewed it for the *AHR* and who privately praised the young author for having "certainly carried our Negro scholarship to another milestone. . . . I am afraid we are showing up the few white men who have dealt with our topic."[140] And for a few years (1943-46) Franklin's name appeared frequently in the affairs of the ASNLH—as a speaker at conventions and with essays published annually in the *JNH*.[141] In fact, it was Woodson who first encouraged Franklin's research into the career of George Washington Williams. Thereafter, Franklin was less involved with the ASNLH, while Quarles in the long run was considerably more active in the organization's affairs. The significance of both men in Woodson's eyes is evident from the fact that—in his usual way, without consulting them—he carried their names as assistant editors of the *Journal.* Yet the two men neither grew close to Woodson, nor did they become involved in any controversy with him. One member of Woodson's inner circle summed up the situation when he recalled: "Franklin was not close to Woodson, and Quarles would just smile and have no trouble with him."

When compared with Woodson the two men, though certainly not identical in their perspectives, reveal the drift taking place in the field of Afro-American history during the 1940s, heightening the trends that had been initiated by the more analytical scholars in the Woodson circle. Thus where Woodson celebrated individual black achievement, Quarles and Franklin focused much more on the collective experience of the race. Woodson himself noted this quality in his review of Franklin's first book, and as Franklin pointed out in the introduction to *From Slavery to Freedom,* he had consciously sought "the maintenance of a discreet balance between recognizing the deeds of outstanding persons and depicting the fortunes of the great mass of Negroes," since "the history of the Negro in America is essentially the story of the strivings of the nameless millions." Similarly as Quarles wrote in the preface of *The Negro in the American Revolution,* his aim was "to present a group portrait rather than a study of individuals."[142]

The two men also distanced themselves from Woodson in their greater emphasis on integrating black history with the study of the broader American past. There has been a difference of degree here between Franklin and Quarles. The latter, like those in the Woodson circle, specialized in black history, and like Woodson he employed history as a tool for both raising black pride and educating whites. Asked to prepare an essay for *Social Education* just after World War II (itself a sign of changing sensitivities among white intellectuals), Quarles called for a "Revisionist Negro History" that would correct the omissions and distortions in American history textbooks by depicting the advanced nature of African cultures, discussing slave revolts and the constructive side of Reconstruction, and presenting the achievements and contributions of blacks as early American explorers, as highly skilled craftsmen in the antebellum period, and as citizens and soldiers from Crispus Attucks to World War II.[143] This closely resembled Woodson's approach to white audiences, but Quarles in his monographs was far more emphatic than Woodson in placing blacks at the center of the American historical stage. Moreover, not only were Negroes actors in their own struggle for freedom, but also their actions pushed whites toward the fulfillment of their own values. The bulk of Quarles's writings on the antebellum and Civil War periods has been a twofold exploration of both black contributions to the battle for the fulfillment of democratic values and also the contributions of white allies to that struggle.[144]

On the other hand, Franklin has not identified himself as a specialist in black history, and much of the corpus of his publications has dealt with the history of the South. As Franklin once put it, "I do not teach black history at the University [of Chicago]. I teach the history of the South — black and white." Franklin was interested less in developing race pride than in the more general task of placing the history of blacks within the larger context of American history, illuminating the reciprocal influence of white society on blacks and of the black presence on white America. He consciously wrote *From Slavery to Freedom* with "a continuous recognition of the mainstream of American history and the relationship of the Negro to it." The presence of blacks, he pointed out in his introduction, "vitally affected" the course of American history, and at the same time "the effect of acculturation on the Negro in the United States has been so marked that today he is as truly American as any member of other ethnic groups that make up the American population." Consequently, Franklin aimed "to tell the story of the process by which the Negro has sought to cast his lot with an evolving American civilization." As he expressed it in an article in *Social Education* several years later, "Some Negroes and their sympathetic white friends have seemed, at times, more interested in stimulating pride than in describing in adequate terms the whole story of the Negro and analyzing fully and assessing properly the forces that affect Negro life as well as that of the larger society. They have tended to write rather immodestly about those phases of the Negro's past in which he has been outstanding . . . but have omitted to describe evidences of weaknesses. In failing to relate the history of the Negro, good or bad, to the life of the larger community to which it is inextricably woven, many of these historians have given a vapid and unrealistic picture of the history of the Negro in the United States. . . . It seems unnecessary to labor the point here that the experiences of the Negro did not take place in a vacuum. . . . He was peculiarly affected by everything that transpired in the larger community. In turn, his presence greatly influenced almost every phase of life in America." Until Negro history becomes integrated into the mainstream, "we shall be without a complete and accurate history of our country."[145]

Both Franklin and Quarles, each in his own way, sought to participate in the larger institutionalized world of American historical scholarship. With the 1940 AHA convention having failed to establish a real precedent, these men were exhibiting not only ambition but also a degree of courage. Franklin ventilated the frustrating sense of exclusion that black scholars felt when he wrote Jackson after seeing the program of the SHA's 1946 convention: "An entire session is being devoted to the Free Negro. . . . Too bad the great white fathers in the South couldn't bring themselves to invite

you, Fitchett,* or myself to participate."[147] Given what they saw published
in the major mainstream historical journals, black historians and probably
most whites working in the field easily assumed that there was a negative
bias on the part of editors. And because they could look to Woodson as
publishing the journal of record in Afro-American history, only rarely did
they submit manuscripts to the *AHR,* the *MVHR,* or the *JSH.* (Logan
and Greene, for example, did not do so because they believed the mainstream journals would consider their essays too favorable to Negroes.
Aptheker did once offer an article to the *AHR* but refused to reduce the
manuscript to the format of a research note and never submitted anything
else.)[148] Yet Quarles, not long after receiving his doctorate, sent off a
manuscript to the *MVHR,* becoming in 1945 the first Negro since Du
Bois to publish in a leading mainstream history journal (although he carefully offered an essay on sources of abolitionist income rather than one
dealing directly with the black experience).[149] And the extroverted Franklin
very early in his career established contacts with important white scholars.
Unlike most black historians—including Quarles—he made it a point to
attend regularly professional conventions of the predominantly white organizations. People like Woodward, Stampp, Beale, and Arthur Link quickly
became his friends.† In 1948 Franklin made his first appearance—as a
commentator—at an AHA session. A year later he would be the first
Negro to participate at the SHA, giving a paper at the invitation of program
committee chairman, C. Vann Woodward, and in 1951 would also be the
first black to appear on an MVHA program. By the early 1950s he would
also be accepting invitations for visiting professorships at Harvard, Wisconsin, Cornell, and Berkeley.

From Slavery to Freedom, written from the perspective of integrating
Afro-American history into the broader stream of American history, au-
thoritatively summarizing past research and laying out the main contours
of the field, was a milestone in the history of Afro-American history. For
those teaching Negro history courses in the black colleges, it was a breath
of fresh air, the first really systematic survey based upon a thorough mastery
of the relevant literature; to the growing numbers of whites who were
becoming sensitive to the issue of race, it was the kind of synthesis that
provided recognition and legitimacy for this hitherto neglected field. Far

* E. Horace Fitchett, a sociologist, had done important work on the history of
free Negroes in Charleston.[146]
† Beale caused a considerable stir when he invited the young Franklin, then
teaching at North Carolina College in Durham, to address one of his classes at
Chapel Hill during the academic year 1946-47. Although certain trustees at the
University of North Carolina raised objections, Beale arranged for Franklin to
make a return visit the following year.[150]

more subtly, the appearance of Quarles's 1945 essay in the *MVHR* also made an important symbolic statement. The differences between the two men notwithstanding, they both did much to advance the incorporation of the black past into the mainstream of American history and the consciousness of white historians. Franklin, in fact, given his persona and his extraordinary ability to involve himself in important networks, during the following years would come to occupy an unprecedented and—given his universalistic aims—a somewhat ironic position as the veritable personification of the field, as the individual who most effectively projected its legitimacy and importance.

The reception accorded the work of Quarles and Franklin reflected the changing intellectual milieu of the post–World War II era. The actions of the young Carl Degler symbolized the situation: the first book he bought after leaving the army was Gunnar Myrdal's *An American Dilemma,* and the first book he bought after starting graduate work was Franklin's *From Slavery to Freedom.*

Myrdal's opus, which E. Franklin Frazier called "a scientific charter of his [the Negro's] right to full participation in American Democracy,"[151] had benefited from the published research and advice of an impressive list of scholars, including heavy reliance on black social scientists like Frazier, Ralph Bunche, and Charles S. Johnson. Myrdal elevated to the level of a scientific theory the strategy that black Americans throughout their history had employed in their struggle for social change: appealing to the democratic value system and making whites sensitive to the contradictions between their ideological protestations and social reality. *An American Dilemma,* appearing when it did and receiving considerable acclaim among broad sectors of the philanthropic and intellectual establishment, epitomized changes that had been occurring in the thinking among white intellectuals during the Roosevelt era. Its note of cautious optimism and its appeal to the egalitarian values of the American creed fitted in very well with the spirit engendered by New Deal reformism and World War II. The Myrdalian emphasis on the unifying consensus in American values and the moral dynamic underlying American historical development intersected with the decline of Beardian economic interpretation and thus signaled a development that had profound significance for Afro-American historiography. Although Woodward's Beardian magnum opus, *Origins of the New South,* appeared as late as 1951, what fueled the rising interest in and the increasing legitimacy of Afro-American history was the growing sense of moral indignation about American racism that Myrdal had predicted.

By mid-century racism was no longer an intellectually justifiable position among social scientists at the best northern institutions and at the most advanced southern ones as well. The result of this shift could be perceived in the attitudes of students and faculty of the most prestigious history departments. Stanley Elkins recalls that at the schools where he studied and taught—Harvard, Columbia, and Chicago—doctrines of innate racial differences had lost respectability, historians socialized in the heyday of scientific racism were shedding their old shibboleths, and even southern-born scholars were on the defensive. Thad Tate and George Tindall recall that at the University of North Carolina sentiment tended toward the same direction, with the majority of graduate students supporting the admission of blacks to the university.

The changing intellectual climate was connected with a paradox in the writing of Afro-American history. Growing numbers of white historians, including a few of the most influential scholars in the profession, were now studying the history of race relations and the black experience. At the same time the number of blacks entering the ranks of authors of published scholarly monographs in the field declined. Thus after the publication of dissertations by Greene, Jackson, Logan, Franklin, and Quarles and the appearance of *From Slavery to Freedom* in the 1940s, preeminence in Afro-American historiography passed from blacks to whites. In the 1950s and 1960s nearly all the most influential books on black history and race relations from Kenneth Stampp's *The Peculiar Institution* (1956) to Winthrop Jordan's *White Over Black* (1968) would be by white scholars.

During the 1950s and 1960s among the established black historians most of the older men in the Woodson group were no longer productive; Franklin was devoting himself to southern history—*The Militant South* (1956) and *Reconstruction after the Civil War* (1961); and only Logan, with his volumes on the post-Reconstruction decades, and Quarles, with *The Negro in the Civil War* (1953), his second *MVHR* article, "The Colonial Militia and Negro Manpower," in March 1959, and *The Negro in the American Revolution* (1961), continued to make important contributions to the ongoing development of Afro-American historiography. Only five new young black scholars—including Helen G. Edmonds, Earl E. Thorpe, Frenise Logan, and Arvarh Strickland—published monographs in black history.* What was happening among Negro graduate students at Howard and Harvard universities was symptomatic. At Howard, the men and women who earned M.A. degrees under Rayford Logan and John Hope

* In addition to the frequently cited books by Edmonds, Thorpe, Frenise Logan, and Strickland discussed in the text, the published dissertations on black history included Bernard H. Nelson's *The Fourteenth Amendment and the Negro since 1920*, Catholic University 1945, published the following year.

Franklin around mid-century (almost always with a thesis in black history) and then went on to gain doctorates did not produce published dissertations about the Afro-American past. At Harvard (where no blacks were awarded Ph.D.s in history between 1941 and 1956), of the three Negro men who were pursuing residence work in the 1950s—Otey Scruggs, Ph.D. 1958; Jerome Jones, 1960; and Nathan Huggins, 1962—all did their dissertations on non-black topics.* In a sense, Earl Thorpe's 1953 dissertation on the writings of black historians down to mid-century (published in 1958 as *Negro Historians in the United States*) marked the end of an era.

By the time Woodson died in 1950, this trend was the cause of some concern among leaders in the ASNLH. Logan in his annual report as director observed that "indeed, the scope of interest and the high caliber of the articles submitted [to the *JNH*] by non-Negro scholars constitute a real challenge to the mature and budding scholars of our own race." Wesley, disturbed about this situation, wanted to know "why are our history scholars not more productive?"[152] Some of the black scholars whom we interviewed were also aware of what they labeled a "lost generation" or "a generation gap" in the 1950s and 1960s, but for them as for us its causes seemed puzzling and elusive.

The roots of this phenomenon appear to lie partly in a temporary decline in the number of blacks receiving doctorates in history during the immediate postwar period. While we lack the kind of comprehensive tabulation that Harry W. Greene's *Holders of Doctorates among American Negroes* (1946) provides for the period down to the middle of World War II, the data that we have been able to assemble suggest that a decline did occur. Certainly the kind of substantial growth in the number of black Ph.D.s in history that one might have expected by the late 1950s did not take place.[†] The notable clustering of black females who received their

---

* Youra T. Qualls, a Fisk graduate, received her Ph.D. at Radcliffe in 1956. Both she and Letitia W. Brown, a Tuskegee graduate who would receive a Harvard Ph.D. in 1966, had been in residence at Radcliffe in the 1940s. These two older individuals were typical of their generation. Both held GEB fellowships (and Qualls also had a Rosenwald fellowship), and both did their dissertations in black history. Huggins, coming along later, was twice awarded John Hay Whitney fellowships.

† Our list of blacks earning Ph.D.s in the post–World War II era was drawn from our personal knowledge of the individuals, supplemented by the directories of Rosenwald and GEB fellows (which are listed by race). We have cross-checked this information with the *Comprehensive Dissertation Index*. Our list is of necessity something of an underenumeration. There were undoubtedly some individuals who earned a Ph.D. in history without help from these two foundations,

doctorates during and after World War II* seems to have been a transitory phenomenon, and a substantial flow of Negro women Ph.D.s into history does not appear to have resumed until the late 1960s. World War II often postponed the pursuit of higher education for males. Then in 1947 the Rosenwald Fund closed down its operations, and in 1950 the GEB terminated its fellowship program. Still through the mid-1950s there was a stream of older individuals receiving doctorates in history, whose work had often been facilitated by GEB and Rosenwald awards made during the 1930s and early 1940s. In addition there was a younger group, who frequently undertook their advanced education under the GI Bill of Rights. A few of them benefited from John Hay Whitney fellowships, which in the 1950s functioned in a very modest way in the manner of the earlier, more ambitious foundation programs.

There was another less obvious but more significant dimension to the generational changes involved, as an examination of the dissertation topics chosen suggests. Younger blacks were more likely than older ones to select subjects that were completely outside the field of Negro history. Thus of the twenty-one blacks who completed their dissertations between 1936 and 1943, 62 percent had selected topics in black history. Again, of the thirty-eight whom we have identified as receiving their degrees between 1945 and 1962, twenty-five had been born in 1920 or earlier, and of these almost the same proportion — 60 percent — likewise did their dissertations in black history. On the other hand, of the thirteen who were born after 1920, slightly less than one-fourth wrote their dissertations in black history. Since our data are incomplete, these figures must be used with caution. In addition, paralleling this shift in the choice of dissertation topic, publication in the post–World War II period was far more likely to be on non-black themes than had been the case earlier. Thus ten of the dissertations completed by Negroes between 1945 and 1962 subsequently appeared in book form, and of these, half dealt with non-black topics.

A number of factors appear to have been responsible for this generation gap, some rooted in the institutional world of black colleges and others

and about those we have no knowledge. This is likely to be true of younger people who began work on their degrees after the foundations terminated their fellowship programs. In addition, even among those who did receive a Rosenwald or a GEB fellowship, it is likely that the number of married women who obtained their Ph.D. is underenumerated because they might have received their fellowships under maiden names, which would not be carried in the *Comprehensive Dissertation Index*.

* The most prolific publisher of this group was Merze Tate, history professor for many years at Howard University, who received her doctorate at Harvard in government and was well known for her histories of the early twentieth-century efforts at disarmament.

in the changing intellectual milieu and social attitudes in white academe. These intersected with each other, often in a highly paradoxical fashion, and operated upon individuals in varied ways. In the tangled web of causation it is difficult to say which specific factors were most important, but an analysis of them reveals much about the social context in which the writing of black history was now taking place.

It is likely that the single most important factor accounting for this gap lay in a cautiously optimistic view of the social climate, based upon the changes that began during the Roosevelt era—the view that in the increasingly integrated world of the future, blacks would and *should* be making contributions to all fields of knowledge rather than confining themselves to black studies. The growing enlightenment among white academicians and graduate students, gradual though it was, seems to have encouraged a decidedly integrationist orientation among some Negro intellectuals, expressed among historians as a desire to demonstrate that they could write any kind of history rather than being pigeonholed into a Jim Crow specialty. The integrationist aspirations of black graduate students were illustrated by the way in which those at Harvard in the 1950s did not clique together, and in fact quite deliberately moved in white student circles that were now open to them. Related to this was the perception that with certain white schools beginning to lower their exclusionary employment barriers, writing on a non-black topic might even be professionally beneficial. For some like Franklin and Nathan Huggins such kinds of assessments of the future were quite conscious; others we interviewed suggested that the process might have operated on a subconscious level, providing a context in which one felt free to choose an intellectually stimulating subject without reference to racial considerations.

The employment of blacks in northern institutions of higher education was indeed beginning to grow in these years. At the opening of World War II the number had been virtually nil. (Max Yergan at City College, for example, had worked on a part-time appointment.) But there were inklings of ferment among avant-garde black graduate students. The psychologist Kenneth Clark, although feeling a sense of obligation to teach at a black institution, by the time he earned his doctorate at Columbia in 1940 had set his sights on working at a northern university.[153] The shortage of teachers during the war provided such an opportunity for a few like Clark himself who taught at the City College of New York; with prodding and a temporary subvention from the Rosenwald Fund the University of Chicago had employed two blacks in regular faculty positions by 1943. By 1945-46 the number of such appointments had reached twenty-two (with nearly thirty additional temporary visiting professorships). Roosevelt College, established in 1945 with an explicit racially egalitarian outlook, led the way with four full-time appointments, while New York University, assisted with funding from the GEB, inaugurated a Visiting Professorship in Negro Culture and Education. Over the next decade the number of regular faculty appointments rose to well over a hundred, including positions at Haverford and Olivet colleges and the University of Minnesota. These were scattered across a broad range of disciplines, but interestingly enough except for Reddick, who at the close of the war was supplementing his duties as curator of the Schomburg Collection with teaching at City College and the New School for Social Research, there was not a single historian among them.[154]

During the 1940s Franklin had no illusion that blacks were about to be hired by northern history departments. In fact, the first black appointment to a full-time position in such a department was his selection as chairman at Brooklyn College in 1956. Still to him and a number of other black intellectuals there were hopeful signs of progress during the war and postwar years. As he said soon after going to Brooklyn: "Looking at racial integration, say over the last ninety years the pace is slow. But looking at it over the past decade, you have such considerable acceleration that I would say that the pace is being stepped up substantially, and I hope permanently. Most of the significant gains, after all, have been during the postwar period after World War II. That is a relatively short time. Certainly an historian would regard it as a short time. I am optimistic and I believe that there are so many forces operating, both within and without the country, to propel this movement that there is every reason to believe that it is going to speed up rather than slow down." For many other black academicians, it is true, the perception of the white professoriate as hostile, or at best indifferent, to having blacks as colleagues proved inhibiting: In Franklin's words, "There are still large numbers of people who do not believe that Negroes are competent, . . . you have got to overcome this very serious reservation. Then there is this other very important point, namely, that even where the reservations are overcome, Negroes are sometimes not aware of it and they don't take advantage of moving into areas where they might move. It is understandable. They feel that there is no chance. They stay in their little world."[155] Franklin himself had been more optimistic and self-assured, suspecting that the time would come when his work would bring offers from northern white institutions.

Huggins (b.1927), pursuing doctoral training at Harvard in the late 1950s, though perhaps not quite as optimistic as Franklin, also had universalist goals. Moreover, coming from a northern background, he did not want to go to the South to teach. Although having a personal interest in Afro-American history, he sensed that a position in a northern college might be obtainable as long as he did not become identified with a field that was still not widely regarded as a legitimate specialty. Besides, he recalled, "I had been geared to think of history as being broad, and I was intrigued by intellectual and social history in general." What he wanted was to be viewed first as a historian—"I was anxious that no department could pick up my vita and say, 'Well, he's a Negro historian and that's a field we don't teach.'"[156] Benefitting from a Massachusetts law that forbade identifying an applicant's race on placement forms, he startled his future employers at Long Beach State when he appeared for a job interview in 1962; recovering their composure, they hired him and later talked proudly of their "pioneering step."

Another factor that often helped shape the research directions taken by black graduate students was the role played by key professors at both the undergraduate and graduate levels. Their input was highly varied and was sometimes downright ambiguous or inconsistent. At Fisk, where the inspiring white professor, Theodore Currier, dismissed the notion of Afro-American history as a viable specialty, it is probably no coincidence that of the five publishing historians who studied under him (Franklin, Reddick, Elsie Lewis, Frenise Logan, and David Lewis), only one—Reddick—moved into black history without hesitation, the others either selecting Negro history topics with some reluctance or doing doctoral dissertations in completely different areas. Arvarh Strickland (b. 1930), on the other hand, who was studying at Tougaloo College, Mississippi, in the late 1940s, had his interest in black history awakened by August Meier, who taught the course, and Strickland would go on to take his doctorate at the University of Illinois with a history of the Chicago Urban League. At about the same time at North Carolina College in Durham, the universalistic outlook of John Hope Franklin and Helen Edmonds notwithstanding, the lesson that Earl E. Thorpe (b. 1924) absorbed from their record of publication when he was studying there just after the war was that black history was so exciting that he had no desire to do his research in anything else. Indeed, beginning with his dissertation at Ohio State University in 1953, he has devoted his entire scholarly career to publication in this field.

Such inconsistencies in the professoriate abounded in graduate school, with rather mixed and even contradictory perceptions being expressed by those whom we interviewed. Blacks found some professors encouraging, others indifferent, and still others negative toward their doing research in Afro-American history. The evidence even indicates that among the professors who discouraged their Negro students from choosing black topics, two opposing considerations were operative. Some still felt that blacks could not write objectively about their own past; at Columbia University, for example, one otherwise very liberal academic luminary as late as the end of the 1940s openly averred that for this reason Negro graduate students should write dissertations on anything but Afro-American history.* Others, however, thought that with integration proceeding apace, blacks should first achieve recognition in broader realms of historical inquiry before turning to an investigation of the history of their race.

At Harvard, for example, where an earlier generation had perceived their professors as encouraging research in black history, Negro students in the 1950s regarded the environment as indifferent. The situation contrasted with the days when Hart and Baxter entertained Du Bois and Logan in their homes; or when Schlesinger urged Franklin to submit his seminar paper on the Christian socialists to the *New England Quarterly* and then pointedly informed a class of graduate students that they had a publishing scholar in their midst. Even though Schlesinger encouraged Scruggs to work in Afro-American history, this new generation of black graduate students perceived the Harvard faculty as acting in an impersonal manner. They were also acutely aware that even Schlesinger and Oscar Handlin, for all their liberalism, ignored a discussion of blacks in their courses except for slavery.

At Chicago black graduate students, gravitating to Avery Craven because of his specialization in southern history, found him supportive of their interest in the Afro-American past, and all but Elsie M. Lewis did their dissertations in this area. Thus the long-time Atlanta University professor Clarence Bacote (1906-81), assisted by GEB fellowships, followed in the footsteps of Jackson, Johnston, and Reddick and did his 1955 dissertation on "The Negro in Georgia Politics, 1880-1908." Lewis (b. 1912), who had been a contemporary of Franklin and Reddick at Fisk, was also assisted by the GEB and the Rosenwald Fund; like Franklin she staked out her field as southern history, taking her Ph.D. in 1946 with a study of the secession movement in Arkansas. By the time she succeeded Franklin a decade later as the Howard University department's specialist in southern history, however, her research interests had turned to the study of the

* Howard K. Beale had such persons in mind when in his address to the MVHA dinner at the 1952 AHA convention he said: "Few older historians, whether Northern or Southern, have been free from assumptions that prevented their writing with a sense of balance about Negroes. Yet there has been a strange conceit in us that has led most white historians to feel competent to deal with the Negro but has made them discount writing about the Negro by Negro historians as certain to be biased. Some Negroes like some whites do write with strong bias concerning race. Yet we have John Hope Franklin, Alrutheus A. Taylor and E. Franklin Frazier writing with amazing 'balance' about white people and on the other hand we have leading white historians writing about Negroes with a bias so glaring that what they say on Negroes or whites' relations with them cannot command serious scholarly attention."[157]

black past.[158] Lewis's original decision to focus on the South during the sectional crisis had been hers. On the other hand, even in the late 1950s Vincent Harding, pursuing graduate work in religious history at Chicago, was guided into a non-black topic by his distinguished advisor Sidney Mead, who urged him to establish his reputation in a mainstream subject before following up on his interest in Negro history.[159]

Of the three black graduate students whom we have identified as working on degrees at Wisconsin during the 1940s and 1950s, all did their research on non-black topics. Two, following Quarles, worked not under the liberal Beale or Curti, but under the southern historian, Hesseltine. One of them, George R. Woolfolk (b. 1915), found Hesseltine encouraging regarding his interest in Afro-American history. But for practical and financial reasons Woolfolk decided to choose a topic that could be investigated with the sources available in Madison, writing his 1947 dissertation on *The Cotton Regency, Northern Merchants and Reconstruction, 1865-1880*, published in 1958. On the other hand, Robert L. Clarke (b. 1920), while not sharing in the view of those who regarded Hesseltine as a racist, did not feel that his advisor would have wanted him to work on a black topic. From Clarke's 1948 M.A. thesis dealing with economic carpetbaggers during Reconstruction came a 1953 essay on "The Florida Railroad Company in the Civil War," the first article by a Negro to appear in the *JSH*.[160] Unfortunately, a misunderstanding with Hesseltine over a dissertation topic precluded his obtaining a Ph.D. On the other hand, Curti's student, Elvena Bage Tillman (b. 1924), came to Wisconsin with a solid background in black history but never thought of selecting a topic in this field for her dissertation. After obtaining her M.A. at Howard in 1948, she taught the undergraduate course in Negro history there. As a research assistant for Rayford Logan's *The Negro in American Life and Thought: The Nadir, 1877-1901*, she received credit from him for supplying "much of the most important research."[161] Although Tillman found that both Curti and Beale included black history in their teaching, she felt no push to specialize in it; rather, already knowing a good deal about the black experience, she consciously sought to broaden her knowledge. In this her thinking dovetailed with Curti's own views, and she would ultimately do her 1968 dissertation on a topic in American social history—"The Rights of Childhood: The National Child Welfare Movement, 1890-1919."

The various cross-pressures upon black graduate students could produce very different results, as is illustrated by the experiences of two other black women, both of whom had obtained their doctorates directly after the war in 1946. The northern-born Margaret Nelson Rowley (b. 1917) was the last of the three black females who received doctorates from Columbia University during the 1940s. Originally hoping to do a history of the

NAACP, she was deflected by several considerations: her lack of theoretical knowledge about the sociology of organizations; the view widely shared by her contemporaries that they did not want to be stereotyped as capable only of doing Negro history; and a perception that most of their professors wanted them to avoid that field as a source for dissertation topics. On the other hand, the North Carolinian Helen Edmonds (b. 1911) in pursuing her graduate work at Ohio State University (Ph.D., 1946) did both her master's and doctoral research in black history, even though she has consistently seen herself not as a specialist in that field, but as a teacher and scholar of American history. Her published dissertation *The Negro and Fusion Politics in North Carolina* (1951) notwithstanding, she was never interested in teaching black history as a separate course and has regarded it as a subject that should be treated not in isolation but as an important, integrated part of the mainstream of the American experience.

Another, although somewhat special kind of integrationist impulse, may be seen in the experiences of Otey Scruggs (b. 1929) and Frenise Logan (b. 1920). Like Huggins they grew up in ethnically heterogeneous working-class neighborhoods outside the South, and both displayed considerable intellectual curiosity about their ethnic neighbors. Scruggs, reared in southern California, wrote his 1957 Harvard doctoral dissertation on Mexican-Americans. Logan, consciously aiming to be a historian who was not restricted to writing black history, wanted to do his dissertation at Western Reserve University on the Cleveland ethnics whom he had known as a youth. Instead, he decided to study *The Negro in North Carolina, 1876-1894* (Ph.D., 1954, and published in 1964) at the urging of his professor, Harvey Wish, who himself had a profound commitment to studying the black experience, but despaired of much research being done in the field unless blacks themselves undertook it.

In addition to the influences that encouraged Afro-American graduate students to do their research on non-black topics, there were factors in the life experiences of black academicians and in the Negro college milieu that had negative effects upon scholarly productivity altogether. These of course were impediments that had long discouraged research and publication. For some blacks limited finances delayed doctoral work for years; a few of the older historians, for example, were compelled to postpone their advanced education until funded under the postwar GI Bill of Rights and did not earn a doctorate until they were in their forties, well past the prime age for the creation of productive scholars. As Daniel Thompson's research on the black professoriate at mid-century reveals, Negroes, far more frequently than whites, had to work their way through graduate school, thus retarding their professional development and narrowing their intellectual perspectives.[162] Furthermore, teaching at small, underfinanced southern institutions, with heavy course loads and slender library resources, hardly encouraged the writing of books and journal articles. As poorly funded as these colleges were, superior libraries and substantial leave or free time for research were luxuries that could scarcely be afforded. As one authoritative survey of black colleges (by Earl J. McGrath, commissioner of education during the Truman administration) concluded: "All but a few of the 123 predominantly Negro institutions of higher education . . . are essentially teaching institutions . . . unable to provide their faculties with the opportunity or the resources essential to a continuing program of research." Reddick, writing in 1940, said of the black academicians: "The scholar is burdened with heavy class schedules; his income is low and the unavailability of laboratory and library facilities has become to him a byword. It is not surprising, therefore, that a considerable folklore has grown up around the experience of those, once ambitious, who have surrendered the ideal after going into teaching."[163]

Luther Porter Jackson was in part diverted from scholarship by his civil rights activism, but also, as he once explained his situation to Woodson, "I teach the regular load of fifteen hours. I handle large classes of students, and I continue this process not for nine months but eleven each year. . . . Hundreds of my friends, white and colored, are amazed over what I do accomplish within these limitations." A. A. Taylor at Fisk, which had better research grants than any black college and which was second only to Howard in the quality of its library holdings, had similar cause for complaint: "I suppose it is not to be expected that many persons will in this day, especially in our schools, have broad opportunities for research. At Fisk we have been singularly blessed by affording such opportunities to some people. The Social Science Department has had, of course, unusual opportunities, financed, not merely by the college, under conditions not to be easily reproduced elsewhere. Some men in the sciences have had good opportunities not equal, of course, to those in the social sciences. A few celebrities have had almost unrivalled opportunities for writing. But some have had very little real chance to work effectively. There has seemed never to be available for some, at a given instance, the necessary combination of funds and time." When Horace Mann Bond, president of Lincoln University in Pennsylvania, one of the finest and best endowed of the Negro liberal arts colleges, sought to recruit John Hope Franklin for his faculty, the latter inquired about the teaching load, asking "To what extent is it possible to carry on a program of research and writing . . . ? You know my interests well enough to understand why I have raised these questions." In reply, Bond described the fifteen-hour teaching schedule that was "conventional" at black colleges and conceded: "The Lincoln faculty has been noted for its teaching rather than for its research, and I do think this is of great importance. . . . Certainly research and writing would be encouraged, but teaching is paramount."[164]

Moreover, black scholars, almost all of them at southern institutions, typically faced obstacles when they tried to use state and county archives, local historical societies, and even some major university libraries. On the eve of World War II, Reddick had observed: "Some state and municipal libraries will admit him [the Negro scholar]; others will not. A few of the privately endowed institutions will permit individual Negroes to read 'somewhere in the building'; many of them will not even do this. . . . With the Negro and white scholars of the south separated from each other, and with the Negro scholar further handicapped by the social barriers to his documents, is there any wonder that so little is produced, and little of that little is of the first quality?"[165] Thus in Virginia, Jackson, who had won "absolute entree to anything that the 'white folks' have in this state by way of public records," jubilantly observed: "The wide open reception which is given is nothing less than marvelous." In 1945 Elsie Lewis found that it required the intervention of her advisor, Avery Craven, to obtain access to the Arkansas state archives. Like Horace Mann Bond as far back as 1930, Jackson and subsequently Franklin marvelled at the access they secured from Marie Bankhead Owens, the head of the Alabama State Department of Archives and Senator John H. Bankhead's sister.[166] While the libraries at Emory, Duke, and Chapel Hill were helpful to black historians, Vanderbilt's excluded blacks as late as the 1950s. Franklin had even found the personnel at the North Carolina State Archives ambivalent. To prevent him from sharing the reading room with white scholars and from giving orders to white pages, they provided Franklin both with his own study room and permission to go to the stacks himself. Protests from white scholars, resentful about his special stack privileges, produced an integrated reading room.[167] Access to research collections was thus erratic and uneven, and there was very likely some retrogression during the white backlash of the late 1950s. In any event, the white North Carolina university libraries were probably unusually cooperative. Franklin, for example, found the curator of manuscripts at Duke "extremely helpful." It is perhaps not entirely by coincidence that four of the dissertations by black historians in the 1940s and early 1950s—those by Franklin, Edmonds, Frenise Logan, and Roland C. McConnell—had North Carolina topics.[168]

For those with a scholarly bent there was also the black college ethos that E. Franklin Frazier so savagely satirized in *Black Bourgeoisie* (1957). The limited job options for educated blacks heightened the significance of college teaching as a ladder for economic mobility and social status and thus lessened the importance of purely intellectual aspirations among many of the professors. Moreover black colleges, which were primarily teacher-training institutions whose administrative ranks were disproportionately filled with individuals holding doctorates in education, were interested in securing Ph.D.s for their faculty to meet accreditation standards, and often remained unappreciative of scholarly endeavor.[169] This situation was exacerbated by the white paternalism exhibited at several graduate schools that sometimes granted what many black professors themselves derisively labeled "Negro Ph.D.s," based on the idea that since blacks were locked into teaching at segregated schools, it was unnecessary to hold them to the usual standards. In addition over the years able faculty at black colleges who desired professional advancement were deflected into administration, and the few with doctorates were in great demand for such posts.[170] Not only did Horace Mann Bond, Rufus Clement, and Charles Wesley sooner or later subordinate scholarly interests for careers as college presidents, but A. A. Taylor became dean at Fisk, and the maturation of Quarles's scholarly career was almost certainly delayed by his tenure as dean at Dillard University.

It is true that such considerations had not prevented the flowering of black historical scholarship from the 1920s through the early 1940s, much of it stimulated directly by Woodson's entrepreneurship. Paradoxically, however, during the postwar years an improving opportunity structure that was emerging at the black colleges seems to have had a dysfunctional impact upon the scholarly productivity of some professors. The scholarly elan that the GEB and Rosenwald fellowship programs had stimulated at black institutions diminished as the fellowships were phased out in the late 1940s. At the same time the increase in enrollment at black colleges outran the slow rise in the number of Negro Ph.D.s. This development came as the Negro institutions of higher education were beginning to upgrade facilities to remove themselves from the Jim Crow class B accreditation category to which the Southern Association of Colleges and Secondary Schools had assigned them. Additionally, by mid-century, in the vain hope of heading off the drift of Supreme Court decisions toward mandating desegregation in higher education, southern state authorities bestirred themselves to equalize salaries in publicly owned institutions. The impact of these converging factors placed black schools in sharp competition with each other for the few blacks with doctorates. At the end of World War II there were probably scarcely twenty black historians with Ph.D.s engaged in or available for college teaching positions. Earl Thorpe recalls working in virtual intellectual isolation at Southern University in Louisiana during the late 1950s, where he was the first Ph.D. on the faculty and the only black historian with a doctorate in the state after Quarles moved from Dillard to Morgan State. Given this situation,

in most black colleges a Ph.D. almost automatically brought a full professorship at a good salary. Such a reward system hardly put a premium
on continued scholarly productivity. Morgan State, for example, garnered
five of the black doctorates in history earned between 1936 and 1947;
although they held degrees from important universities—Wisconsin, Harvard, University of Southern California, Michigan, and New York University—except for Quarles these individuals published virtually no scholarly research.

With academic advancement lying only marginally in publication, it is
not surprising that Jackson and Franklin regarded themselves as quite
unusual in their devotion to research and publishing. As Franklin once
told Jackson: "You are to be congratulated for keeping alive the fire of
research along with your many other duties. I'm rather disgusted with the
average Negro scholar in our field and in others. They seem to just sit
down after they get their degrees and rest on their laurels (what laurels!!!)."
Even at Howard University Franklin was distressed: "The most disturbing
thing to me was . . . the lack of their determination to become really and
truly intellectually independent . . . really and truly scholars. . . . Of course,
tied up with that . . . is the way in which the college was operated and
the lack of appreciation of scholarship on the part of those in charge.
They never, almost never created a climate that was congenial to it." He
observed that "it is not without significance that the Howard period is
the period in which I did the least of my publishing. Now to be sure . . . *The
Militant South* is a product of my Howard years. But the research and
writing for the book was done while I was on leave from Howard on
fellowships which I secured, and which Howard did not encourage me
to secure and did not assist me in any financial or any other way once I
had secured them. . . . Then, too, the facilities for research, the teaching
load and all the other things stood in the way of my production while I
was there. . . . [Although] I was getting some stimulation from a limited
number of members of the Howard University faculty," that period was
"intellectually . . . satisfying primarily because of where Howard is located.
I could always steal some time and go to the Library of Congress and
meet large numbers of colleagues who were coming in and out of Washington and get some stimulation that way."[171] Certain envious colleagues
at Howard privately tried to dismiss Franklin as a "D.C.H." ("Distinguished
Colored Historian"), and to this day there is among younger black historians in the profession an oral tradition that Franklin, "because he
worked so hard at research at Howard, was something of an oddity."

Thus the whole reward structure at the black colleges in the postwar
years frequently acted as a subtle motivational mechanism to discourage
scholarly productivity. In short, it would seem that the particular social

milieu at the Negro institutions of higher education converged with changes in the intellectual milieu in the larger American society to create the generation gap in the writing of black history by Afro-American scholars.

The changing milieu of the postwar world, which encouraged some black intellectuals to pursue investigations in topics other than Afro-American history as an expression of their universalistic aspirations, also prompted a growing number of white historians to undertake serious studies of race relations and the black experience.* Unlike their black contemporaries, whose outlook was shaped primarily by their racial experiences, the intellectual roots of the white scholars who contributed to the monographic literature in the field during the decade of the Brown decision and the rise of Martin Luther King, Jr., lay primarily in their socialization in the reformism of the Franklin Roosevelt era. Among those whites we interviewed, nearly all who came to young adulthood by the end of World War II were ideologically left of center and in effect constituted an expansion of the liberal and radical streams of research in which Wish, Aptheker, Wharton, and Woodward had pioneered during the 1930s. A few came from politically conscious radical and liberal families, and for them the events of their own lifetime served to reinforce the commitment

* Paradoxically in sociology during this period, following the appearance of Myrdal's *An American Dilemma* (1944) and St. Clair Drake and Horace Cayton's *Black Metropolis* (1945), the study of race relations and the black experience exhibited a very different trajectory, becoming relegated to a backwater of generally inconsequential scholarship. One can only speculate on the reasons. Partly the situation may have stemmed from the fundamental changes taking place in the discipline itself. Sociology finally cut its remaining ties to the reform impulse that had dominated so much of the field's earlier years, stressed instead objective reporting of social process and social structure, and became largely dominated by quantitative techniques that did not lend themselves to furthering an understanding of race in American society. The waning of research on race may also have had something to do with the passing of the preeminence of the Chicago School and of the community studies that it had encouraged. Chicago's Robert E. Park retired to Fisk to be with his former student, Charles S. Johnson, but Johnson's considerable hegemony over the careers of black sociologists produced virtually nothing in the way of fundamental research. Finally, it seems likely that Myrdal's magnum opus, synthesizing the work that had been done over the years at Chicago, Fisk, and the University of North Carolina, developed and expressed so felicitously the implications of their findings (and the assumptions underlying them), that it functioned as a scientific paradigm. It was almost as if Myrdal made so much sense to the postwar generation of sociologists, that little more in the way of fundamental research seemed called for. Not until the "functions of social conflict" theorists began applying their model to the study of American race relations in the early 1960s would a new sociological perspective on race in America begin to take shape.

to social justice. More typical were persons from conventional backgrounds whose outlook shifted considerably to the left in the social and intellectual context of the New Deal and World War II. In short, most of them were part of the wave of socially conscious youth who were pursuing graduate studies in the postwar years of the Fair Deal and the Truman administration. Many were activists on behalf of civil rights. Moreover, converging both from the radical left and the liberal center, a striking number of them supported Henry Wallace's 1948 presidential bid. On the other hand, the cadre of more conservative whites, who had encouraged the work of the Woodson movement, had virtually no successors.

Underlying similarities notwithstanding, an analysis of individual careers reveals that the white scholars who, motivated by a concern for social justice, found themselves attracted to research in Afro-American history were products of such highly diverse experiences that they defy easy classification. Nevertheless, this group may conveniently be divided into four rough categories: (1) an "old Left" of persons who while coming to intellectual maturity during the Depression had roots in ideologically radical or liberal family traditions; (2) a group more particularly socialized by the Depression and the New Deal that moved gradually to an ideologically liberal position by the end of World War II; (3) a few from the latter group for whom military experiences during the war provided the crucial turning point; and (4) a small number of more conservative older men who, in contrast to the secular outlook of the others, were molded by the particular religious environment in which each was raised.

Slavery was the subject that produced the most innovative research in the 1950s, and the authors of these works—Kenneth Stampp, Stanley Elkins, and Carl Degler—illustrate the range of radical and liberal sensibilities that informed most of the work being done in black history after mid-century. All three, sharing in the underlying intellectual drift toward a racially egalitarian outlook, articulated a negative moral assessment of slavery and race prejudice, while both Stampp and Elkins continued the historical inquiry inaugurated by Wish and Aptheker into the ways that slaves responded to a coercive and oppressive labor system. Yet each reflected the changing climate of scholarly opinion in his own particular way. Stampp was a man of radical antecedents who became interested in the problem of racial injustice, Degler represents the quintescence of enlightened post–New Deal liberalism, and Elkins was one of the advance guard of Jewish scholars who would come to play such an important role in the study of the black past.

Stampp (b. 1912) actually belongs to the generation that included Quarles, Franklin, and Woodward—and like the distinguished white southern historian, Stampp was deeply affected in his social ideology by the Depression.

Reared in Milwaukee in a German socialist family who shared Victor Berger's mixture of radicalism and racism, Stampp moved further to the left during his college days in the early 1930s and like Woodward was intrigued and later repelled by the Communists. Unable to commit himself to revolution, he joined the Socialist party instead; as late as 1948 he thought about supporting Henry Wallace but cast a protest vote for the Trotskyist candidate; not until the presidential election of 1952 did he vote for a Democrat. As an undergraduate and graduate student in residence at the University of Wisconsin during the 1930s, Stampp was attracted to southern history through studying with the stimulating Hesseltine, and given Stampp's cast of mind, this almost inevitably led him into a study of Negro history. Indeed, in his first half dozen articles, published in the early 1940s, he interspersed essays on sectional politics in the *JSH* and *MVHR* with two articles in the *JNH,* most notably "The Fate of the Southern Antislavery Movement."[172] Disenchanted with the traditional southern scholarship on slavery ("The road from Appomattox to the present," he wrote, "is cluttered with scholarly books and articles . . . [that] embellished [the Southern legend] . . . with the trappings of scientific fact"), he realized that he was in a "dissenting minority." Thus when Aptheker's *American Negro Slave Revolts* was published, Stampp in an elegantly written 1944 review essay penned for Dwight McDonald's independent Marxist journal, *Politics,* welcomed the appearance of this fellow "heretic" who was willing to "emphasize the uglier aspects of Negro slavery." Relating his views on slavery to his larger social vision, he concluded that "southern Bourbons are still doing business at the same old stand while poor whites and blacks glare at each other across the color line. Indeed, one might ask as ironically as he likes, What is so 'new' about the 'New South'?"[173]

Stampp's move from the University of Maryland to the University of California, Berkeley in 1946 placed him at one of the most distinguished history departments; the publication of his second book, *And the War Came,* in 1950 established him as a major historian. By then, long impressed with the need for a new general monograph on black bondage, he had undertaken what became his magnum opus. Though it was the prodding of a graduate student that crystallized his decision to do the volume, it is perhaps not entirely accidental that he began *The Peculiar Institution* in 1948, the year of the tumultuous confrontation with the Dixiecrats at the Democratic national convention. The publication of his 1950 AHA paper, "The Historian and Southern Negro Slavery," in the *AHR* in 1952[174] decisively identified this prominent scholar with the field of Afro-American history.

The times were auspicious for the publication of *The Peculiar Institution* in 1956. Coming shortly after the Brown decision, in the middle of the excitement over King's Montgomery bus boycott and Woodward's *Strange Career of Jim Crow* (1955), it struck a responsive chord and quickly became an influential classic. What in 1944 had been the heretical view of a dissenting minority was becoming the standard interpretation, and the man who earlier had found Aptheker a welcome breath of fresh air now saw his own volume similarly greeted by a wider audience. Just months before the book's appearance, David Brion Davis, who spent considerable time with Stampp when the latter was a visiting professor at Harvard in 1955-56, had found his ideas "a revelation." Reading the book, Woodward concluded that it "firmly rips off a lot of flattering unctions . . . and a lot of blindfolds we have used to shut out realities. . . . Left in shreds" were the "legend" of "the gay, carefree black clown," and the myth "of racial harmony under slavery." Enthusiastically he wrote, "It is a rare opportunity for a reviewer to be able to report upon an important undertaking, carried out with intelligence, insight and imagination. Professor Stampp's study of slavery in the South . . . deserves some adjectives rarely earned by historians who tackle a controversial subject in a revisionary spirit—adjectives such as 'objective' and 'thorough.'"[175]

Indeed, since the publication of Elkins's *Slavery* with the assertion that Stampp had in effect scored a "devastating" victory that closed the debate with Phillips, it has become the conventional wisdom to perceive that *The Peculiar Institution* was accepted by the profession with little if any serious questioning. "It is doubtful," Eugene Genovese has written, "that many professional historians had accepted Phillips's viewpoint on the day before Stampp's book appeared; rather, most seem to have been so thoroughly prepared for a new interpretation that they simply breathed a sign of relief when a substantial alternative finally arrived." Representing as it did "the conjuncture of a decade or so of serious [revisionist] scholarship and the force of political circumstances. . . . by the time that *The Peculiar Institution* appeared . . . it was virtually an ideological anticlimax."[176] Yet without denying the basic validity of Genovese's point, one should note that Stampp's book received considerable criticism from well-established historians of the old South. Hesseltine went so far as to write a harsh review that appeared in a Milwaukee newspaper, where Stampp's family could not help but see it. Other scholars with southern sympathies found the book biased, unconvincing, based on unrepresentative sources, and simply too "harsh" in its condemnation of slavery. Even David Donald, who had studied under Wharton at Millsaps College and accepted the view of "every intelligent modern American" that science had demolished notions of inherent racial mental differences, gave *The Peculiar Institution* a decidedly mixed evaluation. It was "admirable in many ways," "a model of accuracy and correctness" in its factual presentation, and arguing its case "with great cogency." "Perhaps the author is most to be praised because he has avoided pussyfooting . . . and has forcefully . . . taken a stand." Nevertheless, Donald pronounced the book "long on morality and short on historical understanding." "Parts of Mr. Stampp's argument rest more upon inference and moral indignation than upon evidence"; the book "contains nothing" that abolitionists would not have said a century earlier. Indeed, "there is in Mr. Stampp's thinking a certain ahistorical turn, so often characteristic of deeply committed liberals."[177]*

From one perspective *The Peculiar Institution* of course represented the fruit of a revisionism extending back nearly two decades to Wish's and Aptheker's work. For blacks, indeed, the book vindicated the position they had held all along.[179] Ironically, the radical sensiblity in which *The Peculiar Institution* was originally rooted went entirely unrecognized, and its real significance lay in its reception as the contribution of a mature and highly respected *liberal* scholar. Not only Donald but also David Potter in a far more favorable assessment made this point: Potter found the study "doubly illuminating, both objectively as a new account of slavery based on a remarkable array of fresh data, and subjectively as a reflex of the degree to which liberal thought has altered prevailing concepts of the Negro." At the other end of the political spectrum Aptheker, in welcoming the volume, pointedly argued that the criticism of Phillips leveled by black scholars and "white radicals . . . could never, by themselves, really penetrate dominant intellectual circles." Stampp "untroubled by [such] . . . disabilities" had succeeded in doing this; that his findings "should be announced now, with the imprint of Knopf, testifies to the profound advances being made in the whole area of Negro-white relations." Thus, given "the context of its production," this "devastating refutation of the moonlight and magnolia mythology" was itself a historic milestone.[180]

A dozen years younger than Stampp, Stanley Elkins (b. 1925) belonged to the postwar wave of liberal intellectuals who took their advanced academic training in the liberal glow of the Truman Fair Deal. His early concern with racial and ethnic prejudices had been reinforced by experiences among the heterogenous student body at his Boston high school and by many vigorous arguments with white southerners during his army service. Later as a Harvard undergraduate Elkins shared the concern for

* Donald's reaction stood in marked contrast to that of Stampp's friend, Richard Hofstadter, who wrote that "you are too gentle, too quiet, too objective, and there are many points at which I wish you were a little more indignant, or quarrelsome . . . [and] let more of your political, and human, feelings shine through. . . . You are far more vulnerable to the charge of icy detachment than you are to that of special pleading."[178]

peace and social justice exhibited by many of his peers, and although subsequently moving to the political center, in 1948 he had worked in Wallace's campaign. Underlying Elkins's approach of course was the anthropological and psychological environmentalism that Stampp had voiced so explicitly. In addition, Elkins's intellectual journey was tinged with the consciousness of his Eastern European Jewish origins and included an avant-garde interest in interdisciplinary approaches to the study of history.

Some historians have theorized that his *Slavery* (1959) was really a way of addressing the problem posed by the limited Jewish resistance to Nazi tyranny, and one may speculate that his interest in slave behavior may have reflected more of a concern with the Jewish experience than he consciously realized; yet in terms of chronological sequence his interest in slavery was first and his awareness of the parallel with the German concentration camps later.[181] On the other hand, his interdisciplinary interests appeared early. Originating during his Harvard years, they were encouraged at Columbia Univeristy (Ph.D., 1959) by his graduate advisor, Richard Hofstadter, who suggested that he study with C. Wright Mills, a sociologist fascinated by the mechanisms mediating between power and personality. Elkins, impressed by the evidence of widespread dependency and docility in slave behavior, at the purely descriptive level found Phillips more convincing than Aptheker; and in Bruno Bettelheim, whose work made it clear that power could infantilize even highly sophisticated people, regardless of race or ethnicity, Elkins saw an attractive environmental substitute for Phillips's racist explanation. (Even Stampp, as early as 1952, had not been unaware of the lessons to be learned from life in the concentration camps: "In the light of twentieth-century experience, when white men have also been forced to submit to tyranny and virtual slavery, it would appear to be a little preposterous to generalize about the peculiarities of Negroes in this respect."[182]) As Elkins has said, "I chose the concentration-camp analogy, because it was dramatic, because it was fresh in our memories, and because it got around the problem of race."[183]

The response that *Slavery* received from fellow historians was almost entirely negative. Across the board Elkins was attacked for his sweeping generalizations and his lack of empirical investigation. The remnants of the pro-Phillips forces were alarmed at his seeming to equate the southern plantation with the concentration camp;[184] the anti-Phillips group was angered by his accepting the Sambo stereotype as a valid description of slave behavior. Donald managed to sum up the feelings all around: for him the concentration camp analogy showed "poor taste and worse logic," and the thesis about " 'the infantilizing tendencies of absolute power' " suffered from "a dubious unstated major premise—that the southern Negro was indeed a Sambo, something that Elkins assumes but nowhere even attempts to prove." Probably the most discerning, if most respectful, evaluation came from John Hope Franklin: "This book is bold and original. . . . One has the feeling, however, that Mr. Elkins not only joins in the old debate he avowedly scorns, but initiates a few debates of his own. In language as strong as any used by Stampp, he tells the apologists of slavery that the institution had a deeply corrosive effect on every aspect of the slave's being. Even so, one is not altogether convinced that the effect was as complete or as permanent as Mr. Elkins asserts. There was enough initiative—running away, revolt, and other manifestations of aspiration—to suggest that, despite the dehumanizing effects of slavery, the personality of the slaves was not destroyed altogether."[185]

Carl N. Degler (b. 1921) represents another variant of postwar liberal tendencies. Raised in a Newark, New Jersey, German family, he came from a social milieu where adoration of Roosevelt's economic policies went hand in hand with the anti-Negro prejudices of many white working-class ethnics. While an undergraduate at Upsala College Degler's leftward drift was encouraged by close friendships with the radical and liberal Jewish students who were fellow commuters to this suburban Lutheran institution. An ardent New Dealer, by his junior year he had developed a serious concern about racial injustices, was a campus leader against the discrimination faced by the college's few black students, and—as an outgrowth of his racial views—was on the way to the feminist position for which he would later become well known. Although he found himself excited by two Marxist works on Reconstruction—Howard Fast's novel *Freedom Road* (1944) and Du Bois's *Black Reconstruction*—his own egalitarian views were rooted in a Myrdal-like awareness of the gulf between ideal and reality in American life.* Degler's social idealism during graduate school days led him to vote for Wallace, but afterward he returned to conventional Democratic party liberalism. His 1952 dissertation was in labor history, but the depth of his interest in the history of race relations and the black experience is revealed by the fact that his first published volume, *Out of Our Past*, appearing virtually simultaneously with Elkins's *Slavery*, had more references to blacks than to any other topic and included an abbreviated version of his seminal essay on "Slavery and the Genesis of American Race Prejudice" that appeared the same year.[187]

If the plantation regime was being demythologized during the 1950s, so also was the role of the white abolitionists in the struggle for Negro

---

* Although Degler by the end of the 1960s would lose some of his optimism, his outlook has been essentially a Myrdalian one. *Out of Our Past* (1959) was not only consciously informed by this perspective but explicitly criticized C. Wright Mills for his negative assessment of the possibility for social change within the existing system.[186]

freedom. Both Larry Gara and Leon Litwack, pioneers in this revisionism, came from radical working-class socialist backgrounds. While Gara (b. 1922) was still in high school in Reading, Pennsylvania, he became a Quaker and developed an interest in jazz that later eventuated in his first book, a biography of the black musician Warren "Baby" Dodds (1959). Three times his higher education was interrupted by imprisonment as a conscientious objector; on one of these occasions he met the black pacifist and future civil rights leader, Bayard Rustin, with whom he participated in nonviolent demonstrations against racial segregation in federal prisons. Litwack (b. 1929), on the other hand, was in many respects typical of those coming from a leftist Jewish background. Shaped by his parents' strong labor and socialist sympathies and by his experiences growing up in a heterogeneous Santa Barbara neighborhood of whites, Mexicans, and blacks, Litwack's interests had also crystallized during his high-school years when he displayed a fascination with black literature and blues, was buying radical books from International Publishers, and familiarized himself with Du Bois's and other Marxist works on Reconstruction. A campus activist during his early years as an undergraduate at the University of California, Berkeley, he supported Wallace in 1948.

In graduate school these two historians had different experiences. Gara took his doctorate at Wisconsin under Hesseltine in 1954, and his dissertation did not touch on black history. In fact, he attributes his curiosity about the Underground Railroad not to his concerns about racial injustice per se, but to the "higher law" views involved in his pacifist beliefs. We also suspect that Hesseltine's skepticism about the motivations of abolitionists and other reformers may have had an unconscious impact. In any event, while still a graduate student, Gara made his first investigation of how whites and blacks functioned in lending assistance to fugitive slaves. A paper presented at the 1952 MVHA convention, "The Underground Railroad: A Re-Evaluation," and an essay that same year in the *NHB*[188] briefly stated the thesis, subsequently developed in *The Liberty Line* (1961), that fugitive slaves usually made their escapes unaided by the white abolitionists. Litwack studied with Stampp, a sympathetic advisor who reinforced the direction his scholarly interests were taking, and he had the good fortune to be Franklin's research assistant when the latter was a visiting professor at Berkeley. Litwack's 1958 dissertation, published as *North of Slavery* in 1961, the same year as Gara's *Liberty Line,* explored the status of antebellum northern free blacks (a topic that had been ignored since the appearance of a handful of state and local studies early in the century) and provided a pioneering analysis of the ambivalences in the racial attitudes of white abolitionists.[189]

Gara never became a specialist in black history as such, and at first neither did Litwack. Despite his interests, such was the temper of the times that Litwack took the advice of a senior professor at Berkeley who urged him to specialize in another field lest he hurt his career. Accordingly Litwack spent his years as a young teacher at the University of Wisconsin unproductively investigating the origins of Jacksonian democracy. It was the social milieu created by the black revolt of the 1960s that would subsequently encourage him to turn once again to his real field of interest.

There were certain individuals like LaWanda Cox and August Meier who came from a democratic-socialist background, but whose research in black history was more directly rooted in the social and intellectual climate spawned by the Depression and New Deal. For Cox (b. 1909) the most decisive influences came from the multifaceted reformer Merle Curti, with whom she worked as a research assistant in the early 1930s, and who brought her into her first personal contacts with Negroes. Pursuing her Ph.D. at Berkeley during the height of the Depression era's radical student activism, she tried futilely to revive the Socialist organization, the Student League for Industrial Democracy, in opposition to the ascendant Communist militants. And amid the highly publicized misfortunes of the southern white and black tenant farmers, she wrote her 1941 dissertation on "Agricultural Labor in the United States, 1865-1900, with Special Reference to the South." Cox's research convinced her that the former slaves were fully justified in believing that they had been promised land. With the struggle against the Nazis reinforcing her social consciousness about race relations, Cox did further study in the disappointing land redistribution policies of the federal government after the Civil War, her findings being published in the *MVHR* in 1958 as "The Promise of Land for the Freedmen."[190]

August Meier (b. 1923), reared in a Newark, New Jersey, professional family, came from a mixed Gentile-Jewish background that represented the convergence of both East European Jewish and German socialist traditions. From his parents, who were democratic socialists turned New Dealers, he absorbed a concern for social justice that, colored by his sense of ethnic marginality, intersected with the increasing salience of the racial issue that marked the World War II period. His undergraduate years at Oberlin College provided an exposure to both intellectual history and the history of nationalism under Professor Frederick B. Artz. At the same time reading in the sociological and anthropological literature on blacks and on race relations served as the route toward an interdisciplinary framework. While teaching at southern black colleges in the postwar years, Meier pursued graduate work at Columbia University, with a 1949 M.A. thesis on black nationalism before Marcus Garvey (which appeared in distilled form in Lorenzo J. Greene's *Midwest Journal*)[191] and a 1957 doctoral dissertation on black racial ideologies in the age of Booker T. Washington, which was published in 1963 as *Negro Thought in America, 1880-1915.* Involvement in the demonstrations of the activists of the Student Non-violent Coordinating Committee at Morgan State College in the early 1960s informed his subsequent writing on the history of the black protest movement.

Strictly in the stream of New Deal liberalism and without radical antecedents—though otherwise displaying very dissimilar routes to their interest in black history—were Francis Broderick (b. 1922) and Richard Bardolph (b. 1915). Broderick, who has described himself as an "[Irish] Catholic well disposed to the reforming urge that inspired the progressive tradition in America and led to the New Deal,"[192] came from a family of ardent Roosevelt supporters, FDR having appointed his father superintendent of state banking in New York and later to the Federal Reserve Board. Bardolph, born into a poor Dutch immigrant family in Chicago, lacked such a coherent liberal outlook; and as far as blacks were concerned, his youthful interactions had been negative—helping to "hustle them out of the local parks." In their teens Broderick was exposed to the racial concerns of the chaplain at prep school and Bardolph to the outlook of a few socially conscious teachers at a Dutch-Reformed parochial school. As an undergraduate and graduate student at the University of Illinois (Ph.D., 1944), Bardolph was attracted to the Socialist professor and outspoken critic of racism, Fred Shannon; an incident early in World War II—overhearing a black woman tell her son why he could not aspire to be a streetcar conductor—aroused Bardolph's moral indignation about racial injustice. By the end of World War II he was a "red-hot New Dealer." Meanwhile Broderick, who did his undergraduate work at Princeton, during his senior year led a vigorous campaign for the admission of black students. An editor of the Daily *Princetonian* in 1942-43, he penned a series of pointed editorials appealing to the wartime enthusiasm for democratic ideology in an unsuccessful attempt to rectify the policies of this conservative, southern-oriented school. Calling upon the university to end "that lip-service to democracy which excludes our Negro countrymen from its most fundamental rights," he observed: ". . . while 13,000,000 Negro Americans look for signs of their admission to a rightful place in American democracy, Princeton continues its principle of white supremacy and, in an institution devoted to the free pursuit of truth, implicitly perpetuates a racial theory more characteristic of our enemies than of an American university."[193]

Their worldviews thus set, Broderick and Bardolph pursued their research and writing on the black experience during the dozen years after World War II. Having completed a senior thesis on the Washington–Du

Bois controversy, Broderick entered Harvard planning to do his doctoral dissertation analyzing the career of the distinguished protest leader Du Bois. By the early 1950s, Bardolph was teaching at the University of North Carolina at Greensboro, where he chaired the local Americans for Democratic Action chapter and was active in the interracial circles that made early steps in desegregating drinking fountains and restrooms in downtown stores. He had also inaugurated his inquiry into the origins of the black elite. The liberal scholarship of these two men bore fruit in 1959: Bardolph's *The Negro Vanguard* and Broderick's *W.E.B. Du Bois: Negro Leader in a Time of Crisis,* the first scholarly biography of this major black figure.

While for a number of scholars wartime sensitivities thus reinforced concerns implanted during the Depression, for others who had been previously oblivious to racial injustice direct experience with racial discrimination while serving in the armed services provided a pivotal turning point. This can be seen most explicitly in Dudley Cornish's *The Sable Arm: Negro Troops in the Union Army 1861-1865* (1956); its dedication to "Eustace" was a poignant reference to a friendly fair-skinned Negro whom Cornish met on his first day in the army, but who to Cornish's dismay was promptly shipped off to a Jim Crow unit when his black ancestry was discovered.[194] Both Elliott Rudwick (b. 1927), whose *W.E.B. Du Bois: A Study in Minority Group Leadership* was published in 1960, just a year after Broderick's biography, and Leslie H. Fishel, Jr. (b. 1921) were disturbed when they saw how the U.S. Navy segregated blacks and relegated them to jobs as messmen and stewards' mates. Rudwick (Ph.D., University of Pennsylvania, 1956) was raised in a New Deal–oriented, nonideological working-class Philadelphia family. His interest in race led him briefly into Wallace's Progressive camp and for a longer period into the field of sociology, which in the 1950s still had the image of being the center of scholarship on race relations and the black experience. Fishel, who came from a liberal Republican background, was a naval officer who took seriously the liberal traditions of his alma mater, Oberlin College. At Harvard he experienced the indifference to studying black history that others have reported; still, working under Handlin and then Schlesinger, Fishel did his important though unpublished 1954 dissertation, "The North and the Negro, 1865-1900: A Study in Race Discrimination."[195] In 1956 he introduced at Oberlin one of the earliest courses in black history in a predominantly white institution. Fishel enthusiastically wrote to the editor of the *JNH:* "My course in the Negro in American History has enrolled almost twice as many students as I anticipated. I am using Aptheker's *Documentary History,* Quarles on the Civil War and Woodward on segregation as the major texts. In addition, I am sending them again and again to the *Journal* for weekly assignments."[196]

The few southerners who joined the expanding ranks of white scholars contributing to the study of Negro history were not only part of the postwar generation of liberal graduate students but also in important respects continued the pattern established by Woodward and Wharton. Three such men — George B. Tindall, Thad W. Tate, and Louis R. Harlan — later rose to prominence in the profession. All were reared in middle-class families of conservative (though not rabid) racial views, and all three arrived gradually at their emancipated position.

Tindall and Tate were natives of the Carolina piedmont who came to intellectual maturity during their postwar years at Chapel Hill. For Tindall (b. 1921) as for Wharton, a devout religious upbringing imparted a value system whose implications provided the underpinning for the development of his racial outlook. Growing up in Greenville, South Carolina, he vividly recalls his fourth-grade teacher chastising his classmates for assaulting black children who insisted on their right to use the sidewalk; in high school he wrote a paper on the inequities of the segregated southern school system and took a course in South Carolina history that left him "haunted" by the miscegenation debates at the 1895 state constitutional convention. An undergraduate professor at Furman University further encouraged Tindall's incipient liberalism, which blossomed in the postwar heyday of Frank Graham's administration at Chapel Hill. For Tate (b. 1924), a native of Winston-Salem, educational experiences — a liberal social science teacher in high school and the University of North Carolina milieu during the 1940s — were also important. Both men were involved in the campaign to get blacks admitted into the University of North Carolina graduate schools, both were active members of the interracial Chapel Hill chapter of the American Veterans Committee, and when it split over endorsing Wallace in 1948, Tindall and Tate both sided with the anti-Communist wing. For Tindall in particular the salience of civil rights in the presidential election that year made a deep impression. His M.A. thesis on race as an issue at the 1895 South Carolina convention[197] was a prelude to his 1951 dissertation, published the following year as *South Carolina Negroes, 1877-1900*. In this volume Tindall consciously did for his native state what Wharton's recently published monograph had done for Mississippi. Tate was working for the Institute of Early American History and Culture in Williamsburg, Virginia, in the period after the Brown decision, at a time when the Institute was inaugurating a series of research projects designed to broaden its focus beyond the colonial elite. He volunteered to study blacks in colonial Williamsburg; though not published until the surge of interest in the black experience after 1960, *The Negro in Eighteenth-Century Williamsburg* (1965) was a product of the 1950s. The scholarly contribution of both men was closely intertwined with their commitment to racial justice. After the

Brown decision, Tate had organized a citizens' group in support of school desegregation. Tindall, though always striving for detachment in his writing, was proud to be working on a subject relevant to his social idealism, and he recalls particularly the exhilaration he felt in discovering (a half dozen years before Woodward's *Strange Career of Jim Crow*) that there was a time when Jim Crow laws had not existed.

Louis R. Harlan (b. 1922) was in the advance guard of southern whites who, becoming liberated from their racist heritage, gravitated to Woodward first at Hopkins and later at Yale. Woodward's appointment at Hopkins in 1946, like Stampp's at Berkeley the same year, was itself indicative of the way in which more liberal views on slavery and race were moving toward the mainstream of the profession. Woodward's own perspective was epitomized in *The Strange Career of Jim Crow* (1955). Originally presented as a series of lectures at the University of Virginia in the autumn of 1954, a few months after the Brown decision, the book deliberately aimed at employing historical data to offer optimistic illumination on the possibilities for peaceful school desegregation. Woodward noted that although he would undoubtedly be making some mistakes, "I feel that the need of the times for whatever light the historian has to shed upon a perplexing and urgent problem justifies this somewhat premature effort" to correct the faulty information on which the debate over the ineradicability of Jim Crow was being carried on.[198] As in his earlier work on Populism, here was another instance of a forgotten alternative that the South might have taken. Actually Woodward's information about the fluidity of post–Civil War arrangements and the relatively late development of segregation laws was not that new. Wharton and Tindall had become very much aware of this and from the purely legal perspective the point had been made as far back as 1910 in Gilbert T. Stephenson's *Race Distinctions in American Law*. But Woodward, with his usual gift of expression, brought these facts to the attention of a wider audience, with a flair and a cogency that scarcely any other historian could have equalled.

For Harlan, the seeds of skepticism about southern racial mores had been sown while he was an Emory undergraduate in the early 1940s. His course readings included Woodward's *Tom Watson,* and there were enlightening exposures such as the time he was hitchhiking and obtained a ride with a black man who startled him by engaging in a highly intellectual conversation. Harlan's naval duty during World War II also provided a broadening melting pot experience that helped him shed his deep South provincialism, while amid the coarseness of most of the ship's crew the dignity and lack of subservience of the black steward's mate left an indelible impression. He returned to the United States "with a new view of what the world should be like." Taking his M.A. at Vanderbilt after the war, Harlan felt constricted by the generally conservative and racist atmosphere of this university. Distancing himself from the racial and sectional parochialism of his southern background, Harlan became caught up in a leftward drift that made him sympathetic to the Wallace progressivism of the present and the Populism of the past. Finding Woodward's books congenial with his emerging worldview, Harlan transferred to Johns Hopkins for the Ph.D. After an initial stab at a labor history topic, he turned to what became his study of the interplay between northern philanthropy and southern racism in the development of segregated public school systems. As he was working on his dissertation in the early 1950s, both his research interests and his social activism dovetailed with the progress of the NAACP's school desegregation litigation. Teaching at a college in rural East Texas, where race relations were so oppressive that the local blacks were still stepping off the sidewalk when whites passed by, Harlan helped organize voters of both races in support of liberal Democratic candidates. By the time he finished his dissertation in 1955, it was clear that Harlan's research, detailing the increasing inequalities in southern public school education early in the century, had obvious relevance to what had become a central contemporary issue. The convergence of his own scholarly work with the progress of the NAACP's campaign made both the publication of his dissertation *Separate and Unequal: Public School Campaigns and Racism in the Southern Seaboard States, 1901-1915* (1958) and the later *AHR* article on desegregation in the New Orleans schools during Reconstruction unusually timely.[199]*

The nexus between research interest and the changing social and intellectual milieu is more nebulous for Emma Lou Thornbrough (b. 1913), the first white woman to publish a scholarly monograph in black history

---

* Other variants on this pattern of change among a new generation of postwar southern white historians are provided by Donald E. Everett (b. 1920) and Samuel R. Spencer, Jr. (b. 1919). Everett's views on race had begun to change as a result of experiences in the student Y movement at the University of Florida and contacts with black servicemen while stationed in England during the war. Pursuing graduate work at Tulane, he briefly moved far enough left to vote for Henry Wallace and wrote a 1952 dissertation on "Free Persons of Color in New Orleans, 1803-1865."[200] Spencer, author of *Booker T. Washington and the Negro's Place in American Life* (1955), early in his undergraduate days had begun to question whether the racist system under which he had been reared in Columbia, South Carolina, squared with his Christian values. This concern was further stimulated at the beginning of World War II when he served as a lieutenant in a black army unit. As a postwar graduate student at Harvard, he chose to do a paper on Du Bois from among a list of topics offered by Schlesinger in his social history seminar. Learning of this interest, Handlin commissioned Spencer to write the volume on Washington for his American biography series.

and to devote her scholarly career to this specialty. Coming from an Indiana Republican family, Thornbrough's route into Afro-American history was partly the result of taking her doctorate in 1946 at the University of Michigan under the historian of antislavery, Dwight Dumond, with a dissertation on legal aspects of slavery in the North. Teaching at her undergraduate alma mater, Butler University in Indianapolis, she next turned to investigating the history of race relations in her native state. As her work proceeded, she became more sensitive to blacks as persons and joined the NAACP. What had begun as a legal study became a broader social history. In addition, her own marginality as a woman historian making her way in a male-dominated profession sensitized her to the situation that blacks faced as a minority. It would appear that her particular personal experiences, occurring in a context of increasing public concern about the race issue, operated in complex and subtle ways to produce her lifelong interest in Afro-American history.

Only rarely among this growing number of white graduate students writing dissertations on race relations and the black experience does one find individuals who did not fit the model of a mainly secular postwar reformism. But two older men, Howard Bell (b. 1913), whose dissertation and pioneering articles on the antebellum Negro convention movement appeared in the 1950s, and Charles Flint Kellogg (1909-80), chronicler of the NAACP's early history, both came from highly religious Christian backgrounds with missionary-oriented concerns about the life and education of non-white peoples. Bell was the son of a Kansas clergyman in the fundamentalist free Methodist church; Kellogg, a descendant of an old Great Barrington, Massachusetts, family, was an ordained Episcopal priest who had once been a missionary-teacher in China. Ray Allen Billington, Bell's advisor at Northwestern University, knowing of his student's interests, consulted John Hope Franklin about possible topics. His suggestion of the convention movement, with its concerns for social and educational progress, and its roots in black church leadership, proved an ideal subject for Bell's 1953 dissertation, "A Survey of the Negro Convention Movement, 1830-1861" (finally published in 1969). Subsequently Bell's desire to serve mankind led him into a teaching career at black colleges in the South. Kellogg, who grew up in the town where Du Bois had been born, and where top NAACP officials were well-known summer residents, undoubtedly came to his dissertation on the NAACP as the result of specific personal experiences. Coincidentally his investigations meshed with the interests of his advisor, Woodward, and some Hopkins fellow students, in exploring the racial views of the antislavery reformers and their descendants.* His earliest publication was a 1959 article on the

* For discussion of this point, see pp. 168-70 herein.

leadership of a key NAACP founder, Oswald Garrison Villard, grandson of William Lloyd Garrison.[201]

Thus it is evident that the white scholars came to their study of Negro history through a number of different routes. Yet, however varied their intellectual biographies, all of them in one way or another were the kind of individuals who proved particularly sensitive to the growing salience of civil rights as a national issue.

The 1950s marked a major watershed in Afro-American historiography. As Franklin observed a decade after the publication of his survey of the field, "The writing of the history of the Negro in the United States has come into its own." "In quantitative terms alone the results have been most impressive," with historians of both races and sections having "produced an enormous quantity of studies," and with programs at the conventions of "every major historical association . . . in the past ten years" having paid "considerable attention to subjects related to Negro history."[202]

Especially obvious had been the major works on slavery and the slaves' response to bondage. Degler's work heralded an interest in an exploration of slavery's interrelationships with race prejudice (including his own comparative study of race relations in Brazil and the United States, *Neither Black nor White* [1969]), and by the end of the 1950s both Winthrop Jordan and David Brion Davis were doing research for what would become major monographs on that subject. Litwack and Gara were about to publish the books that contained their revisionist views of the abolitionists. Quarles and Cornish had placed the study of the Negroes' role in the Civil War on a new footing. Cox prefigured the new kinds of questions that both she and the next generation of scholars would be asking about Reconstruction. Lewis, Broderick, Rudwick, Spencer, Meier, and Beale's student, E. David Cronon—with his *Black Moses: The Story of Marcus Garvey and the Universal Negro Improvement Association* (1955)—were charting new directions in the study of black ideologies and leadership. One of the striking things about the new literature was the willingness to examine the unpleasant and discouraging period following southern "Redemption." The list of studies included not only the research into late nineteenth-century black thought and leadership, but also Fishel's discussion of the northern states after the Civil War, the monographs by Edmonds, Frenise Logan, and Tindall on the Carolinas, and two influential books on late nineteenth-century race relations North and South: Woodward's *Strange Career of Jim Crow* and Rayford Logan's *The Negro in American Life and Thought: The Nadir, 1877-1901*. In short, as Franklin observed, "For the first time . . . there is a striking resemblance between what historians are writing and what has actually happened in the history of the American Negro."[203]

The reception accorded books like Franklin's *From Slavery to Freedom*, Woodward's *Strange Career of Jim Crow*, and Stampp's *The Peculiar Institution* and the increase in the number of dissertations and published monographs in Negro history and race relations had their parallel in the gradual growth of black participation in the affairs of Clio's principal professional organizations: the American Historical Association, the Mississippi Valley Historical Association (which in 1964 became the Organization of American Historians), and the Southern Historical Association.

The representation on convention programs symbolized the changes taking place. Precedents were established at both the MVHA and SHA, while at the AHA there was a small but fairly regular participation. In 1942 Alrutheus A. Taylor had appeared at the AHA on a session devoted to U.S. "Minority Problems"; between 1946 and 1961 Negroes were on programs every couple of years, most commonly with Franklin or Rayford Logan giving a paper or serving as commentator. In part this development reflected the growing salience of the civil rights issue amid the controversy over school desegregation: the AHA meetings in 1955 and 1957 (at both of which Franklin presented a paper) had sessions on the history of segregation that were "heavily attended."* Progress at the SHA and MVHA was more erratic. Franklin was the first black on a convention session at both the SHA and MVHA, presenting a paper at the SHA in 1949 and chairing a session at the MVHA in 1951. Elsie Lewis was the next black historian to receive comparable recognition, giving papers at the SHA in 1952 and the MVHA in 1953. Franklin and Rayford Logan delivered papers at the MVHA in 1954. The following year the SHA sponsored a

---

* Interestingly enough, Philip D. Curtin (b. 1922), future authority on the history of Africa and the transatlantic slave trade and the AHA president in 1983, presented a paper at the 1956 AHA convention on "Racism and the Tropical Colonies, 1833-1852," in a session on "British Imperial History." Curtin was a product of a Quaker high school, Swarthmore College, and Harvard University (Ph.D., 1953); his dissertation had just been published under the title *Two Jamaicas* (1955). Briefly a religious pacifist on the eve of World War II, Curtin has always considered himself as on the political left, a non-Marxist socialist, though he has consistently voted the Democratic ticket. His research interests grew partly out of experiences in various South American and Caribbean countries during his high-school and college years under the auspices of a group known as Experiment in International Living. His concerns about race had been intensified by contacts with black seamen, including the social scientist St. Clair Drake, during service in the World War II merchant marine; and from the beginning of his graduate school days he had always wanted to specialize in the study of the relationship of Europe to the Third World. The subject of his 1956 AHA paper received greatly expanded treatment in his *The Image of Africa: British Ideas and Action, 1780-1850* (1964).

notable dinner session on "The Segregation Decisions" which featured an address by Benjamin Mays, president of Morehouse College. The presence of blacks grew spottier on convention sessions of both organizations toward the end of the decade. (The most notable exception was the SHA's 1958 meeting at Nashville, where Lawrence D. Reddick participated on a session on "Ideologies, Strategies and Tactics of the NAACP, 1909-1958," that drew a capacity crowd spilling over into the corridor.) At the same time, however, all three organizations were according Franklin recognition with committee assignments. During the mid-1950s he served two terms on the AHA's Beveridge Award committee; he was a member of the SHA's membership committee in 1952 and program committee in 1955; and in 1958 he was elected first to the MVHA executive committee and then to the AHA Council, being chosen chairman of the latter two years later.

Much of the explanation for the differential patterns of black participation in the programs of the three organizations and the erratic nature of the participation at the MVHA and especially at the SHA lay in the difficulties presented by the segregation laws and discriminatory hotel policies still prevalent in the southern and border states.[204] For the AHA, which regularly rotated its meetings among New York, Chicago, and Washington, there was no very serious problem. It is true, Franklin recalls, that the situation in the immediate postwar years could be unpredictable, as when he was lodged in a room on the exhibit floor at a New York convention. But the wave of new antidiscrimination legislation in a number of northern states eliminated the remaining difficulties in the convention cities of that section of the country. Moreover, by the end of World War II, even in Washington, the AHA's regular convention headquarters—the Mayflower Hotel—was extending the use of all its facilities to blacks in attendance,[205] and in 1953 the U.S. Supreme Court's decision in the Thompson Cafeteria case spelled the end of discrimination in the city's restaurants and hotels. The situation for the SHA, which never met outside of the South, was the most serious, but the MVHA also faced problems, since its membership contained a sizable southern contingent (including the influential scholars connected with the *JSH,* which was edited during the immediate postwar years at Tulane University) who were not only prejudiced but also felt aggrieved when the organization passed over their region in selecting a convention site. Here in fact was an emotional and highly divisive issue. Distinguished figures in the professional associations, including C. Vann Woodward and Merle Curti, who were anxious to bring about an end to the discrimination proceeded with considerable care, working to rectify the situation without at the same time splitting the two organizations asunder.

Conditions in the SHA during the late 1940s were epitomized by the actions of a handful of black professors at the Birmingham convention in 1946 and at the Jackson one in 1948. At Birmingham they had to wait until the dinner dishes were cleared and then enter the banquet room through the kitchen door to hear the presidential address. At Jackson the black teachers from Jackson State College had to enter the hotel through the back door and—sitting in the rear of the meeting rooms—attended the sessions. By then Woodward, as chairman of the program committee for the 1949 meeting at Williamsburg, was arranging the session featuring John Hope Franklin. Even at this center of Rockefeller philanthropy, however, hotel accommodations were barred to Franklin, the local arrangements committee informing Woodward that the black historian could attend only the official luncheons and dinners. Franklin stayed with friends in town. His participation created a considerable stir. "A lot of the hassle [over trying to secure a hotel room] was done behind my back. . . . It was a lovely November afternoon [when the paper was presented] and the whole thing was quite a spectacle—people were wandering around outside and looking in at me, [and] there was a packed room." Franklin did attend the presidential dinner, but because of the racial attitudes of many SHA members a few of his friends saw to it that only congenial people sat at his table. What occurred at Williamsburg, however, proved a mere slight and temporary crack in the doorway. Two years later, when the SHA met in Montgomery and held a session in the old state capitol building, blacks had to sit upstairs in the gallery of the rotunda.[206]

A second step forward was taken at Knoxville, Tennessee, however, in 1952 when Woodward was SHA president. As usual blacks in attendance, like Franklin and Elsie Lewis, had to obtain rooms and meals with professors and friends in the city. However, the local arrangements committee chairman, LeRoy P. Graf, had secured permission from the headquarters hotel for blacks to attend the dinner preceding the presidential address, a matter of considerable importance to Woodward. But just before the convention opened, the hotel reneged; Graf spent a feverish day seeking substitute facilities, and by the time Woodward arrived the resourceful University of Tennessee professor had arranged to transport the delegates to a club some distance from town for the dinner, which was the first time in SHA history that black members freely participated in this annual affair. (On the other hand blacks were not able to attend the host institution's complimentary luncheon, a standard part of an SHA meeting in those years, and Graf was obliged to take them out to the university campus, where, having earlier been turned down by the Faculty Club, he arranged to have them served in an enclosure off the main cafeteria, with faculty members from related departments serving as hosts.)[207]

Meanwhile the previous year the issue had exploded at the MVHA convention in Cincinnati, when the executive committee reconsidered an earlier decision to hold the 1952 convention in New Orleans, where Curti would be delivering the presidential address. The New Orleans hotel would not even permit blacks to attend the sessions, much less participate in the official luncheons and dinners.[208] For Curti (the sort of person who had taken the lead in the successful battle to break down the exclusionary practices of the University Club soon after he began teaching at Wisconsin), the idea of presiding under these conditions was intolerable. Yet he wanted to avoid splitting the MVHA on this volatile issue, a likely possibility given the strong feelings not only of the southerners, but also because of the powerful support they received from an influential executive committee member like Dwight L. Dumond.[209] During two days of long and emotional executive committee sessions at the Cincinnati convention, president-elect Curti made clear his position that because black members should have at the very least the right to attend official functions, he would not give his presidential address under circumstances where all members were not allowed to be present. Finally, the committee decided to poll the entire membership, presenting them with the choice of meeting either in New Orleans or in Chicago. Curti and his supporters felt confident that the predominantly northern membership would vote for Chicago but accepted this compromise, since it would save face for the Tulane people and "prevent a headon collision in the business meeting."[210] But Curti's close friend and Wisconsin colleague Howard K. Beale (who in 1949 had only with difficulty been dissuaded from creating a confrontation over the issue on the floor of the SHA convention in Williamsburg)[211] found the formula unacceptable. At a tumultuous business meeting he successfully moved that an explanation of the segregation issue should accompany the ballot. With that decision the New Orleans people withdrew their invitation.

Curti and others were deeply worried that the polarization would produce many resignations. A committee appointed to consider the issue, headed by Western Reserve University's Carl Wittke, in 1952 recommended that MVHA meetings should be held only where all members could participate in official functions but avoided "acrimonious debate" by deliberately ducking the housing issue. Yet even this minimal formula was pigeonholed by the executive committee, and another body, headed by the liberal southerner Thomas D. Clark of the University of Kentucky, was appointed to give still further study to the matter. Clark was able to arrange for the 1953 convention to be held in Lexington, Kentucky, where blacks were accorded equal treatment at the headquarters hotel. However, debates and tangled maneuverings over the issue continued for another year until finally in 1954 the executive committee quietly arranged to hold all future meetings at hotels that treated blacks on the basis of full equality. The first such convention was held at 1955 at St. Louis.[212]

For the SHA the solution to the discrimination problem was harder and slower to achieve. Acting on a motion introduced by Woodward, a closely divided executive council in 1954 narrowly passed a resolution committing the SHA in principle to meeting at hotels that accorded equal treatment to black members. The following year the organization did prevail upon the Peabody Hotel in Memphis to serve blacks at the official functions, most notably at the dinner session, which featured the discussion on school desegregation. A few blacks attended under these conditions, but Franklin, who served on the program committee for that year and recognized the efforts of both the committee chairman, James W. Silver, and the SHA president, Bell I. Wiley, to achieve even this partial desegregation, stayed away. He wrote to these officers of the organization, "There are times when one gets weary of inconveniences and risks of humiliation." "Even my thick skin can be wounded by a repetition of the insults and indignities I have received."[213]

Because of the southern white backlash of the 1950s — epitomized by the proliferation of White Citizens Councils throughout the region — it was not possible to carry out the new policy that the executive council had approved. Thus at Houston in 1957 blacks could attend all official functions, but at Atlanta in 1959 it was only with the greatest difficulty that secretary-treasurer Bennett H. Wall could prevail upon the hotel management to permit blacks to attend sessions. The issue, raised now by a small contingent of younger, northern-born scholars teaching at southern black schools, publicly erupted again at that same convention and in the ones held in 1960 and 1961, with the problem only resolved in the early 1960s, when the council quietly decided to follow Wall's choices of convention sites in Miami and Washington and at cooperative hotels in places such as Nashville and Little Rock.[214]

Another index to the changes occuring during the 1950s was the growth in the number of articles by and about blacks in the learned journals. Quarles's second article in the *MVHR* on the use of Negroes in the colonial militias appeared in 1959, but in terms of numbers a more impressive representation of blacks was to be found in the *William and Mary Quarterly* and the *JSH*. The former had four essays by Negroes, all on black topics, most notably Quarles's "Lord Dunmore as Liberator" in 1958.[215] More significant were the six articles by Negroes — four of them on non-black themes — that appeared in the *JSH* between 1953 and 1960, at the very time circumstances virtually barred blacks from attending most of the organization's annual meetings. The first such essay in its pages was Robert L. Clarke's 1953 piece to which we have already referred; Franklin published an essay on "The Southern Expansionists of 1846," and George R. Woolfolk one on "Taxes and Slavery in the Ante Bellum South." Frenise Logan who, given his universalistic orientation, had turned to studying the impact of the Civil War on the cotton industry in India, would have two articles on the subject in the *JSH* in 1958 and 1965. In addition in the late 1950s two students of Avery Craven, Elsie Lewis and Clarence Bacote, each published an essay on the black experience in the post–Civil War South.[216] In all three journals there was a rise in the number of blacks writing book reviews. Here again the *JSH* displayed the greatest representation; beginning with one by Franklin in 1949, between one and four reviews by blacks appeared there annually. With the *JSH* being edited during most of this period at Kentucky by Thomas D. Clark (1949-52) and J. Merton England (1953-58), who had personally done research on the free Negro in Tennessee,[217] its record epitomizes the results flowing from the confluence of a more enlightened attitude among influential individuals in key positions, with the rising number of black scholars who were largely doing their research on American rather than Afro-American topics. In fact the two editors took positive steps to encourage blacks to submit essays to the *JSH*.

At the same time in both the *AHR* and *MVHR* there was a significant increase in the number of relevant articles authored by whites. In the *JSH*, where given its geographical focus, there had been occasional articles about blacks from the beginning, the proportionate increase was slight; but the other two journals from the first time had a good scattering of essays on black history. Most important probably were three articles in the *AHR* prompted by the school desegregation controversy—by constitutional historians Leonard W. Levy and Alfred H. Kelly, followed a bit later by Louis R. Harlan's 1962 article on New Orleans public school desegregation during Reconstruction.[218] A half dozen relevant essays appeared in the *MVHR* during the decade 1950-60, including Fishel's piece on blacks in northern politics, articles by University of Kentucky professors Clement Eaton and Ben Wall, and essays by the first two white women historians to make contributions to the study of the Afro-American past, Emma Lou Thornbrough and LaWanda Cox.[219]

Overall, the participation of black scholars, whether measured by committee assignments, appearances at conventions, or publications in journals, was limited mostly to a rather visible but tiny minority among the small cadre of blacks with doctorates in history. Franklin achieved recognition across the board in the learned organizations and journals, characteristically functioning as one of the "firsts" and "onlies"—a category of achievement that was beloved by Carter G. Woodson but that Franklin in his writings consciously strove to transcend. Rayford Logan (partly because of his

Caribbean and African interests) appeared most often in AHA affairs; Quarles, who tended to eschew attendance at conventions, was to be found mainly in the pages of the *MVHR*, and Elsie Lewis chiefly in the activities of the SHA. Moreover, editors of the three major journals relied heavily on these four when they assigned book reviews. Franklin was far and away the most often called upon, although from time to time other individuals were asked.

The prominence of Logan and Franklin was not surprising. They taught at the finest black graduate school, they had the prestige of Harvard degrees, they were both widely known for at least one book, and they were located in Washington, which facilitated contacts both with researchers at the Library of Congress and with the AHA national office. In addition, they were both active in furthering the integration of blacks into the profession. Franklin regularly entertained visiting historians and would hold parties at his home when the AHA met in Washington. He also attended historical conventions as often as possible. For example, he was one of only three or four blacks who showed up when the AHA met at St. Louis in 1956. This small turnout was a matter of considerable disappointment to Franklin, since in making these arrangements a couple years previously, Curti (then AHA president) and the rest of the organization's leadership had been careful to secure assurances from the hotel management, the council even having "sent the executive secretary to me to ask me if it was all right to go to St. Louis." Although most black historians, still feeling that they had little if any chance in the wider professional world, were conspicuously absent from the mainstream national professional meetings, Franklin's strategy was clear: "that is where you move, that is where you find out whether the door is open. That is the way you move into the great stream of the professional life."[220]

Change was indeed in the air at the professional organizations, and Franklin had a prominent part in it. With *From Slavery to Freedom* having appeared just three years before Woodson's death, Franklin quickly succeeded the ASNLH founder as the leading authority on Negro history. But he played this role in a far more integrated context than Woodson had done, symbolizing the profound shifts that were beginning to occur in the historiography of black America.

What Franklin perceived as the "New Negro History" epitomized the convergence of viewpoint between black historians with nearly a half-century tradition of scholarly writing rooted in their racial experiences, and a growing number of white historians, newly sensitive to the importance of the black past, who came to their researches out of broader radical and liberal reform interests. Franklin himself credited Woodson with "launching the era of 'The New Negro History'" by "exploding the myths" that blacks had no past and by "putting the Negro in his rightful place" in American history.[221] Yet Franklin and Quarles, by moving beyond Woodson in the way they treated the black past as an integral part of the fabric of American history, expressed an orientation that dovetailed with that of the growing number of white scholars who by mid-century were enlisted in "the struggle" for "a more adequate treatment of the Negro in the history of the United States."[222] Undoubtedly a kind of circular causation operated: Quarles and Franklin, sensing the changing intellectual climate, intuitively grasped the opportunity it offered and reached out to the broadening audience of white historians, and in turn the accomplishments of these two Negroes did much to legitimize Negro history among other members of the profession.

In retrospect the evidence confirms Franklin's contemporary assessment of what was happening. By 1960 the landscape had changed considerably. The quantitative increase in research and publication, the scope, depth, and new directions this research was taking, the shifts in the activities of the professional organizations all point to the 1950s as a watershed in the development of the field, a time when the historiography of black America was shedding its previously enforced parochialism. The role of Stampp and Woodward, as highly prominent scholars located at two of the leading graduate departments, epitomized the changes in the professoriate that were moving black history toward the center of the stage. Already, the first students of Woodward and Stampp to publish their dissertations had embarked upon their careers: the future Pulitzer Prize winners of the 1980s, Louis Harlan and Leon Litwack, were the vanguard of what would be a distinguished cadre of scholars who took their Ph.D.s under these two men. At the same time Franklin, although not teaching at a Ph.D.–granting institution, played a parallel role informally, suggesting a topic for Howard Bell, stimulating the interest of Litwack and Herbert Gutman (his research assistants at Berkeley and Wisconsin respectively), and generously offering support and counsel to nearly every one of the younger people who would make their mark in the field over the next decade. Overall it seemed a pardonable exaggeration to say, as Franklin did in 1957, that rather than suffering any longer from neglect "the writing of the history of the Negro in the United States has come into its own."[223] By the end of the 1950s black historiography seemed poised for the burst of scholarly activity that would flower with the civil rights revolution of the 1960s.

CHAPTER 3

Generational Change and the Shaping of a Scholarly Specialty

PART II, 1960-80

THE SCORE OF YEARS BEGINNING in 1960 witnessed an enormous scholarly output in the history of race relations and the Afro-American experience. There was a quickening of publication in the early 1960s, and by the end of the decade Afro-American history had become fashionable, a "hot" subject finally legitimated as a scholarly specialty. At bottom this development was the fruit of the social consciousness that came with the zenith of black activism and the changes in American race relations. At the same time the intellectual origins and trajectories of those historians making contributions to the field became more varied. Satisfactory categorization of individual scholars is more difficult than for earlier periods, given the especially complex interplay between ethnic and family background, ideological orientation, new perspectives and methodologies within the historical profession, and the changes in the larger social milieu. And there was also a greater diversity of interpretation, as scholars responded in highly dissimilar ways to the tumultuous events of the era.

The half dozen years between 1960 and 1966 that corresponded to the climax of the nonviolent, direct-action phase of the black protest movement witnessed a decided quantitative leap in the number of scholars contributing to the historiography of black America. This was an overwhelmingly white group whose intellectual outlook had in most cases pretty well crystallized before the advent of the 1960s civil rights revolution. In only a few instances were the sit-ins and street demonstrations important in shaping the perspective of those who emerged as scholars in the study of the black past during this period. A handful were older individuals whose research was largely rooted in the kinds of radical and liberal sensibilities that had motivated so many of the earlier historians. Most, however, were socialized between the time that Negro rights became an important political issue—during the Truman presidency—and the rise of Martin Luther King, Jr. Indicative of important future trends were two new phenomena: a small number of young scholars who came from highly racist backgrounds, and another group, also modest in size, who unconsciously drifted into their study of Negro history, rather than coming to their research out of an intense social conviction.

Among the older individuals, Richard C. Wade (b. 1922), author of *Slavery in the Cities* (1964), like his contemporary at Harvard, Francis Broderick, came from a well-to-do Catholic family with a tradition of liberal Democratic politics. In Wade's case, this reached back three generations to rural Iowa, where his grandfather had lost a gubernatorial campaign by a slim margin of votes due to Ku Klux Klan opposition. Wade himself, reared in North Chicago's suburbs, knew Negroes only as domestics, but his father had always dwelt on the importance of decent treatment of blacks because white society had imposed such a "special burden" upon them. With Wade's undergraduate years during World War II having provided him with vivid memories of A. Philip Randolph's March on Washington movement and the 1943 Detroit race riot, his interest in civil rights crystallized during the Truman era. He served as a researcher for the President's Committee on Civil Rights and in 1948 took an active part in drafting Hubert H. Humphrey's speech to the Democratic convention supporting the civil rights plank, whose adoption led to the walkout of the Dixiecrats. A couple of years later while doing research in Louisville for his dissertation published as *The Urban Frontier* (1959), Wade's observation of the old slave quarters then still standing prompted him to realize that slavery in the cities would be an important subject for a future book.

Another contemporary of Wade's at Harvard, David Brion Davis (b. 1927), author of the influential *The Problem of Slavery in Western Culture* (1966), also came from midwestern reform Democratic antecedents. A grandfather knew William Jennings Bryan well, and Davis's own parents, while conservative on race, imbued him with a concern for social justice. What awoke Davis to the inequities of the color line was the disturbing segregation and racism that he witnessed in the army. Becoming politically involved while a Dartmouth undergraduate after World War II, he sided briefly with the Progressives when the liberals split over Henry Wallace's candidacy. More directly pertinent to his later scholarship was the campus interest in civil rights generated by Professor Robert Carr, who had served as executive director of Truman's Committee on Civil Rights. Graduate courses at Harvard provided no equivalent exposure to the race issue, but

Davis's social concerns found expression in his early research on homicide and capital punishment. Meanwhile, during the academic year 1954-55 Davis was enormously stimulated by the lectures of visiting professor Kenneth Stampp. Afterward, taking a teaching position at Cornell, he came across the extensive antislavery collection in the university library. Although Davis turned to his monumental study in 1957 in the wake of the Montgomery bus boycott and the Little Rock school desegregation crisis, his decision, rather than being a response to vivid current events, resulted from a convergence of his long-standing ethical concerns, his exposure to Stampp, and the fortunate discovery of a superb collection of relevant research materials.

For the slightly younger Robert L. Zangrando (b. 1932), sensitivity to racial issues was rooted in the intersection of his particular experiences as a working-class ethnic growing up during the Depression and his later observations of the civil rights struggle. Raised in a strongly pro-labor and pro–New Deal household in Albany, New York, Zangrando resented the unfairness of the ethnic discrimination he observed: both the Irish-German-Anglo domination of the city's business and politics and the contempt exhibited by his northern Italian neighbors toward southern Italians. Such perceptions converged with (1) the ethical doctrines inculcated in parochial school and (2) an awareness of social injustice in American society derived from his father's protracted unemployment during the 1930s to produce a strong identity with the oppressed. Stirred by the impressive NAACP court victories that occurred during the years he was working his way through college, Zangrando did his senior paper in 1958 on what would become the subject of his University of Pennsylvania doctoral dissertation five years later—the NAACP's antilynching campaign. Meanwhile he had been a dedicated activist, participating in the 1958 Youth March for Integrated Schools, picketing Woolworth's in sympathy with the southern black student sit-ins of 1960, and four years later spending part of the summer working with the Mississippi Freedom Schools. Zangrando's first article, "The NAACP and a Federal Antilynching Bill, 1934-1940," was published in the *JNH* in 1965, and his 1963 dissertation appeared in revised form as *The NAACP Crusade against Lynching, 1909-1950* (1980).

The intellectual biographies of nine historians whom we interviewed indicate the continuing importance of a diversity of Jewish backgrounds as sources of scholarship in black history. As earlier, several were of radical or liberal origins, but now there were also others who came from non-ideological backgrounds and for whom consciousness of ethnic identity rather than politics was a paramount consideration.

For example, Herbert G. Gutman and Rudolph Lapp represented a somewhat older contingent, born in the teens and 1920s, whose early social consciousness was rooted in the radical Eastern European Jewish subculture; both came from families sympathetic toward the Communists. Lapp (b. 1915) recalls having Paul Robeson for a boyhood hero and carrying banners in Scottsboro parades. Although his graduate research under Stampp at Berkeley was on poor whites of the antebellum South, he was highly conscious of the role of blacks in American history. Teaching at the College of San Mateo, he introduced the first Negro history course in California's colleges and universities in 1959 and uncovered materials on black history in the state that led to his studies of Negroes in Gold Rush California, the first fruits of which appeared in the *JNH* in 1964.[1] For Gutman (1928-85), whose family also moved in Communist circles and who headed the Queens College movement for Henry Wallace in 1948, interest in labor and black history did not stem directly out of his youthful politics. It was the anti-Communist labor historian Henry David who inspired Gutman's interest in history during his senior year; and it was while pursuing his doctorate with Howard K. Beale at Wisconsin in the 1950s that he both completed his disillusionment with Stalinism and came into real contact with Negroes for the first time. John Hope Franklin, with whom he studied when the latter was a visiting professor there in the spring of 1953, stimulated Gutman's interest in black history. Thus, although his specialty was labor history, Gutman was sensitive to the blacks' historical role, and in the early 1960s he wrote important essays on the pioneer Negro socialist Peter Clark and on black coal miners, most notably his analysis of the treatment of blacks in the United Mine Workers.[2]

An exception because he was considerably younger than either of these historians was another scholar of Old Left antecedents who began his publishing career in this period—Philip Foner's precocious nephew, Eric Foner (b. 1943).* The younger Foner's interest in racial justice, rooted partly in his family background, was greatly enhanced by the black protest movement. As a Columbia University undergraduate during the early 1960s, he was a political activist, among other things participating in the five-and-dime store sympathy demonstrations. With Foner's intellectual interests early centering on slavery, the Civil War, and Reconstruction, he did a 1963 senior honors paper on the Free Soil party's attitudes toward blacks, out of which came his two 1965 articles in *New York History* and the *Journal of Negro History* on this topic.[3] His interest in the racial outlook of the antislavery politicians informed Foner's study of Republican party ideology, *Free Soil, Free Labor, Free Men* (1970).

Howard Zinn (b. 1922) was an older individual who came from a nonpolitical family background but was also exposed to radical currents

* His father, Jack D. Foner, is also a historian whose *Blacks and the Military in American History* was published in 1974.

of thought. In his teens Zinn moved to the left, and on the eve of World War II joined the Communist party. Functioning as an active party member for almost a decade, he continued thereafter to be an "independent radical"—an orientation that has informed all of his writings. Given his perspective, when he learned of an opening at a black college in Georgia, he displayed no hesitation in applying for it. In turn, Zinn's civil rights activism and writing came directly out of his experiences while teaching at Spelman College. In the late 1950s he worked with black students and faculty in the Atlanta black colleges to desegregate local public libraries and the galleries of the Georgia legislature; in early 1960 his involvement in the lunch counter sit-ins led to his long association with the Student Nonviolent Coordinating Committee. From this participant observation resulted *SNCC: The New Abolitionists* (1964).[4]

Coming from a Socialist rather than a Communist background, Gilbert Osofsky (1935-74) vividly exemplifies how the matrix of both ethnicity and ideological radicalism propelled an intellectual into writing Afro-American history. His father, a faithful reader of the socialist Jewish *Daily Forward* and an admirer of Eugene V. Debs, often talked about the injustice of discrimination against blacks. Although Osofsky discarded his religious beliefs in high school, from his family background came both a life-long identification with the working classes and an intellectual fascination about anti-Semitism and other kinds of oppression against minority groups. Desiring to make his research relevant to his social ideals, Osofsky first wrote an M.A. thesis on the response of New York's German Jews to the immigrants from Eastern Europe. Then acting upon the suggestion of his advisor, Robert Cross, who urged him to deepen his insights by looking at a different minority group, Osofsky, for his 1963 Columbia University dissertation, chose to examine Harlem as a case study in the evolution of twentieth-century racial segregation in the North. *Harlem: The Making of a Ghetto, 1890-1930* appeared in 1966.[5]

William Berman, Seth Scheiner, and Allan Spear were farther to the right in their intellectual origins. Berman (b. 1932), who came from a household with decidedly liberal New Deal sympathies, feels that his Jewish cultural background encouraged both the universalistic perspective on social justice and the sensitivity to racist oppression that were at the root of his response to the growing salience of the civil rights struggle occurring while he was studying at Ohio State University during the 1950s. A participant in the Woolworth sympathy demonstrations of 1960, this specialist in recent U.S. history was drawn quite naturally to his 1963 dissertation, published as *The Politics of Civil Rights in the Truman Administration* (1970). On the other hand, Scheiner (b. 1933), who was investigating black life in New York simultaneously with (but independently of) Osofsky, does not know how his consciousness about racial matters developed. Although he was from a conventional New Deal–oriented background, certainly his father, with whom he argued repeatedly on the subject, showed not the slightest concern about discrimination against blacks. Possibly Scheiner's sensitivity was rooted in friendships with black teammates during his years as a high-school basketball player. Subsequently in both undergraduate and graduate school he was a campus civil rights activist, and his 1963 dissertation at New York University, published as *Negro Mecca: A History of the Negro in New York City, 1865-1920* (1965), was, like the monographs of the others we have been discussing, an expression of his commitment to the cause of racial justice. Spear (b. 1937), who similarly was doing his research on Chicago at the time that Osofsky and Scheiner were doing their investigations on New York, came from a highly assimilated non-ideological family. Spear attributes his interest to a dual marginality: being both Jewish and gay made him feel "outside the mainstream." His alienation from his peers was evident when as a student in high school he found himself alone in his excitement about the Brown decision. At Oberlin College in the mid-1950s, he took Leslie Fishel's course in black history, joined in campus demonstrations against a discriminatory barber shop, and participated in an exchange program with Fisk University, where he experienced life in the black milieu of a southern city. At Yale he was active in the highly militant New Haven chapter of the Congress of Racial Equality (CORE), wrote all his papers on black history topics, and, turning to an urban subject, did his 1965 dissertation (published two years later) on *Black Chicago: The Making of a Negro Ghetto, 1890-1920.*

As our discussion has suggested, the politics of the Truman era did much to stimulate an interest in Negro history, and one of Truman's actions, desegregation of the armed forces, had an important long-range impact. Experiences in the desegregated Army, Navy, and Air Force would open minds and reshape attitudes and could even lead a scholar quite directly into his research topics. Four people—Andrew Buni, William M. Tuttle, Richard Dalfiume, and Joel Williamson—illustrate this phenomenon particularly well. They were from diverse geographial, ethnic, and socioeconomic origins and were alike only in the racism of the environments in which they were raised.

Buni (b. 1931), the son of a Ukrainian-Catholic textile mill worker in Manchester, New Hampshire, was reared in a milieu of white working-class racism. The first stage in his evolving social consciousness was the admiration he developed for Franklin Roosevelt as a result of family poverty during the Depression. What opened his eyes about racial matters was the positive experience he had with black soldiers after steps were taken to desegregate the Army during the Korean War. Later a Negro roommate at the University of New Hampshire furthered his education about black life, but it was the lunch counter sit-ins, which broke out when he was studying for the doctorate at the University of Virginia, that provided the catalyst for his 1965 dissertation, published in 1967 as *The Negro in Virginia Politics, 1902-1965.*

Tuttle (b. 1937) was the son of a conservative Detroit surgeon with rather negative views about blacks. But even as a youth, Tuttle was open on the subject of race, rooting for Jackie Robinson at baseball games and finding himself terribly upset when a stone-throwing mob tried to drive a black family from a nearby neighborhood. But the pivotal experience was his tour of duty with the integrated Air Force, 1959-62, where he developed close friendships with two black fellow officers. He started graduate work at Wisconsin, planning to specialize in black history, and his 1964 M.A. thesis on the Chicago race riot of 1919 reflected the Myrdalian assumptions and hopefulness about the future of American race relations that imbued the thought of so many intellectuals who went to college during the 1950s. (Revisions made prior to publication in 1970 under the title *Race Riot: Chicago in the Red Summer of 1919* would reflect Tuttle's radicalization during the late 1960s and the influence of the new working class history.)[6]

During 1959-61, at the time that Tuttle was in the Air Force, Dalfiume (b. 1936), an enlisted man, had equally positive experiences with his black sergeant and lieutenant in the Army. The grandson of an Italian immigrant tenant farmer and the son of a small-town Louisiana grocer with highly conventional southern racial attitudes, Dalfiume nevertheless, even as a child, started to question privately the discrepancy between the abilities of the blacks with whom he played and the way in which society treated them. The Army years, however, were the crucial ones. Afterward, while he pursued his M.A. at San Jose State, reading C. Vann Woodward stirred an empathy for the Populists; participating occasionally in NAACP marches kindled an interest in that organization; and researching in the politics of the Truman administration further informed his views. Dalfiume's interest in the Truman presidency and civil rights, his tour of duty in the desegregated Army, and his awareness of the NAACP's importance fitted together, and by the time he went to the University of Missouri in 1963 to work on his Ph.D., he already had in mind the topic that became his 1966 dissertation published three years later as *Fighting on Two Fronts: Desegregation of the U.S. Armed Forces, 1939-1953.*

For Williamson (b. 1930), a stint in the Navy during the 1950s provided a vital broadening experience in which he overcame his South Carolina parochialism. The way in which black servicemen were functioning competently in an integrated setting impressed the young white southerner, and he found himself disturbed by the amount of racial injustice that still survived. But he had not become a crusader for civil rights. Indeed, the march of events from Montgomery to Greensboro during the years he was doing graduate work at Berkeley did not further affect his consciousness. Williamson's decision to do his 1964 dissertation on blacks in Reconstruction South Carolina under the direction of Kenneth Stampp came about simply because it was a viable topic in southern history, his chosen field of interest. Williamson's real commitment to racial justice grew out of the crucible of writing his manuscript while teaching at the University of North Carolina in the early 1960s, with the waves of black activism swirling all around him. Although only at the end of his chapter on segregation did he allow his feelings to become explicit, an intense passion informed all the writing in *After Slavery: The Negro in South Carolina during Reconstruction* (1965). Interestingly enough, what impressed him about the civil rights revolution's heady days was not the progress being made, but the obdurate racism of the white South. The book's discussion of segregation, with its challenge to the optimism of Woodward's *Strange Career of Jim Crow*, was not a mere historiographical debate. Williamson's pessimism — most recently exhibited in his *The Crucible of Race: Black-White Relations in the American South since Emancipation* (1984) — reflected his concern about the depths of racism in America.

Actually, Woodward's own hopeful assessment had already undergone significant modification. *The Strange Career of Jim Crow* in its revised editions (1957, 1966) was tempered by his recognition of the pervasiveness of racism in American history and the prevalence of segregation in the antebellum North. By the end of the 1950s Woodward was also exploring the way in which racial ambivalences among abolitionists, missionaries, and Radical Republicans had stood in the way of the egalitarian hopes for Reconstruction. This was not simply an antiquarian exercise, for Woodward was then also skeptical about the depth of the commitment to equality that underlay the northern pressures behind what he and others described as the "Second Reconstruction of the South."[7] Woodward's critical and ironic analysis of the nineteenth-century northern reformers intersected with the critiques of the abolitionist myth in the monographs by Larry Gara and Leon Litwack, which he pointedly praised.[8] Moreover, his interest in the subject also converged with the researches of several students who obtained doctorates under him at Hopkins and Yale during the early 1960s — Bertram Wyatt-Brown and Tilden Edelstein with their respective biographical monographs (*Lewis Tappan and the Evangelical War against Slavery* [1969] and *Strange Enthusiasm: A Life of Thomas Wentworth Higginson* [1968]), and three whose books were particularly germane to black history, James McPherson, Willie Lee Rose, and William McFeely.*

Woodward's role in providing inspiration for these studies was a subtle one. He was never a professor who pressed particular research topics upon students, and these individuals believe that he did not influence their choice. Yet they were all greatly inspired by him, most were attracted to Woodward in the first place partly because of his position on racial issues, and they were of course *au courant* with his latest concerns and publications. All were impressed by his ironic view of history, including the ironies in black-white relations. Such ironies were exactly what Edelstein perceived in Woodward's book on a southern white reformer, *Tom Watson,* a volume that influenced his own approach to Thomas Wentworth Higginson. Willie Lee Rose in undertaking her study of the South Carolina Sea Islands during the Civil War was certainly conscious of both Woodward's concerns and the contemporary relevance of what she was doing. As she wrote at the time: "There would seem to be little doubt about the timeliness of such a study. For the first time in nearly a hundred years liberal opinion in the North is again actively demanding that far-reaching changes be effected in Southern race relations. The New Reconstruction, to use Professor C. Vann Woodward's apt phrase, inevitably exacts a reappraisal of that other Reconstruction and raises new questions. The reactivation of the old American dream of equality brings us to ask why it was so quietly laid to rest. . . . May we not at last venture to ask how fully the aim of equality was accepted by Northern liberal opinion?"[9]

Rose (b. 1927), a native southerner from the Virginia Piedmont, had imbibed the views of her unusually liberal mother. At Johns Hopkins, her first choice for a dissertation topic had been a biography of the antislavery figure, Charles Francis Adams, Jr., who like Higginson had headed a Negro regiment during the Civil War, but who subsequently shared the latter's ambivalences about blacks and became disillusioned with the Reconstruction process. Then, opting for a broader inquiry into the changing attitudes of northern "liberal" opinion on southern Reconstruction, she ultimately decided to write about the Sea Islands as a manageable case study. Her

* Two earlier studies on northern white reformers had been completed under Woodward at Johns Hopkins during the 1950s: Suzanne C. Carson, "Samuel Chapman Armstrong: Missionary to the South" (Ph.D. diss., Johns Hopkins University, 1952), and Otto H. Olsen, whose 1959 dissertation was revised and published in 1965 as *Carpetbagger's Crusade: The Life of Albion Winegar Tourgee.* Although Carson's manuscript exhibited a skeptical stance about the motivations of Hampton Institute's founder, Olsen's study was of a different genre. It arose from his interest in the history of Reconstruction in North Carolina, and in fact Woodward was initially skeptical about the choice of Tourgee as a dissertation topic.

research produced a subtle analysis of the behavior of the missionaries, philanthropists, and other antislavery reformers, with all its ambiguity and complexity. But *Rehearsal for Reconstruction* (1964) was much more. This influential monograph cast in a new perspective the story of federal policy toward the ex-slaves and sensitively examined the attitudes and actions of the freedmen themselves. As David Brion Davis observed, "Perhaps Mrs. Rose's richest contribution to our understanding of the first phase of Reconstruction lies in her portrayal of the Negro himself."[10]

Where Rose, Edelstein, and Wyatt-Brown emphasized the ambiguities and ironies in the white abolitionists' racial attitudes, McPherson (b. 1936) focused on their constructive role in the struggle for racial equality. Having pursued his undergraduate education in Minnesota at a time when civil rights and Senator Humphrey were much in the news, McPherson arrived at Johns Hopkins in 1958 strongly conscious of the race question. At the very time that he was casting about for a dissertation topic in the spring of 1960, McPherson was among the Hopkins graduate students picketing in the sit-in demonstrations that Morgan State College students had mounted in downtown Baltimore. Struck by the parallels between white civil rights activists of 1960 and the white abolitionists of 1860, he decided to investigate the latter's role in the campaign for equal rights during the Civil War and Reconstruction. A study of the sources convinced him that the abolitionists were genuinely concerned not only with emancipation but also with the far more radical goal of citizenship rights and full racial equality in American society. *The Struggle for Equality* (1964) departed from earlier monographs on the antislavery movement in its systematic and integrated treatment of the role of both blacks and whites. McPherson's second volume, *The Negro's Civil War* (1965), interwove documentary selections into a coherent narrative about the blacks' views and activism during the great conflict.

On the other hand, William S. McFeely (b. 1930), who received his doctorate at Yale in 1966 with a dissertation on General O. O. Howard and the Freedmen's Bureau, was the Woodward student who produced the most negative assessment of a nineteenth-century northern white reformer. McFeely's relatively conservative Republican parents were uncomfortable with the rationalizations offered by their southern relatives for keeping blacks "in their place"; taught him to be decent and fair to Negroes; and disagreed pointedly with neighbors who wanted a Negro child in his school excluded from a class picnic. By the time McFeely received his B.A. from Amherst in 1952, he had developed a profound interest in the race question, and it was this that attracted him to work with Woodward after he had matriculated at Yale. Where Rose had started out focusing on white reformers and arrived later at an examination of the freedmen's views and actions, McFeely, doing his dissertation at the height of the 1960s black protest, came from the opposite direction. His original interest was in studying what the transition from slavery to freedom meant to the southern blacks themselves. However, as his research proceeded and he uncovered the Howard Papers, his inquiry shifted, and he became involved in scrutinizing how much a man like Howard was actually committed to racial equality. Yet *Yankee Stepfather* (1968) not only treated Howard from the perspective of how he failed the ex-slaves but also, in its discussion of the Memphis and New Orleans race riots of 1866 and especially of the development of the sharecropping system, made other important contributions to the study of the Afro-American experience.

These students of Woodward epitomize the way in which moral concerns over the issue of racial discrimination were drawing larger numbers of young white scholars to the study of race relations and Afro-American history. Equally striking was a new phenomenon — whites drifting into their research in this area without an ideological commitment. Jane H. Pease (b. 1929) and William H. Pease (b. 1924), whose work on the Port Royal, South Carolina, experiment and on the ambivalent attitudes of the abolitionists paralleled the studies of scholars like Gara, Litwack, and Rose, came to their research virtually by accident, choosing what they found to be interesting and challenging topics.[11] Winthrop Jordan (b. 1931) recalls that about 1958 he somehow simply "backed into" what appeared to be the interesting intellectual question of how prejudice toward Indians and blacks developed in America. Though publishing his seminal articles in the *William and Mary Quarterly* in the early 1960s[12] and writing *White Over Black* (1968) in the midst of the climax of civil rights activism, Jordan consciously distanced himself from contemporaries whose research interests in the origins of American slavery and race prejudice seemed so clearly a response to "modern tensions."[13] It was only after his book was written that Jordan at the close of the decade became an activist in recruiting black students and championing black interests on the Berkeley campus. For Constance Green (1897-1975), investigation into Afro-American history was a spin-off from her long-standing specialization in urban history, and she was not thinking of race in the 1940s when she embarked upon her Pulitzer Prize–winning history of the nation's capital. Blacks came to her attention simply because they were so large a part of the District of Columbia's population; yet her two volumes on Washington's history, which appeared in the early 1960s, were at the time unusual for the amount of space devoted to the Negro inhabitants and race relations.[14] Green's decision in 1964 to write *The Secret City* (1967), a more detailed, separate volume on blacks, quite possibly resulted from the timely convergence of her research and the climax of the black revolt. Certainly it was while she was working on this book that Green came to develop a serious concern about civil rights.

Among those who originally arrived at their research into Afro-American history without a strong ethical concern were others whose decision was prompted by the interests or suggestions of their professors. Robert McColley (b. 1933), as an M.A. student at Harvard in the mid-1950s, was so impressed by visiting professor Kenneth Stampp that he followed the distinguished scholar to Berkeley. McColley's monograph, *Slavery and Jeffersonian Virginia* (1964), was stimulated by Stampp's interest in slavery rather than being rooted in a personal concern on McColley's part about racism or the peculiar institution as problems for American society. Recommendations made by their teachers provided pivotal motivation in the case of both Joe M. Richardson and Thomas Cripps, who, like Joel Williamson, became emotionally committed to the cause of racial justice *after* they had selected their research topics and while they were doing their writing amid the activism of the early 1960s. Richardson (b. 1934), pursuing graduate work at Florida State University in the late 1950s, adopted a professor's suggestion and did his M.A. thesis on the Freedmen's Bureau in Florida. From this he moved to the broader study of Negroes in that state, which was published in 1965 as *The Negro in the Reconstruction of Florida, 1865-1877*. Completing the dissertation while teaching at the University of Mississippi during the confrontation over the admission of James Meredith, Richardson became committed to the study of the Afro-American past and, returning to teach at his alma mater, lobbied successfully for the introduction of a black history course in 1965. Cripps (b. 1932) had been raised in a family that was—for his native Baltimore— relatively tolerant toward blacks, but there was nothing in his college and early graduate school years to suggest that he might become a specialist in Negro history. Indeed, the race relations struggles of the time were only vaguely at the periphery of his awareness. But taking his doctorate at the University of Maryland, he was drawn into undertaking research in Negro history by Patrick Riddleberger, a former Stampp student (who after moving to Southern Illinois University would in 1962 introduce one of the early courses in black history at a predominantly white institution). Riddleberger, by urging Cripps to examine the Booker T. Washington Papers at the Library of Congress, provided the initial impetus toward what became Cripps's dissertation on blacks and the southern lily-white Republicans. Just after deciding upon this topic, Cripps, in an equally unpremeditated way, made the pivotal decision to teach at the black school, Morgan State College, it being simply the first institution within a reasonable distance of the Library of Congress to offer him a position. Teaching there during the early 1960s, he developed a profound concern with

racial issues. Meanwhile, his fortuitous discovery of extensive materials in
the Washington Papers about black protests against the racist film, *Birth
of a Nation,* converged with his own long-time enthusiasm for the movies
to lead to subsequent research on blacks and the motion pictures, his first
essay on this subject appearing as early as 1963.[15]

This contingent of whites who found their way into black history
without originally entertaining a deep concern about racial injustice illuminates certain important aspects of the dynamics behind the groundswell
of interest in the subject. On the one hand, the seemingly accidental,
serendipitous — occasionally even unconscious — way in which these individuals came to their work in the field and the decline in the notion
that a dissertation in black history could stand in the way of one's professional career suggest the field's growing legitimacy (as did the way in which
Riddleberger and Richardson felt confident enough to press successfully
for the introduction of courses in the subject). On the other hand, the
experiences of most of these persons do demonstrate how events continued
to shape a scholar's consciousness — albeit in a new fashion — by adding
a sense of social commitment to what at first was an unemotional intellectual interest. Certainly the manner in which these scholars were swept
up in the cause of racial justice as their research and writing intersected
with the demonstrations and confrontations of the early 1960s is a striking
phenomenon.

In the era of mass marches and mass arrests, of King's campaigns at
Birmingham and Selma, of northern school boycotts and job demonstrations, of the 1963 March on Washington, the Civil Rights Act of 1964,
and the Voting Rights Act of 1965, there were other manifestations of
the rapid growth of both scholarly and popular awareness of the importance of the black historical experience and of the Negroes' active role
in shaping the country's historical development.

Indications of the changing social consciousness among historians between 1960 and 1966 can be seen in the activities of the professional
organizations. Progress was uneven, being most noticeable in the AHA
and SHA. Both now regularly had sessions on the history of blacks and
race relations — usually one each year at the AHA and two to four annually
at the SHA. In these two organizations there was also now a greater black
presence at conventions, evidenced by the participation of Negroes as
authors of papers, commentators, and chairpersons. Although the *AHR*
had only two articles relevant to black history in the 1960s,[16] the *JSH*
was publishing from one to four essays annually on black history and
carried the one article by a black[17] to appear in a mainstream journal in
these years. Negroes also functioned on committees in both organizations.

The AHA, after Franklin's first term on the council expired, continued to have black representation on committees, most notably the appointment of Merze Tate and Rayford Logan of Howard University to the program committee for 1963 and 1964, respectively. Meanwhile at the SHA, Clarence Bacote served on the 1962 program committee and two years later became the first black elected to the council. On the other hand, for some reason, in the MVHA black representation was sparser. Essays in the *MVHR* relevant to black history continued to be more sporadic than in the *JSH*, and from 1961 through 1963, MVHA convention programs had neither sessions on black history nor black scholars as participants. Yet by the mid-1960s the program committees of the SHA and the MVHA were consciously seeking to arrange sessions on black history and to secure the participation of Negro scholars. Thus in 1964 (the year in which the MVHA became the Organization of American Historians) the program committees of both organizations, lacking persons with expertise in the area, called upon Louis R. Harlan to develop sessions for them. And in 1966 Franklin was tapped for the editorial board of the *Journal of American History* (the former *MVHR*)—the first black to serve in this capacity in any of the leading historical organizations. On the other hand, there was only a slight broadening in the number of blacks involved. Whether one looks at committees, convention programs, or reviews in the journals, there was still a tendency to rely on a few highly visible individuals— Rayford Logan in the AHA; two of Avery Craven's students, Clarence Bacote and Elsie Lewis, in the SHA; and John Hope Franklin in all three organizations.

Certainly under the impact of current events, there was a rising awareness of the importance and legitimacy of studying the past history of race relations and Negroes in America. The generation of scholars discussed in this section had come to intellectual maturation during the 1950s. Still the relevance of "modern tensions" to specific subjects chosen for historical research was evident in both the concern with nineteenth-century white attitudes and black activism during the "First Reconstruction of the South," and also in the attention to more recent events in the politics of civil rights in such studies as Zangrando's on the NAACP and Dalfiume's and Berman's examination of the Truman era. The impact of the freedom struggle can also be seen in the topic chosen by the one young black scholar who completed a published doctoral dissertation in Negro history during the early 1960s. Arvarh E. Strickland (b. 1930), who finished his dissertation in 1962 at the University of Illinois during the cresting of black activism, had decided to study the Chicago Urban League. This was one of the most important and militant affiliates of the National Urban League, and the fact that it possessed a large corpus of records going back nearly a half century obviously encouraged Strickland's choice. His *History of the Chicago Urban League* (1966) was the first scholarly treatment of the history of a local racial advancement organization.

Strickland's monograph can also be viewed as part of the flowering of black urban history during the early 1960s. Actually, it is difficult to account for the nearly simultaneous appearance of several pioneering and seminal works on this subject. At first glance it might appear that this development was related to the rise of urban history as a specialty, but only the monographs by Wade and Green stemmed from this interest. The one thing that can be said is that Wade, Spear, Osofsky, Scheiner, and Strickland all came to their monographs out of their concern about black advancement and civil rights, and it does not seem likely that even Green's *Secret City* would have been written had it not been the era of the "Second Reconstruction."

Another dimension to the changing consciousness among white historians — especially among graduate students and younger scholars — in this age of dramatic black activism was the increasing value being attached to the use of black historical sources and to the analysis of how Negroes themselves felt and acted. During the 1950s Stampp's book had sought to view slavery from the slaves' perspective, and he was a pioneer among white scholars in employing previously spurned ex-slave autobiographies as one tool for understanding slavery (a research strategy that did not go uncriticized). At the same time Howard Bell and Elsie Lewis, in effect taking up where Woodson's *Mind of the Negro as Reflected in Letters Written during the Crisis, 1800-1860* (1926) left off, had combed unused minutes of black conventions and black newspapers. The publication of August Meier's *Negro Thought in America, 1880-1915* in 1963, followed soon after by Rose's and McPherson's books that carried further Bell Wiley's and Benjamin Quarles's conscious attention to the blacks' role in shaping the struggle for equality during the Civil War — and in McPherson's case tapping black-written sources of previously unrealized richness — marked an important stage on the road to studying the black experience from the black perspective. One member of Woodward's first seminar at Yale in 1962-63 recalls how the students were eager to look at Emancipation and Reconstruction from the freedmen's vantage point and to unearth whatever black sources were available. A couple of years later one of the authors of this volume, participating in a conference on Reconstruction historiography at the University of Illinois, was struck by the warm response that graduate students in the audience gave to his call for analyzing Reconstruction in terms of asking "how Negroes actually functioned . . . keeping in mind that Negroes were not chiefly bystanders to events in which whites were the actors, but were also people who were themselves active participants in our history."[18]

Paralleling the growth of interest among professional historians during the early 1960s was a simultaneous groundswell of popular interest in the Afro-American past—especially in the black community—that was directly stimulated by the drama of the protest movement. In retrospect it now seems evident that the generation gap we have observed among black historians also had its counterpart in popular thinking; for example, in the 1950s Negro History Week was often ignored in predominantly black schools in the North and West, and ASNLH meetings in the 1950s were only sparsely attended. (Interestingly enough so few black college students were electing courses in Negro history during the 1950s that by the middle of the decade sales of Franklin's survey had nearly reached the vanishing point.) However, the heroism and the victories of the civil rights demonstrations in the early 1960s generated a new social climate. Sensing the "Negro Mood," the journalist Lerone Bennett wrote a series of articles on Afro-American history for *Ebony* and soon after brought them together in his popular volume, *Before the Mayflower* (1962). That same year the future Northwestern University professor and historian of black nationalism, Sterling Stuckey, at the time a Chicago high-school teacher, founded the highly successful interracial Amistad Society to foster the study of black history. As the nonviolent direct action movement attained its crest in 1963-64, across the North and West there was a wave of popular adult education courses and special lecture series in black history. In the search for a usable past, movement activists introduced black history units into the curricula of the "freedom schools" that accompanied the school integration boycotts in the North and the Mississippi Freedom Summer in the South. Meanwhile, boards of education began to address themselves to "the racial imbalance and neutralism of pusillanimous textbooks designed to appeal to Southern as well as Northern school adoption committees." When Chicago's board of education dragged its feet, Stuckey's group led a hundred black students and teachers in picket lines with such placards as "Teach Us About Us!" In 1964 New York City's school board published a thick pamphlet for teachers, *The Negro in American History*, and Detroit's social studies teachers produced their own booklet, *The Struggle for Freedom and Rights: Basic Facts about the Negro in American History*. The following year Franklin, surveying the activities among publishers, teachers, and school boards, called these beginnings of curriculum revision "one of the most significant by-products of the current Civil Rights Revolution."[19]

The relationship between these developments at the grass roots—among activists, school personnel, and a lay adult audience—and what was transpiring in the scholarly world is of course indirect. Yet given the context of social change in the early 1960s, Negro history was now the object of unprecedented excitement and attention among wide segments of the American population, black and white. In academe nothing epitomized this growing legitimacy of black history better than the way in which certain scholars of both races, who had previously been ambivalent about being identified as specialists in the field, now reversed themselves.

Thus Frenise Logan, assuming an academic career after a stint in the diplomatic service, not only secured publication in the *JSH* of his two essays on the impact of the Civil War on Indian cotton production but also decided to revise for publication his 1953 doctoral dissertation on blacks in late nineteenth-century North Carolina. An award in 1960 from the North Carolina Historical Society for an article drawn from his dissertation encouraged him to do further research, and the expanded monograph entitled *The Negro in North Carolina, 1876-1894* appeared in 1964.[20] It is true that as late as 1963 a white professor was advising John W. Blassingame to avoid black history if he wished to have "a future in the historical profession."[21] Yet more indicative of how things were going was that 1964-65 marked a turning point for two of Kenneth Stampp's former students at Berkeley—Nathan Huggins and Leon Litwack. The changing intellectual milieu seems to have permitted Huggins, whose original intention of specializing in African and Afro-American history had been overruled by practical considerations, to move into what became his long-range commitment to the field. By 1965 when his interest in intellectual history found expression in the idea of doing a book on the Harlem Renaissance, the factors that earlier would have discouraged such a study on his part had dissipated. For Litwack the return to Negro history was an especially vivid experience, and he recalls the day he made a guest appearance at the University of Rochester, lecturing on his current investigations in Jacksonian democracy. Some graduate students in the audience, sensing that his heart was just not in that topic, urged him to undertake research once again in the field to which he had already made an important contribution. By the time he joined the faculty at Berkeley in 1964, he had settled on the study that became *Been in the Storm So Long* (1979). In short, both Huggins and Litwack now felt able to dismiss the professional considerations that had loomed so large in their earlier decision to work in other specialties and to identify themselves with what had hitherto been a marginal field of inquiry.

During the late 1960s—in the years following the civil rights legislation of 1964 and 1965, the civil disorders in the northern ghettos, the rise of Black Power ideologies, and the assassination of Martin Luther King—Afro-American history achieved a central place in the writing and study of the American past. The number of predominantly white schools offering courses in black history continued to grow and then mushroomed after King's death until by the early 1970s the majority of colleges and universities included such courses in their curriculum. From 1966, history departments, propelled by their own sense of guilt, the demands of black students, and pressures from sympathetic white students, not only began to introduce such courses but also with growing intensity actively recruited black faculty and graduate students. Numerous doctoral candidates, both black and white, elected to do their dissertations on topics in Afro-American history. Fellowship-awarding agencies encouraged this research. Convention programs now had numerous sessions on the black experience, and in the early 1970s the *JSH* was reading almost like a *JNH*. In several instances scholars with established reputations in other areas of American history undertook studies of the black past, and some produced major monographs. In short, the social climate had wrought new attitudes among both young black intellectuals and many white historians, attitudes which completed the revolution in the mainstream scholarly view of the role of Negroes in American history that had begun around the middle of the century. The enormous impact of the events of the 1960s is epitomized by the way in which even conservative individuals, becoming sensitive to the issue of racial justice, were attracted to the study of black history.

Certain long-range trends within the profession, independent of the changing context in race relations, also helped to account for this florescence of writing and publication in black history during the late 1960s and 1970s. For one thing, there was the sheer number of graduate students producing a flood of dissertations across the whole range of history. Of greater consequence was the fact that liberal and left perspectives now became the ideological mainstream of the profession. Largely the product of the wave of post–World War II Ph.D.s now entering middle age, this trend was accentuated by New Left doctrines prominent among graduate students during these years. Enhancing this development were intellectual influences stemming from the new social history: perspectives offered by the Annales School in France, the new working-class history in England, and the methodological revolution in quantitative techniques that opened up hitherto inaccessible sources for the study of the inarticulate. "History from the Bottom up" came of age, adding reinforcement to the impetus for the study of an oppressed minority.

While the majority of historians publishing monographs in the field in the late 1960s and early 1970s continued to be overwhelmingly white — and male — the number of blacks — and women — grew substantially both absolutely and as a proportion of publishing scholars in the field. With nearly all the blacks who obtained doctorates in these years doing their dissertations either in African or in black American history, and with several

Negroes who had specialized in other fields now turning to the study of the Negro past, the generation gap of the 1950s and 1960s disappeared. The first published books in Afro-American history by this new corps of black historians appeared quite suddenly—between 1970 and 1972, with the arrival of David L. Lewis's *King: A Critical Biography* (1970), Mary Frances Berry's *Black Resistance/White Law* (1971), B. Joyce Ross's *J. E. Spingarn and the Rise of the NAACP* (1972), and John W. Blassingame's *The Slave Community* (1972).

All in all, the turn of the decade into the 1970s was an exhilarating time for those undertaking their first work in the field. The great majority of those who now emerged as published scholars were born between 1940 and 1947—with a decided clustering of birthdates between 1943 and 1945 among those we interviewed—and they exhibited an elan rooted in the socialization they experienced during their college years in the early 1960s when the black protest demonstrations were at their height. To paraphrase the comments of two of the women we interviewed, Nell Painter and Nancy Weiss, they saw themselves as working on an exciting frontier, engaged in exploring a newly legitimized field, perhaps the liveliest one within all of American history, a specialty with infinite possibilities for pioneering and innovative research.

The individual life trajectories and the ways in which they intersected with both the course of the black protest movement and the changes going on in the profession were now more heterogeneous than ever.* At first glance in fact, there seems to be a multifaceted array of highly diverse intellectual biographies that collectively explain, to use Carl Degler's phrase, "Why Historians Change Their Minds."[22] Yet certain patterns do emerge. Not only did blacks once again become a major component among the publishing scholars in the field, but also the increase of representation from white southerners (virtually all of native Protestant background) was striking. The proportion of scholars of Jewish origin remained high, and those of Catholic background were still quite rare. Overwhelmingly both the blacks and the Jews were from families who voted Democratic and supported the liberal Democratic legislative agenda. (Moreover, it is scarcely coincidental that about half the individuals in each of these two subgroups reported experiences as activists in the cause for racial equality, compared to only one-fifth of the white non-Jews.) In contrast to the Jews and blacks, nearly two-thirds of those from white Christian backgrounds (and fully three-fourths of the southern-born whites) reported that their parents

* Among both blacks and whites, about half were from professional and business family backgrounds. Somewhat under half came from lower-middle class and working-class environments, and a small percentage—all but one of them black— were from genuinely poor families.

were ideologically conventional or conservative. This white group of conservative family background is especially significant. Offering the most vivid examples of a dramatic change in racial views, it reveals particularly well the impact of the new legitimacy that historians now accorded black aspirations for equality and the study of the Afro-American past.

Although only a minority, the proportion of white scholars who became interested in black history even though they were reared in prejudiced family backgrounds was unprecedentedly large. With a few exceptions, conservative parental ideologies were generally associated with negative views about blacks. For example, Charles Dew (b. 1937), the student of industrial slavery, absorbed from his parents, who were conventional southerners, a decidedly conservative view of race and the social order. Knowing blacks only as cooks or yardmen until he went north to Williams College, Dew had not questioned the system of racial segregation in which he had grown up. Far more extreme was the experience of Charles Martin (b. 1945), author of *The Angelo Herndon Case and Southern Justice* (1976), whose Mississippi-born father was a Goldwater Republican and hated Martin Luther King, Jr. Instances of this sort were not limited to those born in the South. David Gerber (b. 1944), who wrote *Black Ohio and the Color Line, 1860-1915* (1976), was an unusual case of a person from a politically conservative Jewish background. He recalls that in debates with his father, an attorney who was an enthusiastic Goldwaterite, the race issue was at the cutting edge of the generational conflict. Walter Weare (b. 1938), author of *Black Business in the New South* (1973), a social history of a major black corporate enterprise (the North Carolina Mutual Life Insurance Company), came from a Colorado working-class family and had a rabidly racist father who virtually regarded his son as a traitor to the white race for studying the history of a people whom he regarded as inferior.

Among this generation of scholars, the relative prominence of individuals who were raised in anti-black environments reflects the long-range changes in racial attitudes among college youths. The brightest students, especially in history and the social sciences, were in the vanguard of those articulating racially egalitarian views, and among the historians we interviewed those who attended northern and western colleges and universities in particular, no matter what the section of the country in which they had been raised, found it impossible to sustain a racially prejudiced outlook if they wanted acceptance as intellectuals. Dew vividly recalls that as early as 1954, "When I went to Williams College I had tried to defend the Southern position at first, but as time went on, as national events ran on in the field of race relations and the civil rights movement, I became aware of the bankruptcy of segregation. . . . I realized that the racist system just had no intellectual defense. And I wanted to be an intellectual." The televised events from Little Rock to Greensboro completed his conversion and eventually his racial views intersected with his specialization in southern economic history to produce his 1974 *AHR* article, "Disciplining Slave Ironworkers in the Antebellum South: Coercion, Conciliation, and Accommodation." Another southerner, Robert Morris (b. 1942), who has written on post–Civil War education for the ex-slaves (*Reading, 'Riting and Reconstruction: The Education of Freedmen in the South 1861-1870* [1981]), came from a prejudiced Virginia family. He recalls how during his freshman year at the University of New Mexico in 1960-61, the shift in his views crystallized when he realized that "an educated person just isn't a Southern racist." Raymond Wolters (b. 1938), author of *Negroes and the Great Depression* (1970), who was raised in an ultra New Deal–hating southern California background, found that studying in the intellectual milieu at Stanford in the late 1950s and then at Berkeley in the 1960s changed his political outlook, and his first two books were sympathetic to the protest movement.

Rarer were individuals of conservative families whose parents were relatively enlightened on racial issues, instilling a mind-set that in some cases was reinforced by the college milieu of the late 1950s and 1960s. Willard Gatewood (b. 1931), the son of a wealthy North Carolina tobacco farmer, and Pete Daniel (b. 1938), whose father was a small-town South Carolina sawmill owner, illustrate the directions that certain types of southern paternalism might occasionally take. Gatewood's father, though prejudiced, believed that blacks should be given "a fair chance," lent his tenants money to send their children to college, and did not perceive the NAACP as a subversive organization. Daniel's father, while also believing in segregation, earned the respect of his black workers by his fair and even-handed treatment. Both scholars thus got to know their parents' black employees in a context unusual for southern whites. The young Daniel in particular found the blacks often more intelligent than his father's white workers, and subsequently his egalitarian tilt was reinforced by a circle of liberal faculty and intellectual students he found in the relatively open atmosphere at Wake Forest College in the late 1950s. Gatewood, in the course of his research, gradually awakened to the possibilities in black history. Thus in the mid-1950s while writing a dissertation on an early North Carolina state superintendent of education, he was impressed upon discovering archival materials detailing activities of the highly literate black officials in the department. Later, when Gatewood became involved in his study of Theodore Roosevelt, the importance and relevance of that president's actions on racial matters were obvious to this southern scholar, and his research led to two *JNH* articles in 1968[23] and to his 1975 monograph, *Black Americans and the White Man's Burden, 1898-1903*. Daniel, specializing in southern history at the University of Maryland in the latter part of the 1960s and working with Louis Harlan, chose to do his dissertation on peonage, published as *The Shadow of Slavery: Peonage in the South, 1901-1969* (1972).

There were also rare cases of northerners whose family backgrounds combined political conservatism with a more liberal view on race. David Rankin (b. 1945), a David Donald student who specialized on blacks in Reconstruction New Orleans,[24] came from a family of conservative California Republicans "with a social outreach": his grandfather, a Methodist minister, had taken a missionary interest in the black churches of Oakland; his father, a secondary school principal, made special efforts to encourage black youths to obtain at least a high-school diploma. Eric Anderson (b. 1949), who received his doctorate under John Hope Franklin at the University of Chicago in 1978 with a monograph on *Race and Politics in North Carolina, 1872-1901* (1981), came from a conservative Seventh Day Adventist background and is to this day a Reagan Republican. The Adventist church, although against slavery at the time of its origins, in the twentieth century was hardly among the more advanced Protestant denominations on civil rights. But Anderson's parents, conservative on other subjects, interpreted the church's moral teaching as a call for racial equality. While still a student in high school, this psychiatrist's son was writing Barry Goldwater, urging him to vote for the 1964 civil rights bill. Anderson took his undergraduate degree in the late 1960s at Andrews University, an Adventist institution in Michigan well outside the academic mainstream. Nevertheless, he found reinforcement for his views there, since the brighter students were by then profoundly concerned with the contradictions between racial practices and Christian teaching—the interest in race and civil rights was, he recalls, "the mood of my generation."

At the time that whites of conservative family origins were coming to play such a significant role in Afro-American historical scholarship, those who had experienced Old Left politics constituted a smaller proportion of the scholars first making their mark in the field than at any time since before the Depression. The parents of Robert Starobin were prominent Communists. George Rawick in the late 1940s and 1950s was active in a succession of progressive, socialist, and Trotskyist organizations that informed his understanding of the civil rights movement and the black past. For others, however, the connection between such exposures and the study of Afro-American history was now likely to be tenuous and indirect. Robert Fogel and Eugene Genovese had been Communists in the late 1940s and 1950s, but both undertook their studies on slave life long after they had left the party—and as a spin-off from other research concerns rather than being inspired by their belief in racial equality.

A number of whites came from environments that ran the gamut of various liberal perspectives. These were virtually without exception people of northern origins—although J. Morgan Kousser (b. 1943), who grew up in Nashville, owed a great deal to the "diffuse sense of social consciousness" expressed by his mother who, given her southern rearing, was remarkably liberal. Peter Wood (b. 1943), author of *Black Majority: Negroes in Colonial South Carolina from 1670 through the Stono Rebellion* (1974), was raised in an elite professional family from New England with FDR-Democratic sympathies; considerably more enlightened than their acquaintances in St. Louis where Wood grew up, they welcomed the Supreme Court's Brown decision. Thomas Webber (b. 1947), a student of southern slavery who wrote *Deep Like the Rivers: Education in the Slave Quarter Community, 1831-1865* (1978), was the son of an activist Episcopal minister who worked among blacks in the interdenominational East Harlem Protestant parish; and in high school Webber himself was involved in tutoring and recreational activities among black children of the neighborhood. However, liberal families were most frequently to be found among people of Jewish ancestry. Michael Homel (b. 1944), a Franklin student who received his Ph.D. from Chicago in 1972 and whose revised dissertation was published as *Down from Equality: Black Chicagoans and the Public Schools, 1920-41* (1984), came from a highly assimilated suburban Chicago background; his parents, who had joined a Unitarian church, were deeply interested in interracial activities. Peter Kolchin, Todd Savitt, and Carl Brauer were representative of people who came from liberal Jewish families in the New York metropolitan area. For Kolchin (b. 1943) the racial views of his moderately socialist parents were reinforced by a stint as an undergraduate research assistant to James P. Shenton of Columbia College, who was studying blacks during Reconstruction. Obtaining his Ph.D. under David Donald at Johns Hopkins, Kolchin did his dissertation on Alabama Negroes during presidential Reconstruction, published as *First Freedom* (1972). Savitt (b. 1943) as a high-school student had been quite concerned about race relations, an interest that was rekindled in medical school where he worked as a research assistant to a microbiologist studying sickle-cell anemia. Transferring to the University of Virginia for graduate work in history, he did his dissertation under Willie Lee Rose on the broader subject of *Medicine and Slavery: The Diseases and Health Care of Blacks in Antebellum Virginia* (1978). Brauer (b. 1946), who took his doctorate at Harvard with a dissertation published as *John F. Kennedy and the Second Reconstruction* (1977), was the son of decidedly antiracist Adlai Stevenson Democrats; in high school during the early 1960s he was friendly with middle-class blacks and was both interested in jazz and fascinated by the highly publicized works of James Baldwin and Malcolm X.

This relative prominence of liberals of Jewish origins—a phenomenon that had its parallel in the prominence of such people in the civil rights movement in the early 1960s—underlines the continuity in the disproportionate role that individuals from Jewish backgrounds have played in Afro-American historical scholarship. The cause of this is not entirely clear. Although only a couple of individuals in this category whom we interviewed dismissed the notion of any connection between their scholarship and their ethnic origin, the others, who thought that there was a decided connection, expressed puzzlement about the precise dynamics of this relationship. Most of those we spoke with felt that their Jewish background, though important, operated subconsciously. In any event, a number of factors appear to be involved. For one thing, in the course of our interviews it was often noted—on the basis of general impressions—that historians of Jewish extraction seem disproportionately represented in the profession and, given Jewish tendencies toward overachievement, have attained high visibility in the ranks of publishing scholars generally. Moreover, perhaps because of their marginality, they have figured particularly in various specialties within social history. The evidence from the interviews is mixed with regard to the impact of the Holocaust and the identification with blacks as another oppressed minority group. For example, Carl Brauer and Lawrence Levine, virtually the only ones we found who came from religiously Orthodox backgrounds, perceived a direct connection—in Brauer's phrasing, slavery had been for blacks what Hitler's final solution had been for Jews. Elizabeth Pleck and Peter Klingman, who were from more secular liberal backgrounds, also recalled that consciousness of themselves as members of a minority group, experiencing snubs and social alienation as a consequence, sensitized them to the issue of racial injustice. On the other hand, Allan Kulikoff feels that although "the Jewish social ethic" supports liberal political and social policies, for Jews of his generation the Holocaust was no longer a significant motivating factor. Certainly for himself, the crucial consciousness-raising events were the civil rights movement, the fight against poverty, and the protests against the Vietnam War. His interest in blacks was part of a larger attraction to social history and to the problems of the dispossessed that was widespread among his peers.

Religious beliefs per se thus seem quite irrelevant as an explanation for the fact that so many individuals of Jewish background were interested in black history. All but a handful of those we interviewed came from highly secularized backgrounds, and, as Ira Berlin suggested, black history may have been a kind of surrogate—usually subconscious—for people who had disentangled themselves from the synagogue culture, and who as a group had little if any scholarly interest in Jewish history. (For example, Pleck and Kulikoff, who took their doctorates at Brandeis University, did not find Jewish history intellectually viable.) Moreover, black history did indeed function as something of a surrogate for the study of Jewish history in the case of the occasional person who consciously sought in the black experience an understanding of his own perplexities as a member of a minority group. For Gerber, a powerful influence underpinning his interest in black history was his own alienation from the values that his parents shared with other prosperous, upwardly mobile Jews from Chicago's suburbia. In college Gerber concluded that if he could understand the black experience—how blacks could be patriotic and committed to the American dream—he could understand the background from which he himself came. William Toll (b. 1941), who joined the ranks of the New Left at Berkeley in the late 1960s and did a monograph on black thought, *The Resurgence of Race: Black Social Theory from Reconstruction to the Pan African Conference* (1979), had originally wanted to write a dissertation on Jewish history. However, he became excited about black history as a graduate student reading Du Bois: "Du Bois spoke to a lot of psychological problems that disturbed me. He was an intellectual who spoke for the problems of a minority group—and I identified with him. . . . Du Bois was meaningful as a parallel—having to understand the world through a veil—the sense of difference that blacks felt—that was parallel to me."

For the scholars of Jewish background, ethnic and cultural marginality rather than a religious outlook thus provided the context in which individuals were attracted to Afro-American history. On the other hand, a religious upbringing provided an important ingredient in the motivations of several of the white Protestant scholars. A case in point is northerner William Chafe (b. 1942), whose sensitivity was first aroused by divinity students who directed his Baptist youth group. Later as a Harvard undergraduate, activity in the Baptist campus student organization, coming at the time of the southern lunch counter sit-ins, reinforced his interest in civil rights, and he took his B.A. in 1962 with an honors thesis on Du Bois. Although disillusionment with the organized church aborted Chafe's plans to become a minister, his concerns with race and other social issues survived. In his 1968 *JSH* essay, "The Negro and Populism: A Kansas Case Study,"* he presented a pathbreaking analysis that by picturing the alliance between blacks and Populists as based on political convenience undermined the Woodward conceptualization of interracial working-class solidarity.

The influence of religious values was more pronouned in the South, where they continued to function for a significant minority of scholars as a mechanism of emancipation from Dixie's racism. Thus Linda O. McMurry

---

* This article was based on his 1966 Harvard M.A. thesis, but it seemed more appropriate to discuss Chafe in this section than in the preceding period.

(b. 1945), whose 1976 dissertation at Auburn University was a biography of *George Washington Carver: Scientist and Symbol* (published in 1981), grew up a devout Methodist in suburban Atlanta, where she came under the influence of racially emancipated Emory University divinity students. As a child she had been emotionally moved by the Brown decision and in high school wrote term papers on black topics. One of her vivid memories was attending a Methodist-sponsored "race relations weekend," where she heard a black student touchingly describe experiences and problems in being among the first to integrate the Atlanta high schools. Charles Martin took seriously the biblical morality that he absorbed from his ultraconservative evangelical Protestant Texas environment. Dan T. Carter (b. 1940), the author of a volume on another Communist cause célèbre, *Scottsboro: A Tragedy of the American South* (1969), was a South Carolina Baptist for whom the vocabulary of Christian ethics proved important, even though his church made a sharp disjuncture between personal righteousness and solving social problems. At the University of South Carolina during the early 1960s, he found interracial activity led by deeply religious social-gospel types, who were heirs of the southern interracial movement of the 1920s. Their talk of doing "the Christian thing" provided a conceptualization that facilitated the painful process Carter underwent as he broadened his comprehension of what Christian ethics were all about.

As in previous decades, the blacks entering the ranks of publishing historians during the 1970s were more likely than the whites to have come from essentially nonideological backgrounds. For them, racial concerns were rooted in intense and direct personal experience with prejudice and discrimination, rather than deriving from a broad philosophy of social justice. With Negroes being an important part of the Democratic party coalition, nearly all of them were raised in an environment supportive of the Fair Deal–New Frontier programs, although in this respect they functioned more as members of an interest group than as part of an ideological vanguard. Among the black historians we interviewed, however, there was a handful of individuals who had been exposed to more radical ideologies early in their lives. One was Nell Irvin Painter (b. 1942), whose family's racial consciousness prompted them to vote for Henry Wallace in 1948 and later led them to live and work in Ghana for several years.

Another was Sterling Stuckey (b. 1932), who as a Chicago high-school teacher during the latter part of the 1950s not only exhibited a mastery of the literature of Afro-American history but also articulated a radical socialist and cultural nationalist ideology. As a youngster in Memphis he had been exposed to the Woodson tradition through Negro History Week celebrations. But the years of the cold war and McCarthyism, when he was in high school and college in Chicago, were pivotal for him. He had an uncle who was a Communist, and as a high-school student the young Stuckey became personally acquainted with two prominent Communist sympathizers, Du Bois and Paul Robeson. In that era of anti-Communism and assimilationism Stuckey and his circle were exceptional in their enthusiastic admiration for these two men who at the time were distinctly suspect among blacks as well as whites. Not only were Du Bois and Robeson victims of the cold war hysteria, but their thinking also contained a prominent strand of cultural nationalism, which was then at a low ebb in the outlook of black intellectuals and racial advancement organizations. Even as a teenager Stuckey had read Woodson and Du Bois, resonating to their interest in Africa and their belief in the existence of African cultural survivals. (Stuckey's depth of feeling about Du Bois is reflected in a 1957 letter he wrote after visiting the latter's home: "You remain now as always my greatest single inspiration, for you represent not only the New Negro in his finest form but, more importantly, through your breadth of knowledge and universality of humanity, you point the way.")[25] He also studied the works of Herbert Aptheker, whose *Documentary History* introduced him, among other things, to the existing career of the nineteenth-century nationalist, Henry Highland Garnet. Stuckey knew that his radical orientation and his fascination with black history and the unique aspects of Afro-American culture made him atypical of the black intelligentsia during the 1950s. For him that decade marked a profound discontinuity in blacks' consciousness of their past, and he recalls feeling how unfortunate it was that in the era's optimism about the possibility of full inclusion in American society, so many blacks avoided calling attention to Negro history and culture because they feared that doing so would militate against achieving integration.

For at least a few among the new generation of black scholars, the interest in Afro-American history reflected the long-range impact of Carter G. Woodson's influence. This was true, even though in contrast to the earlier Negro historians who had laid the foundations for the field, only about one-third of the younger historians took their undergraduate degrees at black colleges, where the likelihood of exposure to black history, either through formal instruction or through the celebration of Negro History Week, was certainly higher.

The continuity in the tradition of Negro history teaching stemming from the Woodson movement was exemplified both by the encouragement that Howard University's history department was still offering at the graduate level during the 1960s under Elsie Lewis and Rayford Logan and also by the kind of influence coming from Richmond's Virginia Union University somewhat earlier under the inspiring undergraduate instruction of people like Tinsley Lee Spraggins. Spraggins (b. 1910) himself had trained at Howard (M.A., 1935), later taking his doctorate at American University (1957) with a dissertation on "Economic Aspects of Negro Colonization during the Civil War." In both his social activism and teaching and research he modeled himself on an older Virginia scholar whom he greatly admired, Luther Porter Jackson. At the opening of the 1950s, Arnold H. Taylor, whose work in black history would be appearing in the mid-1970s, had been inspired by Spraggins. Toward the close of the decade Raymond Gavins (b. 1942), author of a biography of Jackson's close friend, the Commission on Interracial Cooperation and Southern Regional Council leader Gordon Blaine Hancock (*The Perils and Prospects of Southern Black Leadership*, [1977]), had come to his interest in a similar fashion.

John W. Blassingame (b. 1940), taking his B.A. at Fort Valley State College (Georgia) in 1960, had experienced Negro History Week celebrations and had had a strong component of black history in his American history courses under the instruction of two other Howard University M.A.s.* Blassingame himself went to Howard for his M.A. under Rayford Logan. His contemporary there, Mary Frances Berry (b. 1938), had originally been introduced to Negro history by an inspiring high-school teacher in Nashville. Although Berry majored in philosophy as an undergraduate, her interest was reinforced by Logan and Elsie Lewis, under whom she pursued her M.A. degree in 1961-62. Encouraged by these two older historians to prepare for the new professional opportunities that were opening up for blacks, both went on to further graduate work. Berry took a Ph.D. in constitutional history and a doctorate of jurisprudence at the University of Michigan, a specialization reflected in her *Black Resistance/White Law* (1971). Blassingame took his Ph.D. with Woodward at Yale, with a 1971 dissertation on a social and economic study of blacks in Reconstruction New Orleans (*Black New Orleans, 1860-1880* [1973]). Although far more disposed to a radical ideology than either Blassingame or Berry, John H. Bracey, Jr. (b. 1941), growing up in Washington during the 1950s, had also been decidedly influenced by the Woodson tradition. The ASNLH had its headquarters there, and both that organization and the environment provided by Howard University, where his mother taught, had been enormously stimulating. The way in which Albert N. D. Brooks,

---

*One was David W. Bishop (b. 1921), who had imbibed an interest in black history from his schoolteacher mother and did a pioneering 1950 M.A. thesis under Rayford Logan on the role of the Interstate Commerce Commission in the evolution of the separate-but-equal doctrine. Bishop's 1961 dissertation at Catholic University, however, reflected the orientation of many black history doctoral candidates around mid-century and was on a non-black topic—an examination of the ICC as a regulatory agency.

his junior high-school principal and Woodson's successor as editor of the *Negro History Bulletin,* virtually celebrated Negro History Week "all year long" remained a vivid memory for Bracey.

Diverse as were the backgrounds of the scholars who began their careers in the late 1960s and 1970s, there was one underlying unity in their experiences: their exposure to the black protest movement of the 1960s. Most of the individuals whose dissertations and first published books appeared in this period were college undergraduates during the early 1960s, and for virtually every one, those years provided a vital consciousness-raising experience that accentuated the growth of interest among white scholars and decisively ended the generation gap among black historians. Blacks and whites alike, fascinated by the drama of the sit-ins, freedom rides, and marches, were glued to the mass media's reports of developments. Many, even occasional white southerners, were swept up in direct participation in the civil rights struggle.

Some of the whites we interviewed had especially specific recollections of how the vivid events associated with the black protest of the 1960s decisively shaped their research interests. Among them was George Fredrickson (b. 1934), a somewhat older scholar with an established reputation in the history of the Civil War period. In the manner of many college intellectuals of the post–World War II era who came from conservative families, he had become more liberal over the years, but the crises of the early 1960s—from the Freedom Rides to the confrontation at Selma— enormously stimulated his sympathies. His Harvard dissertation, published as *The Inner Civil War: Northern Intellectuals and the Crisis of the Union* (1965), touched on racial issues; then during his first year of teaching at Northwestern in 1966-67 he introduced a course in southern black history and inaugurated the research that led to his well-known *The Black Image in the White Mind: The Debate on Afro-American Character and Destiny, 1817-1914* (1971). Other younger scholars who began the decade of the 1960s as conservative Republicans, like the northerner Carl Osthaus and the southerners Charles Martin and Lester Lamon, received indelible impressions from the naked hatred of white racists and the dignity of civil rights demonstrators in the face of brutal physical assaults that filled the television screens. Such scenes aroused feelings of moral indignation over the way in which people "in a just cause with the law on their side" could receive such vicious treatment in the United States and ultimately paved the way for a broader commitment to the cause of social reform. Osthaus (b. 1943) wrote his senior thesis at Kalamazoo College in black history. His doctoral dissertation was done under John Hope Franklin at the University of Chicago (1971) on the Freedmen's Bank and was published in 1976 as *Freedmen, Philanthropy, and Fraud: A History of the Freedmen's Savings Bank*. Martin, a warm supporter of Barry Goldwater's bid for the presidency in 1964, moved leftward politically, doing an M.A. thesis on blacks and the National Recovery Administration and his Ph.D. at Tulane in 1972 on the black Communist Angelo Herndon. Lamon (b. 1942), who came from a Republican home in Marysville, Tennessee, entered Vanderbilt University as a freshman in the autumn of 1960, at a time when the controversy swirling over the university's expulsion of black divinity school student James Lawson for his civil rights leadership was still current. Nashville was also the home of Fisk University and American Baptist Theological Seminary, centers of civil rights activism, whose activities raised issues that compelled Lamon to confront crucial questions of segregation and integration. While teaching high school at Oak Ridge, Tennessee, in the mid-1960s, he developed curriculum materials in black history in response to the comments and questions of black students. Later, pursuing a doctorate at the University of North Carolina, he decided to write his 1971 dissertation on blacks in Tennessee during the early decades of the twentieth century, a topic encouraged by his professors, George Tindall and Joel Williamson, and published as *Black Tennesseeans, 1900-1930* (1977).

For some black scholars the protest of the 1960s was not only an important consciousness-raising experience but also resolved identity questions. In the case of Otey Scruggs (who, as we have observed in Chapter 2, had earlier avoided black history) the events of the period proved to be a decisive turning point. While teaching at Santa Barbara in the early part of the decade, he was president of the local NAACP, but as late as 1964 or 1965 he declined to offer a course in black history. In his American history survey classes he had found it unpleasant to discuss topics like slavery and to present a separate course in Afro-American history seemed to conflict with his integrationist goals. But the affirmations of the Black Power years and the enlarging exposure of service in the Peace Corps produced a sharp reversal in his thinking. On returning to the United States, he discovered that teaching black history, which he began doing in 1968, was "a liberating experience." Subsequently his publications and much of his teaching have been devoted to the study of the black past. Presently Scruggs is writing a history of Afro-Americans through the experiences of his own forebears (whom he traces back to the early 1800s on his mother's side and to the late antebellum period on his father's). Using many of these experiences, he would like to demonstrate that blacks as a people did not fall to pieces but endured and overcame the countless obstacles they faced.

The black protest also left a lasting imprint on Charles Vincent (b. 1945), author of *Black Legislators in Louisiana during Reconstruction* (1976). Born in a highly repressive area in rural Mississippi, he recalls the buses with the 1961 Freedom Riders speeding by near his family's small farm. Because of his father's apprehensions, Vincent did not become an activist while an undergraduate at Jackson State. Nevertheless, he credits the SNCC program with teaching him to cherish black history and to demand equal rights, including the right to attend any of the South's best graduate schools. Accordingly, he pursued his graduate work at Louisiana State University. In his courses he found that the Reconstruction period—a time when as in the 1960s blacks were pressing for civil rights and political power—stirred his imagination. Expanding on a seminar paper on blacks in the Louisiana constitutional convention of 1867-68 written under Charles Dew, Vincent did his 1973 doctoral dissertation on black political leadership in Louisiana during Reconstruction. For him, black history was more than an intellectual inquiry—it was also a journey into self and roots. Seeing himself as in the tradition of Du Bois and Franklin in countering the Dunningite stereotype of black incompetence, he sought to show that— as he knew from his own experience as the son of a farmer, church deacon, and Sunday School superintendent—blacks could run affairs with skill and proficiency.

Albert J. Raboteau (b. 1943), a Catholic brought up in a predominantly white environment, felt doubly isolated from the black community and its cultural traditions. It was at Marquette University in Milwaukee, where he enrolled in 1966 with the intention of becoming a seminarian that he began his search for identity. His involvement in student efforts to increase black representation in the university helped awaken his race consciousness. Teaching in 1968-69 at the black Catholic Xavier University in New Orleans was an experience that led him to come to grips with what became his real vocation—to teach and investigate the black past and especially the largely black Protestant religious tradition. Out of his dual marginality and his search for racial and religious roots came a 1974 dissertation in religious studies at Yale published as *Slave Religion: The "Invisible Institution" in the Antebellum South* (1978).

Alfred A. Moss, Jr. (b. 1943), was the same age as Raboteau and like him entered graduate school and forged his sense of identity during the Black Power era of the late 1960s and early 1970s. But he experienced a very different trajectory—and one that is particularly instructive, revealing as it does in such a striking way both the ambiguities and ambivalences prevalent in the thinking of many black intellectuals in the 1970s and the ebb and flow of the ascendancy of integrationist and nationalist tendencies among them. As an undergraduate at Lake Forest College (B.A., 1965) during the integrationist period of the early 1960s, Moss had found the secular Jews on the faculty especially friendly and influential on his thinking. Yet, affected by the social changes occurring in the middle of the decade, Moss concluded that to continue with his plans for advanced work in Russian studies would be a flight from his identity. Quite suddenly, deciding to seek social involvement, he went to divinity school at Harvard, where he found considerable interest in race relations. Subsequently the Episcopal church assigned him to the campus ministry at the University of Chicago and charged him with the task of bringing together North Shore white civic leaders and inner city blacks. Frustrated by the failure of this effort and the reactionary attitudes of diocesan leaders, he concluded that he needed to study more about the black past if he were to understand the present. This was at the time when Episcopal priest Nathan Wright was among the most articulate spokesmen among Black Power ideologists, when Vincent Harding was recruiting intellectuals for his newly established Institute of the Black World. Alienated from the white church establishment and fascinated with Black Power groups, Moss was friendly with militant blacks who were urging him to join Harding's Institute. But older friends in the academic world advised him that he could maintain a radical outlook while pursuing advanced work at a major graduate school. The years in Chicago's history department working under Franklin provided a "re-integrating experience." As a result his 1977 dissertation on the elite group of turn-of-the-century intellectuals took the form of a nonideological historical monograph published as *The American Negro Academy: Voice of the Talented Tenth* (1981).

Other blacks reflected the impact of the protest movement on their thinking and scholarship in various ways. Clayborne Carson (b. 1944) had been so excited by the southern freedom movement of the early 1960s that he twice visited the South to observe events firsthand. Then, during the middle of the decade, while completing his undergraduate work at UCLA, he participated in direct action demonstrations and joined a black culture and history study group that was a forerunner of the university's militant black student union. Although it was this latter experience that sparked his interest in studying the black past, in a larger sense "my study of Afro-American history [was] an outgrowth of the changes wrought by SNCC in my consciousness,"[26] and this organization became the subject of his 1975 dissertation, published as *In Struggle: SNCC and the Black Awakening of the 1960s* (1981). Darlene Clark Hine (b. 1947), attending Roosevelt University in the mid-1960s, was influenced by the group of militant black revolutionary nationalists in the student body there and for a period was attracted to the Black Muslims. But in the end she opted for neither separatism nor revolution. Her research topics, reflecting the influence of the black protest movement on her thinking, focused on the ways in which blacks of the professional class have historically sought to dismantle the barriers of discrimination.[27] Sharon Harley (b. 1948) at the height of the black separatist and revolutionary tendencies of the late 1960s was selling Black Panther newspapers. Both she and Hine were subsequently influenced in their outlook and research interests by the feminist movement. Harley co-edited with Rosalyn Terborg-Penn the anthology *The Afro-American Woman: Struggles and Images* (1978), and did her 1981 dissertation at Howard University on "Black Women in the District of Columbia, 1890-1920: Their Social, Economic, and Institutional Activities." Hine embarked upon seminal work concerning the history of blacks in the nursing profession.

The impact of the protest movement of the 1960s propelled many of the scholars we have interviewed into an activist role (and for some, as we shall explicate below, this activism was intertwined with radical ideological shifts toward militant black nationalism and the New Left). For example, Harvard Sitkoff (b. 1940), whose 1975 Columbia University dissertation appeared three years later under the title, *A New Deal for Blacks: The Emergence of Civil Rights as a National Issue,* was the son of old-fashioned New York Jewish liberals and a prominent undergraduate leader at Queens College at the turn of the 1960s. He helped found a campus NAACP chapter and as student council president was involved with the National Student Association's efforts to assist the southern black college student demonstrations during 1960-61; he himself had a "brief sojourn in the Southern black freedom struggle of the early 1960s. With other northern white students I had gone to march, to picket, to sit-in. I did a bit. Mostly I waited, and waited."[28] Rosalyn Terborg-Penn (b. 1941), a black woman who was a contemporary of Sitkoff's at Queens, was active in the NAACP and the Northern Student Movement, picketing Woolworth's and later tutoring young blacks from low-income areas. While working on her M.A. at George Washington University, she was engaged in the fight to eliminate discrimination on campus. Becoming sensitized by the feminist movement, she did her 1977 dissertation at Howard University on "Afro-Americans in the Struggle for Women's Suffrage, 1830-1920," and subsequently co-edited with Harley the previously mentioned anthology on black women's history. Although Peter Klingman came from a northern liberal background, it was the "rural, redneck" system of southern segregation that he observed as a University of Florida undergraduate that changed his life. Joining a Gainesville student group trying to desegregate local restaurants during the high tide of direct action in 1963, Klingman became interested in studying the historical roots of the Negro's status and wrote his dissertation on *Josiah Walls, Florida's Black Congressman of Reconstruction,* which was published in 1976. Elizabeth

Pleck (b. 1945), spurred initially by her parents' liberal outlook, participated in the suburban Chicago open-housing demonstrations while she was in high school. As a freshman at Berkeley, where she joined Friends of SNCC, Pleck also involved herself in the job demonstrations at San Francisco's Sheraton Palace Hotel and Auto Row in 1963-64. Transferring to Brandeis where she obtained a Ph.D. in 1974, Pleck participated in a number of civil rights and other activist causes, including the Boston school boycotts and the antiwar and feminist movements. Pleck's early fascination with black history functioned as an academic counterpart to her activism in the civil rights movement and led to undergraduate and graduate research papers on Boston Negroes, culminating in her dissertation published in 1979 as *Black Migration and Poverty: Boston 1865-1900*. Lawrence W. Levine (b. 1933), somewhat older than most of the others undertaking research in black history at this time, was well-known for his monograph on William Jennings Bryan—a subject about as far removed from black history as one could imagine. Originally from a nonpolitical background, Levine's politics had been shaped not only by his knowledge of the Holocaust but also by the perspective of postwar campus liberalism. After obtaining his Ph.D. from Columbia in 1962 and joining the history department at Berkeley, he became deeply involved in CORE activism in the Bay area. Three years later, and shortly after joining other historians on Martin Luther King's Selma to Montgomery march, Levine embarked upon the project that culminated in the influential *Black Culture and Black Consciousness: Afro-American Folk Thought from Slavery to Freedom* (1977).

Just four of the activists we interviewed were native southerners, two whites and two blacks—Dan T. Carter, Charles W. Joyner, William H. Harris, and Thomas Holt. For Carter, the change in racial views came gradually as an undergraduate at the University of South Carolina between 1958 and 1962. During his freshman and sophomore years, while working part-time as a reporter for the Florence *Morning News*, his experiences covering civil rights demonstrations began to undermine his stereotypes of black leaders. Transferring from Florence to the university's main campus at Columbia in 1960, he soon found himself attending his first interracial meeting. There a black minister's eloquent defense of the sit-in demonstrations was an unsettling experience and caused Carter to reexamine his whole position. During the next couple of years he helped found the South Carolina Student Council on Human Relations through which he came to know undergraduates at black colleges and, after attending training workshops of the Southern Christian Leadership Conference, became involved in voter registration work among blacks. This activity provided him with a taste of the intimidation that southern black activists faced. Alienated from the white South, Carter took his M.A. at the Uni-

versity of Wisconsin with a thesis on the convict lease system. But unhappy
with the kind of student radicalism reaching its peak there, he transferred
to the University of North Carolina, where he did his doctoral dissertation
in 1967 on Scottsboro under George Tindall.

Carter's friend at the University of South Carolina, Charles W. Joyner
(b. 1935), also moved quite gradually from his family's conventional southern ideas about race toward an emancipated view concerning blacks as
well as his native South. This shift in intellectual perspective came to
maturity while he was an M.A. student in 1956-58. At that time a deep
interest in jazz acquired while he was an undergraduate at a small Presbyterian college converged with the intellectual challenge posed by the
stimulating and argumentative University of South Carolina historian Howard Quint. Quint vigorously questioned the provincial views of his southern
white students, and soon Joyner found South Carolina history too parochial
a subject for research. His M.A. thesis, which grew out of Quint's seminar,
was on a topic in social and reform history, the Western Federation of
Miners. Meanwhile, Joyner was acquiring a knowledge of black literature
and the folk music of various protest movements, and subsequently, during
his tour of Army duty his closest friendships were with black musicians.
Studying once more at the university in the early 1960s when the southern
black student protest was at its crest, he became one of the founders —
and the first president — of the South Carolina Student Council on Human
Relations. This activity, combined with contacts among civil rights leaders
in the Southern Christian Leadership Conference (SCLC) and with the
influential southern white liberal James McBride Dabbs, provided a vital
experience. Talks with SCLC people like Ella Baker and Andrew Young
brought him to a new and more subtle appreciation of the Christianity
that he had come to question as an undergraduate. Dabbs, who held that
"The South" included blacks as well as whites and that segregation must
end if the region was ever to reach its potential, provided a viewpoint
that liberated Joyner from a hatred for his native South. By 1966 he was
also exploring southern folklore in a paper discussing the interracial exchange of folk culture as being basic to understanding what the southern
experience had been — a segregated society with an integrated culture. This
formed the basis for what became his first book, *Folk Song in South
Carolina* (1971). Believing that folklore was essential to an understanding
of the black and white South, Joyner, nine years after receiving his first
doctorate at South Carolina, obtained a second one in folklore and folklife
from the University of Pennsylvania. The principal thesis of his 1977
dissertation, a study of slave culture in the All Saints Parish area of tidewater
South Carolina, appeared in an essay entitled "The Creolization of Slave
Folklife" in *Reflexions Historiques* (1979) and the revised dissertation was

published as *Down by the Riverside: A South Carolina Slave Community* in 1984.

William H. Harris (b. 1944), as an undergraduate at Paine College in Augusta, Georgia, between 1962 and 1966, led the campus NAACP in sustained voting rights campaigns, sit-ins at local restaurants, and a series of Sunday forays to desegregate the city's white churches. Combining movement activism with leadership in the campus student government, Harris was able to draw large undergraduate turnouts at demonstrations. Participation in the civil rights movement awakened him to an awareness of the importance of the relationship of the United States to the non-white world, epecially to the new African states, and he originally entered Indiana University intending to study diplomatic history. However, Harris decided to switch to Afro-American history, and drawing upon his movement experience he wrote a seminar paper on a comparison of the 1963 March on Washington with A. Philip Randolph's March on Washington Movement of 1941. From this, Harris proceeded quite naturally into his 1973 dissertation on Randolph's leadership in the Brotherhood of Sleeping Car Porters, published as *Keeping the Faith* (1977).

For Thomas Holt (b. 1942), the relationship between his activism and the development of his scholarly interests was more complex. In the early and mid-1960s, while taking a B.A. and M.A. in English at Howard, with a thesis on Shakespeare, Holt participated with the campus SNCC affiliate in the campaign to desegregate Maryland's restaurants, joined in the mass marches held in the face of a brutal policy of repression in his hometown of Danville, Virginia, in 1963, and spent a summer organizing migrant workers on Maryland's Eastern Shore. Subsequently he worked with the Office of Economic Opportunity helping seasonal farm laborers, and with the SCLC's Poor People's Campaign that followed the assassination of King. After he enrolled in Yale's American studies program in the autumn of 1968, Holt continued to work for a consulting agency involved in the New Haven model cities project. Ultimately these interests eroded his commitment to literary studies, and he moved into Afro-American history, taking his doctorate under C. Vann Woodward. About the time he made this shift in 1969, Eugene Genovese was a visiting lecturer giving a course on comparative slavery; Woodward was talking about the importance of studying emancipation in a cross-cultural comparative perspective; and Holt himself was serving as a research assistant in the undergraduate Afro-American history survey course that William McFeely had just introduced. (Ironically, Holt's initial impression of Woodward, who was skeptical of the quality of most of the research done in American studies, had been unfavorable, and it was McFeely who smoothed the way for a fruitful relationship between the two men.) In short the exposures offered by

McFeely, Genovese, and Woodward, all coming together, served to crystallize Holt's decision to make a comparative examination of the Emancipation experience, starting with an investigation of black political leaders during Reconstruction. In addition, the direction of his research enabled him to address in a historical context the kinds of issues raised by his experiences as an activist—how social change came about and how blacks functioned in a political environment that, though dominated by white elites, accorded them some voice. The first product of his long-range investigations into the Emancipation experience in the New World was his 1974 dissertation on black political leadership in South Carolina, which was published as *Black Over White* three years later.

Epitomizing the web of interrelationships among the consciousness-raising events of the early 1960s, civil rights activism, and the changes in the profession occurring in the most elite academic circles was the situation at Princeton University. It was a sign of the times that the institution that Francis Broderick had unsuccessfully sought to desegregate two decades earlier should now have both students and faculty in the vanguard of scholarship in the history of American race relations and the Afro-American experience. On the faculty during the 1960s were at least four historians very much interested in these subjects: Eric Goldman, who both as a professor at Johns Hopkins during World War II and in his *Rendezvous with Destiny* (1952) had displayed an avant-garde interest in the integration of black materials in the writing of American history; Martin Duberman, whose play *In White America* was a Broadway hit in 1963; and two Woodward students, southerner Sheldon Hackney (author of *Populism to Progressivism in Alabama* [1969]), and James McPherson. (Moreover, McPherson and his colleagues in the American civilization program at Princeton would produce the most sophisticated of the several bibliographies on the black experience that appeared in the 1970s.)[29] Among the students who were attending Princeton at the time were David Gerber, Robert Engs, J. Morgan Kousser, and Gary Nash, all of whom would make contributions to the study of the history of blacks in America.

Robert F. Engs (b. 1943) first developed a racial consciousness when he was an undergraduate at Princeton between 1961 and 1965. Since his highly assimilated parents had taught him nothing about Afro-American history, his knowledge of the field began in his sophomore year when he worked as Martin Duberman's research assistant helping to gather materials for *In White America*. Soon Engs was organizing the handful of black undergraduates and operating in a coalition with white campus liberals; their civil rights activities during the heyday of direct action included desegregating Princeton barbershops. By his senior year Engs was working with low-income young blacks in Princeton's Upward Bound program.

Convinced that the civil rights movement "had to be about" the black poor, after graduation he spent a year running the project. Engs had long since discarded his earlier goal of becoming a State Department official and, influenced by McPherson, went to Yale where, as a Woodward student, he chose the Hampton black community for the subject of his 1972 dissertation, published as *Freedom's First Generation: Black Hampton, Virginia, 1861-1890* in 1979.

Engs's friend and classmate at Princeton and Yale, the white southerner J. Morgan Kousser (b. 1943), had come to college already committed to civil rights. As a youth his intellectual proclivities had alienated him not only from the lower-middle class children in his neighborhood, but also from the wealthy and prejudiced classmates he met as a scholarship student in a prestigious prep school. He thus found himself in rebellion against his white southern environment—and, as he observed, for a person in revolt against the white South, the first thing to rebel against was the racial system. While completing high school in Nashville in 1960, he was fascinated by the sit-ins, and although fear of expulsion from school inhibited his participation, he got to know the black student demonstrators at Fisk and Tennessee A. & I. At Princeton, where he, like Engs, became involved in student activism, he did a senior thesis on Tennessee politics and the Negro, 1958-64. Visiting SNCC and SCLC projects as an employee of the U.S. Civil Rights Commission's Memphis office during the summer of 1965 further enriched his knowledge. By the time he went to Yale to study under Woodward, he had moved ideologically from being a Lyndon Johnson liberal into opposition to the Vietnam War. His 1971 dissertation, published three years later as *The Shaping of Southern Politics: Suffrage Restriction and the Establishment of the One-Party South, 1880-1910*, was a study of racial disfranchisement at the turn of the century.

Gary B. Nash (b. 1933) as a high-school student had shed the racial prejudices of his rather conservative parents, and at Princeton in the early 1960s participated in the group trying to improve conditions for migrant agricultural workers. He also wrote a seminar paper for Goldman on the beginnings of Negro Harlem. His interest was accentuated as a result of his taking a teaching post at the racially heterogeneous University of California at Los Angeles in 1966, shortly after the Watts riot. Here he became involved with Operation Bootstrap, a black-led job-training organization that was a spin-off from the local civil rights movement. Nash founded a white support group for Bootstrap that held weekly consciousness-raising sessions in the heart of the Watts ghetto, exploring the implications of white racist attitudes. Bringing his concern about race prejudice into the classroom, he devised a course on the evolution of racism in America that regularly drew enrollments among the largest in the UCLA history department during the late 1960s. Out of this interest came his book, *Red, White, and Black* (1974), a study of the interaction of the races in the colonial period. Moreover, from his research in the social structure of colonial cities developed his studies on urban blacks in early America.[30]

As many of the illustrations in the preceding pages indicate, the development of scholarly research in Afro-American history was for many individuals intertwined with an ideological shift to the left. In the case of those whites who became either more liberal or more radical, the dynamics involved were largely a matter of the black protest movement of the early 1960s awakening people to the whole question of social and economic injustice. In addition, there were those, both black and white, who were deeply affected by the Vietnam War and by the radicalism that loomed so large on university campuses during the second half of the decade. Moreover, movement to the extreme left was partly a function of the disillusionment that set in for some individuals, as the improvement in the Negro's status in the course of the 1960s notwithstanding, they became painfully aware of the depths of white prejudice and concluded that the eradication of both racial discrimination and poverty would require fundamental changes in the American social order. A number of those we interviewed considered themselves radical historians, frequently vaguely socialist rather than Marxist. Several of the whites were profoundly influenced by the New Left movement and a few of them became highly politicized activists in Students for a Democratic Society (SDS). Among certain blacks, the radicalization took the form of a militant nationalism (sometimes tinged with Marxist or socialist ideas) that functioned as an ideological counterpart to the New Left politics among the whites. Although he never became a black nationalist, William H. Harris epitomized the change in thinking that affected so many of the scholars we interviewed: an optimistic nonviolent activist and a Lyndon B. Johnson Democrat in the mid-1960s, he became an opponent of the Vietnam War and a pessimistic critic of capitalist society.

Among those we interviewed, twelve whites were very much attracted to the New Left for a period during their undergraduate and/or graduate careers. All were northerners; otherwise their social and political origins covered a broad gamut. Just two came from Old Left backgrounds; all of the others experienced a leftward transformation in their ideologies. For all, both concern for the poor and opposition to the Vietnam War reinforced the consciousness-raising impact that came from both the salience of the black protest movement and from the peer group influences exercised by fellow intellectuals. Generally a concern about civil rights either preceded or went hand in hand with the shift to a radical perspective; rarely did prior interest in other New Left issues provide the vehicle for the creation of an interest in Afro-American history. Some were at the peripheries of the New Left movement; others were deeply involved. Some were attracted by its early moderate phase, others by its later radical phase. Only seven were actually members of SDS at one time or another in that organization's increasingly radical trajectory.

Among those on the fringes of the New Left were David Gerber and John Dittmer. For Gerber, the temper of Princeton's academic environment was such that race was "*the* domestic issue," but his break with parental conservatism during his undergraduate years also propelled him to the edges of the student counterculture and to a fascination with the participatory democracy of early SDS. Dittmer (b. 1939), who came from a fundamentalist Lutheran Republican family, was exposed as an undergraduate at Indiana University not only to news of the black protest movement, but also to the liberal views of the campus's brightest students; he graduated in 1961 a Kennedy Democrat. After he returned to the campus for graduate work two years later, Dittmer attended SDS meetings and enthusiastically concluded that college youth could indeed bring on a nonviolent social revolution that would truly help poor people. He never joined SDS, but to this day he is a "neo-Populist" and an independent socialist. Family responsibilities prevented him from joining the southern freedom movement, but his desire to do something socially worthwhile led Dittmer in 1967 to take a job teaching at the black Mississippi school, Tougaloo College. Choosing a research project that would give intellectual expression to his social conscience, he turned to the study of race relations in early twentieth-century Georgia, his 1971 dissertation being published in revised form as *Black Georgia in the Progressive Era, 1900-1920* (1977).

Epitomizing the way in which the radical student subculture of the 1960s was intertwined with much of the scholarship subsequently published in Afro-American history was the experience of Ira Berlin (b. 1941). Raised in a nonideological but Democratic New York Jewish family, Berlin as a high-school student had become aware of the inconsistency between the lessons of the civic classes and social reality. At the University of Wisconsin, where he attended undergraduate and graduate school in the late 1950s and the 1960s, the radical intellectual environment was enormously exciting. There was the peer group pressure to read Marx and become politically literate, and like so many of his contemporaries Berlin became deeply concerned about the conditions of the "common people" and wanted his scholarship to reflect his social idealism. Although Berlin never became a doctrinaire ideologue, he was exceedingly sympathetic toward the New Left and became caught up in the intense desire to remake the world. Berlin's interest in black history, though stimulated by the civil rights movement, was inchoate at first; his 1963 M.A. thesis under Leon Litwack was on Jacksonian politics. But in the Wisconsin milieu at the peak of the black protest movement and the escalation of student radicalism amid the Vietnam War protests, his concerns about racial justice crystallized into a research concentration in Afro-American history. Berlin originally considered studying the abolitionists (who impressed him as the nineteenth-century counterparts of the white civil rights activists), but ultimately he settled upon his study of free blacks in the Upper South; with considerable additional research, this 1970 dissertation became the basis of his *Slaves without Masters* (1974).

Theodore Kornweibel (b. 1942) followed an atypical route, since his interest in racial injustice and black history came relatively late in his brief radical career. Born into a moderately conservative southern California Republican family, Kornweibel moved leftward as a student at the University of California, Santa Barbara, in the early and middle 1960s, rising to a top leadership position in the campus Free Speech Movement. It was this role that in turn led him into Santa Barbara's CORE, which used the campus as a recruiting base for its direct action projects. Subsequently a year of teaching at Prairie View College in Texas provided a "black milieu" that encouraged him to do his first serious reading in black history. Given Kornweibel's interests, an analysis of the radical circle connected with A. Philip Randolph's *Messenger* magazine was a logical topic for his dissertation in American studies at Yale in 1971, published four years later as *No Crystal Stair*.

John B. Kirby (b. 1938), though from a conservative Republican background, as a youth had positive associations with blacks. The only white newsboy in his prosperous neighborhood, he mingled with black newspaper carriers and later developed a close friendship with a black teammate on his high-school football team. With alienation from his parents' conservatism having begun before he went to college, during his undergraduate career at the University of Wisconsin (B.A., 1962) he was attracted by Litwack's lectures on the labor movement, developed New Deal and socialist sympathies, and participated in Woolworth sympathy and fair-housing demonstrations. Studying for his M.A. at the University of Michigan, he pursued his interest in labor history under Sidney Fine, was active in more open-housing demonstrations, and joined protest marches against John F. Kennedy's handling of the Cuban missile crisis. Over the next three years he underwent a series of experiences that radicalized him further and involved him deeply in the black community. Spending a year as a welfare worker in southside Chicago where he became active in the school boycotts, Kirby also participated in SNCC's 1964 Mississippi Freedom Summer and helped to organize welfare mothers. Enrolling at the University of Denver in 1966 for graduate work, he was swept up in SDS activism and quickly expelled for his role in the occupation of the chancellor's office. Ultimately he secured his Ph.D. at the University of Illinois with a 1971 dissertation published as *Black Americans in the Roosevelt Era: Liberalism and Race* (1979), which had crystallized out of his interest in the New Deal and his commitment to black advancement.

Russell Menard (b. 1942) came from a family of mixed French-Canadian and Irish-Catholic background, moderately racist and conventionally urban Democratic in political sympathies. Excited by the idealism associated with Kennedy's New Frontier and moving leftward as a University of Delaware undergraduate, Menard shifted from indifference on racial issues to sympathetic support as a result of the black protest demonstrations. The Vietnam War teach-ins of 1965 further radicalized his perspective, as did the climate of opinion among faculty and students during his graduate years at the University of Iowa, where he was very active in both SDS and Friends of SNCC. Although his principal involvement was in the antiwar struggle, he also campaigned for the recruitment of more black students and was selected to teach the first Afro-American history course there in 1969. On the other hand, sensitive though he was to the importance of studying the black experience, Menard's research interest in the field would come later, flowing from a more general investigation of social structure in the Chesapeake colonies.

Mark Naison (b. 1946) was reared in a Jewish socialist and trade-union environment. Although his parents never shared his concern with racial injustice, Naison early developed sympathies for the less fortunate, and while still in high school participated briefly in the militant Brooklyn CORE demonstrations of 1961-62. At this point Naison was far more interested in competitive sports than in social activism. But by the time he was a Columbia University sophomore, he was tutoring black junior high-school students, and as a member of the campus CORE chapter he helped organize Harlem tenants for rent strikes. (His senior honors' thesis was an analysis of that movement, which provided the basis for his first published article, "The Rent Strikes in New York," in *Radical America* in 1967). Subsequently he was involved in a lengthy love affair (over his parents' vehement opposition) with a black woman; did an M.A. thesis at Columbia on the interracial Southern Tenant Farmers Union; and worked in the university-sponsored Upward Bound program designed to orient black high-school youth toward college careers. The trust he gained from blacks through his participation in this program proved useful in 1968, when he acted as liaison between blacks and the white SDS militants during the student revolt at Columbia. Further radicalized by this crisis, Naison joined SDS, becoming an active leader and a member of the defense squad who beat up people interfering with the organization's work. He was almost expelled from Columbia for knocking out a right-wing student and was arrested for assaulting a policeman. Naison's particular series of radical experiences left a strong mark on his subsequent research, which was on the Communists in Harlem. Having become convinced that SDS should reach an accommodation with the militant black separatists of the Black Power years, Naison began his Ph.D. dissertation (1975) that focused largely on the complex interactions between black nationalists and the Communists in Harlem during the 1920s and 1930s. Considerably amplified, and including a description of the Communists' relationships with the integrationist advancement organizations like the NAACP as well, his study was published in 1983 as *Communists in Harlem during the Depression*.

Finally, mention should be made of a smaller group of New Left scholars who themselves came from a radical Old Left family background. Eric Foner's interests in the history of the black experience flowered at the end of the 1960s when he taught the first course in black history offered by Columbia University. While preparing to teach it, he put together his anthology, *America's Black Past* (1970). Subsequently his *Nothing But Freedom* (1983) would add illumination to the study of Emancipation. Robert Starobin (1939-71), like Foner, was no stranger to the cause of racial justice. His Communist parents knew Paul Robeson and Herbert Aptheker and provided him with many interracial experiences. Still, his real commitment to radical ideas and civil rights did not develop until about 1960 when, as an undergraduate at Cornell, he rebelled against the latter-day stodginess of the Old Left. At Berkeley, where he was a leader in the Free Speech Movement and a participant in both Friends of SNCC and in the militant mass civil rights sit-ins of the era, he took his doctorate under Kenneth Stampp in 1968 with a dissertation published as *Industrial Slavery in the Old South* (1970).[31]

The interviews we had with the publishing black historians who emerged during the 1970s indicate that they were less likely than the whites to develop a systematic political viewpoint. As one of them put it, he is "blissfully free from ideology." Still, amid the social and intellectual change occurring in the middle and late 1960s, a minority came to espouse highly nationalist ideologies. In certain instances these were fused with Marxist perspectives. For those nationalists socialized in the integrationist milieu of the early part of the decade, disillusionment with the course of events produced the shift to a separatist position. For others the intellectually formative years came at the crest of the nationalist sentiment at the end of the 1960s. Especially instructive are the intellectual biographies of John H. Bracey, Jr., Sterling Stuckey, and Vincent Harding, all of whom in one way or another have remained deeply influenced by the nationalist perspective to which they became committed. Although they differed widely, the three were similar in that each developed a systematic radical vision about the destiny of black men and women in America.

Bracey (b. 1941), although far from unique in articulating a complex amalgam of Marxist and nationalist thinking, was rare among the publishing historians in his advocacy of a genuinely revolutionary nationalist outlook.[32] The crucial period in his development was his undergraduate years at Howard and Roosevelt universities, 1959-64. Howard exposed Bracey to a variety of intellectual influences: the paradoxical fascination with the nationalist and often Marxist African independence movements exhibited by the highly assimilationist bourgeois faculty; the African leaders who visited the campus; the highly visible presence of West Indian–Pan-African intellectuals in the student body; and the activity of Michael Thelwell, Stokely Carmichael, and others in the local SNCC affiliate whom Bracey knew personally. Roosevelt University, with its nucleus of radical ideologists, and Chicago, as a major center of civil rights activism, proved just as stimulating as Howard University and Washington. A founding member of Stuckey's Amistad Society, Bracey also established a Negro History Club at Roosevelt. At this institution professors St. Clair Drake, August Meier, and others provided a long-range influence in demonstrating that activism and good scholarship "were not polar opposites." Bracey joined the Chicago Friends of SNCC—a group well in advance of SNCC itself in the shift toward nationalism—and participated (and was arrested) in some of the most militant demonstrations sponsored by CORE and other civil rights organizations. At the same time he was exposed to the thinking of white left sectarian organizations and of black intellectuals who sought to apply a Marxist-Leninist analysis to the problem of racism. As a matter of fact, he interacted with a broad spectrum of Marxists: Ishmael Flory, who for years had been the leading Negro Communist in Chicago (and who, curiously, like some of Bracey's bourgeois Howard University professors coupled his interest in Africa with a negative view of domestic black nationalism); the two black Communists whom Elijah Muhammad employed to edit *Muhammad Speaks* and to direct the Black Muslims' University of Islam; the writings of C. L. R. James and his followers in the interracial Trotskyist splinter group, the Facing Reality Committee, whose members contended that the black movement was the vanguard of revolutionary change in the United States; and Akbar Muhammad Ahmad (Max Stanford) of the Revolutionary Action Movement (RAM), and Robert Williams (the former NAACP branch president of Monroe, North Carolina, ousted for advocating armed black self-defense), both of whom called for organized violence as the way to revolution.

For a period Bracey felt uncertain about where he stood, as he sorted out these ideas. For him, the views held by the Communists and Trotskyists were relevant purely because of their revolutionary Marxism and not their interracialism. He did not perceive Marxism as mandating interracial cooperation, either in Africa or the Caribbean or the United States; rather he considered it unfortunate that the white Marxists saw the black struggle as but an aspect of the working-class struggle for a socialist society. In fact, if any view about white workers was being expressed in Bracey's circle, it was that these whites were more race-conscious than class-conscious and were therefore hardly likely allies in the blacks' fight for freedom. For Bracey, the lesson to be learned from the Marxists lay not in their integrationism but in the nationalist implications to be drawn from their works on black history. Herbert Aptheker's *American Negro Slave Revolts* was an "indispensable" book, an antidote to the view that blacks lacked a history of struggle or that their struggle was limited to legal and nonviolent forms. Aptheker's *Documentary History of the Negro People in the United States* "opened our eyes to the complexity of our history and to the immense talents of our forebears who seemed to have anticipated the form and content of every strategy or tactic that we thought we were inventing for the first time." In the period from 1963 to mid-1965 Bracey sought to synthesize SNCC activism, Malcolm X's nationalism, and Williams's advocacy of armed struggle. In Bracey's circle of young and angry black militants, SNCC was greatly admired for its courage and skill in organizing southern Negroes, but criticized for its nonviolence and integrationism. He found the Black Muslims and the various surviving Garvey groups inactive politically and burdened by religious mysticism; but he greatly admired the Muslims' ex-leader Malcolm X, who fused a nationalist position with a call to examine the strategy of revolution. Ultimately Bracey found the key to the synthesis toward which he was groping in the early essays of Harold Cruse,[33] with his critique of American Marxists, his analysis of the dilemma of the black intellectual attracted to the revolutionary nationalism of the Third World but reluctant to adopt such a program for Afro-Americans, and his articulation of the concept of "domestic colonialism." Cruse* also offered an explanation of the class divisions

* Cruse himself was an ex-Communist and no stranger to Marxist sectarian warfare. Indeed, his experiences in the Communist party had led him to conclude that while American society could be restructured, the white radical left was incapable of performing this task.[34] (Moreover, the concept of "domestic colonialism," which seemed like such a new idea in the 1960s, had actually been first developed by Communists during the 1920s.) Cruse's *The Crisis of the Negro Intellectual* (1967) produced a considerable stir among black and white intellectuals when it appeared and reinforced the trend toward seeing the black experience in cultural terms. Yet Cruse's role in shaping the views of professionally trained historians has been surprisingly difficult to trace, and only rarely have individuals we interviewed pinpointed his work as significantly influencing their own scholarship. One was William Toll, who consciously utilized Crusean cultural analysis in *The Resurgence of Race,* a revisionist volume on black ideologies in the age of Booker T. Washington.

within the black community and "challenged us to join the struggle with the masses of our people." As Cruse had said as early as 1962, it was "impossible for American society as it is now constituted to integrate or assimilate the Negro," and "the American Negro is the only potentially revolutionary force in the United States today." As long as segregation remained a "built-in characteristic of American society," nationalist ideology would continue to grow, probably ending in "racial wars."[35]

With Malcolm X's death and the Watts conflagration, Cruse's insights seemed to be confirmed. Bracey recalled, "What we thought we were in was the first stage of armed struggle for the national liberation of Black America." He joined the radical nationalist organizations, RAM and the Republic of New Africa, and played a leading part in the militant black student activism at Northwestern University in the late 1960s. Not long afterward Bracey published a succinct statement of the intellectual synthesis underlying his own view of Afro-American history in a documentary history of black nationalism in America.[36]

Sterling Stuckey came to the 1960s with an orientation toward radical Marxist politics and cultural pluralism that would provide underlying unities to the changes in his perspective over the following years. In the vanguard of the surge of interest in the Afro-American experience engendered by the events of the first half of the decade, Stuckey's Amistad Society had a program that was directed toward a lay audience but that at the same time showed a scholarly sophistication consonant with his extensive knowledge of the literature and his long-range professional objectives. Although Stuckey, a CORE activist, had been swept up in the enthusiasm of the nonviolent integrationism of the period, at the same time he was reaching a different segment of black people through a series of 1963 articles in *Muhammad Speaks* on black revolutionaries and nationalists like David Walker, Nat Turner, and Henry Highland Garnet.[37] By the time he embarked upon his graduate work at Northwestern University in 1965, Stuckey had become convinced that freedom involved more than the elimination of racism, and that in addition to breaking down the chains of discrimination blacks must learn to prize their cultural distinctiveness and uniquely humane spiritual values. Articulating ideas expressed by his youthful heroes Du Bois and Robeson, he criticized blacks who wanted "white people to believe that Negroes were psychologically and spiritually just like them." Du Bois, he pointed out, "did not think it desirable for Negroes to so aspire," but believed that attainment of equal rights meant being both "free and black. . . . He meant that black men did not come seeking freedom empty-handed but possessed gifts the country could not afford to reject."[38]

For Stuckey (Ph.D., Northwestern University, 1971), the rise of Black

Power ideology in the mid-1960s confirmed his instrumental view of history: that blacks had to explore their own past in order to conduct their struggle effectively, and that freedom involved the conscious cultivation of the singular values in black culture. It now appeared to him that "the promise of integration" had been unjustifiably "blown sky high" and "bleached white" by civil rights leaders like Roy Wilkins, and he welcomed the urban summer violence as a sign of "the first revolutionary activity among black people." For a period at the height of black separatist sentiment, Stuckey's thinking took a more "narrowly racial" turn: trying to transform the larger American society seemed irrelevant and Stuckey's enthusiasm for the Robeson–Du Bois contention that blacks had a valuable contribution to make to the Western world was temporarily submerged. Meanwhile his scholarly explorations took two directions: the study of the early nineteenth-century black nationalists, and the investigation of the Afro-American cultural tradition. He found the first topic to be of contemporary relevance: the historical record "seems to suggest . . . that those people of color . . . who believed in the absorptive powers of America were vastly more deluded than those blacks who decided to depend mainly on their own people, their own energies in a hostile land." Better known has been Stuckey's contribution to the examination of black culture. He believed that the roots of Afro-American nationalism were to be found in the culture that the slaves had generated, and drawing upon ideas he had seen expressed years before by Du Bois and Robeson, Stuckey, in one of his best-known essays, "Through the Prism of Folklore," in the late 1960s made a pioneering plea for the use of folklore materials as a key to understanding the black experience in bondage. Moreover, as he put it at the opening of the 1970s, blacks themselves must develop their own African-oriented values in the context of the non-Western age that was dawning.

Subsequently, however, as the tide of separatism receded, Stuckey would by the mid- and late 1970s adopt a more universalistic view, emphasizing, as Robeson and Du Bois had done, the spiritual gifts that blacks had for white America; that, as Du Bois had put it in his 1897 paper on *The Conservation of Races*, "we are Negroes, members of a vast historic race," with "a contribution to make to civilization and humanity, which no other race can make" — "the harbinger of that black to-morrow which is yet destined to soften the whiteness of the Teutonic to-day." In short, as Du Bois had held, black spirituality rooted in Africa would supply a humane leaven for the harshness of materialism of the whole Western world.[39]

Vincent Harding was also greatly inspired by the prophetic voice of Du Bois, but where Stuckey's views were informed by a secular and radical socialist perspective akin to that of the former *Crisis* editor, Harding came to his civil rights activism and writing of history out of a deeply religious worldview. Harding (b. 1931) was reared in the messianic tradition of a black Seventh Day Adventist denomination. Educated at City College of New York and at the Columbia University School of Journalism, he spent a disquieting two years in the Army during the mid-1950s, "a pivotal experience" that led him into the pacifist and interracial Mennonite church. While studying at the University of Chicago for a doctorate in religious history (which he would receive in 1965 with a dissertation on "Lyman Beecher and the Transformation of American Protestantism, 1775-1863"), Harding served for several years as a part-time lay pastor for the Mennonites and in 1961 undertook an assignment as their field representative to the southern freedom movement. In this capacity he worked in numerous communities across the South, principally as a lecturer on nonviolence and as a mediator with local white leaders. Harding was arrested in the massive jail-ins at Albany, Georgia, and in the spring of 1963, coming to Birmingham at King's request, performed his most important mediation work in helping end the crisis in that city. Along with King and other fellow activists, he shared the faith in American democratic institutions that was the hallmark of the time. Although aware that the secularized young leaders of SNCC were increasingly uncomfortable with talk of love and nonviolence, he believed that there was hope especially in the many instances when whites joined blacks in their demonstrations, and he welcomed signs that slowly some whites were "begin[ning] to see the logic in the Negroes' claim: 'We march to free you as well as ourselves.' "[40]

Subsequently Harding, like many black militants disillusioned when the limited scope of the movement's victories became evident, modified his perspective. Two essays, penned in late 1965 and 1966, catch him at the crossroads of the movement's transformation and reveal Harding grappling with the question of the continued relevance of love and nonviolence for the black struggle. "Where Have All the Lovers Gone?" is a sensitive evocation of the decline of King's dream of the "beloved community." For a time the love-your-enemy approach, whether seen in the ideological terms expressed by King or viewed as simply a practical strategy, had worked in the South. But the movement's successes were hedged in with paradoxes, and the perception grew that the victories came not from the redemptive power of sacrificial love, but from the power of economic boycotts and especially from the federal pressures that the protest demonstrations had engendered. Love therefore was forgotten; by the end of 1965 power had become the new theme; and almost inevitably there occurred "the transformation of black radicals from the singing, integration-directed marchers of Montgomery, Alabama, in 1955 into the avowed guerrilla fighters and alienated rebels of the late 1960s."[41] Harding's concerns as a religiously motivated participant in the southern movement were also reflected in a paper he delivered at the 1966 OAH convention, "Religion and Resistance among Antebellum Negroes, 1800-1860." In this analysis of the complex ambiguities of the role that religion played in slave responses to white oppression, he conceded that Christianity in large part functioned as the otherworldly opiate that an older generation of black scholars had described. But reviewing the evidence from a number of slave rebellions, he contended that it had also provided the seedbed of messianic revolt. As Harding put it elsewhere, Nat Turner—"The Jesus of Southampton"—"leaps forth as a religious mystic, a single-minded black believer with a powerful sense of messianic vocation."[42]

Harding's years as a professor at Spelman College in the second half of the 1960s were transitional ones, during which he moved away from the ideology that King represented and embraced Black Power. Partly Harding's radicalization, like that of many others in the civil rights movement, stemmed from his opposition to the Vietnam War. In addition, both as a teacher at a southern black college during the upsurge of the Black Power movement and as an individual who maintained his personal relationships with militants in the struggle, he found himself "in accord with many of the basic concerns" expressed by "that powerful Black symbolism." He also believed that the issues of racism and war had to be linked in "an independent Black critique of American life and American foreign policy . . . encouraging the upsurge of a Black cultural renaissance." While hoping that a way might be found to reconcile the contrasting perspectives of King and the Black Power advocates, Harding concluded that the former failed to provide an effective answer to the black radicals' convictions "that this nation will not allow black men the freedom, opportunity and restitution needful for meaningful lives without a total, violent disruption of the society."[43] Notwithstanding his growing reservations concerning King—and a growing appreciation of Marcus Garvey and Malcolm X— Harding served as the first director of the Martin Luther King, Jr., Memorial Center from 1968 to 1970. Eventually his ambivalence about violence and his nationalist inclinations, both at odds with the martyred leader's beliefs, prompted a split with King's widow and his departure from the center. By then he had established the Institute of the Black World, an Atlanta-based think-tank—"a community of scholars and artists, coming out of the Black experience, coming together for giving their intellectual gifts over to understanding the past and present and trying to set guidelines for the future of Black people." It was founded on the premise "that the whole study of the Black experience that was being pressed up as a result of the struggles . . . ought to be essentially defined by Black people"— specifically from the perspective of the most radical wing of the black protest movement whose spirit had prompted the institute's establishment.[44]

Even more than Stuckey, Harding, the prolific essayist, is known for his hope that blacks, given "our moral superiority," could play the vital role in reforming an evil, materialistic, racist, and undemocratic American society—a message that he was articulating even at the height of black separatist sentiment at the turn of the 1970s. Because white society was so morally bankrupt, he dreamed that blacks were destined to be the agent of purification; since "white America has clearly lost its spiritual grasp," it was up to blacks to lead the way to "radical, life-affirming change." Although offering hope more than certainty about the future, Harding seemed firm in his messianic vision of the blacks' struggle: the evidence forces "those who write Black History to the only logical conclusion: Black-led, radical, perhaps revolutionary change for America."[45] This revolutionary program, grounded in race rather than class, and spiritual rather than materialist in its analysis, was anything but Marxist. Although Harding came to respect black Marxist intellectuals, he nevertheless remained convinced that "Marxism simply cannot serve as the fundamental grounding for the necessary revolution in the world's major post-industrial welfare/warfare/racist state":— "[I]ts tendency to set aside the life of the spirit actually cripples it as a tool for dealing with much of the Black experience."[46]

Harding's dual role as prophet and historian—a combination akin to the role essayed by Du Bois whom Harding so much admires (though for his messianism rather than for his socialism)—went hand in hand with the uneasy fusion of Malcolm X and Martin King that derived from his own experience in the southern freedom movement. All this propelled Harding into a long-term study of the history of black radicalism, which he viewed as a wide river of resistance that had existed since the arrival of slaves in the New World.[47] Evidently intended chiefly for a black lay audience, *There Is a River* (1981) is suffused with a rhetorical tone, a sense of Old Testament moral righteousness, and a celebration of the indestructible quest for freedom. For him, blacks like Frederick Douglass and others who appealed to the moral sensibilities of white America were both unrealistic and insufficiently radical. Instead, Harding sided with those who shared the apocalyptic conviction "that there could be no ultimate deliverance for Blacks (or whites) without a Black-led rebellious movement, which would involve levels of anguish and blood-letting surpassing those of the Civil War." It was to be hoped, however, that blacks could play their messianic role through an essentially nonviolent transformation; already the post–World War II freedom movement provided them with a new sense of direction that had enabled blacks to open the way for the antiwar, feminist, and student movements that challenged the status quo.[48] Harding's messianic nationalism, like Du Bois's, thus lies beyond separatism: like mid-nineteenth-century nationalists in Western Europe and the United States, his view is one of a chosen people destined by God to inaugurate a millennium of universal freedom and justice. This conceptualization represents the ultimate resolution of his ambivalent fascination with pacifism and violence, with Malcom X's militant nationalism and Martin Luther King's beloved community.

Other blacks reflected the ideological currents of the 1960s and 1970s in various ways, and for some who experienced the impact of the nationalist surge, its effects upon their thinking and published writings have been more subtle than they were for Bracey, Harding, and Stuckey. Clement A. Price (b. 1945), a specialist on blacks in New Jersey and the compiler of *Freedom Not Far Distant* (1980), a documentary history of Afro-Americans in that state, had a decidedly activist bent: a leader in the southern freedom movement while a freshman at St. Augustine's College (Raleigh, North Carolina), he subsequently headed the University of Bridgeport NAACP and led the campaign for black studies and black faculty there. Black Power crested during his graduate years at Rutgers University, where he wrote his 1975 doctoral dissertation on "The Afro-American Community of Newark, 1917-1947: A Social History." Rather than destroying his commitment to traditional civil rights agitation, Black Power added new dimensions to his thinking: a stress on black unity and an affinity for the cultural nationalism of Imamu Baraka and Cruse. Subsequently, while not shedding what he found valuable in a nationalist perspective, interaction with white faculty colleagues led him to see the black experience as having much in common with that of other oppressed minorities, and he moved toward a broader humanitarian concern. Joe William Trotter, Jr. (b. 1945), who came to intellectual maturity when he attended Carthage College in Wisconsin during the late 1960s, was also an activist, heading the campus Afro-American society that pressed for the introduction of black faculty and black studies. An admirer of Baraka and Ron Karenga, he had become a nationalist by his senior year. Yet this perspective was always laced with considerable ambiguity. As the vulnerability and limitations of the Black Power movement became evident during the 1970s, Trotter, while remaining close to the nationalist perspective, carefully followed the nationalism-versus-Marxism debates in the *Black Scholar* and came to recognize the need to incorporate class considerations into his analysis. With his outlook also informed by the new working-class history, he introduced into his 1980 University of Minnesota dissertation (published in 1984 as *Black Milwaukee: The Making of an Industrial Proletariat, 1915-45*), a fresh conceptual framework for black urban history: an analysis of "proletarianization" and the transformation of peasant migrants into an urban working class.

Intertwined with the radical trends in the profession and further accentuating the impact of the black protest was the rise of the new social history that became so prominent by the end of the 1960s. This development was the fruit of two mutually reinforcing factors, one intellectual and the other technological. There were, on the one hand, the streams of influence emanating from the French Annales School and more especially from the English practitioners of working-class history, particularly E. P. Thompson; these in turn intersected with the leftward trend among historians to produce the excitement over writing "history from the bottom up."* On the other hand, there was the popularization of quantitative techniques facilitated by the computer, a development that encouraged going beyond the study of elites to the analysis of whole communities, and through the use of manuscript census materials, tax records, and estate inventories—all of which could be quantified—provided a new tool for approaching the study of the inarticulate. In the following pages we examine four leading scholars—David Katzman, Kenneth Kusmer, Nell Painter, and Peter H. Wood—whose careers illustrate the ways in which the new social history interacted with the other aspects of the changing social and intellectual milieu that we have been describing.

Katzman (b. 1941) has had an intellectual trajectory that exhibits the intertwining of several factors previously identified with the development of interest in Afro-American history among white historians—a liberal Jewish background, the salience of the black protest movement, and the rise of the New Left—as well as the emergence of the new social history. His liberal family, owners of a jazz-booking agency in New York, not only introduced him to black musicians but also deliberately provided interracial experiences by sending him to a mixed YMCA summer camp. At the same time the many Communists and fellow travelers living near where he grew up provided an exposure to radicals that was reinforced by the circles in which he moved during the 1960s, first as an undergraduate at Queens College and then as a graduate student at the University of Michigan. At Queens he participated in NAACP demonstrations against job discrimination in the building trades unions, and later, although not joining SDS, he was active in antiwar teach-ins and demonstrations, moving steadily leftward. Although ultimately alienated from the left on the subject of

---

* While much of the credit for popularizing this phrase in the late 1960s goes to Jesse Lemisch, it is interesting to note that Stephan Thernstrom employed it in *Poverty and Progress* ([1964], 3, 7). Thernstrom cited the use of this phrase first made by Carolyn F. Ware and Constance M. Green in Ware, ed., *The Cultural Approach to History* ([1940], 273, 275).

Israel, he retained his deep interest in the common people and the dispossessed. At Queens he specialized in sociology and economics and was introduced through European history courses to the work of the Annales School. This rich background in social history and the behavioral sciences, combined with his ethical commitment, enabled him to grasp opportunities that came about almost accidentally at Michigan. Excited at finding the manuscript census schedules while working on his first seminar assignment, he immediately realized their potential as a tool for studying the inarticulate classes. A summer job researching the history of blacks in Ann Arbor revealed the "fantastic" possibilities for black community studies in Michigan. He proceeded to read widely in black history and sociology, finding his interests especially akin to those exhibited in the black urban community monographs written by the earlier giants of black social science from Du Bois to St. Clair Drake. Katzman wanted to analyze both race relations and the nature of the black community (and he already had a conceptualization of community studies derived from his knowledge of sociology and the writings of the Annales School); he was interested in both process and social class, the latter reinforced by reading Thompson's *The Making of the English Working Class* soon after its publication. In short, as a result of his ideological leanings and academic training, he had a sense of doing history from the bottom up even before Jesse Lemisch's paper popularized the idea.[49] All this went into the making of Katzman's 1969 dissertation on blacks in nineteenth-century Detroit, published in 1973 as *Before the Ghetto*.

For Kusmer (b. 1945), who also contributed to the study of black urban communities, the influence of the new methodologies and European traditions of history-writing was considerably less direct. As a youth growing up in a Cleveland working-class neighborhood in ethnic transition, Kusmer had had many black friends. The civil rights movement of the early 1960s, the antiwar movement later, and the radical atmosphere at Oberlin College all reinforced his youthful nonideological social concerns, and while never an ideologue, he came to identify himself as a left-liberal. There was nothing inevitable at that point about his embarking upon the study of black history, but Meier's presence at nearby Kent State University provided an opportunity. Arriving at Kent with a strong undergraduate background in intellectual history, Kusmer perceived Meier's interdisciplinary approach as in effect transforming intellectual history into social history. Stimulated by the earlier sociological works on urban blacks, Kusmer, like Katzman, became part of the wave of young social historians interested in community studies. His 1970 M.A. thesis on Cleveland blacks in the late nineteenth and early twentieth centuries underwent substantial revisions over the next five years, a period in which Kusmer mastered quantitative techniques and developed the comparative approach that lent sophistication to his 1976 book, *A Ghetto Takes Shape.*

Like Katzman, Painter (b. 1942) had radical leanings and was influenced by the Annales School. In addition, having imbibed from her parents a strong feeling of identification with West Indian and African blacks, there has been an important strain of nationalist—or what she describes as "Pan-Africanist"—thinking in her outlook. An activist while taking her undergraduate degree in anthropology at Berkeley, she had participated in sit-ins and become a supporter of the black nationalist-Marxist Monroe Defense Committee, organized to aid Robert Williams. In the mid-1960s she spent two years at the Institute of African Studies of the University of Ghana, and African history remained a field of concentration throughout the rest of her academic training. Discussions at the University of Ghana had further exposed her to Marxist politics; in the long run, however, although sympathetically disposed toward socialism, she was unable to embrace the Marxist model with its preoccupation about class and its slighting of race. A year studying medieval history in France had earlier (1962-63) introduced her to the perspective of the Annales School. And while formulating the direction of her 1974 Harvard University dissertation on the Kansas exodus of 1879, she was stimulated by suggestions from the innovative Herbert Gutman, who did so much to popularize among American scholars the ideas of the English historians of the working class. Painter's monograph, published as *Exodusters: Black Migration to Kansas after Reconstruction* (1977), reflects the range of these varied intellectual influences. There was her interest in the nationalist colonization movements to Africa and the historical relationship between them and internal black migration movements within the United States. There were also her concern with the life of the common people, her emphasis on indigenous leadership arising from the masses, and her criticism of elite black leaders who opposed the exodus from the South—a viewpoint that was an expression of her social radicalism and at the same time reflected the inspiration she received from the new social and working-class history.

Wood, by the time he went to Harvard, had some awareness about racial matters, as we have indicated. But as an undergraduate he was absorbed in sports and school work, and it was not until he returned to Harvard in 1966 after studying in England on a Rhodes scholarship that his concern about race relations really took shape. By then both the social landscape and historiographical trends in colonial history—the field he had chosen for specialization—had changed considerably. The new forms of black militance made him acutely aware of the race issue, the Detroit riot of 1967 crystallizing his desire to do a dissertation in black history; and his knowledge about the black experience was considerably enlarged when he served as a teaching assistant in the black history course introduced under Frank Freidel's direction in the academic year 1968-69. Meanwhile, he was experiencing a broadening of social consciousness on two other fronts: the interaction he had with radical undergraduates while resident director of Eliot House, and his fascination with the demographic and community research being done at Harvard in colonial history. He found demographic studies inherently radicalizing, since they required that one deal with all the people in a community rather than with only the elite. Searching for a topic that would combine his interests in both black and colonial history, he came to do his 1972 dissertation on slavery in early South Carolina, published two years later as *Black Majority*.

Thus the salience of the black protest movement, the ideological shift in the profession in a liberal and radical direction, and the development of new historical perspectives and methodologies all were instrumental in bringing black history to the foreground as an area of research. These factors were of course mutually reinforcing: as several of those we interviewed observed, for example, the new social history and Afro-American history "fed on each other." In any event, propelled most obviously by the events of the 1960s that culminated in the sense of crisis precipitated by King's assassination, black history became a legitimate and even popular academic specialty.

The mainstream legitimization of the study of the black experience, evident in the explosion of research and publication that occurred, decisively distinguished the late 1960s and 1970s from earlier periods. This development was the culmination of a long-term trend going back at least to mid-century, as the evidence presented in this volume has indicated. Still there had been a dramatic shift even from the situation at the opening of the 1960s, when it generally still required strong motivation and ideological commitment for whites to work in the field. By 1965 or 1966 it had become clear that to do a dissertation or book in Afro-American history was no longer thought to be pursuing an unconventional topic that might place one in scholarly limbo. By 1968 the subject of black history had become downright "fashionable."[50] Courses proliferated; fellowship programs encouraged research; formerly indifferent and skeptical publishers rushed books into print; and an unprecedented number of papers appeared on convention programs and in learned journals.

Numerous scholars of both races perceived black history as a lively field with endless opportunities for exciting investigations on the frontiers of historical research. Moreover, in a circular way, the field's newfound legitimacy reinforced the surge of scholarship. However, in supplying such reinforcement, this newly established legitimacy tended to operate in rather different ways among whites and among blacks.

Among whites there was more of a tendency than ever before for individuals to more or less "back into" their research topics, rather than choose deliberately to do such research as an expression of their social commitment and ethical concerns. Representative of this group was Nancy J. Weiss (b. 1944), who came from a highly assimilated Baltimore Jewish family. Although her parents voted for liberal Democratic candidates, they were essentially nonideological. Weiss herself recalls that as an undergraduate at Smith College she was active principally in campus affairs. Although she had a well-defined concern about race relations, her entry into black history in the late 1960s was rooted in a feeling that it was a stimulating new field of research. A *Time* cover story about Whitney Young and the National Urban League precipitated the decision to write her 1970 dissertation on the history of that organization, a topic that fitted very well with her interest in the subject of twentieth-century reform.[51] Weiss sees her scholarship in black history as her way of making a contribution to the understanding of race relations in America. Yet she rather "fell into" the field that has dominated her research, rather than having the sense of being a conscious pioneer with the kinds of motivations that would entail.

For a number of whites the example of particular professors at leading graduate institutions was a decisive factor. By the mid-1960s there was a growing number of historians in prestigious departments who had a profound interest in the subject and who attracted or inspired many young scholars. At Chapel Hill George Tindall came to occupy a niche comparable to the one C. Vann Woodward and Kenneth Stampp had filled at Johns Hopkins and Berkeley earlier. Chicago brought John Hope Franklin to its faculty in 1964; and although he eschewed teaching black history as a separate course, his presence at the university symbolized the field's new legitimacy and brought numerous students into it. At Princeton, as we have seen, the constellation of prominent historians doing work relevant to the subject by the 1960s was especially striking, and in addition Weiss joined the department at the end of the decade. At Berkeley the presence of Stampp, Litwack, Jordan, and Levine provided another strong concentration of interested professors. Yale, with Woodward and David Brion Davis, the art historian Robert Faris Thompson, and the anthropologist Sidney Mintz, offered comparable opportunities. In the spring of 1969 the history department there sponsored a course on comparative slavery by visiting professor Eugene Genovese, and two years later John Blassingame obtained an assistant professorship, adding further strength to Yale's already well-established interest in Afro-American history and related topics. Things had certainly changed from the time when, only a decade earlier,

Yale's John M. Blum, seeking to comprehend a white graduate student's unusual preoccupation with the study of the black experience, exclaimed to Allan Spear: "Oh, you people from Oberlin are all alike!"

Several of those we interviewed spoke appreciatively of the way in which their major professors stimulated their interest in black history. For example, Walter Weare, even though as a youth he had disagreed with his parents' racist opinions about the school desegregation crisis of the 1950s, possessed no strong emotional commitment or research interest until he pursued his graduate work with Tindall in the late 1960s. By then not only was civil rights the key domestic issue, but also Tindall with his profound humanism was the inspiration that paved the way for Weare's history of the North Carolina Mutual Life Insurance Company. Similarly Gerald (Michael) Mullin (b. 1938) had drifted away from the conservative outlook of his parents by the time he was doing his doctoral studies at Berkeley in the 1960s. He originally intended to concentrate in British history until the stimulation provided by Winthrop Jordan turned him to the study of American colonial and black history, and into his 1968 dissertation on the relationship between acculturation and forms of slave resistance in late eighteenth-century Virginia that was published as *Flight and Rebellion* (1972). Loren Schweninger (b. 1941), who earned his Ph.D. at the University of Chicago in 1972 with a biography of Alabama's only black congressman, published as *James T. Rapier and Reconstruction* (1978), had had varied experiences with blacks: hostile interracial conflicts at one of Los Angeles's roughest junior high schools, followed by close friendships with a couple of Negro football teammates at the University of Colorado in the early 1960s. Yet even though he had received some passing exposure to aspects of black history as an M.A. student there, he had not experienced the profound consciousness-raising that characterized so many whom we interviewed. He was not even committed to American—let alone Afro-American—history when he started doctoral work in the middle of the decade. Rather, it was the personal inspiration offered by Franklin that turned Schweninger into a specialist in black history.

Another University of Chicago Ph.D., Howard Rabinowitz (b. 1942), also credits Franklin's personal qualities with leading him into black history. Even though Rabinowitz has a strong sense of Jewish identity and was socialized to a considerable extent by the college radicalism of the 1960s, he is not conscious of either factor being causally related to his choice of black history research topics. As a high-school athlete in Brooklyn, he moved in groups that regarded fellow students who picketed Woolworth stores in the spring of 1960 as "freaks," and he entered Swarthmore College as a varsity basketball player with a quite "conventional" frame of mind. Fortuitously assigned to a dormitory where many radical activists resided—

people involved in the civil rights demonstrations and in the nascent SDS—Rabinowitz became more sensitive to social issues. By the time he went to graduate school at the University of Chicago in the mid-1960s, he wanted to investigate the history of Populism, which was then an active field. At Chicago the combined influence of Richard Wade, who awakened his interest in urban history (a subject then also at the height of its popularity), and of Franklin, who provided an exposure to the post–Civil War South, proved decisive. Franklin's 1967 seminar on Reconstruction involved the class in a two-week research trip to North Carolina; desiring to examine a racial topic, Rabinowitz, at Wade's suggestion, studied blacks in Raleigh after the Civil War. Fascinated with his findings, Rabinowitz was thus established on the road that led to his 1973 dissertation published as *Race Relations in the Urban South, 1865-1890* (1978) and his subsequent edited volume, *Southern Black Leaders of the Reconstruction Era* (1982). For Rabinowitz, it was the inspiration offered by Franklin rather than moral sympathies or a sense of guilt that had crystallized an interest in black history.

An occasional white southerner also illustrated the way in which the legitimization of the field encouraged a scholar to undertake research in black history. Gary B. Mills (b. 1944), one of the few individuals of Catholic background who has specialized in Afro-American history, grew up in heavily black and rural Bolivar County in Mississippi. Attending college during the height of the Mississippi freedom movement, by the time he took his bachelor's degree he had decided that the racist system under which he had been raised was invalid. Still, he embarked upon graduate work at Mississippi State University without the slightest intention of going into black history. Subsequently observing that courses in this field were being introduced at the state's predominantly white institutions of higher education, Mills concluded that the black experience was a legitimate area of inquiry. Switching from his original interest in French history to American, he drifted toward the study of the area around Natchitoches, Louisiana, where his mother's French forebears had lived. Funded by a local history buff to study Melrose, the ancestral home of the Metoyer family, he subsequently extended his research into a 1974 dissertation on this well-known clan of slave-owning *gens de couleur libre*, published as *The Forgotten People* (1977). Leonard P. Curry (b. 1929), a native Kentuckian, came to Afro-American history late in his scholarly career. A specialist in the nineteenth century, he arrived at his research in black history by a circuitous route in the late 1960s. A chapter on urban history in a proposed text on the antebellum period became a book-length project and, in turn, plans for a chapter on blacks in the cities became a full-length monograph. *The Free Black in Urban America, 1800-1850* (1981) dealt with a manageable and publishable topic in an unexplored area of an important field. Moreover, both the course of public events and Curry's research developed his sensitivity to racial issues. Although his work was not in any conscious way the product of the civil rights movement, by the 1970s he shared the general view among historians that since blacks were a part of American society their past could not be ignored.

The economists and cliometricians Robert W. Fogel (b. 1926) and Stanley Engerman (b. 1936), who met each other while graduate students at Johns Hopkins University around 1960 provide, perhaps, quintessential examples of individuals whose selection of a black history topic originated essentially in a desire to address an important and timely research question. Fogel had met his black wife in the Henry Wallace presidential campaign during his Communist party days. Engerman, who came from a nonideological family background, during the 1950s became more liberal and aware of racial issues; he was among the Hopkins graduate students joining the Morgan State students on the picket lines in 1960. Nevertheless, both scholars perceive their collaborative work on slavery, which began about 1966, as in no way rooted in their moral concerns. Rather it came about by accident, flowing from the debate that had resulted from the pioneering econometric research on slavery's profitability of Alfred H. Conrad and John R. Meyer.[52] Indeed Fogel and Engerman's *Time on the Cross* (1974) is an amoral portrayal of planter paternalism, which some have condemned as reading like proslavery apologetics.

For blacks, the legitimization of the study of the black experience provided new professional opportunities that reinforced the consciousness-raising impact of the black protest movement that did so much to attract Negroes into studying their own past. Motivated both by the demands coming from black students and their own growing sense of guilt, white history departments and university administrations began to recruit actively black faculty and graduate students and to inaugurate courses in black history. In 1968-69, the year of the great wave of decisions to introduce these courses, predominantly white institutions were making a determined effort to staff them with knowledgeable people, both black and white. But by 1970 the combination of black student demands and affirmative action policies of the federal government had led colleges and universities to virtually restrict the search to black candidates. It is true that given the small number of Negro Ph.D.s, "A.B.D.s" were often employed for these courses, but the attainment of the doctorate and scholarly publication were duly rewarded. In effect the policies of the predominantly white schools, reinforced by the expanding fellowship opportunities and the policies of book publishers, constituted an affirmative action program that had significant effects on Afro-American historiography.

There was a tendency among the black individuals whom we interviewed to see the job opportunity structure as operative for others but irrelevant for themselves as far as motivating people to do research in black history was concerned. There was, in fact, some ambiguity on this point. For example, a couple of persons who in speaking with us discounted the significance of the new opportunities as a factor shaping the choice of research topics, have complained to white colleagues in their departments about the tendency to recruit blacks only for jobs in Afro-American history and to expect them to publish only in this field. But, as others told us, the fact that nearly all the writing by black historians in recent years has been in black history is rooted both in the interests of white institutions and in the desires of blacks themselves. Thus, as Raymond Gavins of Duke University said, young Negro intellectuals went into Afro-American history both because of the socialization they underwent in the 1960s and also because white administrators and white colleagues expected them to specialize in the study of their own past. In short, as he put it, the impact of the social activism of the decade and the needs and desires of the white schools made "a nice fit." Another black scholar who has written on both black and non-racial topics perceived the same mix of factors, though with less generosity toward the white administrators: blacks themselves wanted to work in black history, but there was often a feeling in predominantly white institutions that black history was a peripheral field where it would be acceptable to employ young blacks without doctorates and thus to restrict them in effect to working in their own segregated specialty.

The most explicit evidence of the way in which new opportunities encouraged black historians to write monographs in Afro-American history is to be found in the role played by publishers. The careers of Edgar A. Toppin (b. 1928) and Arnold H. Taylor (b. 1929) illustrate this point. Both of them, as previously noted, had done M.A. theses on black topics but for various reasons wrote dissertations on other themes. For Toppin, the turning point back came in the 1960s when he was offered a contract by Doubleday for a book in their Zenith series of black history volumes under the general editorship of John Hope Franklin.[53] The publication of Taylor's 1963 dissertation (on *American Diplomacy and the Narcotics Traffic, 1900-1939*) by Duke University Press in 1969 put him in a good position to pursue his longstanding interest in black history. Financially supported like others, with research grants and fellowships from ACLS, the National Endowment for the Humanities, and the Ford Foundation, he began work on what became *Travail and Triumph: Black Life and Culture in the South since the Civil War* (1976). Particularly striking was the career of David L. Lewis (b. 1936), a product of Fisk University who had been trained in French history at Columbia University and the London School of Economics. He came into black history quite by accident when a Fisk classmate, who was a college professor in England, recommended him to Penguin Books for a biography of Martin Luther King, Jr. Once Lewis had written *King: A Critical Biography* (1970), he realized that there was a large unmined area of twentieth century Afro-American cultural history to be investigated, and while by no means discarding his interest in European history, Lewis turned to what became his monograph on the Harlem Renaissance, *When Harlem Was in Vogue* (1981).

Moreover, the legitimization of black history had ramifications in the policies of publishers and foundations and in the activities of learned societies that functioned in a circular way to reinforce the swelling tide of research and publication in the field on the part of scholars of both races.

Among the publishers, Hill & Wang had been the only firm to embark upon a deliberate program of issuing books in black history and culture prior to the 1960s. Lawrence Hill and Arthur Wang came from radical political perspectives that provided the source for their interest in the subject. By the end of 1959 they had laid plans for publishing reprints of selected literary classics by black authors and a new survey volume on American Negro history.* Despite the idealism behind their effort, Hill and Wang were not "dummies" and correctly sensed that such books would have reasonable sales, although not until the end of the 1960s would they become really substantial. A few years later André Schiffrin, a Jewish refugee from Nazi-occupied France and an old socialist and admirer of Norman Thomas, also deliberately sought to publish significant books on black history and the civil rights struggle when he became director of Pantheon Books in 1962, even though at the time he did not anticipate that they would make much money. His efforts were part of a larger social interest that also led him to publish other major works on the history of the underclasses.

Then, in 1965-66, Oxford University Press and Atheneum decided to make Afro-American history an area of concentration. Although Alfred

---

* Wang and Aida Donald decided to commission a short survey of black history for the series in American history that she was editing for the firm. Approaches were made first to Rayford Logan and John Hope Franklin, neither of whom was in a position to undertake this task in view of the books they had already published covering similar ground. At this point they turned to August Meier, then an unknown historian who, while a graduate student at Columbia University, had come to the attention of Aida Donald's husband, David Donald. Because of his interdisciplinary approach, Meier later asked Elliott Rudwick, who was trained in sociology, to co-author the book that became *From Plantation to Ghetto* (1966).[54]

Knopf, Jr., president of Atheneum, had inherited from his parents and from his youthful contacts with blacks an appreciation of the significance of the field, the impetus for developing a series came from a young editor, Robert J. Zenowich, whose inquiries among history professors had revealed a need for books in black history. Similarly at Oxford it was not a matter of sentiment or moral purpose, but of a sensitive editor looking for books on important historical issues and becoming aware relatively early that here was a significant area of interest. Sheldon Meyer, soon after his arrival at Oxford in the mid-1950s, had arranged to have Woodward's *Strange Career of Jim Crow* put into paperback, and a year or two later had commissioned Benjamin Quarles to write *Lincoln and the Negro*. Yet though both books sold well, it was still some time before Oxford decided to make black history a major area of concentration. By the time it did so, Richard L. Wentworth, director of Louisiana State University Press, was similarly alert to the way things were moving. With his press having on its list a substantial number of relevant titles, which had been accumulated as a by-product of its publishing program in southern history, he decided it would be worthwhile to have an exhibit at the ASNLH's 1966 convention in Baltimore. Wentworth thus established a precedent that other white publishers followed when black history became a truly "hot field" in 1968.[55]

Such efforts paved the way for the major publishing programs that emerged by the 1970s: Oxford, LSU, and, after Wentworth moved from Baton Rouge to Urbana, the University of Illinois Press. Pantheon, which had brought out James McPherson's *The Negro's Civil War* in 1965, had also become a major publisher in the field, though known less for the number of books on its list than for their importance. Then by about 1968-69, simultaneously with the explosion in black history and black studies courses, numerous book publishers jumped on the bandwagon. By the 1970s publishers without books in black studies found themselves in an awkward and embarrassing position. For example, distinguished university presses like Princeton and Harvard, which had just about ignored black history over the years, during the late 1970s and 1980s were issuing important monographs in the field.

Meanwhile by 1970 fellowship-granting agencies from the NEH to the Ford Foundation were also giving decided encouragement to research in black history both through the rapidly expanding regular grant programs and through specific fellowships designed to support work in black and/ or ethnic studies, as well as the somewhat later affirmative action programs for minority scholars. Although these agencies could not supply us with systematic information, acknowledgments in dissertations and published monographs, as well as information from our interviews, make the scholarly debt to them very evident. Indeed, it is not too much to say that the role of the NEH and the Ford Foundation in particular had an impact analagous to that of the Rockefeller philanthropies and the Rosenwald Fund more than a generation earlier.

The legitimization of black history as a scholarly specialty was also evident in the activities of the learned and professional organizations. One aspect of this was the substantial white participation in the latter part of the 1960s at the ASNLH conventions. Beginning in 1966, at the invitation of the energetic program chairman, Walter Fisher of Morgan State College, white scholars, including prominent individuals like C. Vann Woodward, Willie Lee Rose, and Arthur Schlesinger, Jr., appeared on programs that were now being attended by hundreds of people of both races. Only a change of policy around 1970, associated with the rise of black separatism, reversed this pattern. More significant in the long run were participation of blacks and the attention to black history evident in the activities of the predominantly white professional historical organizations.

In the period 1967 to 1969 there was a decided leap in black participation, especially at the SHA, but also in the AHA and the OAH, and this trend was consolidated during the 1970s. How much the development was due to black pressures and how much to the new social consciousness of white historians would be difficult to state. It is worth noting, however, that the kind of highly orchestrated black demands and angry confrontations that occurred in sociology, for example, never developed among historians, and blacks with whom we have spoken have remarked upon the relative openness of the historical profession. Certainly there was nothing in any of the other scholarly disciplines that even remotely approximated the position of John Hope Franklin, who was elected to a second term on the AHA Council at the end of 1969 and served as president of the SHA in 1971, of the OAH in 1974-75, and of the AHA in 1979.

In regard to officeholding, 1967 marked something of a breakthrough at the SHA: in addition to Clarence Bacote, who was still on the council, four blacks held committee posts, including Franklin on the nominating committee and Elsie Lewis on the program committee. The following year Franklin chaired the nominating committee. And in 1969 Jimmie L. Franklin (b. 1939, a specialist in Oklahoma history who would publish a history of blacks in that state in 1982),[56] served on the program committee; Elsie Lewis was elected to fill a vacancy on the council, and John Hope Franklin was chosen as president-elect. During the late 1960s the OAH and AHA moved more slowly. Franklin was finishing his term as an editorial board member for *JAH* and beginning his second term on the AHA Council, but otherwise blacks were holding only minor posts in the two organizations. Since then, however, all three associations have made a conscious effort to secure black representation and participation.

This attempt was most explicitly evident in the record of the OAH, where the nominating committee often paired blacks against blacks and women against women to guarantee representation. Edgar Toppin, Mary Berry, and Nathan Huggins all served terms on the OAH Council during the 1970s. The record does show that where blacks were paired against whites in OAH elections, they lost; on the other hand, when Blassingame was elected to the AHA Council at the end of 1973, he was the top vote-getter on the slate of candidates. In 1978 Huggins was chosen for the *AHR* editorial board and a few years later also joined the AHA Council. After the AHA structure was reorganized at the end of the decade, Berry became one of the three vice-presidents. Blacks were now fairly regularly elected not only to councils but also to program, nominating, and other committees. The SHA, for example, had an unbroken record of blacks serving on the program committee beginning in 1971, and two were on that committee both in that year and a decade later. In this organization, moreover, two more blacks, Edward Sweat and Jimmie Franklin, served on the council, and the SHA was also notable in that Jimmie Franklin and Arvarh Strickland each served a term as chair of the nominating committee. (On the other hand, the first black to serve on the *JSH* editorial board would be Thomas Holt in the early 1980s.) John Hope Franklin deliberately chose a black as chair of the program committee each time he was an organization's president—Edgar Toppin at the SHA, John Blassingame at the OAH, and the Africanist Joseph Harris of Howard University as co-chair at the AHA. This growth in the number of blacks active in the affairs of these associations was partly a reflection of the rising number of Negro historians. Yet there was still a marked tendency for this participation to be largely concentrated among a few names— Bacote and Lewis until they retired from teaching; John Hope Franklin, Blassingame, Berry, Strickland, Jimmie Franklin, Huggins, and Toppin; and, beginning at the end of the 1970s, Nell Painter.

As noteworthy as the record of officeholding were the consolidation of the black presence on convention programs and the numerous sessions devoted in whole or in part to papers relevant to Afro-American history. As Lawrence Towner, chair of the AHA's program committee in 1968, reported: "I doubt . . . that there has been an Annual Meeting in the past ten years where at least one aspect of Negro history has not been discussed. But, in 1968, Negro history has become 'Black' history, and it abounds." With the ballroom session commemorating the centennial of Du Bois's birth, chaired by Woodward, "for openers, there were at least eleven other sessions that dealt with race in America and in the world. The only subject more popular was the scarcity of 'Black' historians possibly open to job offers."[57] In part, both the increasing attention to black history and the growing number of black participants reflected the flowering of doctoral research in the field that began in the late 1960s, but it also was rooted in the conscious efforts of the learned societies to respond to the issues raised by blacks, feminists, and New Leftists. It seemed that if history was going to deal with subjects from the bottom up, it needed to have new faces, unknown but potentially productive scholars—in short, to recruit convention participants from the bottom of the profession as well as the top.

This kind of response to the new realities of the profession was made especially explicit in the case of the SHA. In this organization black attendance had visibly increased starting with the Richmond meeting in 1965. Black participation on convention sessions rose gradually from two in 1966 to eight in 1969. For 1970 the program committee chair, Richard Current, made a special effort to see that Negroes and women were well represented, though with disappointing results on both scores, the number of black participants falling to three. On the other hand, ten of the sessions dealt in whole or in part with black Americans and race relations. The next year under Franklin's presidency, and at his directive, the search for fresh faces was intensified. For the first time the program committee sent invitations to submit proposals not only to the usual select group of institutions but also to departments in all four-year colleges in the South and to most of those outside the South. Toppin, who was chair of the program committee, reported, "Heeding President Franklin's plea to try to increase representation of women and blacks, the committee included on the program fourteen black men, ten white women, and one black woman."[58]

About the same time at the AHA the democratization of the process by which participants were chosen also benefited blacks, who were predominantly to be found among the less well-known younger scholars. The program committee chair for 1972 reported that "it is fair to say now that all remnants of 'old boyism' or any other form of favoritism have been cast aside in light of the fact that a large part of the last three programs originated in letters to the committee." Moreover, in an effort to "serve a broad spectrum of interests" and represent the areas in which "some of the most substantial and rewarding research [is] currently under way," the 1972 program had a heavy emphasis on social history, psychohistory, and black studies.[59]

Although the information available concerning OAH conventions during the 1960s is erratic and incomplete, it is clear that both black historians and Afro-American history were now fairly consistently represented at the annual meetings of all three organizations. In addition to sessions devoted solely to Afro-American history, there were often papers dealing with the black experience on panels concerned with broader themes—a sign of the degree to which black history was becoming more integrated into the mainstream of the writing of U.S. history. It is true the number of sessions and papers relevant to Afro-American history and the number of black participants fluctuated considerably from year to year—evidently largely a function of the conscientiousness of the program committee member charged with responsibility for this area. Still at the AHA in 1979 there were at least seven sessions on black history and eighteen Negro participants. At the SHA during the mid- and late 1970s there were often as many as a dozen blacks on the program, and they represented only a small proportion of participants on sessions devoted in whole or in part to some aspect of Afro-American history.

The legitimization of the field was further seen in the space accorded to black history in the pages of the learned journals. People identified with black history were now being appointed to the journals' editorial boards. These included not only Franklin and Huggins, but also whites like Rose, Williamson, Harlan, Meier, and Rabinowitz. All of the major journals had an unprecedented number of articles on or related to black history. Ten such essays appeared in the *AHR* in this period. The *JAH* carried relevant articles in all volumes except two. These included three Pelzer Award essays, a sign of the profound interest in black history among so many graduate students at the time. And for a period in the early and mid-1970s, the *JSH* almost read like a *JNH*, with a high of eleven articles on black history in 1976. Journals such as *William and Mary Quarterly* and the *Journal of Social History* also served as vehicles for the publication of important scholarship on black topics.

It is true that virtually all of this output came from white scholars. Ironically, the growth in the number of Negro historians notwithstanding, articles by blacks in the mainstream learned journals were fewer in the 1960s and 1970s than they had been in the 1950s. For whatever reasons, to the disappointment of journal editors, blacks seldom submitted manuscripts to these publications; rarer still were the contributions that survived the rigors of the refereeing process. Negroes were reviewing books in increasing numbers, however. But outside of Franklin's presidential addresses, blacks were represented in the journals of the three major professional organizations only by Blassingame's two essays in the *JSH*.*

Paradoxically, the legitimization of the study of the black past at the end

* Except for Franklin's presidential address, the first essays by blacks to appear in the *JAH* since Quarles's two were Armstead L. Robinson's "Beyond the Realm of Social Consensus: New Meanings of Reconstruction for American History," *JAH* 68 (Sept. 1981); and David L. Lewis's "Parallels and Divergencies: Assimilationist Strategies of Afro-American and Jewish Elites, 1900 to the early 1930s," ibid., 71 (Dec. 1984).

of the 1960s—the recognition among white historians of its importance both as a specialty and as an integral part of American history—coincided with the cresting among some black historians of a nationalist and separatist perspective. At the very time that whites were more interested than ever before in exploring the black experience, this separatist line of thinking called into question the very propriety of whites undertaking research in black history altogether.* Nationalist historians, calling for a new "black history" as contrasted with the old "Negro history," criticized the hopeful integrationist assumptions underlying the writing of preceding generations of black historians.

Harding and Stuckey—who had spent some months at Harding's Institute of the Black World—were prominent among the proponents of the new black history. Both perceived a radical disjuncture in the kind of history-writing that Woodson and his successors had done and the kind of history-writing that the era of Black Power demanded. In Harding's words, just as the "political" struggle was being transformed from "a battle in which we sought to be accepted on the terms by which this nation defined itself" to a "struggle for the power of self-definition and self-determination," so the old "Negro History" was being challenged by the new "Black History." The two men acknowledged the debt that the present generation owed to the earlier generations of black historians. Yet, as Stuckey maintained, with the waning of the blacks' faith in America, "The Negro history movement has had its day." Since the time of George Washington Williams, Harding observed, scholarly "Negro History" had been characterized by "its attempt to reveal the 'contributions' of blacks to the American saga"; its emphasis on black heroism in the wars; its call for racial pride and for continued struggle to enter the mainstream of American life; its claim to be primarily interested in objective truth, while "writing history through tears." Stuckey had a similar evaluation: "The historians of the Negro History movement, though critical of America, did not condemn America for her crimes against black people. So strong was racism in American life that all of those involved in this movement concentrated their efforts on using history to prove the black man's humanity and to demonstrate to the larger society that their people were Americans entitled to the rights and privileges of all other Americans." Thus, wrote Harding, "Negro History almost never questioned the basic goodness and greatness of American society." Quarles, for example, wrote history as a way of creating "bridges to interracial harmony"; and the "final impact" of Franklin's work was "one of optimism about the movement of blacks into the mainstream of America, carrying with them certain gifts, but bearing no essential threat to the status quo."[60] In the view of

---

* See Chapter 5 for discussion of the "insider-outsider" controversy.

both Harding and Stuckey, Du Bois with his radical critique of American society (most notably in *Black Reconstruction*) had been a splendid but isolated exception.

In contrast, the proponents of the new "Black History," socialized in a later period, were unable to look at the historical record and still believe in America. They refused "to write with detachment from the agonies of our people. We are not satisfied to have our story accepted into the American saga." Stuckey declared, "As we move away from 'integrating' blacks into American history, we must concern ourselves increasingly with examining that larger society which arrogantly calls itself the mainstream.... Black History must become a searchlight flashing over the terrain of the American night, illuminating hidden horrible ruins." "Black History," wrote Harding, "does not seek to highlight the outstanding contributions of special black people to the life and times of America. Rather our emphasis is on exposure, disclosure, and reinterpretation of the entire American past." "Black History is the constant demand that the cancerous state of America be seen and known." As Harding pointed out, where earlier the tendency was for blacks "to stand with Frederick Douglass, to confess love for a land that refused to love, and to believe that the Black Experience would ultimately be recorded as an evidence in favor of America.... Black History says to Douglass: We are judgment and testimony against the American society." Instead of the Douglasses, the true heroes were the rebels and nationalists who "have stood in judgment upon America"—David Walker, Nat Turner, Martin Delany, and Henry Highland Garnet.[61] Yet for Harding and Stuckey black history was far more than a vigorous critique of American society. It was also the history of the struggle of blacks for control over their lives. For both men the new black history has been celebratory—but not in the old Negro history's way of publicizing individual achievements. Nor is it celebratory in recounting the progress from slavery toward freedom and justice. Rather black history has celebrated the collective accomplishments of the race—the cultural creations of the black folk and the indomitable spirit of black resistance.*

The excitement generated during the late 1960s and early 1970s by the advocates of the new black history has left an ambiguous legacy. Although

---

* Actually in their effort to distinguish between the old Negro history and the new black history, Stuckey and Harding blurred the important differences between Woodson, on the one hand, and Quarles and Franklin, on the other. Moreover, in significant ways, Stuckey and Harding themselves marked something of a return to Woodson's perspective, both in the underlying celebratory quality of their work and in their perception of Afro-American history as particularly the province of black intellectuals.

for a period this perspective won widespread support among younger black intellectuals, it has not informed a great deal of the monographic work of publishing scholars. Harding's *There Is a River* is an attempt to restructure fundamentally the writing of black history. Yet this work of prophesy aimed at a mass audience has thus far had negligible impact on the mainstream of scholarship in the field. Stuckey made a pioneering plea for the study of black—especially slave—culture, but, as the discussion in Chapter 4 indicates, the intellectual roots of the community-and-culture studies of the 1970s are complex and highly diverse. Among black scholars addressing themselves to the other major theme of the new black history—the severe indictment of American society—the most notable work has been Mary Berry and John Blassingame's *Long Memory: The Black Experience in America* (1982). Yet Berry owes much intellectually to Woodson and especially to Rayford Logan, whose books she greatly admires. Although during the early 1970s Berry negatively assessed the capacity of white scholars to write black history, Blassingame was among those who publicly took issue with this kind of separatism, and he was never identified with the proponents of the new black history. Most of the publishing black scholars were never separatists. For some who were deeply affected by the nationalist impulse of the late 1960s and 1970s, this perspective was characterized by considerable ambiguity and even transience, and over the course of the 1970s a number of individuals shifted from a separatist toward a more universalistic orientation. Moreover, well before the end of the 1970s, separatist sentiment was on the wane, and the ideological debate among those scholars who were concerned with such issues was not over nationalist versus integrationist interpretations but rather over a racial versus a Marxist (class) analysis. In the final analysis the impact of the Black Power era, as far as historical scholarship was concerned, seems to have functioned principally like that of the freedom movement of the early and middle 1960s—to raise the consciousness of both black and white intellectuals and to stimulate further an interest in black history, not to establish a particular kind of interpretation.

Although Afro-American historiography was anything but monolithic during the dozen years under consideration in this section, there was indeed a shift in overall perspective and general interpretation. Essentially this was rooted in the new consciousness generated by the black protest movement, reinforced by perspectives from the new social history and by looking at the experience of the oppressed from the bottom up. The very period when black intellectuals had become more severe than ever in arraigning the virulent racism of white society witnessed the appearance of a handful of pathbreaking, monumental studies of the history of that racism by white scholars. Yet at the same time, and more important, there was the culmination of the movement away from looking at black history as largely a question of what whites were doing about blacks, to looking at the experience from the perspective of blacks themselves. Finally, the oppressiveness of white racism notwithstanding, studying the actions of blacks themselves involved a shift from stressing the pathological effects of that oppression (the victimization model) to emphasizing the creative ways in which blacks coped and survived: the cohesiveness and cultural continuity, and the distinctiveness of the black community.

Our next chapter constitutes a case study in the development of the treatment of black culture and community, as evident in the scholarship on slavery. At this point, however, some words are in order about the nature of the broader shift in emphasis from focusing on what whites were doing about blacks to the actions of blacks themselves. Actually the widely held view of a drastic change in emphasis having occurred in this regard[62] is something of an oversimplification. From Woodson and Du Bois on down, black scholars especially have written of the strengths that blacks demonstrated, their achievements in the face of adversity, and the ways in which they expressed their humanity. And while it is true that interested and sympathetic white scholars in the 1950s and 1960s often tended to be concerned with the *status* rather than the *activities and thinking of blacks,* as we have seen there were also significant monographs, notably the studies of black leaders and ideologies and the books on the Civil War era, which focused directly and specifically on what blacks themselves did and said. Still, the events and the new social and intellectual climate of the latter part of the 1960s and the 1970s led to a major transformation in emphasis. The distance traveled is suggested by looking at the scholarship of Leon Litwack — from *North of Slavery* (1961), notable chiefly for its portrayal of discrimination, to *Been in the Storm So Long* (1979), his account of the southern black Reconstruction experience, with its emphasis on how the ex-slaves acted and felt and its refutation of the assumption that they lacked a culture and a cohesive community. The shift can be seen also in Joel Williamson, whose *After Slavery* (1965) dismissed the idea of a distinctive black subculture, even in tidewater South Carolina, but whose *New People: Miscegenation and Mulattoes in the United States* (1980) takes an opposite position. Perhaps the change in perspective is most dramatically illustrated by the views now widely held about the significance of the African background for the Afro-American culture, and the acceptance of the point of view concerning African cultural survivals that had been advanced by Woodson and Du Bois early in the century and had been developed by the anthropologist

Melville J. Herskovits in the early 1940s, but which for years had been dismissed by all but a few liberal white and black intellectuals.[63]

There were several mutually reinforcing reasons for the earlier tendency to undertake a race relations approach with its relatively heavy emphasis on white racism and black social disorganization. Black scholars and intellectuals themselves, from Du Bois to Kenneth Clark,[64] in the effort to expose the evils of racism and promote acceptance of blacks in the American social order, did much to popularize the victimization and pathology model. At the same time most black intellectuals denied the existence of a distinctly black culture (whether derived from Africa or not), whose existence would have posed yet another argument against—and barrier to—the Negroes' assimilation into the mainstream of American society. For historians there had been the salience and obvious importance of the slavery issue and the need to refute Phillips's picture of benign planter paternalism and happy-go-lucky slaves. Then, as the NAACP's desegregation litigation was progressing through the courts, sensitive white historians scrutinized the Jim Crow regulations that had replaced slavery as a mechanism of racial control. Ghettoization, a form of segregation that was perhaps the most obvious manifestation of northern racism, was another important theme for those white scholars who were becoming increasingly sensitive to the issue of discrimination. Historians of the northern black ghettos, drawing to a considerable extent upon the older community studies by black social scientists from Du Bois's *Philadelphia Negro* to St. Clair Drake and Horace Cayton's *Black Metropolis* (1945), examined with varying degrees of emphasis, not only the mechanisms by which American racism created residential segregation and ghetto "pathology" but also the ways in which blacks coped through their own institutions and advancement organizations (although one can scarcely claim that Drake and Cayton's lively description of the black subculture in Chicago functioned as a model for historians). The change in historical perspective during the 1960s and 1970s can be observed in the difference between Gilbert Osofsky's *Harlem: The Making of a Ghetto* (1966) and his 1968 *JAH* article, "The Enduring Ghetto," both of which focused on white oppression and black victimization, and the respective volumes on San Francisco blacks and Negro alley dwellers of Washington by Douglas Daniels and James Borchert, both published in 1980, with their emphasis on the richness and vitality of the life-styles in the black community.[65]

Another dimension to the challenge of looking at the Afro-American past from the viewpoint of blacks themselves lay in the utilization of black-generated sources. The extent to which earlier scholars had found it necessary to rely on readily available white-generated materials—plantation manuscripts, public records, white abolitionist writings (published and

unpublished), and easily accessible periodical and newspaper files—
limited what would be written about how life looked from the black
perspective and the interior dimension of the black experience. (Some
recent research, however, such as Herbert Gutman's use of Freedmen's
Bureau and plantation documents in his *The Black Family in Slavery and
Freedom: 1750-1925,* demonstrates the kind of relevant information that
can be teased out of such sources.) Of course, the recognition of the
significance of using black resources to understand what blacks were
thinking and doing was certainly not unprecedented. To cite just a few
examples: Woodson had made an important beginning in collecting Negro
manuscript materials; Frederic Bancroft had undertaken interviews with
ex-slaves; and the scholarly studies of black thought and leadership that
appeared in the 1950s and early 1960s depended primarily on black sources.
Yet the awareness of the importance of studying how blacks felt and
acted—which we have seen was rising in the early 1960s—now grew
rapidly, and the self-conscious effort to use black sources and exploit
hitherto neglected types of materials that had emerged during the early
1960s accelerated enormously.

A brief review will indicate how over the half century since the ASNLH's
founding the expansion of available sources facilitated the exploration of
the black past from the perspective of blacks themselves. Involved were
three interrelated phenomena: the availability and accessiblity of black-
generated sources; the legitimacy and validity that historians attached to
many of these sources; and technological changes that enhanced the possibilities of using previously neglected materials.

Research into what blacks were saying and doing had been facilitated
first by the acquisitions of three black bibliophiles, whose efforts provided
the base of the valuable library collections that virtually made possible
serious research into the history of race relations and Afro-Americans.
Jesse Moorland's personal library, supplemented later with the books by
black authors that the white NAACP official Arthur Spingarn collected,
formed the nucleus for the extensive holdings developed by Howard
University. Arthur A. Schomburg, whose collection was bought by the
New York Public Library in 1926 with a donation from the Carnegie
Corporation of New York, provided the base for the equally large and
better-known Schomburg Collection. Similarly the books and pamphlets
gathered by Henry Slaughter, an employee of the U.S. Government Printing
Office, greatly augmented the holdings of Atlanta University, which pur-
chased them in 1946. To this day these depositories, along with the less
extensive materials at Fisk University, comprise the largest collections of
book and pamphlet materials by and about blacks.

Technological change provided a major breakthrough after World War

II, with the Negro newspaper microfilming project sponsored jointly by the American Council of Learned Societies (ACLS) and the Library of Congress. Originally proposed at the 1940 ACLS Conference on Negro Studies by L. D. Reddick, then curator of the Schomburg Collection, the project was made possible by a grant from the GEB just after the war. This series of nineteenth-century black newspapers (including complete runs of papers started before 1900 and since discontinued) was available by the middle of the twentieth century. Making widely accessible mostly rare files from scattered locations, this venture revolutionized research into Afro-American history for just about every topic except slavery and opened important windows on the activities and thought of black Americans.[66]

Then came the great age of manuscript collecting. Woodson's donation of materials to the Library of Congress Manuscript Division had been augmented over the years by acquisitions at Schomburg, Atlanta, Fisk, and especially Howard. In 1941 Yale University, with a gift from Carl Van Vechten, had inaugurated its James Weldon Johnson Collection. But this development really hit its stride when the Library of Congress opened the Booker T. Washington Papers at mid-century.[67] By the 1960s the Library of Congress's pursuit of black manuscript and archival collections was itself a sign of the way in which Afro-American history was moving into the mainstream of historical study. Other libraries also actively sought Negro manuscript materials, and an important new depository, the Amistad Research Center, was established in New Orleans. Still, the Library of Congress's subsequent accessions made it the most important single depository.

The microfilming of black newspapers and the scholarly libraries' acquisitions of Negro manuscript collections together provided unprecedented access into what blacks had thought and done, even though these materials shed light chiefly on the elites and contained little about slavery. One source for studying the black view of slavery—the nineteenth-century autobiographies of fugitive slaves and post–Civil War freedmen—had long existed. But Phillips and other white historians dismissed these recollections (which scarcely supported the view of slave and plantation life to be found in *American Negro Slavery*) as biased and propagandistic, often ghost-written by white abolitionists and thus of doubtful validity. As late as the 1950s some historians had questioned Kenneth Stampp's use of even a select group of the best of these volumes.

Of more recent vintage were the transcripts of interviews with ex-slaves, conducted under the auspices of Fisk University and the WPA–Federal Writers' Project.[68] In 1929 Charles S. Johnson, shortly after becoming director of the Fisk University Social Science Department, launched a program of interviewing ex-slaves that ultimately encompassed areas of

Tennessee, Kentucky, and Alabama. Simultaneously John C. Cade, while a professor at Southern University (Baton Rouge), independently interviewed former slaves in Louisiana, publishing a summary of his findings in the *JNH*. In 1934, about the time that both of these programs ended, Kentucky State College professor L. D. Reddick, who had participated in the Fisk project, secured endorsements from Johnson and Woodson and convinced the Federal Emergency Relief Administration to sponsor further interviews. Then in the period 1936-38 came the extensive interviewing done by staff members of the Federal Writers' Project. The folklorist B. A. Botkin published excerpts from the WPA transcripts in 1945, and Fisk University at the same time made the best of its materials available in a mimeographed edition.[69] Still the ex-slave interviews were long ignored by historians.[70] In addition to the view of slavery from the Big House that was regnant in the profession at the time, historians as a group remained leery of utilizing such recollections, particularly since they were obtained so many years after the events described. Consequently Frederic Bancroft stood for decades as a lonely exception to historians' virtual neglect of oral history.[71] Not until the late 1960s, when the use of interviews and oral tradition came into its own, did the potential of these Fisk and WPA materials for understanding the black experience under slavery become widely recognized. By then historians were also beginning to see the possibilities for approaching the study of the mind of the slaves and of the inarticulate black masses in the post-Emancipation period through mining other kinds of oral tradition—spirituals, blues, tales, proverbs, and other forms of folklore.*

The use of such hitherto ignored sources converged with another trend that we have already discussed—the rise of cliometrics, which provided

---

* There had been interest in black folklore, especially among missionary teachers in the South, in the post-Emancipation era; Hampton and Tuskegee, despite their emphasis on instilling white middle-class life-styles, cultivated this interest. During the 1920s this kind of concern was an important ingredient in the intellectual movement known as the Harlem Renaissance. Woodson himself in the middle of that decade advocated the study of black folklore as a way of understanding the question of African survivals in the New World, and for a period helped to finance the research of that noted student of black folk culture, Zora Neale Hurston.[72] Nevertheless, folklore materials remained outside the range of sources utilized in historical monographs. As late as 1969 Gilbert Osofsky, in seeking to convince other historians of the usefulness of the nineteenth-century ex-slave autobiographies as historical sources, refrained from including in his discussion "corroborative materials from the rich folklore of slavery." In "A Note on the Usefulness of Folklore," he explained, "As the published antebellum narrative literature itself has been questioned as a useful historical source, I chose not to further cloud the issue by suggesting that historians take seriously another type of traditionally overlooked source—traditionally overlooked by professional historians, that is."[73]

an effective way of handling the enormous quantities of information to be found in census returns, tax records, estate inventories, voting records, and legislative roll calls. Much of this material was white-generated, but under slavery white records often provided more data about black slaves than about average whites. In any case, these sources offered important information about blacks — both inarticulate and elite — ranging from the structure of the black family in slavery to opinions and behavior of black legislators in Reconstruction South Carolina.* The use of such kinds of material was not unprecedented. J. Franklin Jameson and Carter G. Woodson had been aware of the possibilities in manuscript census data; Luther Porter Jackson had combed the records of numerous county courthouses; John Hope Franklin had also exploited such materials; David Katzman had laboriously recorded and counted by hand the census data on blacks in nineteenth-century Detroit. Now at the end of the 1960s computer technology facilitated a revolution in the writing of black history comparable to the impact that microfilming had about two decades earlier.

The availability of this computer technology intersected with the fresh kinds of questions historians were asking in their quest for knowledge about the life of the inarticulate masses in general and about the black community in particular. In short, heightened sensitivities about both racial and class injustice and technological change simultaneously led students of black history to utilize materials — from census data to conjure tales — that previously had been virtually ignored by historians but were now recognized as providing rich resources for the study of the black experience. Indeed, the impact of the ideological trends among both blacks and whites working in Afro-American history can be regarded as prompting historians to tap the great storehouse of evidence documenting the existence of community, solidarity, and a distinctive cultural tradition in both slavery and freedom.

On the other hand, latent within the dominant historiographical emphases of the 1960s and 1970s were certain paradoxes. For one, amid the call for exposure of white racism, many scholars were faulted for focusing too much on that phenomenon and failing to deal adequately with the life of the black community. At the same time there was a tendency among the very Negro historians who were most desirous of unmasking the sins of white America to pay little attention to that task in their own monographic writings. For example, historians like Darlene Hine and Vincent

---

* Quantitative studies also revolutionized the study of the transatlantic slave trade, a topic that we have not included in our purview. See especially Philip D. Curtin, *The Atlantic Slave Trade: A Census* (1969). Actually most of the statistical work for this volume, completed before the widespread use of computers by historians, was done with a calculator.

P. Franklin,* although feeling strongly about the importance of exploring this subject, in their respective monographs on the struggle against the southern white primary laws and on black education in Philadelphia focused not on the exposé of white oppression but on reporting how blacks creatively organized themselves to battle discrimination.[74] Moreover, in certain of the most valuable studies of black culture and community—volumes like Gutman's *The Black Family in Slavery and Freedom, 1750-1925* (1976) and Borchert's *Alley Life in Washington* (1980)—the emphasis on the strengths of that community and the uniqueness of its culture obscures the impact of the oppressive white society in which it developed.[†]

In addition, within the research addressing itself to the theme of black community, culture, and solidarity were tendencies that have led in important new directions. First, in studying the inarticulate as part of the total black community, historians could not in the long run ignore class divisions and tensions between the masses and the elites. In the late 1960s the themes of unity, solidarity, nationalism, and community inhibited exploration of such class divisions (even though critiques of black elites to be found in E. Franklin Frazier's *Black Bourgeoisie* [1957], Nathan Hare's *Black Anglo-Saxons* [1965], and the works of Frantz Fanon enjoyed considerable vogue among militant black activists). For example, in 1968 at the Johns Hopkins Institute of Southern History, David Rankin's paper on class divisions among New Orleans Negroes during Reconstruction received a hostile reception from both black and white participants. Yet at the very time, important research on such cleavages was under way. Katzman, like the black members of the caste and class school of behavioral scientists from Allison Davis[75] to St. Clair Drake, emphasized both class and community. By the early 1970s Thomas Holt was beginning to examine the very important questions of social class and color divisions among blacks in Reconstruction South Carolina; Nell Painter soon followed with her critique of the national black leadership elite for its opposition to the Kansas Exodus. In time the existence of internal class tensions within the black community became widely recognized among historians, although paradoxically attention to these cleavages appeared in two very different contexts: as part of a radical-nationalist critique of the mainly moderate and assimilationist elite,[76] and also as part of a nonideological functional analysis of black leadership.[77]

---

* Vincent Franklin, who has been involved in some of the more significant research into the history of blacks and the public school systems, declined to be interviewed for this book.

† There are signs that a more skeptical look at the slave community may be in the offing. See a critique of the trend "toward celebration and even mystification of slave life" in Peter Kolchin, "Reevaluating the Antebellum Slave Community: A Comparative Perspective," *JAH* 70 (Dec. 1983), 581.

In addition, a serious examination of the American black cultural tradition inevitably led scholars to grapple with the degree to which that culture is uniquely black (and to what extent ultimately African) and the degree to which it shares the cultural patterns of white America. Since the end of the 1960s, there has been a movement beyond the study of black culture and community per se to the examination of the process of acculturation (a topic that has been of interest to students of black life in the Caribbean and South America for years). John W. Blassingame touched upon the issue in his treatment of *The Slave Community*. Gerald (Michael) Mullin's *Flight and Rebellion* was perhaps the first monograph to look systematically at the acculturation process. Subsequently came seminal works of Peter Wood, who studied the reciprocal black-white cultural interaction in colonial South Carolina; of Herbert Gutman, whose findings indicated that under the impact of the plantation environment in the southern colonies the slaves by the eighteenth century had refashioned their African social institutions to establish a distinct Afro-American kinship system; of Lawrence Levine, author of the most comprehensive description of the blacks' acculturation from slavery into the twentieth century; and of Ira Berlin, who showed how the complex interweaving of demographic, economic, and cultural factors had by the end of the eighteenth century produced three distinctive Afro-American subcultures—in the North, in the Chesapeake area, and in the Deep South—with their diverse patterns of both assimilation to and distinctiveness from the dominant white social order.[78] Taken together, these studies constitute a sophisticated approach that provides new dimensions to the perennial question faced by historians of the black experience—the way in which that experience is both different from and yet part of the mainstream of American culture and history.

Although certain interpretive trends achieved salience, the study of the black history was characterized by more diversity than ever, as the explosion of scholarship produced an outpouring of articles and monographs on what seemed like virtually every aspect of the black past. Perhaps the most fruitful work was done on slavery (and the slave trade). Certainly judged by book sales and the intensity of scholarly debate, no area was livelier, and a flood of important books on the subject reached its apogee in the mid-1970s. The black urban experience continued to receive attention, and the production of major works on this subject also crested in the mid-1970s. The exploration of the ghettoization process reached its climax, and there appeared several studies on race riots and the beginnings of an investigation into the history of the black industrial proletariat. Following in the path blazed by David Brion Davis and Winthrop Jordan, major works on the history of race relations and comparative race relations in the New World continued to appear. There was a revival of interest in the history of free blacks in the antebellum South; new studies on the interactions between blacks and Indians; and significant probes into the political and economic aspects of the post-Emancipation experience. Books on black leaders and protest movements also loomed large — from the black abolitionists through Booker T. Washington, Marcus Garvey, and A. Philip Randolph to Martin Luther King, Jr. There were especially notable investigations of black activism in the twentieth century, and a significant effort to move beyond the most celebrated individuals and look at the careers of lesser but nevertheless influential figures. There was also a burgeoning of serious interest in such hitherto virtually neglected topics as blacks and the Communist party, the black image in popular culture, black education, the role of black women, and the history of the Negro family.

Thus as black history achieved legitimization as a specialty, and as — along with other forms of social history — it moved to the center of the stage of American historiography, it has become a highly pluralistic field. It was a paradox that this legitimization was achieved at the time that the black separatist viewpoint crested — a situation that would, as we indicate in Chapter 5, lace that newfound legitimacy with some ambiguity. Paradoxically also, at the very time that black history-writing was, probably more than ever before, infused with explicit value judgments, important historical work on the Afro-American experience was also being done with singular detachment along purely functional lines. Full of vitality, black history exhibited a diversity of approaches and subject matter that augured for a lively future.

CHAPTER 4

The Historiography of Slavery:
An Inquiry into Paradigm-Making
and Scholarly Interaction

IN THE PRECEDING CHAPTERS we have described how historians, their personal intellectual trajectories intersecting with the changing social milieu, came to their interest in and research on blacks in America. We have sought to illuminate the process by which Afro-American history moved from the peripheries into the mainstream of American history. We have also observed how, at the same time, the transformation of the social and intellectual environment in which historians were working encouraged shifts in the major lines of interpretation about the Negroes' role and experience. In addition, we have had something to say about the debt that certain contributors to the field owed to their professors and other scholars. But we have not systematically examined the way in which individual historians working in black history interacted with each other and the extent to which such interaction shaped the changing modes of analysis and interpretation.

The query we raise here is to what extent fresh schools of interpretation—or new paradigms, if one pleases—are the product of a general social climate impinging upon the consciousness of a number of individual historians, and to what extent they were the fruit of seminal works shaping a generation of scholarly research and creating a new wave of historiographical interpretation. Given the amount of scholarship on slavery, the particularly dramatic changes in interpretation, and the virtually universal acceptance by the early 1970s of a new viewpoint about the nature of the peculiar institution and the life of the bondsmen, an analysis of slavery historiography over the past several decades provides a particularly useful case study through which to examine this question.

Reviewing the historical literature of the last half century, one can identify three distinct bursts of slavery scholarship. The investigation of slave resistance crystallized in the late 1930s. The landmark monographs by Kenneth Stampp and Stanley Elkins appeared in the 1950s. And studies of slave culture and the slave community came to prominence at the beginning of the 1970s.

Slavery studies had been very much on Woodson's agenda,[1] although except for Lorenzo J. Greene and J. Hugo Johnston, the Woodson group focused their research primarily on free blacks. In the view of ASNLH's founder, the chief problem with U. B. Phillips and his followers was that they wrote from the perspective of the masters rather than the bondsmen. Woodson castigated *American Negro Slavery* for its "failure to understand what the Negroes have thought and felt and done . . . the failure to fathom the Negro mind."[2] In Woodson's desire to write the history of "Slavery from the Point of View of the Slave," he had hoped at one time to gather systematically documents and testimonies from former bondsmen, but the project had to be shelved for "lack of funds."[3] At the ASNLH's 1936 convention L. D. Reddick summed up the perspective of this generation of Negro scholars when he declared that the vein of research depending upon plantation records and travelers' "superficial impressions" had been "virtually exhausted," and that with the publication of Helen T. Catterall's volumes of judicial cases, there were "but two important aspects of the field unexplored. First, there is need for a thorough study of the attempts to break the system by the slaves through suicide, flight, individual resistance and group insurrection. Secondly, there is not yet a picture of the institution as seen through the eyes of the bondsman himself."[4]

Such observations, although they foreshadowed much of the future research, had no discernible influence on subsequent publications. On the one hand, the effort to examine the slaves' perspective through interviews with living survivors of southern bondage — an enterprise in which Reddick himself participated — would not inform historical monographic publication until about 1970. On the other hand, at the very time Reddick was speaking, revisionist research on slave resistance was actually already underway, being undertaken by graduate students in certain northern universities. Especially notable was the work being done by Harvey Wish and Raymond and Alice Bauer[5] in Melville J. Herskovits's seminar at Northwestern and by Herbert Aptheker studying at Columbia. As we have suggested in Chapter 2, it seems reasonable to infer that this kind of convergence of research interests, like that involved in the studies of black abolitionists being undertaken autonomously about the same time by Benjamin Quarles, Philip Foner, Aptheker, and Charles H. Wesley, was related to the liberal reformism and radical agitation of the Depression era.

Although the well-known and often-cited studies of Wish, the Bauers, and Aptheker were developed quite independently of Woodson, their findings appeared in the *JNH* and were warmly welcomed by Woodson and other black historians. In turn this material was synthesized in the chapter on "That Peculiar Institution" in John Hope Franklin's *From Slavery to Freedom* (1947). Reflecting the view of slavery held by both black and the few sympathetic white historians at the time, Franklin described a harsh and brutal institution that undermined family life and made the bondsmen a dependent class living in a barren world; and yet in the face of this oppression, many slaves had succeeded in sustaining family ties and demonstrated courageous resistance to the system. Franklin's discussion thus anticipated Stampp's by nearly a decade, even though the climax of this revisionist scholarship of course did not come until the appearance of the latter's *The Peculiar Institution* in 1956.

It is a curious, though unnoticed fact that the two major books on American slavery published during the 1950s—those by Stampp and Stanley Elkins—were by scholars who both had close relationships with Richard Hofstadter, himself the author of the first systematic critique of Phillips's methods: the incisive essay "U. B. Phillips and the Plantation Legend," which appeared in the *JNH* in 1944.

Like much of the sympathetic white scholarship of the Roosevelt era, this article was rooted in a distinctly radical political outlook. Hofstadter (1916-70), who came from a mixed East European Jewish and German Gentile background, had been deeply engaged in the student radicalism of the 1930s as an undergraduate at the University of Buffalo and as a graduate student at Columbia University, where he joined the Communist party. This perspective included a sensitivity to the race issue that was evident in his 1936 senior tutorial thesis at Buffalo, a Beardian-type analysis of "The Tariff and Homestead Issues in the Republican Campaign of 1860," which listed Woodson's *The Negro in Our History* in its bibliography. Two years later Hofstadter's 1938 M.A. thesis at Columbia was on a subject of considerable concern to American radicals at the time, the unfortunate fate of southern sharecroppers under the New Deal's Agricultural Adjustment Administration. Continuing with his Ph.D. at Columbia under Merle Curti, Hofstadter in the spring of 1939 wrote a paper on the abolitionist radical Wendell Phillips (which later became the basis for the essay in *The American Political Tradition* [1948]). It was while teaching at the University of Maryland after receiving his doctorate that Hofstadter composed his most important—and final—discussion of race and slavery in the United States.[6]

"U. B. Phillips and the Plantation Legend" was informed by Hofstadter's lingering radical sensibilities (he had left the Communist party early in 1939) and by his interdisciplinary interests. Both were reinforced by the group of congenial colleagues at Maryland during World War II—Frank Freidel, Stampp, and the sociologist C. Wright Mills. Possibly precipitated by an awareness of Aptheker's recently published volume on slave revolts, the article criticized Phillips on both methodological and ideological grounds. It took Phillips to task for his nearly exclusive reliance on an unrepresentative sample of slaveholders (the large plantation owners) and for allowing his racist assumptions to lead him to virtually ignore readily available accounts like Frederick Law Olmsted's, which failed to fit his preconceptions. Hofstadter also urged an interdisciplinary approach and called for writing from the slaves' perspective: "Let the study of the Old South be undertaken by other scholars who have absorbed the viewpoint of modern cultural anthropology, who have a feeling for social psychology . . . who will not rule out the testimony of more critical observers, and who will realize that any history of slavery must be written in large part from the standpoint of the slave—and then the possibilities of the Old South and the slave system as a field of research and historical experience will loom larger than ever."[7]

Although all who were conversant with the *JNH* felt greatly indebted to this essay, at the time it certainly did not influence the views about slavery held by the general run of American historians. Nor, concluded Arthur Schlesinger, Jr., in assessing Hofstadter's work at the end of the 1960s, did the essay seem to have "much specific" influence on the major monographs on slavery that came later.[8] Yet not only was Stampp a friend and colleague when Hofstadter wrote the article, but Elkins knew him as his doctoral advisor at Columbia during the early 1950s. Moreover, Stampp and Elkins, although their books were published three years apart, were working on their monographs simultaneously, and from a perusal of the printed evidence, it is easy to infer that both authors were working out— in different ways—methodological approaches urged in Hofstadter's article. Indeed, Hofstadter's close relationship with both Stampp and Elkins and the timing of their work raise a tantalizing question about the possible lines of interaction and influence that existed among the three scholars.

At the time that Hofstadter composed "U. B. Phillips and the Plantation Legend," Stampp had just started teaching southern history, was at work on *And the War Came,* and had not the faintest idea of writing a book on slavery. Although one might surmise from the virtual simultaneous appearance of Hofstadter's piece and Stampp's review of Aptheker's *American Negro Slave Revolts* that interaction between the two Maryland professors was likely, Stampp has no recollection of any such discussions. In any event Stampp's decision to do *The Peculiar Institution,* made in 1948, arose not from his earlier contacts with Hofstadter but out of his intense feeling as a radical teacher of southern history that a new synthesis was imperative. On the other hand, in embarking upon this project Stampp quite consciously turned to Hofstadter's critique. In a paper on "The Historian and Southern Negro Slavery," delivered at the 1950 AHA convention, Stampp called attention to his friend's plea for " 'a materially different version' " by scholars with "different points of view and different assumptions" than those that informed Phillips's work. He then proceeded to explore key points raised by Hofstadter: the need to study small as well as large slaveholders; the need to view slavery "through the eyes of the Negro as well as through the eyes of the white master" and to examine how blacks responded to their bondage; the availability of "scattered sources" like ex-slave autobiographies that could be exploited to illuminate the experience and behavior of the bondsmen.[9]

By the time this paper was published in the *AHR* in the spring of 1952, Elkins and his close friend Eric McKitrick were already developing their own approach to the study of American slavery. Hofstadter, as their advisor, encouraged their interdisciplinary orientation, but he had no role in stimulating their interest in slavery and abolition. Their first documentable concern with the subject of slavery—including the germ of the theses Elkins developed in his famous volume—was in a lecture course, interdisciplinary in conceptualization, on selected topics in American history, first offered by both McKitrick at Columbia's School of General Studies and Elkins at the Fieldston School in 1952-53. The syllabus for this course included a treatment of abolitionist behavior, a comparative analysis of New World slavery, and a discussion of "the sociological development of a stereotype." Adumbrating what became Elkins's well-known Sambo thesis, the course plan utilized Harry Stack Sullivan's interpersonal theory of the "significant other" and contained the observation: "Barrack leaders among prisoners in concentration camps: took to behaving like SS Troopers—literally aped their manners."[10]

As they were working on this syllabus, Elkins and McKitrick were likely aware of the Stampp essay in the *AHR*, although Elkins does not specifically remember reading it. It is true that they shared Stampp's racial egalitarianism and psychological environmentalism and that both they and he were interested in slave personality and behavior. But with their ideas germinating quite independently of Stampp, they went in a very different direction. They were self-consciously interdisciplinary in their approach, and apart from that the sources for their ideas seem, if anything, to have been right at Columbia. Their course syllabus shows that their treatment of the abolitionists was at least partly influenced by the kind of question raised in Columbia Professor David Donald's controversial analysis of abolitionist motivations; their attention to comparative slavery was inspired by the work of another Columbia professor, Frank Tannenbaum;[11] and their focus on Sambo undoubtedly owed something to an issue that had been agitating students at colleges in New York City since 1949—the use of Sambo as a synonym for slaves in the widely adopted text, *Growth of the American Republic,* co-authored by Columbia Professor Henry Steele Commager.* Certainly in the early 1950s it was a slightly daring and intellectually exciting thing to argue that Phillips could have been right but for the wrong reasons.

For Elkins, Phillips seemed descriptively more persuasive than Aptheker, but the southern historian's racist explanation of that accommodating behavior was anything but satisfactory: "A generation of research in anthropology and sociology, not to mention one's own experience, offered overwhelming evidence to the contrary. If the American slave was dependent or docile, the explanation had to lie within the system itself."[12] Bruno Bettelheim's essay on the behavior of prisoners in the German concentration camps, which Elkins had read while a Harvard undergraduate, was now recalled as providing an arresting analogy. During the summer of 1954 he and McKitrick were in and out of Hofstadter's office, and their professor would thus have known a great deal about how the thought of these two graduate students was developing. At that very time Hofstadter was himself engaged in critiquing the draft chapters of Stampp's monograph, which the Berkeley historian was sending along as he finished them. Commenting in a letter that summer on the chapter, "To Make Them Stand in Fear," Hofstadter observed: "One of the things I have been struck with . . . is the similarity between the parent-child relation between masters and slaves and the *deliberate* infantilization of the slaves. No doubt you have run into the expression 'They're just like children' over and over again. Seems to me this was a statement of wish that was translated into fact by the planters. They wanted to keep the Negroes childlike, and then of course complained, when they succeeded, that the slaves were irresponsible."[13] It would appear altogether likely that Hofstadter had picked up Elkins's idea and tried it out on Stampp, who rejected it.†

---

* The offending passages were in volume 1, written by Harvard's Samuel Eliot Morison, and were uttered in the context of a Phillipsian evaluation of American slavery (rather curious since Morison's daughter was married to the son of Joel E. Spingarn, president of the NAACP). The evaluation of Reconstruction in volume 2, authored by Commager, reflected the revisionism of Francis B. Simkins and Robert H. Woody's *South Carolina during Reconstruction* (1932).

† It is conceivable that Hofstadter's query might have suggested the passing reference in *The Peculiar Institution* where, speaking of the masters' paternalistic affection for their pet slaves, Stampp wrote: "The slave who had most completely lost his manhood, who had lost confidence in himself, who stood before his master with hat in hand, head slightly bent, was the one best suited to receive

The evidence thus indicates that Hofstadter's influence on the development of slavery historiography was negligible; at most his 1944 essay provided Stampp with some methodological pointers, while his interdisciplinary interests reinforced those of Elkins and McKitrick. Nor did Elkins and Stampp, though they were receiving the benefit of his criticisms simultaneously, have any influence on each other. Moreover, the first chapter of Elkins's *Slavery*, which implies that Stampp by closing the debate on Phillips had thus cleared the way for new directions in slavery scholarship, is misleading. (Because it is misleading, as knowledgeable a scholar as David Brion Davis was prompted to observe that "even for Elkins, Stampp opened the way for new and more dispassionate modes of inquiry.")[15] This particular part of the book was written last, after Stampp's volume was published but also long after Elkins's ideas had crystallized. As a literary device that dramatized what Elkins was saying, it actually obscured the autonomous nature of both men's scholarship.

For all of their differences Stampp and Elkins both wrote from the perspective of the anthropological and psychological environmentalism that by the end of World War II was generally accepted among behavioral scientists. It is true that Stampp wrote a book implicitly suffused with moral judgment while Elkins, equally convinced of the injustice of slavery and racism, consciously sought to make a value-free analysis. Yet each in his own way was the product of a growing racial egalitarianism that was rooted in the reform impulses of the Roosevelt era.

It is important to note, however, that Stampp, though emphasizing patterns of resistance rather than accommodation, was far from insensitive to the wide range in the patterns of slave behavior, and he was concerned with the question of slave personality. In addition, Stampp made a pioneering effort to deal with what has since become known as the "cultural question." The chapter, "Between Two Cultures," was the least successful in the book. It missed the richness of both the slaves' culture and the pervasiveness of strong family ties that recent scholarship has uncovered, and it minimized the existence of African survivals. "In slavery," Stampp wrote, "the Negro existed in a kind of cultural void. . . . The average bondsman, it would appear, lived more or less in a bleak and narrow world."[16] Given the perspectives of nearly all black and sympathetic white intellectuals at the time, Stampp's conclusions were probably inevitable. Although E. Franklin Frazier had done pioneering research on the devel-

the favors and affection of a patriarch. The system was in its essence a process of infantilization—and the master used the most perfect products of the system to prove that Negroes were a childlike race, needing guidance and protection but inviting paternal love as well."[14]

opment of stable patriarchal families under slavery,[17] the stark victimization model portrayed in his *The Negro Family in the United States* (1939) was the accepted view. The existence of black folklore was recognized, but its potential for understanding black life under slavery was not. The one exception, Miles Mark Fisher's *Negro Slave Songs in the United States* (1953), was generally dismissed because of its highly speculative generalizations that seemed to "defy common sense,"[18] and although it was published under the AHA's sponsorship with a grant from the Carnegie Corporation's Revolving Fund for Publications, it had no discernible influence on the course of slavery historiography.* Stampp himself studied Herskovits's work closely, only to discard the distinguished anthropologist's thesis about African survivals in American Negro culture as relevant to an understanding of slave life. Given the milieu in which Stampp was working, it seems almost inconceivable that he could have been led to believe that Herskovits, condemned by most black intellectuals because his findings seemed to lend latent support to racist claims of Negro unassimilability, could have been correct.† That Stampp had dealt with the cultural question the way he did was a reflection of the intellectual milieu, both among blacks and whites of his generation. In retrospect, that Stampp even made the attempt to analyze slave culture is itself the significant thing about the chapter.

Representing the climax of the revisionist scholarship that had been underway since the late 1930s, *The Peculiar Institution* was at the time widely perceived to have functioned much the way in which Stampp himself saw it — as an account that treated slavery from the bondsman's perspective. The volume was warmly received by blacks. Franklin wrote Stampp an enthusiastic letter soon after the book was published; for years the Berkeley professor was called upon to speak at Negro History Week observances; to younger black scholars coming along in the 1950s and early 1960s, *The Peculiar Institution* was, as John W. Blassingame found it to be — "a very liberating experience." On the other hand, Stampp himself had no feeling of being influenced by a Negro historiographical tradition. He did not depend on the work of black historians whose contributions

---

* Fisher, who received his Ph.D. in church history from the University of Chicago in 1945 with his dissertation on spirituals, was a well-known black minister who was the pastor for many years at the White Rock Baptist Church in Durham, North Carolina.

† There had been a heated debate between Frazier and Herskovits on the subject of African survivals at the ACLS's 1940 conference on Negro studies, which reportedly almost ended in a physical confrontation. In any case, one suspects that if Herskovits's interpretation had found its way into Stampp's analysis, it would have served to encourage doubts about the soundness of the work and thus have undermined the effectiveness of his critique of Phillips.

to the subject of slavery were pretty much limited to the colonial and early national periods[19] rather than examining the institution in the South during the antebellum generation on which Stampp focused. Instead, Stampp was writing out of his own radical sensibilities; his monograph was well received because it converged both with the blacks' perspectives on the subject and with the egalitarian views that were achieving acceptance among white intellectuals during the postwar years.

Elkins's 1959 volume, although conceived before *The Peculiar Institution* appeared, functioned as a sharp departure from the Stampp synthesis. It was a book that, while initially not well received, enjoyed a considerable vogue in the mid-1960s, only to serve as a storm center of historiographical controversy in the latter portion of the decade. Indeed, it raised important and challenging questions that at first glance seem to have shaped the nature of the historical debate over the bondsmen's response to the slave system. It has been frequently observed that Elkins, although wrong, provoked a rich vein of historical inquiry; that nearly every work on slavery in the late 1960s and early 1970s was either explicitly or implicitly attacking him or grappling with the problem he posed. As Stampp, for example, asserted in 1971: "It is no small tribute to Elkins' achievement that his essay should have provided the focus for virtually all scholarly discussion of slave personality for the past decade."[20]

Yet the fate of Elkins's work—initial skepticism on the part of most of the profession, then a brief but extraordinary vogue, followed finally by the furor of intensive and searching criticism—indicates that more was involved than a stimulating intellectual exercise precipitated by a provocative thesis. Actually by the end of the 1960s *The Peculiar Institution* also seemed to be less and less satisfying, and it even became the object of overt attack from younger blacks—Stampp himself recollecting that the criticism descended rather "abruptly" at the spring 1969 Wayne State University Convocation on the Black Man in America. At that meeting black militants, creating a confrontation over the legitimacy of white scholarship in the field, told Stampp to his face that he had no right to do his book. Indeed, one suspects that if the Elkins volume had not been a lightning rod deflecting criticism away from Stampp, *The Peculiar Institution* might well have become the principal focus of the debate rather than ultimately becoming largely ignored. Just as the contributions of Stampp and Elkins were the products of the rise of a racially egalitarian viewpoint during and after World War II, so the perception of the inadequacies inherent in the Stampp synthesis and the bitter criticism of Elkins were rooted in the new social climate created during the 1960s.

As indicated in Chapter 2, the initial reception to Elkins's book in the profession, as represented in reviews by major historians (few of them with any significant expertise in the study of Afro-American history), had been overwhelmingly unhappy with both his model and his methodology. In addition other negative assessments appearing in journals not seen by most historians came close to the heart of the kinds of argument that would dominate the later debate. There was the review by the anthropologist and Caribbeanist Sidney Mintz, which dissected the unwarranted assumptions in Elkins's cross-cultural analysis and prefigured later criticisms regarding the nature of Latin American capitalism and servitude. There was the critique in *Science and Society* offered by the then unknown Marxist, Eugene D. Genovese, written from his neo-Hegelian point of view. Finally, there was the essay in the *Negro History Bulletin* by Earl E. Thorpe, who, pursuing his interests in psychohistory in his own way, produced an avant-garde critique containing the most thoroughgoing challenge to the concentration camp analogy that had yet been published. Slavery in the New World, argued Thorpe, was simply a very different kind of institution than the concentration camp where death was always imminent. Slaves did not suffer destruction of their personality or become infantilized; rather, expanding on a concept formulated by Stampp, Thorpe argued the slaves found in the system enough "elbow-room" to lead relatively normal lives.[21]

Among black intellectuals the early critiques offered by Thorpe and Franklin were unusual. Frazier in the preface to the paperback edition of *Black Bourgeoisie* in 1962 wrote that "slavery was a cruel and barbaric system that annihilated the Negro as a person, a fact which has been well-documented and substantiated" in Elkins's recent book.[22] With unconscious and pardonable exaggeration Sterling Stuckey would later remark in dismay: "It is particularly worth noting that his [Elkins's] work went virtually unchallenged among Negro historians. Apart from brief but incisive comments from Ralph Ellison, there was no substantial challenge from blacks."[23] Moreover, certain sympathetic white historians, especially among the younger generation who were not yet widely known (and some of whom were still in graduate school), found the book not only provocative but also suggestive. For example, Carl Degler, August Meier, William Chafe, Robert Zangrando, and Howard Zinn found the volume's interdisciplinary and cross-cultural approaches stimulating; more important, by offering an environmental explanation of slave behavior, it eliminated the need for demonstrating extensive rebelliousness to vindicate the equality of races and the humanity of the Negro. For them the concentration camp was not an accurate description of slave society, but a useful analogy that helped explain one extreme variety of slave behavior, and, together with the comparative analysis of New World slave societies, presented a suggestive, heuristic explanation of why slave revolts in the United States were relatively infrequent. In addition, the way in which Elkins accounted for accommodating behavior on the part of many slaves suggested the plasticity of human behavior. As Zinn put it in 1964: "The 'Sambo' personality which Stanley Elkins so provocatively discussed in his book *Slavery* . . . becomes explainable as the product of the plantation's closed society. That personality also becomes, Elkins suggests, reversible. And indeed, the proud Negro demonstrator today appears by the thousands in exactly those little towns and hamlets of the Black Belt that produced silence and compliance half a generation ago."[24]

That Zinn, the militant activist who had been intimately involved with the southern freedom movement, should credit Elkins with having "helped me to find a direction for my own thoughts,"[25] at first appears surprising; yet his comment dovetailed with the apogee around 1964 of the popularity of the victimization model among blacks and their white allies. As we have observed in Chapter 3, that model had long been propagated by black social scientists. Discussions of the Negro family and of conditions in the urban ghettos owed much to their monographs. Perhaps the most influential had been Frazier's *The Negro Family in the United States* (1939), an analysis whose roots can be traced back to W. E. B. Du Bois's *Philadelphia Negro* (1899) and *Atlanta University Studies*.* Moreover, Frazier's description of the *Black Bourgeoisie* (1957), portraying the life-style of the black elite as a pathological exaggeration of what was worst in white upper-class society, was widely admired among young activists. It was scarcely coincidental that Kenneth Clark's influential contributions to the pathological model of black behavior under the stresses of white racism — his psychological study of the harmful impact of segregation on black children's personalities, *Prejudice and Your Child* (1963), and his somber discussion of life in the Harlem slums, *Dark Ghetto* (1965) — appeared amid the cresting of the wave of guilt feelings that the nonviolent civil rights demonstrations were arousing among many whites. In this context, Elkins's Sambo thesis functioned as a counterpart to the behavioral scientists' victimization thesis. Nearly simultaneously with the publication of Clark's *Dark Ghetto* appeared two widely read popularizations of this victimization model that did make use of Elkins: Charles Silberman's *Crisis in Black and White* (1964) and Daniel P. Moynihan's famous report, *The Negro Family: The Case for National Action* (1965).

Elkins's appeal at this juncture in the history of American race relations lay in his very use of the analogy of that symbol of authoritarian op-

---

* For example, in *The Negro American Family* (1908) Du Bois wrote of the slave system's "deadly work of disintegrating the ancient Negro home and putting but a poor substitute in its place."[26]

pressiveness: the concentration camp. Here was a theme that, however uneasy people were about the Sambo stereotype, converged both with the arguments of black militants, who were arraigning white racism in increasingly harsh terms, and with the guilt feelings now to be observed among many whites. As Genovese observed, "If Elkins' defense of the Sambo stereotype disturbed blacks and white liberals, it also reinforced some of their own major arguments." The precedent for employing Elkins's thesis to arouse white guilt feelings had been established in 1960 in Nathan Glazer's review of *Slavery* in *Commentary*. Distorting what Elkins had written and elevating the concentration camp to much more than analogy, Glazer framed the question not as "Why Sambo?" but as "Why was American slavery the most awful the world has ever known?"[27] At the time the message was not popular and the book itself had only lackluster sales—a total of 1,800 copies during the four years following its publication. Then, by the time Grosset and Dunlap issued a paperback edition in the spring of 1963, the whole civil rights movement, both North and South, had exploded and sales promptly took off, averaging about 25,000 copies annually over the next few years. The volume had numerous class adoptions, partly because it was a highly provocative teaching tool, whether or not a professor agreed with it, but even more because its cogently presented historical argument provided an intellectual basis for the rising tide of white concern that was helping to legitimate black aspirations. To an audience far broader than the one Elkins reached directly, Silberman in 1964 presented an extended summary of what he called "the most brilliant and probing study of slavery in the United States." The *Fortune* magazine journalist explained: "Nothing could be more foolish or more damaging to the Negro cause, than to refuse to face the harsh reality of what three hundred fifty years of white oppression have done to Negro personality and behavior. Uncomfortable as we all may find the truth, the truth is that . . . the 'Sambo' of Southern folklore, was a reality and to a considerable extent still is." Finally, the height of the popularization of Elkins's thesis came with the prominence Moynihan accorded it in his controversial report, arguing that slavery greatly contributed to the contemporary "pathology" and "instability" of the Negro family and reiterating Glazer's notion that U.S. slavery was the "most awful the world has ever known."[28]

For two or three brief years Elkins continued to be in vogue. Indeed, those scholars among our interviewees who used *Slavery* in their classes did not at first find even black students taking exception to it. One black professor teaching at northern colleges during the mid-1960s recalls that Negroes in his classes actually responded positively to the book; they liked it because they hated slavery, and Elkins's discussion made the white man guilty.

Yet at the very time when the victimization model was enjoying its greatest vogue, when the views of writers like Clark and Silberman were commanding widespread attention, and even before the release of Moynihan's report to the general public, developments in the civil rights movement and changes in the Negro mood were prompting a reassessment. The protest movement itself, through its courageous actions and its victories, stimulated race pride among blacks — a spirit of self-worth, a sense of the possibility of social change that could be effected through black collective efforts, an affirmation of the uniqueness of Afro-American culture, and a celebration of the blacks' life-styles, their capacity to endure, their singular contribution to religion and music, their special speech and food, ethics and psychology. Such ideas, spurred in part by the fiery nationalist rhetoric of Malcolm X, were being discussed in movement circles as early as 1962-63, although at the time the movement's major thrust, epitomized by the tactics of Martin Luther King, Jr., was to expose the unfair burden of white racism. Meanwhile, white activists, impressed by the militance of the blacks with whom they interacted, also developed a negative assessment of the victimization-pathology model: it certainly did not fit the Negroes whom they knew on picket lines and freedom rides or in southern jails. Moynihan's report seemed to many blacks and white supporters less an indictment of white society than a case of "blaming the victim." Thus dictates of protest strategy, fused with the swelling sense of pride and militance among blacks and the growing salience of nationalist sentiments, rendered illegitimate the pathological model of Negro behavior and spelled the downfall of the Elkins thesis that had been so fashionable. As a matter of fact, it would seem to be scarcely coincidental that the Elkins thesis became the object of systematic attacks not long after the appearance of Moynihan's report. What had happened was that, as Elkins later recalled, "without anyone's quite realizing it the entire 'damage' argument — as applied to Negro life in America — had become ideologically untenable."[29]

Paralleling the shift in outlook among the activists was the development of a significant body of literature affirming the existence of a viable Afro-American culture. There were two volumes on black music—LeRoi Jones's *Blues People: Negro Music in White America* (1963), and the white ethnomusicologist Charles Keil's *Urban Blues* (1966). Joseph R. Washington's *Black Religion* (1964) stressed the folk origins of black religious belief. Ralph Ellison also made a contribution to the discussion when in 1964 he finally published the assessment of Gunnar Myrdal's *An American Dilemma* that he had composed twenty years before. This influential review essay was critical of the black and white social scientists, epitomized by Myrdal, who had seen the distinctive aspects of Negro culture and personality as a product of social pathology and had ignored autonomous black cultural development. Discussing the positive qualities in black lifestyles, Ellison observed: "Much of Negro culture might be negative, but there is also much of great value, of richness, which, because it . . . has made their lives more meaningful, Negroes will not willingly disregard."[30] At this juncture, another figure from the era of Myrdal's study, St. Clair Drake, whose classic *Black Metropolis* had certainly gone far beyond the victimization model, made a similar point. Writing in a prestigious anthology, interestingly enough co-edited by Clark, Drake dealt explicitly with both victimization and the "distinctive ethos" of a viable black subculture.[31]

A number of behavioral scientists were quick to draw their cue from the black protest movement. The debate over both the Moynihan report and the 1966 White House Conference "To Fulfill These Rights" provided the occasion for sociologists, both black and white, to point out the "strengths" in black families and the evidence of stable institutions and group cohesion in the black community. Urban anthropologists like Charles A. Valentine as early as 1966 were scathing in their criticism of the notion that blacks had a pathological life-style rooted in a "culture of poverty." The well-known Berkeley sociologist Robert Blauner wrote vigorous statements supporting the concept of a black subculture. Moreover, scholars like the sociologist John Horton and the specialist in sociolinguistics Thomas Kochman published their researches on specific aspects of a vibrant culture shared by black slum dwellers.[32] Such views, it should be noted, had been formulated well before the intellectual stir over black culture that was created by the arguments in Harold Cruse's 1967 volume, *Crisis of the Negro Intellectual*. In short here was a perspective on black life that had crystallized among many movement people and behavioral scientists in the middle 1960s, but that would not appear prominently in the publications of historians until the early 1970s.

On the other hand, it is important to recognize that beginning in 1966 historians like other scholars were living in a new social climate. The late 1960s and early 1970s were the era of Black Power, of the cresting of nationalist sentiment, with its assertion of pride in black distinctiveness and black culture, of widespread talk about a separate black community with values, life-styles, and interests that were different from those of the white community. It was also the period of Lyndon B. Johnson's War on Poverty and the widespread discussion of the necessity of community organization and community action among blacks and other dispossessed groups. In this general context, the slave community and culture formulation took hold, even though the climax of the historical scholarship it inspired would not appear until the War on Poverty was being dismantled, and black separatism and nationalism were on the decline.

In the final years of the 1960s, as historians reassessed the institution of slavery, the sales of Elkins's book soared to new levels, although this was undoubtedly due primarily to the frantic search for suitable supplementary readings, as college professors quite suddenly felt that they had to make their courses relevant to the black revolution. Still it was at this time that the volume became the focus of historiographical debates over the peculiar institution. The critiques of Elkins, coming from a number of directions, were formulated in 1966-67 and began appearing in published form in 1967-68. At first, however, the argument that the evidence of a viable slave culture disproved Elkins's thesis was distinctly peripheral to the discussion. George Fredrickson and Christopher Lasch argued that a prison was a more fitting analogy than a concentration camp. Eugene D. Genovese emphasized the complexities and contradictions in slave behavior and pointed out that Elkins had described not the typical personality of slaves but the limiting case of the slavish personality. In 1970 Stampp in effect brought this kind of discussion to a climax and summed up much current thinking on the subject in his SHA convention paper, "Rebels and Sambos: The Search for the Negro's Personality in Slavery." Aptheker and Elkins, he explained, had "define[d] the two extremes—the outer limits—of possible slave behavior." Over the years Stampp's analysis had grown more subtle than the views articulated in *The Peculiar Institution*: he had developed some skepticism about the methodological shortcomings and overdrawn picture of slave resistance in Aptheker and had come to recognize that he himself was in considerable agreement with Elkins's description of slavery as a closed system, exerting powerful pressures toward dependent, infantilized personalities. "But I would reject his assertions that the master's power was absolute . . . and that southern slaves were almost totally dehumanized. . . . [P]lantation life enabled most slaves to develop independent personalities—indeed provided room for the development of a considerable range of personality types."[33]

In a sense Stampp's paper and the publication the following year of Ann J. Lane's anthology, *The Debate over Slavery: Stanley Elkins and His Critics* (1971), can be regarded as virtually closing the argument with Elkins. One reason for this sense of closure was that by then the discussion of slave behavior was shifting to entirely fresh grounds. The new awareness of black identity and black culture offered a quite different perspective from which scholars, intensifying Stampp's effort to look at slavery from the bondsmen's viewpoint, were able to approach an old problem. By the opening of the 1970s, a rather novel and more satisfying way of looking at the slave response—focusing on the existence of a slave culture and community that in turn functioned as a means of resistance to white oppression and hegemony—was about to sweep the field. As Elkins later observed, the tide of debate had turned again: "Interest is now focused almost wholly upon resistance, resistance to the degradations of the slave regime that took a variety of forms, and upon something that was of scant concern . . . a generation ago, the growth under slavery of a black culture. The two have become inseparable, culture itself functioning as a form of resistance." Of the literature of the first half of the 1970s, "None is primarily concerned with damage; all are preoccupied with resistance and culture."[34] Blassingame's *The Slave Community* (1972) and to a lesser extent Genovese's 1970 article in the *New York Review of Books,* "American Slaves and Their History," have been widely credited with marking the new departure. George Rawick's *From Sundown to Sunup: The Making of the Black Community* appeared the same year as Blassingame's study, and there followed in quick succession over the next half-dozen years Genovese's *Roll, Jordan, Roll* and Peter Wood's *Black Majority* in 1974, Leslie Owens's *This Species of Property* and Herbert Gutman's *The Black Family in Slavery and Freedom* in 1976, Lawrence Levine's *Black Culture and Black Consciousness* in 1977, and Albert Raboteau's *Slave Religion* in 1978.

Given the intensity of scholarly activity on slave life and culture, and the relative suddenness with which the new way of looking at the peculiar institution emerged, the development of this line of interpretation provides an unusual opportunity to explore the extent to which crystallization of such a viewpoint—or perhaps paradigm, if one may call it that—is the fruit of interaction along scholarly networks. At the same time examining how this way of looking at slavery came to be widely accepted as virtually a common sense solution to the debates over slave life and slave behavior illuminates the way in which diverse factors can converge to produce a new line of generally accepted interpretation. To speak schematically, by 1970 the fact that one could now deal with slaves without regarding them principally as victims released black historians from the inhibitions that had seemingly helped to discourage earlier generations of Negro scholars from giving detailed attention to slavery research. At the same time the celebration of black culture provided both white and black scholars an analytical tool that supplied an intellectually satisfying answer to the kinds of questions raised by Elkins about slave resistance. In retrospect the general outline of what happened seems clear. Yet our interviews with the authors of these works revealed a great deal about the complex dynamics involved in the creation of the new consensus concerning what slavery was all about.

Although Stampp had employed the term "slave community" in *The Peculiar Institution,* the first historian to make this formulation central to his analysis and to call for a cultural approach to the slave experience was George P. Rawick (b. 1929), and he had done this eight years before the virtually simultaneous publication of Blassingame's *The Slave Community* and his own introductory volume to the WPA ex-slave narratives. The views on slave behavior held by this radical civil rights activist had undergone a decided shift since mid-century. A supporter of Henry Wallace while an Oberlin College undergraduate, Rawick during the 1950s became a left-wing democratic socialist. He was attracted to pacifists and socialists like A. J. Muste, Bayard Rustin, Dave Dellinger, Michael Harrington, and Merle Curti, his doctoral advisor at the University of Wisconsin. At the time Rawick had been unhappy about what he perceived as a seeming lack of militance among blacks, and about the small number of Negroes he met in an activist organization like the Congress of Racial Equality (CORE). This situation prompted him in 1958—at the time that Elkins was putting the finishing touches on his book—to develop a lecture arguing that the repressive slave system had created among Negroes a dependent personality type. Although they knew nothing of each other, both men were teaching at the University of Chicago at the time; Elkins, hearing of the lecture, requested a copy and then asked Rawick to critique his manuscript.[35] Rawick had a very high opinion of it and was certainly untroubled by the Sambo model, since he too accepted the idea that slavery had been so pernicious that it had all but destroyed people's personalities, a legacy still evident, he felt, a century after Emancipation.

Then during the early 1960s Rawick's views changed sharply as a result of his exposure to the radical escalation of black militance and to fresh intellectual ideas. He remained a CORE activist after moving to Detroit, where he got to know militant young blacks who would later become leaders in the nationalist League of Revolutionary Black Workers, and, more important, he became associated with the interracial Trotskyist splinter group, the Facing Reality Committee, with its connections to the West Indian revolutionary and historian of the Haitian Revolution, C. L. R. James. As early as the spring of 1961 Rawick had reversed his judgment on Elkins—whose book he now regarded as a "brilliant" but "perverse [and] wrong-headed" analysis.[36] In 1963-64, at the very time that the nonviolent direct action movement reached its zenith, Rawick spent several months in London, associating with British Marxists. There he became friendly with James, and with E. P. Thompson. James, who believed that oppressed peoples constantly resisted their oppressors even when they did not openly rebel, reinforced Rawick's disillusionment with Elkins's analysis. Thompson, whose magnum opus had recently been published, supplied

Rawick with the fruitful conception of "working-class culture" for understanding slave life and behavior. For Rawick, as for his friends in the Facing Reality group, the new black militance demonstrated that Negroes were to be the revolutionary vanguard of the American working class. Exploring this thesis in a 1964 essay on "The American Negro Movement" in the English Marxist quarterly *International Socialism,* he ascribed the origins of black militance to the unique aspects of Afro-American cultural development. He now argued that the southern bondsmen had not become brutalized and infantilized and that their opposition to oppression had been rooted in their "community" and culture, especially in the "African cult meetings" that were the seedbed of slave resistance. Four years later in an essay in the journal *Radical America*—and in phraseology that now sounds very familiar—Rawick wrote that slaves "fashioned their own independent community through which men and women and their children could find the cultural defenses against their oppressors," and he iterated his views about the relation between the slaves' religion and their resistance to bondage.[37]

Rawick had arrived at his conclusions too early to be influenced by the Black Power doctrines and the surge of black nationalism in the second half of the 1960s. Indeed, even though Rawick's analysis of the slave community had been formulated at a time of rising feelings about black cultural identity in important sectors of the protest movement and amid the excitement surrounding the Black Muslims, Malcolm X, and the latter's Organization of Afro-American Unity established in 1964, the radical white historian had been explicit about the class basis for his thinking: "Those who think that American Negroes will follow the banner of 'a separate Negro nation' are unable and unwilling to understand the experience of the Negro in America."[38] In short, he believed that the black cultural tradition provided the groundwork not for nationalism, but for making blacks the spearhead of a general revolt of both black and white workers against their capitalist oppressors.

Thus Rawick was neither influenced by nor at the time familiar with the ideas on slave resistance being articulated as early as 1966 by the emerging nationalist scholars, Vincent Harding and Sterling Stuckey, which first appeared in print in 1968 and 1969. Rawick's ideas about a distinctive slave worldview and particularly about religion as a source of slave resistance did bear obvious similarities to those of Harding and Stuckey. But even though—like Rawick—the perspective of these two black historians was in considerable part shaped by their movement experience, and even though Stuckey had long had radical socialist sympathies, he and Harding came to their interpretations through intellectual routes very different from that of the white radical.

Harding, like certain other academicians, white and black,[39] had been impressed with King's success in using Christian symbols and values to inspire resistance to the racist system in the South and with how this undermined the widespread view, articulated most notably by the black scholars Benjamin Mays and E. Franklin Frazier,[40] that black religion had served historically as a mechanism of otherworldly accommodation to the social order. Harding's "Religion and Resistance among Antebellum Negroes," first presented in 1966 and published in 1969, pointed to the prominence of slave preachers and exhorters in virtually all of the slave conspiracies and rebellions about which much was known. Discussing the influence of the spirituals, he conceded that often they had functioned in an otherworldly way but argued that for many slaves "the music and the faith it expressed—and engendered—filled them with a sense of God's awesome calling for their present moment, and supplied new determination to struggle, build, and resist here."[41]

Harding, while keenly aware of the importance of black folklore and subscribing to the view that there was a distinctive black ethos, has never explored systematically in his writings the subject of black culture and the way it both represented and made possible a sense of community. Indeed, the discussion of slave protest in his major opus, *There Is a River* (1981), has a decidedly old-fashioned air. Despite Harding's emphasis on the messianic content of slave religion, his presentation in this volume owes a good deal to the anti-Phillips genre of history-writing of the 1930s and 1940s, and nothing at all to the resistance through culture arguments that loomed so prominently by the 1970s. Instead, it was Stuckey who, in his essay, "Through the Prism of Folklore: The Black Ethos in Slavery," more explicitly developed the thesis that the slaves fashioned "a life style and set of values—an ethos—which prevented them from being imprisoned altogether by the definitions which the larger society sought to impose."[42]

Originally presented at a conference of southern civil rights activists in the spring of 1966, this paper reached a scholarly audience at the ASNLH's 1967 convention and was published in the *Massachusetts Review* the following year. Contending "that the process of dehumanization was not nearly as pervasive as Stanley Elkins would have us believe," Stuckey opened up new perspectives by focusing his attention not on any theoretical discussion of personality types or on comparing U.S. slavery with other systems of oppression, but on the existence of a slave folklore whose "variety and depth" undermined "stereotypical theories of slave personality." Inspired, as we have observed, by Du Bois and Paul Robeson, and impressed with the work on Negro folklore of Alan Lomax and Sterling Brown, Stuckey examined the Negro spirituals as exemplifying a cultural tradition of resistance and protest. He held that overemphasis on the Christian spirit of patience obscured the important reality that "Christianity, after being . . . recast by slave bards, also contributed to that spirit of endurance which powered generations of bondsmen." The evidence in these songs suggested "that the humanity of people can be asserted through means other than open and widespread rebellion." Looking through the prism of folklore, one could witness the slaves "opposing their own angle of vision to that of their oppresssor, fashioning their own techniques of defense and aggression in accordance with their own reading of reality." Thus "slave folklore, on balance, decisively repudiates the thesis that Negroes *as a group* had internalized 'Sambo' traits" and "affirms the existence of a large number of vital, tough-minded human beings who, though severely limited and abused by slavery, had found a way both to endure and preserve their humanity in the face of insuperable odds."[43]

Rawick's thinking, appearing in radical sectarian journals of limited circulation, did not, with one important exception noted below, influence the subsequent development of the monographic literature on black culture and community. On the other hand, we had originally assumed that Harding's and Stuckey's papers were central to this discourse, exercising a profound effect in shaping the new perspective that triumphed in the 1970s. To our surprise this perception was not shared by the scholars we interviewed. Overwhelmingly, even specialists in the history of slavery recalled reading Harding's and Stuckey's essays only after their own views had crystallized. The ideas of these two men — especially those in Stuckey's widely reprinted essay — would be informing the thinking of younger historians coming along in the 1970s. But those who were examining slave life in the late 1960s found in Harding and Stuckey confirmation of conclusions they had already reached on their own.

The one exception to this generalization was Eugene D. Genovese. Genovese (b. 1930) was unusual among historians of the black past. Although during his high-school and college years he had been an important functionary in young Communist circles, ideologically radical concerns were not what led him into his study of slavery. Moreover, Genovese was virtually unique among historians of the black experience in the way in which he learned from other scholars, engaging in a vigorous and fruitful Hegelian-like dialectical exchange of viewpoints with them. In this way both Stuckey and Rawick in particular were influential in shaping Genovese's conceptions about slave life and slave behavior.

Genovese came to his examination of slave life and culture somewhat circuitously. He first was attracted to the study of the planter class, an interest that arose out of the convergence of exposures provided by two Brooklyn College undergraduate teachers — Arthur Cole, the historian of the South, and Hans Rosenberg, the authority on the Prussian Junker class—and by a professor at Columbia's graduate school, Frank Tannenbaum. From Tannenbaum he drew something quite different than Elkins and McKitrick had done; where they were struck with the Latin Americanist's portrayal of the relative openness of Latin American slave systems, Genovese was impressed with Tannenbaum's emphasis on the organic relationship between bondsmen and masters. Here was a conception that made sense to the young Hegelian, and also, it turned out, helped make sense out of Phillips's portrayal of the southern slaveowners' paternalism. In a lengthy review of Stampp's *The Peculiar Institution* for the Marxist journal *Science and Society* in 1957, Genovese dwelt primarily on an issue of interest to slavemasters—profitability. He praised Stampp's opus for exposing the "inherent cruelty of the system" and explicating the deleterious effects it had on the family and other aspects of slave life, but he sided with Phillips on the profitability argument. Genovese concluded, "Curiously, his racial bias helped him to see the economic plight of the South. Since he regarded slavery as necessary to make the inferior Negroes work, he did not feel the need to defend the system as an economically profitable one." (Interestingly enough, Genovese was also debating the matter with his fellow student at Columbia University, Robert W. Fogel, who sided with Stampp's conclusions on the issue.)[44]

Genovese received his doctorate in 1959, the year that Elkins's *Slavery* appeared. For Genovese the volume was fascinating but disquieting—even "shocking"—and he would be grappling with the issues it raised for more than half a dozen years before he came to a satisfying resolution of the problem. In his paradoxical way Elkins accounted for the kind of slave personality that the racist Phillips had described and provided an environmental explanation that helped make sense of Genovese's own skepticism concerning Aptheker's findings of pervasive rebelliousness. As he would write later: "Phillips' view of the Negro slave, with its racist underpinnings, comes out close to the Sambo whom Elkins seeks to explain. His views of slavery present a firmer basis for Elkins' social-psychological analysis than do those of Stampp, whose emphasis on brutality fits into Elkins' controversial and dubious concentration-camp analogy."[45] From one perspective Genovese's own views about planter hegemony and paternalism thus led logically to Elkins's conclusions about slave personality, yet still he felt there was something faulty with Elkins's reasoning, and Elkins had certainly provided no description of the totality of slave behavior. In reviewing the book in 1961 the only alternative explanation Genovese could offer was to adopt Hegel's abstract conceptualization of master-slave relationships centering on the internal contradictions of a system that produced unstable personalities who had the potential for being both rebels and Sambos. Half a dozen years later he had advanced no further. Analyzing "Rebelliousness and Docility in the Negro Slave," a paper presented at the ASNLH convention in 1966 and published the following year in *Civil War History*, he wrote: "I propose to show . . . that Sambo existed wherever slavery existed, that he nonetheless could turn into a rebel and that our main task is to discover the conditions under which the personality pattern could become inverted and a seemingly docile slave could suddenly turn fierce." The slave was the "product of a contradictory environment, all sides of which he necessarily internalized. Sambo, in short, was Sambo only up to the moment that the psychological balance was jarred from within or without; he might then well have become Nat Turner, for every element antithetical to his being a Sambo resided in his nature."[46]

All during the early and middle 1960s Genovese was still seeing the problem in the framework set by Elkins. By 1963 he had become convinced that he would have to give his attention to studying in depth the slaves as well as the masters. In his recollection this decision was rooted not in the excitement generated by the sit-ins and freedom rides and Birmingham, but in the challenge that Elkins posed. Appropriately enough Genovese's original working title was "Sambo and Nat Turner." The volume took a decade to do and in the end turned out to be something far different than would have been possible for Genovese earlier. For by the end of the 1960s he had found a perspective that simply transcended the questions Elkins was asking.

The path to *Roll, Jordan, Roll* was rocky, however. During the second half of the 1960s Genovese recalls being "buffeted around" by various currents and found himself debating on several fronts. He was, as we have seen, still grappling with the issues raised by Elkins. His efforts to rehabilitate Phillips brought criticism from a broad range of blacks and white liberals and radicals. He was not only debating with Stampp, but was also engaged in a vigorous dialogue with the emerging black nationalist historians. Out of the dialectical process would come a new and important synthesis.

To rehabilitate Phillips meant of course to challenge much of Stampp's work. Although the Berkeley historian receives only a couple of passing references in Genovese's *The Political Economy of Slavery* (1965), the book served to enlarge upon his original *Science and Society* critique of Stampp's view of the peculiar institution as a highly profitable capitalist enterprise. In a series of papers over the next two years, Genovese set forth his unabashed admiration for the southern historian.[47] The only problem with Phillips was that his racism had blinded him to the class analysis implicit in his perceptive treatment of slaveowner paternalism and of the organic nature of the plantation community and had led him to see race as "the central theme in southern history." Phillips, Genovese averred, "came close to greatness as a historian, perhaps as close as any historian this country has yet produced." His racism "alone accounts for his lapse from greatness," inhibiting him "from developing fully his own extraordinary insights." Hofstadter's and Stampp's critiques of Phillips were dissected and found wanting: in regard to the matter of slave resistance and docility, for example, "the principal historical questions remain unanswered . . . , but if we must choose between two one-sided views, it is difficult not to regard Phillips' as closer to the norm."[48] On the other hand, Genovese hedged in his praise with so many qualifications that Stampp was led to retort, "With admirers like Genovese, who needs critics?" Although Stampp found unconvincing Genovese's case for a pre-bourgeois planter class,[49] to a remarkable degree Genovese's radical credentials enabled him to single-handedly legitimize Phillips's magnum opus as a work to be taken seriously whether or not one agreed with it. As David Potter wrote, Genovese's "general commitment to a position on the left enabled him to give freshness, originality, and a new focus to ideas that would have seemed mere apologetics if they had been put forward by someone who grew up in the South."[50]

Although native southerners like Potter and C. Vann Woodward accorded his approach a respectful hearing, Genovese's rehabilitation of Phillips was negatively assessed by most historians seriously concerned with studying the black experience. Nor did his open rejection of the view of slave resistance portrayed by Aptheker and Stampp endear him to such scholars. In a paper presented at a 1966 Socialist Scholars Conference he not only pointed to the relative paucity and small scale of slave revolts in the United States as compared to Latin America, but he also dismissed the evidence of day-to-day resistance as constituting not rebellion but "individual and essentially nihilistic thrashing about." He averred that under U.S. slavery "we find the formation of a tradition of recalcitrance but not revolution, action but not politics, dim awareness of oppression but not cumulative ideological growth."[51]

Genovese's bold effort to restore Phillips and to undermine the kind of consensus about slavery that had crystallized following the appearance of *The Peculiar Institution* ran athwart not only of what was now the standard treatment of the subject but also of the views of the rising cohort of black nationalist historians. The paper at the Socialist Scholars Conference, presented just after the slogan Black Power had burst on the national consciousness, launched him into a spirited and extended dialogue with Harding and Stuckey on both the future of black nationalism and the nature of slave behavior.* Genovese recalls that he had first argued with the two black nationalist scholars as early as the ASNLH convention in 1966, and he was certainly present at that organization's meetings the following year and spoke up at the session in which Stuckey read an early version of his paper, "Through the Prism of Folklore." The public record contains only glimpses of the debate over the next few years[52] (and the personal contacts between Genovese and the two black scholars were far more cordial than one might suspect on the basis of the written word). But it is evident that with Harding's emphasis on overt rebellions functioning as a refinement on the older perspective epitomized by Aptheker, Stuckey's approach proved more stimulating, and Genovese's intellectual interaction with the latter was especially intense. It was Stuckey who insisted that Genovese would have to examine the cultural dimension of slave life and forcefully urged him to utilize the insights about the bondsmen's culture offered by Du Bois in his essay on the spirituals in *Souls of Black Folk* and in *Black Reconstruction*. Meanwhile, Genovese continued to take the Black Power phenomenon seriously. He concluded that "so long as white racism persists, separatism will command respectful attention. Far more than the integrationist tendency, black nationalism has expressed the need to overcome a slave psychology and to repudiate all forms of paternalism. . . . Black nationalism reflects, more accurately than integrationism, the historical uniqueness of the black experience in America."[53]

With Genovese's thinking in flux, an encounter with Rawick in October 1968 proved to be decisive. Both men testify to the lengthy and intensive conversations they had over a two- or three-day period at that time. Rawick's vigorous advocacy of the study of slave culture brought Genovese "up short." In substance what happened was that Rawick, arguing from a conceptual framework in which slaves exemplified a working-class culture, enabled Genovese, with his own affinity for Marxist class analysis, to integrate into his thinking Stuckey's insights about slave culture and how it enabled the bondsmen to resist the system. Moreover, Rawick's belief, derived from James, that oppressed peoples found ways of fighting back whether or not they engaged in overt insurrection converged with Stuckey's contention that through their culture slaves were able to express their resistance to oppression in ways other than open rebellion. Genovese now realized that he had to both re-read the plantation records in a new light and examine black sources such as the WPA interviews, folklore materials, and ex-slave autobiographies. In short, as Genovese has publicly acknowledged, he found "the critique of George Rawick indispensable."[54]

---

* The misinformed discussion of the history of black nationalism and the unsolicited advice on the course of the current nationalist wave in this paper, "The Legacy of Slavery and the Roots of Black Nationalism," raised additional hackles among Black Power militants.

In the spring of 1969 Genovese was at Yale, lecturing on comparative slavery in the New World, and that autumn he took up his duties as department chair at the University of Rochester. Rochester at the turn of the decade, with Robert Fogel, Stanley Engerman, Herbert Gutman, and Genovese all on the faculty, was a stimulating milieu for slavery studies, particularly until Gutman and Genovese came to a bitter parting of the ways. The four scholars, lunching together frequently, engaged in lively intellectual discussions. Partly this took the form of exchange of information and data; partly it took the form of mutual criticism; most important was the mutual reinforcement of certain ideas to which all were moving independently. Genovese and the econometricians had much in common in their concern about economic questions, and the latter succeeded in reversing Genovese's views on slavery's profitability; they also turned up data revealing the substantial number of slave overseers, confirming what Genovese was coming to conclude about their importance. Together Gutman and Genovese led Fogel and Engerman to include within their purview a range of sociological and anthropological issues as well as a purely econometric analysis, and Engerman called Gutman's attention to some of the data upon which he based his analysis of slave family structure on the plantations.* For Genovese the year or two of interaction with Gutman was fruitful. He learned a lot from the latter's way of working and the questions he was asking, and Gutman's exciting new perspectives on the black family sharpened Genovese's views on the subject.[55]† Finally,

---

* Fogel and Engerman's *Time on the Cross* (1974) is essentially a study in economic history. Although it contains a section on the slave family, the book pictures the bondsmen as assimilating white norms of economic behavior. The authors' interactions with Gutman and Genovese notwithstanding, their book, despite its importance in the debates over slavery, is not concerned with the nature of the slave community and its indigenous culture.

† Gutman's views reinforced the drift in Genovese's thinking that had been stimulated when the latter first read Bobby F. Jones's 1965 University of North Carolina dissertation, "A Cultural Middle Passage: Slave Marriage and Family in the Ante-Bellum South." Jones (b. 1932), a native white southerner, had come circuitously to his research on the subject. A paper on a state railway, which among other things dealt with the use of slave labor, led to an M.A. thesis (1961) on the North Carolina black codes, and the discovery of the WPA slave narratives, with their data contradicting the prevailing view of the slave family as matriarchal and unstable. In Jones's view, it was to the slavemasters' self-interest to encourage stable patriarchal family relationships as a way of building slave morale and thus increasing the efficiency of plantation agriculture.[56] Gutman, like Genovese, was also indebted to Jones, although the latter's analysis was more relevant to Genovese's perspective, with its stress on planter paternalism. Jones himself was numbered among those historians who, originally indifferent toward blacks and anything but sympathetic toward the Brown decision, during the course of his research became emancipated in his racial views, and by 1965, as a professor at Tennessee Technological University, was teaching one of the earliest black history courses introduced into the curriculum of a southern white school.

it would seem likely that Gutman, steeped in the scholarship of the English historians of the working class, reinforced the kind of perspective that had been supplied by Rawick.

Genovese's thinking crystallized in a 1970 paper, "American Slaves and Their History," which he first presented at a black studies conference at Sweet Briar College. It was at Gutman's urging that he sought to have it published, and it appeared in the *New York Review of Books* at the end of the year. Without minimizing the originality of the essay, dealing as it does with life in the slave quarters, the nature of slave religion, the resilience of the slave family, the culturally assimilating role of the house servants, and the functions of the slave drivers, one can say that it reveals Genovese at the convergence of various lines of influence. In addition to the stimulus provided by Rawick, there were the obvious input of Fogel and Engerman in his illuminating discussion of slave overseers; the acknowledgment to Gutman in connection with his discussion of the slave family; his debt to LeRoi Jones who "in his brilliant book, *Blues People,* argues convincingly that field slaves had forged the rudiments of a distinct Afro-American culture, whereas the house slaves largely took over the culture of the whites"; the perspectives he received on slave religion not only from Stuckey and Harding, but also from discussions with Lawrence Levine, who was then fashioning his influential analysis of slave religion. Addressing himself to the question of slave resistance, Genovese underscored Harding's point about slaves fashioning the Christian message into one of messianic revolt; took a leaf from James's views about the nature of working-class protest; and followed Stuckey in reasoning that "a distinctly black religion, at least in embryo, appeared in the slave quarters . . . [and] enabled them to survive as autonomous human beings . . . within the white master's world. . . . [T]he most ignorant of the field slaves who followed the conjurer on the plantation was saying no to the boss and seeking a form of cultural autonomy."[57] All this of course represented a distinct shift from the Genovese of the middle 1960s: the nagging question of rebelliousness versus docility had now been resolved through the concept of a resilient slave culture of the bondsmen's own creation.

Although Genovese is not aware of any significant intellectual debt to Thompson (and in fact in the recent book co-authored with Elizabeth Fox-Genovese, *Fruits of Merchant Capital* [1983]), he is critical of what he regards as the romantic view of lower-class culture in the writings of many of the new social historians), it is hard to avoid the conclusion that his analysis represented a fusion of perspectives from both black nationalist and working-class history. As the discussion in the *New York Review of Books* essay itself suggests, Genovese's synthesis indeed stood at the confluence of these two streams of interpretation. In any event, just as in his earlier defense of Phillips, Genovese now, in his treatment of slave life and culture, fused class and racial conceptualizations. He set the findings of his magnum opus, *Roll, Jordan, Roll* (1974), in the context of planter hegemony and paternalism, and he portrayed slave culture as exemplifying a "proto-nationalism." It is true that for Genovese the contradictions inherent in planter paternalism still had their counterparts in slave behavior and that all slaves were potentially both rebels and Sambos. But more important, it was the slaves' insistence on their own autonomy, as evident in their distinctive culture with its particular reinterpretation of Protestant Christianity, and what for Genovese was its underlying nationalist thrust, that revealed their ceaseless resistance to the system.*

Although Genovese and Gutman both profited from the intellectual exchanges at Rochester in 1969-70, Gutman's basic perspective about the black family had crystallized some time before he joined the faculty there. As we have observed, his interests as a specialist in labor and working-class history had long been informed by an awareness of the importance of the black experience. While Gutman does not argue that slaves were a class in the Marxist sense, this early and influential disciple of Thompson employs methods that are applicable to all exploited classes. It was the debate over the Moynihan report, impinging on Gutman's sensitivity to both the importance of black history and the study of the culture of the working classes, that turned him to examining the historical development of the black family. He thus provides a particularly instructive example of the way in which the social milieu can influence the course of scholarly inquiry, and of how a specific public controversy, intersecting with the emergence of a line of scholarly interpretation, can raise a research question that results in a major and seminal monograph.

Gutman's first work on the subject, written in the mid-1960s in collaboration with Laurence Glasco, one of his graduate students at the State University of New York at Buffalo, was a paper on the free Negro family in that city. Based on manuscript census data, this study revealed an overwhelming predominance of stable two-parent households.[58]† By the

---

* Genovese has subsequently shifted once more in his views about slave resistance and the scholarship of Aptheker. In the introduction to the new edition of *In Red and Black* ([1984], xlv), he writes: "I now believe that, specifics apart, he [Aptheker] had been much closer to the truth than I on the way in which slave revolts and militant black resistance have to be understood."

† Laurence Glasco (b. 1940), who haled from the antebellum black community of Xenia, Ohio, had as a youth been interested in Afro-American history. As a senior at Antioch College in the early 1960s, he had done a paper on the AME Bishop and Wilberforce University founder Daniel Alexander Payne. Though as a graduate student at Buffalo at the height of the direct action movement he took his M.A. in Latin American history, Glasco was a student activist and the moving

end of the decade Gutman had uncovered valuable information about slave marriages in the Freedmen's Bureau records. In the early 1970s, encouraged by Woodward, Franklin, and Engerman (who brought the Good Hope Plantation birth register to his attention), Gutman shifted his focus to an investigation of the structure of the slave family itself. Making an original and creative use of the small numbers of relevant plantation documents that had survived, Gutman discovered that an institutionalized slave kinship structure, different from the white kinship system, had taken shape by the eighteenth century. For Gutman, this exemplified the way in which a particular working-class culture was formed. He conceived the slave family as essentially an autonomous institution, developed in spite of the master's actions rather than being significantly shaped by slaveowner hegemony and planter paternalism. His conclusions not only contradicted the Elkins-Moynihan victimization-family disorganization model but also converged with the findings of the growing number of scholars who were stressing the self-generating nature of slave culture and institutions.

Like Gutman, other scholars also came quite autonomously in the late 1960s to their own conclusions about the nature of slave life. Thus Blassingame's views had crystallized by about 1969, around the same time that Genovese's had. Blassingame had studied Phillips and Stampp, of course; as a social science teacher at Howard University he had developed a knowledge of personality theory, and he had found himself unhappy with Elkins when he first read the latter's book in 1964. Five years later, having done considerable reading in the published ex-slave autobiographies, his ideas about life in the slave quarters had taken shape, and he recalls presenting them to a somewhat skeptical audience of colleagues at the University of Maryland at that time. When *The Slave Community* appeared in 1972, cognoscenti who were aware of the most recent tendencies in slavery studies regarded his volume as having a somewhat familiar ring and even faulted him for a failure to cite Genovese's 1970 essay in the *New York Review of Books*. But actually Blassingame's ideas had matured over a year before this pathbreaking article had appeared. Similarly Stuckey's call for the use of folklore reinforced rather than sparked Blassingame's own interest in such sources. Instead of being indebted to other scholars, *The Slave Community* was rooted in the way in which Blassingame's

figure behind the Negro History Week observances. It was Gutman who steered him into social history, and the seminal paper on the antebellum black family in Buffalo grew out of Gutman's seminar. For Glasco, however, institutional pressures happened to work against his doing a dissertation on black history: Employed to help compile the Buffalo census data, he wrote a 1973 dissertation comparing the city's Irish, Germans, and native whites—the black population being too small to make a comparative judgment about them. Subsequently he turned to his long-standing interest in miscegenation and the color line within the black community.

intellectual development intersected with the revolution in black consciousness that occurred in the late 1960s—though the book is not itself a nationalist interpretation. Blassingame himself saw the volume as something quite new: "Historians have never systematically explored the life experiences of American slaves," he wrote in the preface. "In terms of emphasis, it [the book] breaks sharply with American historiographical tradition."[59]

In any event the appearance of Blassingame's volume signaled the entry of the culture-and-community perspective into the mainstream of historical interpretation. Both the seeming familiarity of its ideas to those best informed about slavery scholarship and its ready acceptance by the profession at large in turn reflected the existence of ongoing research by a number of historians, all of whose perspectives had crystallized virtually simultaneously but independently at the very end of the 1960s.

Thus Lawrence Levine, who since the middle of the decade had been doing the groundwork for a book on the history of black thought, by 1967 had been drawn to an exploration of black folk culture as a way of moving beyond the thinking of the elites and grasping the outlook of the masses. In this connection he found Ellison's *Shadow and Act* exceedingly stimulating. Thus the perspective and methodology of Levine's *Black Culture and Black Consciousness* had been developed well before Stuckey's "Through the Prism of Folklore" was published, and the first fruit of Levine's investigations had appeared in his AHA paper on slave spirituals by 1969. Willie Lee Rose, who even in her *Rehearsal for Reconstruction* in 1964 had evinced a sensitive awareness of the evidence for strengths in slave families, delivered a 1970 OAH paper "Childhood in Bondage," exploring the role of slave mothers and fathers in the socialization of their children.[60] Leslie H. Owens (b. 1944), who in *This Species of Property: Slave Life and Culture in the Old South* (1976) was attempting "to get inside the slave's experience as much as possible, to convey a mood as well as offer an analysis,"[61] feels that his approach developed naturally out of his experience as part of the black community. There was, for example, the oral tradition in his large family about how his forebears survived generations of Mississippi slavery and how the local black community helped his grandfather narrowly escape a lynching. Uncomfortable with Elkins's views, Owens as a graduate student in 1968 had written a paper on slave personality, and by the time he read Stuckey and Harding at the end of the decade and Genovese's "American Slaves and Their History" essay soon after, he simply found them strengthening his own thinking. He had met Blassingame in 1970 at the time both were researching their books, but he recollects that the latter had mentioned nothing about his investigations. Owens's 1972 dissertation at the University of California at Riverside thus owed nothing to Blassingame, whose book did not appear until that year. Owens found it therefore ironic that some historians have wrongly perceived *This Species of Property*, with its anti-victimization model, as somewhat derivative from *The Slave Community*. Along the same lines, Albert J. Raboteau recalls the publications of Harding, Stuckey, and Levine—whose paper on the spirituals he found particularly exciting—as reinforcing what he himself was already doing. Blassingame, it is true, was somewhat more of an influence: studying under him at Yale, Raboteau learned much about methodology. But by then he already knew that he was going to write a sociocultural history that became *Slave Religion: The "Invisible Institution" in the Antebellum South* (1978). Finally Peter Wood, motivated both by the consciousness-raising events of the 1960s and the new demographic social history, independently arrived at his approach to the culture of the colonial slaves. Indicative of the isolation in which all these individuals were working and the very different routes by which they arrived at their portrayal of slave life is Gutman's apt comment that Wood was writing about the formation of a working class but did not realize it.

Overlapping in time with the evolution of Wood's approach to the study of black colonial history and sharing much of his methodology, yet independent in its development, was the emergence of the Chesapeake School of historians. Strictly speaking this was not a school but a group of junior scholars working at the Maryland Hall of Records in the late 1960s and early 1970s. Lois Green Carr, around whom the group coalesced socially, recalls 1969-74 as years of particularly fruitful and exciting interchange. All were interested in quantitative research, Maryland's colonial archives being especially rich in the kinds of documentation, including tax records, estate inventories, quitrent rolls, and manuscript census returns, that lent themselves to the study of the inarticulate. The scholars who came to work with these materials were almost inevitably drawn toward the study of slavery, even if it was not their original intention. With their interests centering on economics, demography, and social structure, they were led to the examination of topics such as slave prices, comparative analysis of the migration and the fertility of white indentured servants and black bondsmen, and slave kinship structure. Out of this came the notable essays by Russell Menard[62] and Allan Kulikoff[63] on slave demography and the black family. Menard, though radicalized in the course of the 1960s, like Genovese (who strongly influenced his work) arrived at his researches on blacks out of a larger interest in studying southern social structure. For Allan Kulikoff (b. 1947), who came from a conventional Democratic Jewish background, the critical shaping events had been the civil rights movement, Johnson's Great Society reforms, and the Vietnam War. Like Wood, his route into his investigations of colonial Afro-American demography and society resulted from a merger of ideological and methodological interests. Intersecting quite coincidentally with the work of the other students of colonial slave culture and community was Gerald (Michael) Mullin's monograph on the Chesapeake area in the postcolonial era, *Flight and Rebellion: Slave Resistance in Eighteenth Century Virginia* (1972). Informed by his anthropological training, the book was essentially a study in acculturation, casting new light on the relation between the degree of cultural assimilation and the patterns of slave resistance. However, by the time the manuscript was ready for publication, it was clear to Mullin how much his perspective converged with that of the new breed of social historians, with their commitment to looking at slavery from the bottom up, to studying slave life and behavior through the eyes of the bondsmen themselves, and to examining the slaves' worldview and the content of their culture.[64]

Meanwhile Gilbert Osofsky, reflecting his own sensitivity to the intellectual and social developments of the 1960s, in the introduction to his edition of selected ex-slave autobiographies, *Puttin' On Ole Massa* (1969), came to articulate many of the ideas being expressed by students of slave culture and community. As we have indicated in an earlier chapter, Osofsky's previous books, *Harlem: The Making of a Ghetto* (1966) and *The Burden of Race* (1967) and especially his 1968 *JAH* essay, "The Enduring Ghetto" had all been known for conceptualizing his ideas in the framework of the victimization model. But by the middle of the decade, dissatisfied with Elkins's approach and impressed with the humanity and cultural distinctiveness exhibited by blacks in the face of cruel and dehumanizing oppression, he was moving in a different direction. *Puttin' On Ole Massa* was completed at about the time when Blassingame was also studying the nineteenth-century ex-slave autobiographies as the primary basis for his own monograph on the slave community and when Levine was formulating his treatment of slave religion. In his book Osofsky not only argued for the validity and usefulness of these narratives for an understanding of slave life but also employed the information they contained to demonstrate the importance of such themes as flight and resistance and the unique and autonomous nature of slave religion. Moreover, at the time that Levine was starting to exploit folklore, Osofsky was also steeping himself in such materials, discovering (as he reported in *Puttin' On Ole Massa*) much in the songs and stories to corroborate what he found in the published ex-slave narratives. Indicating also his sensitivity to the general importance of history from the bottom up, he observed: "Anyone interested in working-class history, or the attitudes of the 'masses' . . . must devise techniques to analyze actions and institutions of people who left few written records of their feelings. . . . If one is ever to know about their [the slaves] visions, their quests, their 'mind,' it is obviously necessary to turn to the oral record: the songs, spirituals, and folk tales."[65]

Osofsky was certainly not alone in his willingness to use hitherto unorthodox sources to explore and understand slave life. Other professionally trained historians were independently exploiting these same sources. For example, Stanley Feldstein (b. 1937) finished a doctoral dissertation at New York University in 1969 (published as *Once a Slave: The Slaves' View of Slavery*, 1971), in which he used the published autobiographies to study the slave experience. Somewhat earlier, the desire to understand and ex- - plicate that experience had prompted a few interested students to exploit the WPA interviews with former slaves. Although in the 1970s these materials would become heavily mined, during the 1960s they were utilized only by an adventurous few, largely outside the ranks of professionally trained historians. Rawick in his 1964 article in *International Socialism* argued that the WPA narratives offered a wealth of valid data. But Rawick's monograph, accompanying the publication of the WPA narratives themselves, would not appear until 1972. By then, Charles W. Joyner had come across the WPA materials in pursuing his doctorate in folklore, his earliest publication drawing from this source being a 1971 essay in the *Keystone Folklore Quarterly* entitled "Soul Food and the Sambo Stereotype: Foodlore from the Slave Narrative Collection." Meanwhile, also in the mid-1960s, two non-historians, Julius Lester and Norman R. Yetman, were using these materials. Lester, a former SNCC activist, employed both the WPA interviews and the published ex-slave autobiographies in *To Be a Slave* (1968), written for a popular audience. Yetman's 1969 dissertation in American studies at the University of Pennsylvania, "The Slave Personality: A Test of the 'Sambo' Hypothesis," unlike most subsequent investigators found in the interviews substantial confirmation of the slavish personality described by Elkins. Yetman's volume of selections from the WPA narratives, *Life under the "Peculiar Institution,"* appeared the following year.* All three men — and Feldstein as well — were working virtually simultaneously but independently: Yetman, for example, knew nothing about Rawick's interests until the latter got in touch with him after reading his 1970 anthology.

It is thus clear from the evidence that although the most important monographs on slave culture and community did not begin to appear until 1972, they represented a perspective that had crystallized in the thinking of a variety of scholars coming from diverse intellectual backgrounds before

---

* For Yetman's analysis of the use of the ex-slave interviews in recent slavery historiography, see his "Ex-Slave Interviews and the Historiography of Slavery," *American Quarterly* 36 (Summer 1984).

the end of the 1960s. Stampp remained thoroughly conversant with the most recent stirrings in slavery historiography. In his 1970 paper, "Rebels and Sambos," he revealed the impact of this new scholarship and how he had moved toward a resolution of the cultural question raised in *The Peculiar Institution*. He now recognized that the oppressiveness of the slaveholders notwithstanding, "the system nevertheless permitted them [the slaves] a degree of semiautonomous community life"; that "it was customary for them to live in family groups"; that Christianity functioned not only as a "means of control," but as interpreted by the slaves provided "subtle ways of protesting their condition" — "a system of beliefs that comforted and sustained them in their bondage . . . [and an] additional means of self-expression that helped them retain their psychic balance." Stampp did not "believe that a truly autonomous Afro-American subculture developed in slavery days," but he recognized that "some of the ingredients for one were certainly there," so that after Emancipation the freedmen "[t]hrough their churches, their music, and a great variety of organized social activities" did indeed create a distinctive way of life.[66]

Stampp's new perspective was the fruit of intellectual influences coming from scholars as diverse as his critic, Eugene Genovese, and his colleague at Berkeley, Lawrence Levine.* Yet the striking thing about the way that this consensus had crystallized by 1968-69 was that it had come about generally without intellectual interaction among the several scholars involved. With the notable exception of Genovese, individual scholars, both black and white, came to their portrayal of slave life out of their own particular constellations of ideas. The new slavery historiography stood at the convergence of a heightened sensitivity in the profession about race discrimination and the importance of the black experience, the cresting of black nationalist ideology, the rise of quantitative and demographic history, and the vogue of research on the history of the inarticulate.[67] Out of their diverse experiences, historians of slavery were responding in their separate ways to this complex of social and intellectual forces rather than drawing their inspiration from one another. On the other hand, the very convergence of factors we have just mentioned in the professional milieu of the early 1970s meant that the new way of looking at life in the slave quarters was accepted among historians without question.

In short, given the changes in perspective to be found among members of the profession generally, and the shift to social history that paralleled and was intertwined with the legitimization of black history, the community-and-culture model conformed to a whole new way of looking at the Afro-American past. At the same time this model solved the problem

---

* Stampp was not aware, however, of what Blassingame, whose ideas would not appear in print for another two years, was doing.

presented by Phillips and the dilemma so painfully posed by Elkins. While Aptheker's older revisionism still retained considerable currency, it was widely accepted that servile insurrections were relatively rare in the United States, and that what best demonstrated the slaves' unremitting resistance to the system was the way in which they had retained a good deal of autonomy, shaping their own institutions and creating a folk-culture that expressed their own worldview. Paradoxically, the popularity of this view of slave life was enhanced by the fact that it appeared valid whether (siding with Stampp or Blassingame) one viewed the plantation regime as extremely harsh, or (siding with Genovese and Fogel and Engerman) one perceived its rigors as mitigated by slavemaster paternalism.

At first glance the obvious consensus about what the history of slavery was now all about might seem to indicate the emergence of a genuine new paradigm. Yet given the diversity of routes by which individual scholars arrived at this agreement on what life was like as viewed from the slave quarters, and the variety in conceptualizations that had been involved, it would be difficult to see this consensus as constituting a true paradigm. There are those who came from a quantitative, cliometric approach to social history; those interested in history from the bottom up who conceived slave life in the terms of working-class history; those whose treatment was informed by a nationalist perspective; and those whose work was the fruit of the new racial consciousness of the 1960s, but did not involve conscious ideological and theoretical conceptualizations. Raboteau aptly describes the monographs of Blassingame and others, as well as his own book on slave religion, when he says that he is simply telling the story of people. Among those we interviewed there was a perception that, as one historian put it, while there was "some point in lumping together those scholars who use a common vantage point in looking at things from the perspective of blacks rather than whites, and from their interest in common folk," the historians of slavery in the 1970s were really writing from quite divergent points of view.

In this connection the reception accorded Genovese's *Roll, Jordan, Roll* is instructive. It did not receive the universal acclaim that greeted Wood's *Black Majority* or Levine's *Black Culture and Black Consciousness,* neither of which addressed themselves to issues such as planter paternalism or the implications of slave culture for black nationalism. Some students of the black past were impressed with Genovese's challenging heuristic resolution of the paradox of master control and slave autonomy, and many admired his discussion of slave religion. A few, like Ira Berlin and Leon Litwack, were (as we shall explain below) significantly influenced by Genovese. But most found Genovese's model of planter hegemony and considerable slave dependence too redolent of Phillips to be acceptable. The majority of writers, though theoretically recognizing that the presence of the master class had a role in shaping slave institutions and the bondsman's worldview, virtually ignored this role in their own analyses. In effect, they treated the slave community and way of life as a mechanism for coping with an oppressive system, but otherwise unaffected by it.* Certainly Genovese's discussion, his belief that his conceptualization was congruent with a nationalist analysis notwithstanding, did not find a high degree of acceptance among black nationalist historians. Stuckey, for example, had certain reservations, impressed though he was with the way in which Genovese had now done his homework and had immersed himself in black cultural materials. Harding, more interested in messianic rebellions than in other kinds of black resistance, joined with Aptheker in vigorously attacking the volume's major themes.[68] Genovese seemed defensive about criticism from these perspectives. Even though Genovese did not name them in the acknowledgments to *Roll, Jordan, Roll,* he later publicly declared: "whatever such black colleagues as Harding, Lester, . . . or Stuckey think of my book . . . , I could not have written it without them."[69]

Curiously, although the consensus over slave culture and community was almost entirely spawned during the nationalist zeitgeist of the late 1960s, Genovese's is the only book-length monograph that seeks to place the development of slave culture in a nationalist framework. From Blassingame and Rawick to Raboteau and Thomas L. Webber—author of *Deep like the Rivers: Education in the Slave Quarter Community, 1831-1865* (1978)—the other scholars simply did not see a conceptualization cast in nationalist terms as relevant to their analysis. Indeed, given Genovese's unique position in this regard, he found himself on something of a limb. One can detect a note of frustration in his review of the Raboteau

---

* For a succinct critique of Genovese from the perspective of a scholar who emphasizes the oppressive nature of the system and considers genuinely paternalistic relationships as rare, see Paul D. Escott, *Slavery Remembered: A Record of Twentieth-Century Slave Narratives* (1979). In Escott's view the slaves and masters lived in two separate worlds. The slaves' mental environment was not one they shared with the slaveowners; rather they responded creatively to their milieu without being shaped by the planters' worldview. As in the works by Blassingame, Gutman, and others, the existence of "elbow-room" (Stampp's phrase) or social space is assumed, but there is no analysis of just how in a basically oppressive planter-dominated environment enough autonomy or social space existed to account for the development of a separate culture and community.

Paradoxically, Genovese's concept of a planter paternalism rooted in the aristocratic ethic of an alleged precapitalist economic system accords best with the views of Fogel and Engerman, even though they paint a picture of planters not as aristocrats motivated by a sense of noblesse oblige, but as enlightened profit-seeking entrepreneurs, savvy managers of the workers in their factories in the fields.

and Webber volumes at the end of the 1970s, when it was becoming evident that separatist impulses were on the wane, and that a nationalist perspective would not dominate slavery scholarship. Sharply criticizing these two historians, he observed: "Raboteau and Webber unfortunately follow current trends in one way they ought not to. It is perfectly clear that the history of the slaves, with its delineation of a rich and distinctive cultural legacy, sheds much light on political problems — specifically the problem of black nationalism. One might therefore expect that those who write this history would meet their responsibility to make a considered political evaluation. . . . Those who, like Raboteau, Webber and most recent writers, have discerned a black cultural development with a wide range of autonomy have generally fallen silent on the political implications of their findings, which clearly support some of the black nationalists' main contentions. This silence does no one any good, and we may hope that it will soon be broken." But few historians of the slave community saw it Genovese's way, and a few years later he lashed out against Gutman and his admirers for failure "to notice that their social history lends support to the black nationalist interpretation of the black experience. It is especially unfortunate that Gutman ignores the work of Sterling Stuckey, Vincent Harding, [Imamu] Amiri Baraka and other black scholars whose work on black cultural history compels all who write on black history to confront the national question."[70]

The burden of our argument is that the emergence of an interpretative consensus on slave life and behavior arose not from the influence of one or two seminal volumes, but from the way in which various scholars, each interacting in his own manner within a larger social and intellectual milieu, simultaneously but autonomously arrived at conclusions that at a descriptive level had a great deal in common. We do not mean to say that interaction and cross-fertilization were entirely absent, Genovese being a prime example of their effects. On the other hand, the inference we draw from our data is that for all the sound and fury over Elkins's thesis, it was less a cause of the scholarly investigations into slave behavior and slave life than a convenient target for those whose concerns and perspectives arose out of the zeitgeist of the late 1960s. Without an Elkins the arguments would have been phrased somewhat differently, but the behavioral and cultural questions on which the discussion focused would have had to be addressed and resolved.

Even more indicative of the primacy of the general intellectual and social milieu over the role of a seminal thinker was the way in which the climate of opinion in the late 1960s rescued the reputation of Herskovits. As we have previously pointed out, Herskovits's thesis about the presence of African cultural survivals among American Negroes had been scorned by most black intellectuals for a quarter century after the appearance of his controversial *Myth of the Negro Past* in 1941. True, Du Bois and Woodson had earlier asserted that African traits were to be found in much of the institutional and cultural life of U.S. blacks, but this view, even though Herskovits fortified it with impressive ethnological work, received little credibility. Although Woodson regarded Herskovits's findings as "scientific," and the black linguist Lorenzo Turner, author of *Africanisms in the Gullah Dialect* (1949), was a warm ally, Herskovits for the most part was accorded a reception ranging from indifference to hostility by most black and sympathetic white intellectuals. Generally, African survivals were regarded as negligible, outside of some elements in black dance and music, the Gullah dialect of the Sea Islands, and the faint echoes of voodoo and conjuring among lower-class folk in the South. Among historians, Stampp, after carefully studying the matter, ended up reflecting the perspective of most black intellectuals. The authors of the three principal surveys of Afro-American history that appeared in the quarter century after the publication of Herskovits's volume (Franklin's *From Slavery to Freedom,* 1947, Quarles's *The Negro in the Making of America,* 1964, and Meier and Rudwick's *From Plantation to Ghetto,* 1966) all discussed African survivals in their respective chapters on the West African background, but none integrated such material into the main body of their books. Then with the rise of Black Power rhetoric, the questioning of the assimilationist ethic, and the new interest in the distinctive aspects of the culture of the black working class, the view that there were important elements of African culture in the way of life and thinking of American Negroes took on a new respectability. Yet neither the suggestions made by Du Bois and Woodson nor Herskovits's extensively researched monograph was influential in bringing about this development. Rather intellectuals, having reached a new perspective, found in Herskovits's writings the material that reinforced what they had already concluded was the historical reality. Thus Levine's *Black Culture and Black Consciousness,* which served as a brilliant demonstration of the validity of what Herskovits wrote, contains only a scant handful of passing references to the distinguished anthropologist. Levine had discovered Herskovits after he had formulated his own ideas and had no feeling that he was working out of any earlier intellectual tradition.

Collectively the community and culture studies of the 1970s marked the end to a period of major debate and the creation of an intellectually satisfying resolution of the thorny questions surrounding slave behavior and slave resistance. Then, having become something of a new orthodoxy, the community-and-culture perspective had a vital impact in shaping scholarship on other aspects of the black experience, as historians—extending their investigations both forward and backward in time—applied the lessons learned from the slavery studies. Perhaps the outstanding examples of this can be seen in Leon Litwack's *Been in the Storm So Long: The Aftermath of Slavery* (1980) and in Ira Berlin's *AHR* essay, "Time, Space, and the Evolution of Afro-American Society on British Mainland North America." Deriving much of his viewpoint and inspiration from both Gutman and Genovese and drawing heavily on Thompson's views of the development of working-class culture, Berlin, intersecting with the interests of Mullin, Wood, and Levine, fashioned his tripartite model about the differential development of Afro-American society and culture in the Deep South, the Chesapeake region, and the North.[71] Litwack, employing newly legitimized sources such as the WPA interviews, pictured the early Reconstruction experience as laying the foundation for a genuine black community, and his subtle treatment of the ambiguities and complexities in the attitudes and behavior of freedmen, planters, federal officials, and missionaries can be regarded as representing a synthesis of the perspectives offered earlier by both Willie Lee Rose and Genovese. Thus, although our argument is that the culture and community consensus arose out of a convergence of historians coming mostly independently to their conclusions, it is also evident that this scholarly consensus, once it was reached, in turn did much to influence the course of subsequent research.

We would not dismiss the evidence of interaction among scholars nor would we minimize the impact that widely read scholars from Aptheker and Stampp through Stuckey and Blassingame to Gutman, Wood, and Levine had on the perceptions of the broader scholarly community. Yet we believe that the evidence indicates that the repeated crystallization of new perspectives on slavery over the decades did not flow from intellectual interchange among students of the subject. Rather it flowed from the ways in which individual historians, coming out of varied intellectual origins and theoretical assumptions, and arriving at their conclusions through diverse routes, each in his own fashion responded to the social and intellectual climate of his generation.

Moreover, given the autonomous nature of the way in which most of the involved scholars came to their conclusions, and given the variety of intellectual underpinnings for what appears to be a consensus about slave culture and community, we think that it would be inaccurate to consider this seeming unity of perspective as a genuine paradigm.

CHAPTER 5

On the Dilemmas of Scholarship in Afro-American History

NEARLY A QUARTER CENTURY AGO, amid the intellectual ferment engendered by the cresting of the civil rights movement, John Hope Franklin wrote one of his most significant essays, "The Dilemma of the American Negro Scholar." The black scholar, Franklin observed, faced "numerous and complex dilemmas." First was the formidable task of "seek[ing] recognition in the general world of scholarship." Pushed by circumstances into research that would advance the race, black intellectuals through diligence and determination had produced impeccable scholarship and had won professional standing by treating the race problem with objectivity. Yet it was a "tragedy" that, feeling compelled to devote themselves almost exclusively to the study of the Negro, they became "the victim[s] of segregation in the field of scholarship." Franklin decried the view of many whites that "Negroes had peculiar talents that fitted them to study themselves and their problems"—a kind of " 'mystique' about Negro studies . . . [that] defeated a basic principle of scholarship, namely that given the materials and techniques of scholarship and given the mental capacity, any person could engage in the study of any particular field." Moreover, having chosen to specialize in Negro studies, black scholars found further dilemmas: how to stay calm and objective in the face of forces barring them from membership in the mainstream of American scholarship and how to resist "the temptation to pollute . . . scholarship with polemics." The Afro-American scholar could hardly be insensitive to oppression, but it was essential to recognize "the difference between scholarship and advocacy." On the one hand, black intellectuals must engage in research to refute the misrepresentations propagated by so many white historians and social scientists and to produce the empirical data for the "social engineers" leading the struggle for equality. On the other hand, "There is also a place for advocacy, so long as the Negro scholar understands the difference."

Franklin himself, who in his working paper for the NAACP school desegregation cases, had "deliberately transformed the objective data provided by historical research into an urgent plea for justice," was flattered
by Thurgood Marshall's comment that it read like a legal brief, yet at the
same time "I hope[d] that my scholarship did not suffer."[1]

For Franklin the resolution of both the tension between scholarship
and advocacy and the dilemma of working in what had been a segregated
field while striving for recognition as a scholar regardless of race appeared
plain. Given the pragmatic nature of so much American scholarship, addressed as it was to the resolution of social problems, the proper choice
for black scholars was to employ their knowledge and skills to undermine
discrimination while contributing "to the solution of the problems that
all Americans face in common." It was indeed "a goodly company the
American Negro scholar joins as he chooses to make of the course he
pursues a battleground for truth *and* justice. On the one hand, he joins
those of his own color to make democracy work. On the other hand, he
joins his intellectual kinsmen of whatever race in the worthy task of utilizing
the intellectual resources of the country for its own improvement. A
happier choice could hardly be made."[2] Personally, of course, Franklin has
been mainly a scholar rather than an activist or a polemicist;[3] his Thomas
Jefferson lectures, *Racial Equality in America* (1976), in which he consciously adopted the role of an advocate, were addressed to a lay audience
and were an unusual departure for him. In addition, while making an
important contribution to the study of black history, Franklin has consistently structured his role with an eye toward the mainstream of the
profession. As indicated in Chapter 2, he staked out his particular specialty
as southern rather than black history, and he has constantly striven to
make black history not a Jim Crow specialty, but an integral part of the
fabric of American history-writing.*

Franklin had identified not only the dilemmas facing black historians,
but also the range of dilemmas experienced by all students of the Afro-
American past: the tension between studying Negro history as a distinct—
and separate—field and incorporating it into the larger stream of American
history; the tension between scholarship and advocacy—or more broadly
stated, the tension between the canons of scholarship and the expression
of one's value judgments; the tension between calm and detached scholarship and the pragmatic, instrumental use of history to reform society;

* For Franklin's leanings toward detached scholarship rather than advocacy, see
the views he expressed in his AHA presidential address, "Mirror for Americans:
A Century of Reconstruction History." For a good example of the way in which
he integrates black and southern history, see his SHA presidential address, "The
Great Confrontation: The South and the Problem of Change."[4]

the tension arising over whether Afro-American history is a specialty best done by blacks, or whether it should be a specialty open to all with a serious interest and appropriate academic training. The question of how a scholar should handle his or her ethical commitments in studying the past is, of course, an issue that has long concerned and divided historians. If anything, black history has been a field more infused with value considerations and social purpose than most other historical specialties. The historians of the black experience whom we have interviewed have all perceived a relationship between their values and their scholarship; and all explicitly or implicitly have held up the American democratic value system as the standard against which the status of blacks in American society must be judged. But in other respects historians have resolved the tensions and dilemmas to which we have pointed in highly varied ways.

Thus the pioneering W. E. B. Du Bois and Carter G. Woodson, coming to maturity in an era of intense racism, both utilized their scholarship in an effort to advance the race, but they were otherwise scarcely alike in the manner with which they grappled with most of the dilemmas that Franklin described.

Du Bois's early historical and sociological investigations epitomized the kind of serious scholarship that aimed to reform American society by careful research on the "Negro problem." It was Du Bois's dream that his analytical presentations would command respect from white intellectuals and people of affairs, and in fact he eschewed the emphasis on heroic and individual accomplishments that informed the writings of Woodson and others who concentrated on promoting the study of the black past among Negroes themselves. Especially significant in this connection were Du Bois's 1910 *AHR* article, "Reconstruction and Its Benefits," in which he sought to counter the interpretations of the regnant Dunning school of "scientific" research on the post–Civil War period, and his 1915 synthesis of the black past, *The Negro* (revised and expanded as *Black Folk, Then and Now,* 1939), most notable for its avant-garde discussion of the historical achievements and cultural complexity of African societies south of the Sahara. Within this scholarly framework Du Bois did not always shrink from outright advocacy. There were the explicit moral judgment on the events he described in *The Suppression of the African Slave Trade* (1896) and the policy-oriented recommendations to be found in his sociological studies. But Du Bois was battling against a seemingly irreversible tide of racism; his work commanded attention only among those already convinced and thus did little to further the cause of racial enlightenment. By the time his Reconstruction essay appeared in the *AHR*, Du Bois had resolved the dilemma in favor of a career of activism with the NAACP, which would be his role for the next quarter century. Even the return to scholarship in the 1930s produced a volume, *Black Reconstruction in America,* that was suffused with an impassioned tone more akin to *Souls of Black Folk* and to the editorials he wrote for the NAACP's *Crisis* than to his early monographs.

Woodson also sought to build a field of scholarship that would tell the truth about blacks and their past. But unlike Du Bois he lacked a broad strategy of reform and, as we have seen, consciously and pointedly avoided ideological controversy. His advocacy took two forms. One was popularizing the study of the black past, focusing largely on individual builders and heroes. The other was the campaign to establish Negro history as a viable and legitimate specialty. To this end he secured the help of J. Franklin Jameson and the philanthropists, encouraged the development of a circle of black historians, and provided a publishing medium for interested scholars of both races. It was his singular dedication to both scholarship and popularization that enabled him to make Negro history a definite — if rather segregated — specialty. On both counts Woodson was fostering a veritable social movement, whose institutionalization in the ASNLH, with its journal and its Negro History Week, was the medium through which he reconciled his roles of scholar and advocate.

Yet Woodson's efforts brought him to other dilemmas. One arose from the necessity of depending on foundation largesse to fund a research program. At the start, working with Jameson's support, this had posed no conflict. Later, however, Woodson found himself compelled to tailor the ASNLH's research projects to the economic and sociological policy-oriented interests of the Laura Spelman Rockefeller Memorial. There was also the tension Woodson faced in his attempt to encourage scholarship that would meet the standards he knew at Harvard and, simultaneously, to reach a mass audience of adults and schoolchildren. Though remarkably successful in rising to this challenge, and in balancing the interests of both a lay and a scholarly following, in the final analysis he developed a constituency among public school teachers that was considerably larger than his constituency among scholars. The inauguration of Negro History Week in 1926 was followed by the development of local ASNLH branches. In 1937 came the establishment of a second journal, the *Negro History Bulletin,* "an organ for the schools" aimed explicitly at young pupils and their teachers, and an enterprise sustained even though it was run at a large deficit that absorbed much of the money raised in nickels, dimes, and quarters from the black community.[5] The development of this following involved Woodson in the preparation of textbooks that would have to be sufficiently temperate in tone to be accepted by school administrators in the border and upper South states where they were first adopted. Moreover, the intensive and systematic building of this public school constituency not only saved the organization—and hence the scholarly *JNH*—but also created problems rooted in the divergent interests of advanced scholars and those who were primarily schoolteachers. In the long run it would prove difficult to satisfy both groups. Woodson somehow managed it, but his death weakened the scholarly orientation that the ASNLH had had, and the organization became increasingly directed toward the concerns of people who were teachers rather than productive scholars. Epitomizing the trend was the way in which the *JNH,* probably at the peak of its quality just after Woodson died, subsequently declined under the direction of a teachers' college professor who lacked a doctorate. Ironically, this shift in the ASNLH's orientation took place at a time when black history was moving toward acceptance as a legitimate specialty among the mainstream of academic historians. In the end the schoolteacher constituency, later augmented by personnel from the black studies departments that were created around 1970, have come to dominate the organization.

As the material presented in Chapter 2 indicates, the scholars in the Woodson group also resolved the dilemma between advocacy and scholarship in divergent ways. Among them, Charles H. Wesley, the tireless speaker for the ASNLH before both black and white audiences, perhaps leaned most toward the popularizing side of Woodson. On the other hand, the spirit of Rayford W. Logan's work, exhibiting as it did a commitment to empirical scholarship fused with intense moral condemnation, was most akin to that of Du Bois. But much of the output of these two men, and more especially the monographs of A. A. Taylor, Luther P. Jackson, and Lorenzo J. Greene, were notable for scholarly detachment, undergirded though their monographs were with a desire to set the record straight by correcting racist falsehoods and revealing how blacks against great odds had demonstrated economic mobility and sustained their own social institutions. Jackson with his thorough scholarship, his multifaceted participation in the work of racial advancement, and his activity in promoting the cause of the ASNLH in the public schools of Virginia uniquely combined the scholarly, activist, and popularizing roles. Yet it should be emphasized that for all the members of Woodson's circle, the loyalty to the ASNLH was so intense as to itself constitute a kind of advocacy. As has been pointed out, their dedication to the cause was such that for them black history assumed the dimensions of a social movement, commanding a commitment that transcended the autocratic idiosyncrasies of the ASNLH's founder.

Meanwhile, those liberal and radical white historians who were concerned about the problem of race in American society and who recognized the importance of the study of the black past experienced their own tensions and dilemmas. Reformist by inclination they, like the black historians who were their contemporaries, often sought to vindicate their vision of what American society ought to be. In the case of C. Vann Woodward, for example, the dilemma took the form of a tension between his radical-liberal sensibilities and his devotion to his craft as a historian. As his close friend David Potter observed, Woodward had the "conviction that the historian must reconstruct the past accurately and at the same time make it speak to the present."[6] In his search for a "usable past" that would undermine the seeming historical inevitability of white supremacy, Woodward found in the Populist experience evidence that a different kind of society could have developed after the Civil War, and in "the strange career of Jim Crow" evidence that the southern segregation system could be eradicated. Yet Woodward recognized the fine line that existed between his value-oriented scholarship and social advocacy. As he wrote to an NAACP official when he undertook the preparation of a background paper for the NAACP's desegregation cases: "I should feel constrained by the limits of my craft. . . . I would stick to what happened and account for it as intelligently as I could. . . . You see, I do not want to be . . . delivering a gratuitous history lecture to the Court. And at the same time I do not want to get out of my role as historian."[7]

On the other hand, for the handful of Communist-oriented historians who were emerging contemporaneously with Woodward, there seems to have been no such dilemma. For them advocacy and scientific scholarship were as one. Thus Herbert Aptheker perceived the task of those working in the field as that of correcting the distortions and omissions practiced by most white historians, who "bulwarked the super-exploitation of the American Negro people. Denying them a past worthy of serious study and emulation weakens their fight for equality and freedom." Like Woodson, Aptheker saw himself as engaged in objective scientific investigation: "Nothing can replace this basic procedure [of rigorous, painstaking study] in scientific investigation, and it is only on the strength of such digging and probing . . . that the discipline of historical writing will be lifted above the level of . . . mythology . . . and bigotry, into the realm of fact and reality."[8] It is true that science for Communists was also equated with Marxist ideology, and that the data uncovered by Aptheker dovetailed with Communist views about underclass resistance, while science for historians like Woodson was the methodology they had imbibed at Harvard early in the century. Yet for Aptheker science and ideology coalesced into an approach that in turn meshed with the perspective of the black historians.

Notwithstanding the explicit kind of advocacy that marked the writings of radical white historians who came to the study of the history of race relations and the black experience during the Depression, it should be reiterated that a hallmark of most of the World War II and postwar scholarship in the field was a tendency to strive consciously for scholarly detachment—to place a distance between one's values and one's scholarly publications. This was true of the cluster of black scholars whose monographs appeared during the 1940s, including those associated with Woodson as well as the new generation represented by Benjamin Quarles and Franklin, and of course goes far to account for the respect with which their publications were received. It was also true of the white scholars who were emerging as important contributors to the subject during the 1950s. Undergirding the work of all these historians, both black and white, was a consensus of values about race and the American social order. Still in actual fact the scholars differed in the degree to which these values were to be explicitly found in their works. For Quarles, who was notable for the judicious restraint of his factual accounts, such values helped determine the shape of his published writings more than they did for Franklin. Quarles explicitly wrote from the perspective that "freedom is and always has been America's root concern."[9] Among the slavery scholars of the 1950s, Kenneth Stampp's *The Peculiar Institution,* though criticized by Richard Hofstadter for lacking moral fervor, was informed with enough of it for some commentators to label him a "neo-abolitionist." On the other hand, Carl Degler's essay on the origins of slavery and race prejudice was a model of scholarly detachment, while Stanley Elkins self-consciously sought to transcend moral questions in his social-psychological analysis. Students of black leadership also exhibited differences in the ways in which they handled their values. August Meier deliberately adopted a dispassionate stance and consciously compartmentalized his careers as activist and scholar, believing that the historian's task was to analyze and understand the past rather than make value judgments about it (whatever his personal opinions as a citizen). Moreover, it seemed important to treat with as much detachment as possible the conflicting ideologies within the black community and to deal in a neutral way with both Du Bois, whom he admired, and with Booker T. Washington, whom he did not. Elliott Rudwick, on the other hand, though not hesitating to criticize Du Bois on certain matters, wrote about him with more obvious sympathy. But Francis Broderick, finding the complex Du Bois something of a disappointment and evidently unhappy with Du Bois's conversion to Communism, did not hesitate to present what many other historians regarded as an unduly critical assessment.

Subsequently in the late 1960s and 1970s, the tension between advocacy and scholarship became more acute. Ironically at the very time that black history was attracting scholars who were motivated as much or more by the field's legitimacy as by a deep concern about racial inequality, there were other historians who with unprecedented vigor saw the field in highly instrumental terms. Propelled both by demands of the Black Power militants, and by the general leftward swing in the profession, there was, as Degler has put it, "the emergence of . . . advocacy history."[10] In any event among both black and white researchers in black history there has been and continues to be a continuum ranging from those who, while conscious of the relevance of their scholarship for their social concerns, make a sharp distinction between advocacy and the historical craft, to those who virtually fuse their sense of social mission with their research and writing.

Those with an instrumental view consciously see their work in black history as helping bring about social change. As one white scholar said, "By virtue of doing black history in the first place, a person has indicated that he believes that there are ethical issues which should be examined and some judgments made." Another asserted: "I would place myself in the radical historian category—by that I mean a historian who without giving up the notion of accuracy and honesty has a commitment to radical social change, someone who sees his professional work as part of that commitment." Otey Scruggs, in a paper presented just as black history courses were being introduced in colleges across the country, defended the "desire among Afro-Americans to put history to the service of group uplift"; at the same time he regarded the study of the black past as having important lessons for white Americans, stripping away the "romantic . . . conceit" of white American superiority, so that they would come to question the belief in their "moral omnipotence."[11] Another black historian, a woman, frankly said: "I write history for a purpose. I do not write history for history's sake. I write subjective history, to critique and condemn white America."

Of the black historians who came to prominence in the late 1960s, Vincent Harding and Sterling Stuckey were among the most explicit in their fusion of historical study with social purpose. Harding put it starkly in the introduction to his magnum opus, *There Is a River:* "I knew that my first commitment was not to the ambiguous abstractions of 'objectivity' or 'scholarship,' but to the lively hope and faith of a people in struggle for a new chance to be whole." Stuckey, reflecting the perspective of the advocates of a new black history wrote that Woodson's parading of Negro achievers, on the one hand, and Franklin's and Quarles's judicious restraint, on the other, were alike mistaken for their failure to sufficiently "condemn America for her crimes against black people."[12] Harding and Stuckey see history both as a valuable instrument in the struggle for black autonomy, self-definition, and self-determination and also as part of their messianic view that blacks can function as the vital, humane force for the radical transformation of white America.

On the other hand, a number of those we interviewed explicitly noted that regardless of the values that brought them into the field, once they embarked upon their research "the pride of craftmanship" became paramount. Among white scholars, for example, George Tindall is often cited by his former students as one who urged them not to orate, but "to let the facts speak for themselves." A white woman historian put it in more extreme terms: "I don't use history-writing for a purpose, no matter how admirable that may be . . . you should not use history to indoctrinate. . . . If you use history consciously as a means of black liberation, you will be in danger of selecting evidence." Kenneth Kusmer, in the course of doing additional research and revising his master's thesis for what became *A Ghetto Takes Shape: Black Cleveland 1870-1930* (1976), became increasingly aware of the "ambiguities" of the black urban experience and dropped the highly moralistic tone of the original manuscript. Among black historians Thomas Holt is frequently cited as one who distances himself from his material, even though underlying his interpretation one detects a deep concern with the tragedy of black disunity and class cleavage. Amid the ideological debate at the turn of the 1970s, Nathan Huggins and John W. Blassingame were notable for taking exception to the call for blacks to "create their own myths, [and] call them history." Blassingame maintained that black historians, in challenging the racist assumptions underlying the writing of American history, "must be wary of treading the path of our white supremacy predecessors in distorting history to prove a point. . . . Rather than trying to create myths, the black historian should seek to record the truth." Huggins called for a "realistic" assessment of the black past without mythology or hero-worship. Although it was "not surprising that black people . . . should welcome history as a convenient way to exercise their rage" or that "well-meaning white people . . . welcome Afro-American history as a means of finding substance and focus for their guilt," students, both black and white, "must press beyond the level of wounded sensibility if Afro-American history is to acquire deep, abiding, and constructive meaning."[13] Indeed, most of the younger Afro-American historians whom we interviewed were in essential agreement with this viewpoint, pursuing their own scholarship in what they regarded as a "professional way," telling the historical story and making their analyses without reference to ideological issues.

Still, underlying the view that historical scholarship should not become intertwined with political advocacy was the belief that black history nevertheless had an instrumental role to play in reforming the study of American history itself. Franklin, continuing to articulate ideas he had expressed throughout his career, held that "in the future, Negro American history must not become the exclusive tool for those who want to use it for narrow political purposes. . . . But it must become and must remain

. . . something much more significant than the handmaiden of the political advocate or even the social reformer. It must become and must remain . . . the ground on which American historical scholarship can be tested. From the vantage point and perspective that it provides, it can be a most powerful factor in the continuing movement to revise American history. In this way it will perform much of the task of the political advocate and social reformer." Blassingame believed "that black scholars must challenge the white supremacist tenets underlying American history." Huggins maintained that "one of the most important reasons for studying Afro-American history is that through it we may come to a broader understanding of American history. . . . When we know the Negro's history, we will know the failings of the [American] dream itself." Fusing his call for "realistic" history with his own hopes for a racially democratic society, he concluded: "As we Americans, black and white, struggle to understand how we can survive in peace with one another and how we can finally transform ourselves into a people with a true and inclusive national identity, it is essential that our history encourage us to abandon all fantasies for realistic conceptions of ourselves and our past."[14]

The differences among the black scholars who came to maturity during the late 1960s and 1970s notwithstanding, underlying the thinking of all of them are certain similarities. Like their predecessors, they have all grappled in diverse ways with the task of fashioning a viewpoint that addressed itself to both whites and blacks. Some have conceived their work with the kind of detachment that would appeal to scholars of both races, and at the opposite end of the continuum even Harding's messianism, while addressed primarily to a black lay audience, has a message for whites as well. All would agree that whites need to be educated about the history of race relations and the black experience, both to understand that experience and to face up to the reality of the limitations and failures of their own American dream. Paradoxically, moreover, despite the frequent, vigorous denunciation of American society and the widespread tendency to perceive the black past in terms of a separate community with an ethos of its own, the work of all these historians is deeply informed by American values. The radical transformation of which some of them speak, in essence, boils down to blacks using the history of both their mistreatment and their struggle to bring white America to the fulfillment of its own democratic ideals. In this way they are in the spirit of the whole tradition of black historical scholarship in the United States and of the scholarship of sympathetic whites writing about that experience as well.

With the outpouring of monographic research and publication of the late 1960s and 1970s resulting from the convergence of a number of diverse intellectual streams, few works were actually written from the perspective of the advocates of the new black history. There is a certain irony in this, since with the appearance in this period of major books by black and white scholars both on the history of white racism and on the history of the black community and its culture, the new black history's two principal themes had achieved ascendancy. In addition, the prominence of these twin emphases created its own kind of dilemma. For it has not been easy to integrate both of them in published scholarship — to reconcile a crushing and overwhelming oppression with the assertion of dignity, cultural autonomy, and community cohesiveness. Indeed, there has been a certain bifurcation in the monographs that have appeared, with historians stressing either one or the other. Even a broad survey of the black experience like Blassingame and Berry's *Long Memory,* co-authored by one of the major contributors to the study of the slave community and by one of the leading writers on the theme of white oppression, does not successfully fuse the two subjects, for the book is primarily an indictment of white racism. Nor did Eugene Genovese's attempt to use the concept of planter paternalism to explain the existence of both white racism and black culture and to show how slave behavior was shaped by inputs from both masters and bondsmen prove satisfying to most historians, either. Thus paradoxically, *Roll, Jordan, Roll,* the one major work on slavery that adopted an interpretation attuned to the black nationalist wave at the turn of the 1970s, has been viewed as a decidedly flawed book. But then neither has anyone else successfully synthesized the dual thrust of the new black history.

The new black history was in revolt not only against the black practitioners of the old Negro history, but also against the phenomenon of white scholars having since mid-century done so large a proportion of the publication in the field. The questioning and criticism of the role of these white historians paralleled developments in the civil rights movement where black activists, uncomfortable about the prominent part whites had played, excluded them from leadership and ultimately from membership in organizations like SNCC and CORE. The controversy over white scholarship in Afro-American history can also be seen as a generational rebellion that took a racial form, and to the extent that established white scholars were condemned it was partly due to the fact that they were simply there. (On the other hand, Franklin and Quarles, who were not only criticized occasionally in print but also were privately called "oreos" for their assimilationist outlook, by virtue of their tact and symbolic importance perhaps received less criticism than might have otherwise occurred.) The whole problem was accentuated because of the anomaly created by the generation gap described in Chapter 2, and the discomfort—even among black historians who never joined the ranks of those wishing to banish whites from the field—arising out of the paucity of recent monographs by blacks and the fact that whites had loomed so large in black historiography ever since the publication of Stampp's *The Peculiar Institution.*

It was no accident that this "insider-outsider" controversy coincided with the cresting of the Black Power phase of the protest movement, or that it erupted quite suddenly in 1968-69 just as colleges and universities were introducing black history courses and black studies programs. The argument that blacks because of their experience had superior insight into the study of the black past, that only they could understand black history (a revival in a new form of what Franklin had once labeled the "mystique" of Negro studies), was an epistemological question endemic in the behavioral sciences at the time.[15]

But far more than abstract questions of epistemology were involved. At stake were power and "turf," for there were questions of who was going to control the programs: who would be teaching the courses and who would be setting the agenda for their content. Partly it seemed an ironic injustice that if because of the small number of blacks with doctorates in history, white professors should fill the vacuum created by the need to staff the new courses established at the demand of Negro students. On the other hand, as a black scholar teaching at a northern university in the late 1960s recalls, it was hard to tell how much of the anger exhibited on the issue was genuine and how much was tactical, articulated to obtain the jobs opened up by the black studies programs through intimidation and by playing upon the guilt feelings of white academicians. There was also a political dimension: the push for black faculty—preferably radical— was a corollary of the demand from Afro-American student organizations for a program to build black identity, serve the needs of local Afro-American communities, and enhance the struggle for black liberation and the restructuring of American society. Harding, whose attempt to create at the Institute of the Black World a center that he hoped would shape the future of black studies curricula—and whose efforts at such hegemony were resented by certain blacks who wryly charged him with promoting a "Black Studies Vatican"—put the matter succinctly when he wrote, "We seek for control of our own story."[16] Although neither Harding through the institute nor anyone else was able to determine the content of what remained a highly pluralistic field, blacks did come to possess a virtual monopoly over the teaching of Afro-American history.[17]

Actually this was not the first time the issue of black control over scholarship in Afro-American studies had surfaced. In the early 1930s it was explicitly debated in connection with the Phelps-Stokes encyclopedia project. Before then, whatever ambiguities black historians had about white scholarship in the field, the issue had not achieved salience. Woodson from the start had had a black agenda, and the fragmentary surviving evidence about his initial negotiations with Jameson in 1916 suggest that black control over the direction and sponsorship of research in the field was a matter of concern. Woodson was convinced that "if the story of the Negro is ever told it must be done by scientifically trained Negroes," that in "pursuing the real history and the status of the Negro . . . men of other races cannot function efficiently because they do not think black." (His friend Charles Wesley similarly believed that "no member of the other group can study our group as successfully as one of our group can. They can produce a study, but rarely does it do justice to the case under consideration. The one who feels the pinch can tell the story of the joy or pain more convincingly and truthfully than another.") Still, as Franklin recalled, Woodson welcomed works by white historians, "so long as they were the product of rigorous scholarship and were not contaminated by the venom of racial bias. . . . He would have been appalled with the bickering that enveloped the Association in the 1960s over the question of whether white historians should be permitted to participate in the work of the Association."[18]

In the case of the encyclopedia, as we have seen in Chapter 1, the role that Anson Phelps Stokes projected for whites aroused serious objection. Several considerations were involved in the discussions that took place over this issue. Funding would have to come from white sources that were interested in advancing interracial understanding and believed that a biracial enterprise could best further that goal. In addition, a problem was posed by the role in the project envisaged for suspect whites like Thomas Jesse Jones. Finally, it was Woodson's fear that such a project would undermine the position that the ASNLH occupied in the field of Negro historical scholarship.

In the course of the ensuing arguments over white participation on the encyclopedia, Woodson maintained that studying the black experience was "a task which only the colored man can do. The white man, even when he is honest and sincere, cannot . . . write the history of colored people and portray their present status, when he does not live and move among them."[19] Yet Woodson insisted that he was "in no sense opposed to interracial cooperation, I am very much in favor of it," as the work of the ASNLH demonstrated. "White men contribute to our support and scholars of every race make literary contributions to the Journal of Negro History. . . . The program of the Association for the Study of Negro Life and History, however, is conceived by Negroes; and liberal-minded members of the other race assist us in . . . helping us to help ourselves." As he wrote on a subsequent occasion: "In almost every issue of the Journal of Negro History appears an article written by some white scholar. . . . In these cases, however, the whites are helping us to do what we desire to do in treating scientifically the records of the Negro."[20]

Du Bois at first wished for an entirely black editorial staff and board (with an advisory group of white scholars), since, as he put it, such an encyclopedia should express "temperately but clearly the point of view of the Negro race." "The time is past," he maintained, "for white scholars or any combination of white and Negro scholars to write an encyclopedia 'for the Negro.' The time is ripe when Negro scholarship can and should produce an encyclopedia, with aid and criticism, and in some cases the participation of white scholars." However, nearly all the other blacks involved in the discussions, while leaning toward Du Bois's arguments, nevertheless, for pragmatic reasons, voted for a biracial staff and board. As James Weldon Johnson, the well-known writer and former NAACP executive secretary, put it, "The question was one of effectiveness," of reaching an audience of white influentials. "[I]n the last analysis [the encyclopedia] was not a scientific work in the abstract but propaganda in the highest sense."[21] Du Bois ultimately reversed his position. Impressed with the support he had been able to enlist from prominent European scholars as well as specialists of both races in the United States, he informed foundation officials that "after four years consideration I have changed my attitude. . . . [W]e can expect to have a work which from the beginning will be recognized for its scientific impartiality and will not be simply a document to express the Negro point of view."[22]

The discussions over the encyclopedia revealed virtually unanimous sentiment among black intellectuals that it was preferable for scholarship on the black experience to be done by Negroes themselves. Yet white scholarship unmarked by racial bias was also welcomed, and in fact the question of whites contributing to the field did not become a public issue again for more than three decades. Meanwhile after mid-century the ranks of publishing scholars in the field of Afro-American history became populated mainly by white scholars — without their credentials being questioned by black historians themselves.

The rapidly changing social landscape at the end of the 1960s presented a new perspective. Black intellectuals were showing an unprecedented interest in Afro-American history, while a widespread perception that black history must provide the tools for racial liberation was developing. Equally important in sparking the debate over who was qualified to teach black history was the proliferation of Afro-American history courses both in black studies programs and in history departments. As long as black history had been a rare offering outside of the Negro colleges, there had hardly been occasion to debate the question of racial qualifications for teaching it. But when in 1968-69 history departments were hastily introducing courses on the black experience and sympathetic white historians were retooling and volunteering to teach them, a chorus of protest arose from black student militants and nationalist intellectuals. Regardless of their interests or credentials, the presence of white scholars in the classroom was everywhere sharply questioned by the new generation of students. At Harvard it was Frank Freidel; at Columbia it was Eric Foner; at Wisconsin it was Robert Starobin; at the University of Pennsylvania it was Theodore Hershberg; at Kent State it was August Meier; at Morgan State it was Thomas Cripps. No matter what their perspective, no matter what their expertise, whites teaching the Afro-American history courses were under attack. Thus Starobin's biographer recounts his experience in the lecture hall: "Many black students resented him, felt that the color of his skin disqualified him from teaching the course. They often heckled, jeered, or walked out while [he] lectured. There were days when he felt the pressure was almost unbearable, when he was tempted to yell . . . 'I can't stand the hassle another minute.' "[23]

The controversy thus engendered on the campuses spilled over into learned conferences and the conventions of professional organizations. The issue was particularly salient at the 1969 OAH convention. At one session Harding, Stuckey, and the writer Julius Lester gave papers articulating the black nationalist point of view, insisting that blacks alone were the ones to interpret their own past. According to the official report of the convention, "It would be absurd, said Harding," lumping together all white scholars, sympathetic or not to the blacks' aspirations, "if blacks were now to require validation of their work by the white historian who has betrayed their heritage. Stuckey . . . stated that blacks and whites held too radically different assumptions about the human experience of blacks to conduct a true dialogue. Until a common basis exists, each must go his own way."[24] Significantly at the same convention Woodward devoted his presidential address, "Clio with Soul," to the subject. Conceding that modern white historians, propelled by a sense of guilt, had too often written Negro history as "the record of what the white man believed, thought . . . and did *about* the Negro," and that there was some truth to the claim that those who have undergone an experience understand it better than others, Woodward observed that the white man's version of the nation's history certainly "could profit from an infusion of 'soul.' " Still, "a corrective influence" was one thing, "a mandate for the exclusive preemption of a subject by reason of racial qualification is quite another. They cannot have it both ways. Either black history is an essential part of American history and must be included by all American historians, or it is unessential and can be segregated and left to black historians." The nationalistic "cry that only blacks are truly qualified to write or to interpret or to teach the black experience" was "to subscribe to an extreme brand of racism." John Blassingame, Woodward's student and future colleague at Yale, presented similar arguments; in a paper delivered at the AHA the following December he was even more severe than Woodward in his denunciation of most white scholarship, but maintained that " 'blackness'. . . represents no mystical guarantee of an 'understanding' of the black man's problems, life or culture. Neither color nor earnestness but training must be the test applied to any teacher."[25]

In the meantime, at Wayne State University's Convocation on the Black Man in May 1969 and at the ASNLH convention in October, there were open confrontations about the role of white historians. It was at the Wayne State meeting, Stampp recollects, that criticism of his work seemed to have erupted quite suddenly, with black militants insisting that because he was a white man he had no right to do *The Peculiar Institution*. At the session featuring Starobin's "Privileged Bondsmen and the Process of Accommodation: The Role of Houseservants and Drivers as Seen in Their Own Letters,"[26] Harding stalked out as the paper was being read, while both Stuckey and Lester delivered acid commentaries. Lester, who later regretted his part, recalled: "It was one of those situations that are unavoidable when blacks and whites come together in post–Black Power America, a situation in which people are not individuals, but historical entities. . . . In absolute terms," the view that the white scholar's "presence is unwanted and undesirable . . . is obviously unjust. Historically, it is the present reality, and that day . . . , though I didn't know him [Starobin] . . . I knew what I had to do to him. He had to be attacked and I did so."[27]

Even more dramatic was the scene at the ASNLH convention. Given the fact that beginning in 1966 (when Woodward gave the keynote address), program chairman J. Walter Fisher of Morgan State College had capitalized on the burgeoning white scholarship in black history to arrange for extensive white participation, the 1969 meeting provided an obvious forum for open controversy. Young black militants, unwilling to heed seriously what was being said, shouted down white speakers on the grounds that the latter could not understand what it felt like to be black. There was the reception accorded, for example, Herbert Gutman, who was presenting his early findings on the prevalence of two-parent households among antebellum free Negroes; that his evidence supported the black militants' position on the Moynihan report was ignored. Another white scholar who experienced a similar response to his own paper at this convention recollected: "He [Gutman] was shouted down. And I remember how shattered he was. He told me, 'I'm honest and I am extremely supportive of the black liberation movement—if people would just forget that I am white and hear what I am saying. Actually, what I am saying would lend support to the black liberation movement.' "

The issue was hotly debated over the next few years. As Lester observed, "In these days any white man who devotes himself to teaching and writing about black history must have the fortitude and strength of a bull elephant."[28] One white scholar who seems to have been in the "bull elephant" category was Eugene Genovese. About the time that Woodward delivered his OAH presidential address, Genovese, whose own expertise in black history had been sharply questioned by Harding during a heated exchange over William Styron's controversial novel, *The Confessions of Nat Turner,* penned his *Atlantic Monthly* article, "Black Studies: Trouble Ahead." "The demand for all-black faculties rests on the insistence that only blacks can understand the black experience. This cant," Genovese maintained, "is nothing new: it forms the latest version of the battle cry of every reactionary nationalism. . . . To be perfectly blunt, it now constitutes an ideologically fascist position and must be understood as such."[29] For his part, Stuckey publicly took issue with Woodward's OAH address. The Yale historian, he charged, even though "far more enlightened than the majority of white historians, represents in his thinking, so much that is wrong with the ways in which the past is regarded by white historians." Woodward, Stuckey complained, offered "no indication that he is aware of the role which Negro historians have played vis-à-vis the history of Afro-Americans." And he added: "Of this we may be certain; white historians, save perhaps the most radical of the future, will *never* acknowledge what blacks have done for the country or what Americans have done to blacks."[30]

Eventually the controversy simmered down. Several developments accounted for this. Weary with the bickering and argumentation, the whites who had volunteered to staff the new courses in black history withdrew, while history departments and university administrations, faced with black pressures and anxious to meet affirmative action guidelines, decided to exclude whites from consideration for such jobs in all but a few instances. In the course of the 1970s there was both a decline of separatist-nationalist sentiment and the appearance of a significant corpus of publication by the new generation of black historians, a number of them now teaching in history departments of major colleges and universities. As black historians rose through the ranks and achieved standing as scholars; as some, originally hired in black studies departments, moved into history departments after producing significant monographs; as blacks achieved an unprecedented degree of recognition at meetings of the predominantly white professional organizations, becoming increasingly visible in speaking about their own past at sessions of the AHA, OAH, and SHA; and as, with the ending of the generation gap, Afro-American historians were once again making important contributions to the field, the idea that whites were not qualified to write black history lost a good deal of its urgency.

On the other hand, although certain hurt and discouraged whites turned to other research specialities, the sheer demography of the profession—with blacks continuing to form only a tiny proportion of practicing historians—meant that whites continued to play a prominent part in writing about the Afro-American past. Besides, the important contributions by certain white scholars to the field of community and culture studies converged with the agenda which the new school of black history had set. Given these considerations, as well as the ambivalence in black thinking that has historically always made a consistently nationalist position difficult for American Negroes to maintain, it is not surprising that after several years even the most nationalist of the black historians had, as it is sometimes said, "come to terms with the more complex realities." Virtually all publishing historians in the field now agree that both whites and blacks have contributions to make to Afro-American historical scholarship.

The insider-outsider controversy has largely subsided, certainly among those engaged in serious scholarship. Yet it has left important residues. Some of the critics who have overtly come to terms with the presence of white scholars in the field are not entirely comfortable and feel unhappy because so many whites established themselves as important and influential writers in Afro-American history. In some quarters whites are perceived as dominating the field. Given the many white graduate students and the substantial number of white senior scholars who in the late 1960s and 1970s became excited about doing research in black history and given the small numbers of black Ph.D.s, the white predominance in published scholarship was inevitable. Even after the thin ranks of black doctorates began making their mark as publishing scholars during the 1970s, the prominence of whites—whether measured in terms of books and articles in the major journals or in terms of winning prestigious prizes—was such that Darlene Clark Hine could comment unhappily that "most of the highly-acclaimed historical works were, with a few exceptions, written by white scholars." In fact, she judged that the legitimization of black history had "proved a bonanza for the [white] professional historians already in positions to capitalize from the movement."[31]

In addition, several people we interviewed felt that the tensions associated with the insider-outsider controversy fueled latent anti-Semitism, though there was disagreement on this score. A few black scholars mentioned that resentment at what was regarded as "Jewish domination" in the field of black history was an important, although unfortunate phenomenon in some quarters. Others dismissed it as a rarely discussed topic of little or no significance and thought that, if anything, Jewish prominence in the field was on the wane. On the other hand, some Jewish historians felt that criticism of white scholarship was aimed with special force at them—that as one said, "The signs are up: 'No Jews Need Apply.'"

Moreover, the view that there are distinct (and identifiable) white and black perspectives in the treatment of the Afro-American experience gained wide intellectual currency among scholars of both races during these years, although the white scholars we interviewed were less likely to express this belief than blacks. Blacks tended to see evidence of this difference in the way in which black historians "are more likely to ask the right questions," to have "a better grasp of the black community and its institutions," or to possess "a profound empathy for the black experience, rather than simply dealing with cold facts." That blacks write with "greater depth of feeling," with "a sense of mission," was a common view expressed by black historians. One commented: "Among white scholars there is less of an emotional commitment. In their writing they are much more aloof and remote from the problem. There is not the same kind of fervor." Another black declared: "I can pick up a book and tell if a white or a black wrote it. Whites are concerned with nuts and bolts—their work is drier, more impersonal. . . . Black scholars are into a very people-oriented history— they are not into scientific, or precise quantitative kinds of history. Except for Thomas Holt, black scholars are on the fringes of the current methodology. Black scholars use their history to critique America . . . to pull off the shrouds that hide the contradiction between the American Creed and the country's racism." A white historian made similar observations: "Mostly blacks write history differently from whites because, simply stated, history-writing grows out of a scholar's politics and personal associations. White scholars are much more likely to be exclusively professional in their writing. . . . Black scholars are likely to express their political concerns in their writing. . . . Not too many blacks who write history are in quantification or statistical analysis. Black writers tend to have an intense interest in culture and celebratory-writing." There was also a view expressed by certain scholars of both races that a distinction should be drawn between the history of race relations, which whites were qualified to study, and the history of the black experience, which they were not equipped to understand. One well-known southern white historian asserted that as a white man he simply could never penetrate and understand black culture, and accordingly he limits his research into inquiries about race relations. A younger white scholar, in publishing his findings in 1979 on the slave experience, apologetically wrote, "As a white historian, I have been painfully aware of the problem [of researching a monograph on the black experience]. . . . It is indeed presumptuous of a white scholar to attempt to reveal how black men and women felt about their enslavement." Only that he was working with the words of ex-slaves themselves, he felt, justified his undertaking the task.[32] But compared to other white historians, his was an extreme position. More typical was the view offered by a highly distinguished senior white historian known for his seminal contribution to the field, who, like Woodward in his OAH address, argued that the fact that one indeed wrote with the perspective of an outsider did not mean that his scholarship was of less value. Genovese succinctly summed up this outlook when he noted: "The general reply to it [the position that only blacks can understand the black experience]—if one is necessary— is simply that the history of every people can only be written from within and without."[33]

While there was widespread agreement in abstract terms about differences in racial perspectives, it nevertheless proved difficult for those we interviewed to pinpoint the ways in which these differences were evident in specific scholarly works. Indeed, when asked to indicate how a particular monograph might have differed if done by a scholar of the other race, in most instances individuals with whom we spoke were at a loss to answer and finally said that for many studies at least, neither choice of topic nor method of research nor the way in which the data were handled nor the particular interpretation was identifiable as either white or black. One very prominent white historian who accepted the proposition that there is a black perspective at the same time observed that there were books by black historians such as Thomas Holt and Robert Engs that had "little that is distinctively black." There was, moreover, a certain irony in all the discussion about a black perspective, since blacks themselves say that some of the most important works that exemplify that perspective have been done by white scholars. Peter Wood's *Black Majority,* Herbert Gutman's *The Black Family in Slavery and Freedom,* and Lawrence Levine's *Black Culture and Black Consciousness* in particular are regarded as works that black scholars might have done. As one black historian said of Levine's monograph, "The book is remarkable for any historian, especially by one who is outside of the black group. . . . Levine is an exception—this book has a spiritual quality . . . which works by most white scholars lack." Black historians expressed some ambivalence—a feeling that a Negro should have been the one to do a book like Levine's—but the achievement of such a scholar could not be gainsaid. Stuckey, for example, who had been extremely skeptical of the likelihood that whites could use black folklore materials effectively,[34] was impressed. Indeed, Levine, presenting his paper on slave spirituals at the 1969 AHA convention during the height of the insider-outsider controversy, was pleasantly surprised when the black militant Michael Thelwell, one of the commentators, enthused that it was a real turning point when a white scholar could execute such a study so successfully.

The fact is, of course, that people bring different experiences to their research, and blacks had experiences that whites did not, and vice versa. Still blacks themselves had a diversity of experience, and there was no single black perspective any more than there was a single white perspective, a point Genovese had expressed at the peak of the spirited debates over the matter: "There is no such thing as a black ideology or a black point of view. Rather there are various black-nationalist biases, from leftwing versions such as that of the Panthers to rightwing versions such as that of Ron Karenga and other 'cultural nationalists.' There are also authentic sections of the black community that retain conservative, liberal, or radical integrationist and antinationalist positions. Both integrationist and separatist tendencies can be militant or moderate, radical or conservative. . . . All these elements have a right to participate in the exploration of black historical and cultural themes."[35] It is true that only a black could have written Harding's prophetic and messianic *There Is a River,* but few black scholars write that kind of history. At the other end of the continuum, Thomas Holt was several times cited by blacks we interviewed as one who not only was equipped to handle quantitative techniques, but who produced a book that "could have been written by either a black or a white historian."* There was indeed a considerable overlap between the kinds of things individual whites and individual blacks were writing. Grappling with this situation, one well-known black historian who believes that there is a distinctive black insider perspective nevertheless declared in frustration: "I wish my vocabulary contained more nuanced terms to describe shades of opinion, for 'black' and 'white' are far too simplistic to be accurate. Not all blacks, most notably the neoconservatives, share the orientation that I'm calling 'black.' And not all whites hold what I'm calling 'white' views; Lawrence Levine and Herbert Gutman, for instance, are able to think about history in what I'd call 'black' ways."[36]

We would argue that what is involved here is not so much a question of racial perspective as a question of generational perspective. What occurred in the late 1960s and early 1970s was by no means unique. It was, in fact, not unprecedented for the work of white scholars to be regarded

---

* On the other hand, John H. Bracey, Jr., in critiquing our original manuscript, perceived Holt's book as functioning in a very different way. He wrote: "The issue here is the knowledge of what questions to raise and who feels safe in raising them. Holt's book is about color conflict within the Black community. Few whites would have been the first to write about that for fear of appearing to be minimizing white oppression. Nell Painter's *Black Exodusters* is much more critical of Black leadership than a book by a liberal white would dare to be."

as consonant with the perspective of black intellectuals, even though such white historians arrived at their findings out of their own particular experiences. In the 1940s Aptheker's *American Negro Slave Revolts,* and in the 1950s Stampp's *The Peculiar Institution,* though both rooted in ideologically white radical sensibilities, were virtually synonymous with what black historians said and felt on the subject of slavery. And in the early 1960s Meier's *Negro Thought in America, 1880-1915,* basically rooted in white liberal sensibilities — though informed also by years of living in black college communities and interacting with Negro intellectuals — was seen in similar terms and on occasion was even viewed as written by a black scholar. Given the recurring nature of this congruence in the perspectives of leading specialists of both races; given the rebellion among some of the most recent generation of black historians against both the Negro and white historians of preceding decades; and given the way in which the successful white-authored culture-and-community studies of the 1970s developed autonomously of the call that came form the proponents of the new black history, it would seem quite evident that what we are dealing with here is primarily another manifestation of the generational changes in scholarly perspective with which this book has been so largely concerned.

The heated arguments notwithstanding, one should not exaggerate the polarization among scholars in the field that occurred in the late l960s and early 1970s. As we have noted, the nationalist impulse that crested in these years had relatively little impact on the nature of subsequent published monographic research, and indeed the point of view expressed in most of the books authored by the new generation of black historians was far more universalistic than the intensity of the debate at the turn of the decade might have led one to anticipate.

As the evidence in Chapter 3 indicates, many of these black historians, though socialized and inspired by the protest movement of the 1960s, never became highly politicized or ideological; others moved away from a nationalist perspective in the course of their graduate and teaching careers. While there was a general waning of separatism among blacks, the kind of socialization experienced by the younger black publishing scholars in predominantly white history departments also encouraged a more universalistic outlook. To a significant degree the legitimization and institutionalization of black history were rooted in the radicalization of the profession. Yet paradoxically enough, this very legitimization and institutionalization encourged a shift away from radical objectives to nonideological and professional ones. Our interviews indicated that such changes in viewpoint involved genuine shifts in perception and attitude, as the patterns of race relations and the role of blacks in the profession changed.

On the other hand, the shift in perspective was partly, as some of the blacks with whom we spoke put it, a matter of "strategy." A decade and half ago, an anti-white rhetoric would bring results by striking a chord of guilt among white academicians, while today a black nationalist position is no longer considered "professional." That is, it neither accords with the self-image of scholarly competency that all historians desire to have nor helps one get ahead in the predominantly white professional world that is by now largely committed to affirmative action but is also desirous of hiring blacks with scholarly credentials. One Negro historian observed that there was even a tendency on the part of younger blacks, desiring to "make it" in the history profession, to "ditch themselves" from the black studies departments once their scholarly attainments had secured them a joint appointment in history. It is perhaps no coincidence that nationalist orientations by and large survive most vigorously in black studies departments, where rather few have distinguished themselves as scholars, although here also ideological viewpoints vary considerably. (One individual who perceived the shifting black perspectives as mainly strategic carried this line of analysis a step further, observing that such considerations had also been at the heart of what the earlier generations of Afro-American historians had written. In effect they had adopted a strategy that they hoped would vindicate the race from charges of inferiority and demonstrate that blacks could assimilate into white American society.) In any event the professional urge, the desire to do work that is recognized in the guild as a genuine scholarly contribution, has been an intense one — so much so, in fact, that the strong personal commitments and value judgments of scholars like Darlene Clark Hine and Vincent Franklin were only marginally evident in their published dissertations.

While we would not discount such professional considerations, we would reiterate the importance of both the basically nonideological viewpoint of many of the most recent generation of Negro historians and of the genuine shift in outlook among blacks generally in the course of the 1970s. Also, by the beginning of the 1980s there were two other tendencies, appearing among a small group of black scholars, that epitomized the trend toward a decidedly universalistic perspective. One was the downgrading of race as opposed to class as an interpretative construct, a neo-Marxist approach shared with many of the younger generation of white radical historians. The other was a desire to avoid being identified as a specialist in black history. These two developments are epitomized by Barbara Fields and Armstead Robinson, both of whom declined to be interviewed for this volume on the grounds that since they were not specialists in black history, they did not belong in a book on the study of contributors to the writing of Afro-American history.

Fields, a former Woodward student whose research interests have centered on Reconstruction and the Emancipation experience (and author of *Slavery and Freedom on the Middle Ground: Maryland during the Nineteenth Century* [1985]), has served as associate editor of the documentary history of freedmen during and after the Civil War, a project that is being directed by Ira Berlin. She not only articulates a Marxist class interpretation but also is highly critical of historians for reifying the abstract concept of race. Class, she writes, "refers to a material circumstance; the inequality of human beings from the standpoint of social power. . . . Race, on the other hand, is a purely ideological notion."[37] Robinson, a militant black leader at Yale in the late 1960s, where he did a senior honors thesis on blacks in Memphis during the 1860s, had once been in the avant-garde of those demanding black studies curricula. His 1981 *JAH* article, "Beyond the Realm of Social Consensus: New Meanings of Reconstruction for American History," while essaying a synthesis of class and racial perspectives of the Reconstruction period, nevertheless advocates placing "the process of social class development at the center of the study of Reconstruction politics."[38] Both scholars identify themselves as in American rather than Afro-American history. Fields's position is that her research into the black experience is as much American social history or southern history as is the study of the white experience. Robinson, although director of the University of Virginia's Carter G. Woodson Institute for Afro-American and African Studies, is equally firm in rejecting identification as a specialist in black history.[39] He defines himself as a Civil War and Reconstruction historian and is especially proud of his responsibility for teaching the course on the sectional conflict at a major southern university.

Another dimension to both the ebb and flow of nationalist sentiments and to the professionalization of the new generation of black historians was the fate of the feeble attempt at organizing a black caucus within the mainstream historical organizations. In the late 1960s, as the number of black professors and graduate students in the humanities and social sciences began increasing rapidly, Negro academicians experienced a dilemma over how their advancement in the predominantly white learned societies could be pursued to best advantage. The issue was whether they should work as individuals in a thoroughly integrated way, or whether they should organize racially, with demands for recognition that would advance blacks into the mainstream of these organizations by following a separatist strategy. Black caucuses appeared in a number of specialties—sociology, political science, psychology, psychiatry, and in the African Studies Association—but not in history. There was, it is true, an abortive move among a small group to form a caucus in the AHA, but it disbanded after a meeting or two.

Although some of the black historians with whom we discussed the matter had wondered about it, there was no consensus as to why the experience of the historical profession had differed from that of other fields. Various explanations were suggested, however: the small number of blacks in the predominantly white historical organizations during the 1960s; the existence of an alternative black-controlled organization in the ASNLH; and the relative openness of the historical profession both to studying the black experience and to including blacks in offices and on programs. Certainly the ASNLH (where a rebellion forced a change in name in 1972 to the Association for the Study of Afro-American Life and History) provided an arena of activity for many of the younger black history professors. Certainly also black representation on AHA-SHA-OAH convention sessions and organizational committees and offices increased markedly, without overt demands from the black scholars. As several of the blacks with whom we spoke noted, the fact that historians seemed more open than members of other disciplines inhibited the formation of black caucuses.

Taken together these hypotheses form a viable heuristic explanation, whose convincing nature is suggested by comparing the experience of the historical profession with what happened in the fields of sociology and English.[40] The number of Negroes in the American Sociological Association (ASA) had been far larger than it was in history, and blacks had been considerably more in evidence at conventions. This situation reflected a tradition going back to the era of Robert E. Park with his interest in race relations and the time in the late 1940s when blacks as contributors to the major sociological journals, as members of the board of editors of the *American Sociological Review,* and as presidents of both the American Sociological and Eastern Sociological Associations were represented in a way that simply had no parallel anywhere else in academe. But the shift in interest from social reform to quantified "objective" science had helped make race relations and black life a backwater in sociological research, and black sociologists of the older generation found themselves relegated to a more marginal position within the profession, with all the ambivalences about their place in it that this engendered. Thus, the growth of important historical research on race relations and the black experience during the post–World War II era had no counterpart among sociologists; not until the mid-1960s was a renewed interest reflected in sociological publications. On the other hand, Negro sociologists were numerous enough to form a critical mass that supplied a base for organized activity. The younger militants — their agitation facilitated by the radical tilt that was far stronger among white sociologists than among historians — paved the way, but the ambivalent and somewhat alienated middle-aged black sociologists, who had long held strongly integrationist, universalist perspectives, in time came to support and even lead the black caucus. Exercising a moderating influence, and resisting the demands of the most disaffected youth for withdrawing entirely from the ASA, they pressed with considerable effectiveness for greater recognition within the organization.

In the Modern Language Association (MLA) the number of blacks was even smaller than in the historical societies. This field also had alternative organizations: the all-black College Language Association with its own scholarly journal, and the National Council of Teachers of English (NCTE). The NCTE had far more black college teachers in its membership than did the MLA, and it was far more responsive to black concerns. For example, in the 1950s the NCTE, like the AHA and the MVHA but unlike the MLA, had decided not to meet in southern cities. The NCTE with its substantial black membership among teachers at all academic levels provided the arena for a particularly effective black caucus: within a decade after the caucus had been formed three blacks had served as president of the organization. On the other hand, even after the white radicals and feminists achieved ascendancy in the MLA, black participation, while somewhat improved, remained low.

At the AHA and the other predominantly white historical associations there had been few black members as late as the middle 1960s. The ubiquitous presence of Franklin notwithstanding, black attendance at conventions was a relative rarity, and such participation as existed was limited mainly to a small cluster of individuals. Blacks were still reluctant to join an organization like the AHA and attend its conventions; they quite naturally still felt left out and regarded Franklin, with his wide-ranging contacts, as in a highly exceptional role. Yet beginning with the latter part of the 1960s, hand in hand with the rising number of black doctorates and graduate students and the growing employment of black faculty in predominantly white institutions of higher education, the AHA, SHA, and OAH made conscious efforts to attract and build black participation. Franklin's growing stature itself symbolized the openness of the profession. Both his symbolic role and the obvious increase in black participation together must certainly have served as crucial factors in inhibiting the kind of separatism and confrontation that was found in sociology and political science. Certainly, if an important function of the separatist black caucuses was to further the integration of blacks into the professions, they did not seem essential in the historical associations.

The forces of the black protest of the 1960s and the leftward tilt of many of the younger historians in the profession produced a social consciousness that led numerous departments to introduce black history courses and that prompted many professors to include Negro history more fully in the standard offerings on the American past. The impetus for the inclusion of black history materials and courses in the curriculum of history departments, coming from both blacks and whites, crystallized in the wake of the assassination of Martin Luther King, Jr., in April 1968. The number of departments with a formal offering in the subject, which had been growing slowly in the mid-1960s, now suddenly and rapidly increased. In the summer of 1968 the National Endowment for the Humanities sponsored several workshops around the country for college teachers, designed to help retool historians who were planning to teach these new courses. Harvard introduced a two-semester sequence directed by Frank Freidel in 1968-69,[41] and several schools, including Cornell, the University of Michigan, and the University of Texas, sponsored a lecture series in black history as a stopgap during that academic year, pending the hiring of qualified faculty members.

Yet this institutionalization of black history as an academic specialty, coinciding with the height of the Black Power movement, produced its own dilemmas for the white academicians who had encouraged it. Thus, at the very time that black history was finally achieving legitimacy in the mainstream of American history-writing and instruction, the growth of separate black studies departments raised the question of whether history departments should offer courses in a subject being taught elsewhere in the university. Where black studies was handled as an interdisciplinary, interdepartmental program, this was no problem. Occasionally a black studies department and a history department might both offer courses in black history, but frequently the tendency was for the course to be taught in the former, sometimes cross-listed with history but often not. This development was significant since black studies departments tended to establish their own networks, their own ways of looking at the black experience, their own journals, and their own criteria for promoting faculty members; and likely as not their contact with history departments was negligible. (There are, of course, exceptions to the foregoing generalizations. At the University of Michigan, for example, Thomas Holt not only holds a joint appointment but is currently chair of the Afro-American and African studies department.)

At the same time, given the context in which black history courses were hastily being introduced, history departments faced a serious staffing dilemma—whether standard criteria regarding training and publications should be applied without consideration of a candidate's race or whether to staff the new courses with black faculty members who sometimes lacked the required credentials. Pressures from black student organizations, the force of the insider-outsider controversy, the affirmative action guidelines of the

Department of Health, Education, and Welfare, which could readily be met by employing blacks in black studies courses, and the strong desire among many white academicians to attract Negro faculty members settled this question. The result has been that in only a few institutions are whites to be found teaching black history, and these are principally in history departments in Deep South colleges, where the pressures for employing black faculty were less intense, and elsewhere as token members of black studies departments.

Such exceptions aside, it is obviously ironic that as black history achieved legitimacy and institutionalization in the white academic world, the job opportunity structure in the field functioned to inhibit research in Afro-American history by white scholars. At the time that white historians were showing greater interest in studying the black past than ever before, such hiring practices, reinforced by the severe criticism from blacks at conferences and conventions, discouraged white graduate students from entering the field and encouraged those who had done one monograph in Afro-American history to switch to other subjects. It is true that there had long been a tendency for white historians—especially those who had already established themselves in another specialty—to do one monograph in black history and then move on to another area. Indeed, it says something about the importance of the field that people of the stature of Gutman and Levine, for example, should have moved freely from other areas into their Negro history research during the 1960s, and significant works have continued to come from other prominent scholars not previously identified as being in black history. It would be difficult to know how many of the younger white historians doing their dissertations in the field had planned to devote their careers to black history, but that intention certainly characterized a number who changed fields, either because of criticism from militant blacks or because of the nature of the job market. Frequently these scholars shifted into southern, ethnic, or working-class history. Among those who did continue to write monographs in Afro-American history, and among the declining number of whites who chose to write their dissertation on black topics, the strategy widely adopted was to define oneself as a specialist in other areas. Few whites, in fact, will now identify themselves as being in black history per se. As one professor at a well-known university said, "I am in southern history. Or I could say that I am in the Civil War and Reconstruction Era. Or I could say that I am a nineteenth-century social historian. . . . In recent times it has been difficult for a white person to define himself as a specialist in black history—one doesn't do that for political reasons. It is easier to define oneself in other ways, while granting that I can continue to do research in black history. It is a matter of reality. In our university, we have a department of Afro-

American studies. . . . We in the history department are not to handle such courses . . . for political reasons."

The job market not only discouraged whites from making careers in the field but also diverted some blacks from productive scholarship. Given the gap between the sudden demand for numerous blacks to teach Afro-American history and the limited supply of people available, it was necessary to recruit Negroes from graduate schools before they had completed their Ph.D., thereby retarding their scholarly productivity.[42] Not only did many become immersed in teaching and distracted from research well before their dissertations were completed, but also in certain cases the highly competitive recruitment of blacks proved to be over-rewarding, in effect frequently making research and occasionally even obtaining the doctoral degree unnecessary for professional advancement and recognition. Moreover, nonacademic university needs — the utilization of black faculty in extracurricular matters concerning black students and the lure of administrative job offers as some institutions applied affirmative action remedies to hiring practices outside the classroom — also tended to undermine research productivity.

The impact of the legitimization and institutionalization of black history upon scholarship was also seen in the policies of book publishers. Partly, of course, the outpouring of monographs in black history was one aspect of the general explosion of scholarship that occurred in the late 1960s and early 1970s. But the turn of the decade also witnessed an unprecedented demand for books in the field. Franklin's *From Slavery to Freedom* became something of a "bestseller," and firms like Oxford and Hill & Wang with respectable backlists in black history saw sales mushroom, as others rushed in to fill the gap. Qualitatively the result was a mixed bag: Franklin in recollecting those heady years has observed: "Some writing . . . was stimulated by publishers who were anxious to take advantage of a growing market. Under pressure from . . . editors, some scholars produced works that had the sole merit of having been written with more than deliberate speed." Such books and numerous and hastily compiled anthologies provided "excellent illustrations of how scholars and scholarship can be corrupted by the prospect of monetary gain."[43] By the middle 1970s, as history enrollments dropped and as professors enlarged their interests to include other aspects of social history, the demand for black history books suitable for classroom adoption declined. Yet the competition for scholarly manuscripts actually seemed to increase. Just about all publishers in American history wanted their list to include titles in black history and, if possible, titles by black authors. Meanwhile, the revolution in library book acquisitions, with university libraries placing standing orders with jobbers for all scholarly books in English rather than selecting individual titles themselves, gave rise to a situation where certain publishers exploited this market and issued numerous mediocre books on attractive topics, including black history. The result was that while the intense interest in the field led to the writing of some brilliant, major, and seminal works, there was also an outpouring of lackluster studies. (While this situation was also characteristic of other specialties, it affected Afro-American history writing with special force.) As a consequence of the competition among publishers, library shelves are now lined with numerous pedestrian volumes, some of which—had high standards been maintained—could have been made into truly significant monographs.

Though not often overtly discussed, it is recognized that there has been a sensitive racial dimension to this question of scholarly quality in the monographs and articles that have been published. Some scholars, both black and white, with whom we have spoken have observed that most of the major and seminal works in the field as well as nearly all the prize-winning monographs have been by whites.* To some extent this situation flows from the manner in which, as we have suggested, affirmative action policies have cut two ways—providing opportunities for black scholarly productivity, on the one hand, and yet, through various mechanisms in application, inhibiting the production of research monographs. Principally, however, it is due to the fact that the number of blacks with Ph.D.s working as college and university professors has been and remains very small. Thus in the field of history the proportion of professors (both with and without Ph.D.s) who were Negroes was just under 3 percent in 1970; a dozen years later blacks were still only an estimated 4 percent of the total.[44] In the middle and late 1970s the number of history doctorates awarded to blacks grew slightly. Specifically in American history they rose from eleven in 1974 to between fourteen and eighteen annually over the next four years to twenty-seven in 1979. With the total number of Ph.D.s awarded to people of both races in American history falling from 456 in 1974 to 301 in 1979, the proportion going to blacks rose from 2.4 percent in 1974 to 9 percent in 1979. But by then knowledgeable observers were noting that the number of blacks who were beginning graduate school had been declining since the middle of the decade, as people chose careers in law, business, and government. In any event the total group of Negro professors both in absolute and in relative terms remained very small.[45]

* For example, the Pulitzer Prize winners in history and biography have included Carl N. Degler's *Neither Black Nor White*, Leon Litwack's *Been in the Storm So Long*, and Louis R. Harlan's *Booker T. Washington: The Wizard of Tuskegee*. However, two black historians have been awarded prizes by the historical organizations—Thomas Holt's *Black Over White* was recipient of the SHA's Sydnor Award, and Clayborne Carson's *In Struggle* won the AHA's Beveridge Award.

Given the tiny pool of candidates from which productive black scholars were being drawn, that most of the highly acclaimed books and articles were being done by whites — many of them by senior historians who had been publishing since the early 1960s — is not really surprising.

The complex web of circumstances under which black history became legitimized has shaped the field in a way that leaves one with a degree of disquietude. For one thing, the manner in which Afro-American history is still regarded as a teaching and research specialty particularly suitable for blacks suggests that the field continues to occupy something of a marginal place. One is still uncertain in fact as to just how seriously professors dealing with mainstream American history now take the study of the black past. After all, to no small degree, incorporation of black history and black historians into departments was a political and strategic act and did not represent a genuine commitment among many older scholars. For such people black history has not ever been very important, and one aspect of this attitude was the willingness to establish different criteria for hiring blacks — as long as they were recruited to teach black history. Advocated by many blacks and well-meaning whites as well, this policy, to use Mary Berry's words, had the effect of establishing "the program as something to let the blacks have on campus rather than as an activity to be subjected to strict intellectual scrutiny."[46]

At the very time that black history enjoys unprecedented recognition both as a specialty and as an integral part of the American past, in certain ways the field nevertheless seems to have entered something of a decline. The outpouring of books continues, but fewer articles appear in the major historical journals, and registrations for black history courses have plummeted. Partly this is nothing more than what happens to any subject that becomes institutionalized and legitimized. Thus, the strong ideological motivations associated with the demand for black history dissipated by the end of the 1970s, black students becoming oriented primarily toward practical preparation for a career,* and white students lacking the sense of urgency that the black protest movement had generated among their predecessors. The example of Columbia University, for example, is instructive. Although there was an initial surge of intense enthusiasm and

* Although solid statistics are not available, and although the situation varies from campus to campus, many black studies departments faced a similar situation, and the number of such departments seems to have declined since the early 1970s.[47] While academic officials have often not been committed to such programs, on many campuses black students themselves became less interested. At the same time, at an institution like the University of Massachusetts at Amherst, enrollments have held up very well.

individuals highly qualified to teach black history were on the history department's faculty, since the middle 1970s it has been practicable to offer the course only erratically, at times when student interest has warranted. Moreover, in regard to both teaching and research, the interest in the new social history, which had done so much to encourage study of the black past, now had paradoxical consequences. Black history, which twelve or fifteen years ago was probably the "hottest" field in American history, has now become one of several competing specialties in the wave of enthusiasm for ethnic, women's, and working-class history. Ironically, just as some of the newer textbooks are seriously seeking to integrate the black experience into the study of the American past, teachers are quite likely paying less attention to black history than they were a decade ago. Then, too, the way in which certain factors discouraged a significant number of truly interested historians from working in the area has further accentuated black history's decline from its position in the early 1970s as probably the liveliest and most innovative field within American history.

Nevertheless, the developments of the past quarter century will leave an important impact on the study and teaching of history. Historians who were socialized in the 1960s and 1970s and are still sensitive to the importance of Afro-American history are now moving into the ranks of full professors and are well on the road to becoming the dominant group in the profession. Scholars, both black and white, will continue to produce significant monographs. No longer can the black experience and the role of blacks in the broader American experience be ignored.

ESSAY ON SOURCES

THERE ARE THREE principal kinds of sources on which this book is based: the scholarly monographs and articles that form the corpus of Afro-American historiography; interviews with more than 175 living historians who have done scholarly work in the field (supplemented by interviews with relatives or close associates of eighteen deceased historians); and archival and manuscript collections.

The living historians whom we interviewed were: Eric Anderson, Herbert Aptheker, Richard A. Bardolph, Howard H. Bell, Ira Berlin, William C. Berman, Mary Frances Berry, David W. Bishop, John W. Blassingame, James Borchert, John H. Bracey, Jr., Charles Branham, Carl M. Brauer, Francis L. Broderick, Andrew Buni, Margaret Law Callcott, Shirley Carlson, William F. Cheek, Clayborne Carson, Dan T. Carter, William H. Chafe, Robert L. Clarke, Dudley T. Cornish, LaWanda F. Cox, Thomas C. Cox, Thomas R. Cripps, Harold Cruse, Leonard P. Curry, Merle E. Curti, Philip D. Curtin, Richard M. Dalfiume, Pete Daniel, Douglas H. Daniels, David Brion Davis, Carl N. Degler, James E. DeVries, Charles B. Dew, John Dittmer, Helen G. Edmonds, Stanley M. Elkins, Stanley L. Engerman, Robert F. Engs, Paul D. Escott, Donald E. Everett, Stanley Feldstein, Leslie H. Fishel, Jr., Robert W. Fogel, Eric Foner, Philip S. Foner, Jimmie L. Franklin, John Hope Franklin, George M. Fredrickson, Larry Gara, Willard B. Gatewood, Jr., Raymond Gavins, Eugene D. Genovese, Carol V. George, David A. Gerber, Al-Tony Gilmore, Laurence Glasco, Claudia Goldin, Lorenzo J. Greene, Herbert G. Gutman, Kenneth M. Hamilton, Vincent Harding, Louis R. Harlan, Sharon Harley, Robert L. Harris, Jr., William H. Harris, Janet S. Hermann, Theodore Hershberg, Darlene Clark Hine, Thomas Holt, Michael W. Homel, James O. Horton, Nathan I. Huggins, Sylvia M. Jacobs, Bobby F. Jones, James H. Jones, Winthrop D. Jordan, Charles W. Joyner, David M. Katzman, John B. Kirby, Peter D. Klingman, Peter Kolchin, Theodore Kornweibel, Jr., J. Morgan Kousser, Allan Kulikoff, Kenneth L. Kusmer, Lester C. Lamon, Rudolph M. Lapp, Steven F. Lawson, Lawrence W. Levine, Edwin R. Lewinson, David L. Lewis, Ronald L. Lewis, Daniel C. Littlefield, Leon F. Litwack, Frenise A. Logan, Rayford W. Logan, Robert M. McColley, Donald R. McCoy, William S. McFeely, Linda O. McMurry, James M. McPherson, Charles Martin, August Meier, Russell Menard, Gary B. Mills, Jesse T. Moore, Jr., Robert C. Morris,

Wilson J. Moses, Alfred A. Moss, Jr., Gerald (Michael) Mullin, Mark Naison, Gary B. Nash, Carl R. Osthaus, Leslie H. Owens, Nell I. Painter, Jane H. Pease, William H. Pease, Robert E. Perdue, Elizabeth H. Pleck, H. Leon Prather, Clement A. Price, Benjamin Quarles, Howard N. Rabinowitz, Albert J. Raboteau, Willard Range, David C. Rankin, George P. Rawick, L. D. Reddick, Edwin S. Redkey, Joe M. Richardson, Willie Lee Rose (and William Rose), Theodore Rosengarten, Margaret V. Nelson Rowley, Elliott Rudwick, Todd L. Savitt, Seth M. Scheiner, Loren Schweninger, Otey M. Scruggs, Harvard Sitkoff, Allan H. Spear, Samuel R. Spencer, Jr., Tinsley Lee Spraggins, Kenneth M. Stampp, Arvarh E. Strickland, Sterling Stuckey, Edward F. Sweat, Thad W. Tate, Arnold H. Taylor, Rosalyn Terborg-Penn, Emma Lou Thornbrough, Earl E. Thorpe, Elvena Bage Tillman, George B. Tindall, William Toll, Edgar A. Toppin, Joe William Trotter, David M. Tucker, William M. Tuttle, Jr., Charles Vincent, Richard C. Wade, Clarence E. Walker, Arthur I. Waskow, Walter B. Weare, Thomas L. Webber, Nancy J. Weiss, Charles H. Wesley, Joel Williamson, Raymond Wolters, Peter H. Wood, C. Vann Woodward, George R. Woolfolk, Norman R. Yetman, Robert L. Zangrando, and Howard Zinn.

The following people provided especially pertinent information about deceased historians. Charles H. Wesley, Rayford W. Logan, and Lorenzo J. Greene supplied useful material about Carter G. Woodson. Other individuals who were helpful were Mrs. Clarence Bacote, Mrs. Horace Mann Bond, Mrs. Winfred W. Davis (for Letitia Brown), Lois Green Carr (for Constance M. Green), Luther Porter Jackson, Jr. (for Luther Porter Jackson), Francis C. Jameson (for J. Franklin Jameson), Mrs. Charles Flint Kellogg, Frank W. Klingberg (for Frank J. Klingberg), Mrs. Fred Landon, Marcia Osofsky (for Gilbert Osofsky), Mrs. Kenneth Wiggins Porter, Mrs. W. Sherman Savage, Mrs. Joseph Starobin (for Robert S. Starobin), James Ferguson (for Vernon L. Wharton), Mrs. Bell I. Wiley, C. H. Cramer (for Harvey Wish), and James A. Moss (for Marian M. Thompson Wright). Maggie Jackson of the Indianapolis public school system, searched the files for pertinent information regarding Joseph C. Carroll.

Certain published sources provided invaluable information supplementing other biographical data: Rayford W. Logan and Michael R. Winston, *Dictionary of American Negro Biography* (1982); Michael R. Winston, *The Howard University Department of History, 1913-1973* (1973); Harry Washington Greene, *Holders of Doctorates among American Negroes* (1946); Edwin R. Embree and Julia Waxman, *Investment in People: The Story of the Julius Rosenwald Fund* (1949); General Education Board, *Directory of Fellowship Awards for 1922-1950* (ca. 1952); and *Fellows of the Social Science Research Council, 1925-1951* (1951).

Interviews with several scholars helped us with information on specific questions. Tilden G. Edelstein, Otto Olsen, and Bertram Wyatt-Brown were very informative about certain aspects of C. Vann Woodward's influence with his students. Frank L. Byrne, T. Harry Williams, and Richard N. Current supplied equally illuminating insights into William B. Hesseltine's relationships with his students. David Van Tassel and Merle Curti (as well as John Higham's *History: Professional Scholarship in America* [2d ed., 1983]), were helpful in unraveling for us certain questions about the changing outlook of historians before World War II. Lois Green Carr, in addition to providing information about her mother Constance M. Green, illuminated the work of the so-called Chesapeake School. We spoke with Bennett H. Wall on countless occasions in our efforts to understand the changing position of the SHA in regard to meeting in segregated hotels, and LeRoy P. Graf shared with us his recollections of this subject. Patrick W. Riddleberger of Southern Illinois University–Edwardsville shared with us his experiences in developing one of the earliest courses in black history offered at a predominantly white university. Darwin Turner of the department of English at the University of Iowa provided information on the integration of blacks into the Modern Language Association and the National Council of Teachers of English. J. Walter Fisher enriched our understanding about developments concerning ASNLH convention programs in the late 1960s.

We learned a great deal from talking with publishers and editors who had an active role in the publication of books in black history: Sheldon Meyer of Oxford University Press; Roger W. Shugg, one-time history editor of Alfred A. Knopf; Arthur Wang and former series editor Aida Donald of Hill and Wang; Alfred A. Knopf, Jr., and Robert J. Zenowich of Atheneum Publishers; André Schiffrin of Pantheon; and Richard L. Wentworth, former director of Louisiana State University Press and the current director of the University of Illinois Press. Moreover, J. Merton England, Sanford W. Higginbotham, and Martin Ridge shared with us their recollections of experiences as editors in connection with the publication of articles by and about blacks published in the *Journal of Southern History* and the *Journal of American History*.

One master's thesis and thirteen doctoral dissertations also provided important supplemental information on some of the people and movements discussed in this book: Susan Stout Baker, "Out of the Engagement, Richard Hofstadter: The Genesis of a Historian" (Case Western Reserve University, 1982); A. Gilbert Belles, "The Julius Rosenwald Fund: Efforts in Race Relations, 1928-1948" (Vanderbilt University, 1972); Ann Ellis, "The Commission on Interracial Cooperation, 1919-1944" (Georgia State University, 1975); Linda Forcey's dissertation on Robert Starobin, "Personality in Politics: The Commitment of a Suicide" (SUNY, Binghamton,

1978); Patrick J. Gilpin, "Charles S. Johnson: An Intellectual Biography" (Vanderbilt University, 1973); Janette H. Harris, "Charles H. Wesley: Educator and Historian" (Howard University, 1975); John E. McNeal, "James Hardy Dillard: Southern Humanitarian" (University of Virginia, 1970); James A. Moss, "Utilization of Negro Teachers in the Colleges of New York State" (Columbia University, 1957); Henry Oakes, "The Struggle for Racial Equality in the Methodist Episcopal Church: The Career of Robert E. Jones" (University of Iowa, 1973); Ralph L. Pearson, "Charles S. Johnson: The Urban League Years" (Johns Hopkins, 1970); Daniel Perlman, "Stirring the White Conscience: The Life of George Edmund Haynes" (New York University, 1972); Patricia W. Romero, "Carter G. Woodson: A Biography" (Ohio State University, 1971); Daniel C. Thompson, "Teachers in Negro Colleges (A Sociological Analysis)" (Columbia University, 1956); James Woods, "Alrutheus Ambush Taylor, 1893-1954: Segregated Historian of Reconstruction" (M.A. thesis, Louisiana State University, 1969).

We consulted a number of relevant archival and manuscript collections that are open to scholars. The most useful collections for our purposes were the W. E. B. Du Bois Papers at the University of Massachusetts at Amherst; the archives of the General Education Board and the Laura Spelman Rockefeller Memorial at the Rockefeller Research Center, Pocantico Hills, N.Y.; the files of the Carnegie Corporation of New York at its headquarters in New York City; the personal papers of Julius Rosenwald at the University of Chicago, and the Julius Rosenwald Fund Papers at Fisk University; the Jesse E. Moorland Papers at Howard University; the J. Franklin Jameson Papers at the Library of Congress; and the papers of Luther P. Jackson and J. Hugo Johnston, both at Virginia State College. The Merle E. Curti Papers and the Howard K. Beale Papers, both at the University of Wisconsin, shed important light on the controversy over meeting at Jim Crow hotels during the 1950s. John H. Roper's interviews with C. Vann Woodward and people who knew him, copies deposited with the Southern Historical Collection of the University of North Carolina, Chapel Hill, were enormously helpful on both this and other matters.

Unfortunately, the main corpus of the Carter G. Woodson Papers does not seem to have survived; some useful information was found in two small collections of Woodson Papers at Howard University and the Library of Congress. Rayford W. Logan's papers have been deposited at the Library of Congress but will not be open to scholars until the late 1980s. Nuggets of illuminating information were found in the following collections: Benjamin Brawley Papers, Howard University; Horace Mann Bond Papers, University of Massachusetts at Amherst; Frederic Bancroft Papers and Evarts B. Greene Papers, both at Columbia University; Arthur Meier Schlesinger Papers, Harvard University; Avery O. Craven Papers, Simpson College;

James W. Silver Papers, University of Mississippi; Alrutheus Ambush Taylor Papers, Fisk University; Robert Russa Moton Papers and Monroe N. Work Papers, both at Tuskegee Institute; Emmett J. Scott Papers, Morgan State University; James Hardy Dillard Papers, University of Virginia; Theodore D. Jervey Papers, South Carolina Historical Society; Rockefeller Foundation Archives and Jackson Davis Papers, both at the Rockefeller Research Center; the papers of William E. Dodd, George Foster Peabody, the American Historical Association, and the NAACP, all in the Library of Congress; the Ralph J. Bunche Papers, University of California Los Angeles Research Library; the Phelps-Stokes Fund Archives at the Schomburg Collection of the New York Public Library; the Claude Barnett Papers (containing the archives of the Associated Negro Press), Chicago Historical Society; items in the records of the Organization of American Historians, the American Historical Association, and the Southern Historical Association, located in the offices of the OAH, AHA, and University of North Carolina Library, respectively.

We depended a good deal on several journals. The standard scholarly media consulted included most notably the *Journal of Negro History,* Atlanta University's *Phylon,* the *Journal of Southern History,* the *American Historical Reveiw,* and the *Mississippi Valley Historical Review* (later the *Journal of American History*). In addition, other materials that provided helpful information for certain periods were the *Negro History Bulletin,* the NAACP's *Crisis,* Hampton Institute's *Southern Workman,* the Urban League's *Opportunity,* the *Journal of Negro Education,* and the *Tuskegee Student* and *Tuskegee Messenger.*

EXPLANATORY ESSAY ON NOTES

CERTAIN OBSERVATIONS should be made in regard to the notes that follow. In general we have deliberately been sparing in our use of citations. Wherever feasible we have included the title and date of publication of monographs in the text itself. Where it has proven necessary to cite a book in the notes, we have followed the same form, omitting both the place of publication and publisher. In the case of articles that can be easily located in the journals, we have cited the volume number and date, giving specific page numbers only where there is a reference to a quotation or to a specific point that we are making.

In regard to information about scholarly papers delivered at conventions and the data about officeholding in the learned societies, we have relied upon the standard and readily accessible reports of the organizations involved: the Association for the Study of Negro Life and History, the American Historical Association, the Southern Historical Association, and the Mississippi Valley Historical Association (now Organization of American Historians). Because full citation of this material would have been unwieldy and because the official reports about conventions and officeholding are readily available to scholars, we decided to forego the extensive standard footnoting that would have been required.

Since the interviews with historians were conducted on a not-for-attribution basis, we have rarely cited specific interviews. The principal source of the biographical data for the individuals who are still living (and for Rayford W. Logan and Herbert G. Gutman, who died since we interviewed them) will be obvious; in addition, some of our interviewees furnished observations about other historians "off the record." Interviews with relatives and close friends of historians who died before we did our research, however, are cited in the appropriate places in the notes.

Citations to the General Education Board are to Series I unless otherwise indicated. The citations to the Laura Spelman Rockefeller Memorial Archives will be found in Series III unless otherwise noted.

Chapter 1. Carter G. Woodson as Entrepreneur

1. W. E. B. Du Bois, "A Portrait of Carter G. Woodson," *Masses and Mainstream* 3 (June 1950), 19.

2. Rayford W. Logan, "Carter G. Woodson: Mirror and Molder of His Time," *JNH* 58 (Jan. 1973); Charles H. Wesley, "Carter G. Woodson—As a Scholar," *JNH* 36 (Jan. 1951); Patricia W. Romero, "Carter G. Woodson: A Biography" (Ph.D. diss., Ohio State University, 1971); Carter G. Woodson, "The German Policy of France in the War of Austrian Succession" (M.A. thesis, University of Chicago, 1908); Woodson, "The Disruption of Virginia" (Ph.D. diss., Harvard University, 1912).

3. Woodson to Du Bois, Feb. 18, 1908, in Herbert Aptheker, ed., *The Correspondence of W. E. B. Du Bois*, 1 (1973), 140.

4. John Hope Franklin, "George Washington Williams, Historian," *JNH* 31 (Jan. 1946); Franklin, "George Washington Williams," in Rayford Logan and Michael R. Winston, eds., *Dictionary of American Negro Biography* (1982).

5. W. H. Councill, *Lamp of Wisdom, Or Race History Illuminated* (1898); Booker T. Washington, *Story of the Negro* (1909).

6. Charles H. Wesley, "Racial Historical Societies and the American Heritage," *JNH* 37 (Jan. 1952); James G. Spady, "The Afro-American Historical Society: The Nucleus of Black Bibliophiles, 1897-1923," *NHB* 37 (July 1974); York Russell, *Historical Research* (1912); Arthur A. Schomburg to J. E. Bruce, June [?] 13, 1916 [?], quoted in Tony Martin, "Carter G. Woodson and Marcus Garvey," *NHB* 40 (Nov.-Dec. 1977), 774.

7. *Minutes of the Seminary of Historical and Political Science*, I, Jan. 31, 1890, quotation supplied in Raymond J. Cunningham to authors, Aug. 22, 1982.

8. Ray Allen Billington, *Frederick Jackson Turner* (1973), 436; Charles A. and Mary R. Beard, *The Rise of American Civilization* (1927), 2:38.

9. Wood Gray, "Ulrich Bonnell Phillips," in William T. Hutchinson, ed., *The Marcus W. Jernegan Essays in American Historiography* (1937), 355-57; U. B. Phillips, ed., *Plantation and Frontier Documents, 1649-1863* (2 vols., 1909), including Phillips, introduction, Richard T. Ely, preface, and John Bates Clark, general introduction; John Herbert Roper, *U. B. Phillips: A Southern Mind* (1984).

10. *MVHR* 5 (Mar. 1919), 481.

11. Carol Baird, "Albert Bushnell Hart: The Rise of the Professional Historian," in Paul Buck, ed., *The Social Sciences at Harvard, 1860-1920* (1965), 130; J. Franklin Jameson to Du Bois, June 22, 1910, in Elizabeth Donnan and Leo Stock, eds., *An Historian's World: Selections from the Correspondence of John Franklin*

Jameson (1956), 133; Marion Dargan, Jr., "Clarence Walworth Alvord," in Hutchinson, ed., *Jernegan Essays*, 324.

12. Du Bois, *The Autobiography of W. E. B. Du Bois* (1968), 148; Du Bois, "Albert Bushnell Hart," *Crisis* 32 (Oct. 1926), 284.

13. Baird, "Albert Bushnell Hart," 150; Albert Bushnell Hart, "The Outcome of the Southern Race Question," *North American Review* 188 (July 1908), 51; Hart, *The Southern South* (1910).

14. Albert Bushnell Hart, *Slavery and Abolition* (1906); Walter Dyson, *Howard University: The Capstone of Negro Education* (1941), 415; Hart to Du Bois, Apr. 24, 1905, in Aptheker, ed., *Correspondence of Du Bois*, 1:110; Hart to Du Bois, Apr. 8, 1914, reel 4, Hart to Du Bois, Oct. 10, 1929, reel 28, both in Du Bois Papers.

15. Du Bois, *Dusk of Dawn* (1940), 38; Hart to Du Bois, Nov. 17, 1924, and Du Bois to Hart, Nov. 20, 1924, Du Bois Papers, reel 13.

16. Du Bois, "Albert Bushnell Hart," 284, 286.

17. *Annual Report of the American Historical Association for the Year 1891* (Sen. Misc. Doc. 173, 52nd Cong., 1st sess., 1892), 161-74; *Annual Report of the American Historical Association for the Year 1909* (1911), 36-37; Du Bois, "Reconstruction and Its Benefits," *AHR* 15 (July 1910).

18. R. R. Wright, Sr., "Negro Companions of Spanish Explorers," *American Anthropologist*, n.s. 4 (Apr.-June 1902), and "A Negro Discovered New Mexico," *A.M.E. Church Review* 13 (July 1896). On Wright Jr.'s career, see S. P. Fullinwider, *The Mind and Mood of Black America* (1969), 36-41; Allan H. Spear, *Black Chicago* (1967), 106, 111*n*.

19. Robert Dallek, *Democrat and Diplomat: The Life of William E. Dodd* (1968), 40, 48-49; Benjamin Brawley to Dodd, Oct. 27, 1920, Nov. 25, 1919, Dodd Papers, box 14. For ambiguities in Dodd's racial views, see also Dodd to Brawley, Nov. 12, 1920, Dodd Papers, box 14.

20. C. V. Roman, *A Knowledge of History Is Conducive to Racial Solidarity* (1911), 25-27, 30, 33; A. A. Schomburg, *Racial Integrity* (1913), 5-6; Cleveland *Gazette*, Nov. 12, 1898.

21. Harry Washington Greene, *Holders of Doctorates among American Negroes* (1946), 26.

22. Fisk University *Catalogue* (title varies), *1910-1911*, 31, 44-45; *1911-1912*, 34, 50; *1915-1916*, 36, 56-57. On Haynes's career, see Daniel Perlman, "Stirring the White Conscience: The Life of George Edmund Haynes" (Ph.D. diss., New York University, 1972).

23. *Annual Catalogue of Atlanta Baptist College, 1912-1913*, 28.

24. Michael R. Winston, *The Howard University Department of History, 1913-1973* (1973), 20-21; Rayford W. Logan, *Howard University: The First Hundred Years, 1867-1967* (1969), 172; Jesse E. Moorland to Woodson, Sept. 2, 1915, Moorland Papers, folder 614.

25. Winston, *Howard University Department of History*, 20.

26. Howard University *Catalogue, 1912-1913*, 77; *1916-1917*, 90, 93; *1918-1919*, 126.

27. Woodson to Raymond B. Fosdick, Jan. 16, 1927, GEB, box 205.

28. *JNH* 4 (Oct. 1919), 474; 9 (Jan. 1924), 103-4.

29. Ibid., 20 (Jan. 1935), 4; Woodson, "Some Things Negroes Must Do," *Southern Workman* 51 (Jan. 1922), 36; *JNH* 8 (July 1923), 354; "The Celebration of Negro History Week, 1927," ibid., 12 (Apr. 1927), 105.

30. Brawley, *Negro Builders and Heroes* (1937).

31. For Woodson's views on the CIO, see editorial, "The Right to Work," *NHB* 8 (Oct. 1944), 23; and "On the Road to Peace," ibid., 9 (Nov. 1945), 26, 47. On his views about Roosevelt, see especially editorial, "The Passing of a Great Liberal," ibid., 8 (May 1945), 170, and "Questions Answered" column in ibid., 10 (Dec. 1946), 65. For his skepticism about politicians generally, see ibid., 64, and editorial, "The Third Party and the Negro," ibid., 11 (Mar. 1948), 122, 143.

32. Du Bois, "Portrait of Woodson," 21; *JNH* 1 (Jan. 1916), 98; Woodson, *The Negro in Our History* (2d ed., 1922), 277, 276, 279; *JNH* 30 (Jan. 1945), 88; 22 (Jan. 1937), 109. For view of Woodson as being decidedly anti-Washington and pro–Du Bois, see L. D. Reddick, "As I Remember Woodson," *Crisis* 60 (Feb. 1953), 77.

33. Alrutheus A. Taylor, "Dr. Carter G. Woodson: Inspirer and Benefactor of Young Scholars," *NHB* 13 (May 1950), 186.

34. E.g., Woodson, *The Rural Negro* (1930), 226, 236-38, and "Celebration of Negro History Week, 1927," 105.

35. Woodson, "Ten Years of Collecting and Publishing the Record of the Negro," *JNH* 10 (Oct. 1925), 599; announcement in *AHR* 21 (Apr. 1916), 643; Woodson, "An Accounting for Twenty-Five Years," *JNH* 25 (Oct. 1940), 428-29; "Historical Association in the Celebration of the Twentieth Anniversary Faces the Future," ASNLH press release [Aug. 1935], Barnett Papers.

36. *JNH* 34 (Apr. 1949), 227, 225. See also his praise of NAACP lawyers and A. Philip Randolph's 1941 March on Washington in Woodson, "Workers for Equality and Justice," *NHB* 8 (Mar. 1945).

37. *JNH* 34 (Oct. 1949), 387.

38. Booker T. Washington to Woodson, Oct. 3, 1915, Woodson Papers, Library of Congress (LC), reel 4; and the following in the Moton Papers: Woodson to Moton, June 6, 1917, box 7, June 7, 1918, box 33, Mar. 18, 1919, box 47, "S" to Woodson, Jan. 16, 1919, box 47.

39. *JNH* 12 (Oct. 1926), 572-73; Luther Porter Jackson, "The Work of the Association and the People," ibid., 20 (Oct. 1935), 395.

40. Woodson to Moton, Jan. 6, 1917, box 21, June 6, 1917, box 7, June 7, 1918, box 33, all in Moton Papers.

41. Woodson to Du Bois, Mar. 2, 1923, Oct. 1, 1923, and Du Bois to Woodson, Oct. 4, 1923, reel 11, and Woodson to Du Bois, Nov. 4, 1930, reel 30, all in Du Bois Papers; *JNH* 16 (Jan. 1931), 4-5.

42. Du Bois, "Man of the Month," *Crisis* 4 (July 1912), 120; Du Bois, "The Journal of Negro History," ibid., 13 (Dec. 1916), 61; Du Bois to John Hope, Mar. 25, 1925, in Aptheker, ed., *Correspondence of Du Bois*, 1:312.

43. Woodson to Moorland, Aug. 24, 1915, Moorland Papers, folder 614. On the origins of Woodson's friendship with Jackson, see A. L. Jackson, untitled comment on 50th anniversary of ASNLH, in *NHB* 28 (special summer issue 1965),

182. On Hall's relations with Washington, see Louis R. Harlan, *Booker T. Washington: The Wizard of Tuskegee, 1901-1915* (1983), 98, and ch. 18 passim. On Work's career, see Jessie P. Guzman, "Monroe Nathan Work and His Contributions," *JNH* 34 (Oct. 1949), and especially Linda O. McMurry, *Recorder of the Black Experience: Monroe Nathan Work* (1985), x. For Park's relations with Washington, see Winifred Raushenbush, *Robert E. Park: Biography of a Sociologist* (1979), esp. 41-42, 56-57, and Harlan, *Wizard of Tuskegee*, esp. 290-93. On Woodson meeting Park in the summer of 1915, see his obituary on Park, *JNH* 29 (Apr. 1944), 247, and Logan, "Woodson: Mirror and Molder," 13.

44. Moorland to Park, Jan. 7, 1921, folder 619, to Woodson, Sept. 2, 1915, folder 614, both in Moorland Papers.

45. Woodson to Moorland, Aug. 24, 1915, Moorland to Woodson, Sept. 2, 1915, Moorland Papers, folder 614; minutes of meeting printed in W. Sherman Savage, "Twenty Years of the Association for the Study of Negro Life and History," *JNH* 20 (Oct. 1935), 379-80.

46. Arvarh Strickland, *History of the Chicago Urban League* (1966), 26-31, 40-42; Allan H. Spear, *Black Chicago* (1967), 72-73, 169-74; Nancy J. Weiss, *The National Urban League, 1910-1940* (1974), 30-33, 44-45, 56-57, and ch. 9 passim. On Jackson joining National Urban League staff, see *Crisis* 19 (Mar. 1920), 279.

47. Moorland to William C. Graves, Apr. 21, 1922, Rosenwald Papers, reel 4; Woodson to Moorland, Aug. 24, 1915, Moorland Papers, folder 614; Channing Tobias, "The Colored YMCA," *Crisis* 9 (Nov. 1914), 33-35; "Report on Colored YMCA Buildings Submitted by J. E. Moorland, Jan. 15, 1920," Rosenwald Papers, reel 85; Dyson, *Howard University*, 168-69.

48. *Southern Workman* 45 (Feb. 1916), 80; Woodson to Moton, June 6, 1917, Moton Papers, box 7.

49. Tobias, "Colored YMCA," 33; Moorland, "The Young Men's Christian Association among Negroes," *JNH* 9 (Apr. 1924), 135-36; Booker T. Washington, "A Remarkable Triple Alliance," *Outlook* 108 (Oct. 28, 1914), 485; relevant correspondence in Rosenwald Papers, reel 85, passim; Weiss, *National Urban League*, 82-83; Edwin R. Embree and Julia Waxman, *Investment in People: The Story of the Julius Rosenwald Fund* (1949), 25, 262.

50. Benjamin Brawley, *Doctor Dillard of the Jeanes Fund* (1930), 52-58; John E. McNeal, "James Hardy Dillard: Southern Humanitarian" (Ph.D. diss., University of Virginia, 1970), 112, 148.

51. *Crisis* 4 (May 1912), 26; J. D. Rockefeller, Jr., to Dillard, esp. June 10, 1929, Dillard Papers, box 7.

52. On Dillard's role in organizing the University Commission on Race Relations, a predecessor of CIC, see McNeal, "James Hardy Dillard," 178-80; Charles H. Brough, "Work of the Commission of Southern Universities on the Race Question," *The Annals* 49 (Sept. 1913), 47; for Buttrick being the one to have prevailed upon Dillard to do this, see Dillard's diary, June 8, 1919, University of Virginia, Charlottesville. For origins of CIC, see Wilma Dykeman and James Stokeley, *Seeds of Southern Change: The Life of Will W. Alexander* (1962), 58-59, and Thomas Jesse Jones, *Educational Adaptations: Report of the Ten Years Work of the Phelps-Stokes Fund* [1921], 87-91; Ann Ellis, "The Commission on

Interracial Cooperation, 1919-1944" (Ph.D. diss., Georgia State University, 1975), 7-37. On Dillard's role in CIC see, McNeal, "James Hardy Dillard," 215-18.

53. Leonard Outhwaite to Edwin R. Embree, Mar. 2, 1928, LSRM, box 98; Thomas Appleget to Wickliffe Rose, Mar. 16, 1928, RBF [Raymond B. Fosdick] to JD [Jackson Davis], Nov. 18, 1937, and J. D. memo [to Fosdick], Dec. 3, 1937, with handwritten note by R.B.F., Dec. 6, 1937: "Talked with [Walter] White on phone—told him contribution [to educational discrimination fight] impossible," all GEB, box 257.

54. On funding by Rockefeller philanthropies, see Rockefeller Foundation, Annual Reports, passim, 1918-28. For role of War Work Council of YMCA, see "Appeal of the Commission on Interracial Cooperation," Jan. 24, 1922, LSRM, box 96. On LSRM contributions 1922-28, specific annual grants listed in LSRM, "Appropriations, Oct. 18, 1918 through April 30, 1928," in Rockefeller Foundation Archives, Record Group III, box 910. For Rosenwald, see A. Gilbert Belles, "The Julius Rosenwald Fund: Efforts in Race Relations, 1928-1948" (Ph.D. diss., Vanderbilt University, 1972), 102-3; Will W. Alexander to Rosenwald, Oct. 31, 1929, and Alfred Stern to R. H. King, July 13, 1927, both in Rosenwald Papers, reel 21.

55. Kenneth King, *Pan-Africanism and Education* (1971); James H. Dillard et al., *Twenty-Year Report of the Phelps-Stokes Fund, 1911-1931* (1932).

56. King, *Pan-Africanism and Education*, 30, 25-29; U.S. Bureau of Education, *Negro Education: A Study of the Private and Higher Schools for Colored People in the United States* (2 vols., 1917); McMurry, *Recorder of the Black Experience*, 50.

57. Jones, *Educational Adaptations*, 80-83, 87-91; Dillard et al., *Twenty-Year Report of the Phelps-Stokes Fund*, 16-17, 58-59; William Aery, "Negro Progress and the Phelps-Stokes Fund," *Southern Workman* 61 (Oct. 1932); King, *Pan-Africanism and Education*, 27-43; publications concerning founding of CIC cited in n. 52. On Moton's early involvement in the southern interracial movement, see also Moton, "Signs of Growing Cooperation," *Southern Workman* 43 (Oct. 1914), and Moton, "Racial Cooperation," ibid., 47 (Feb. 1918).

58. Belles, "Julius Rosenwald Fund," 13-16; Charles S. Johnson, "Phylon Profile X: Edwin Rogers Embree," *Phylon* 7 (Fourth quarter 1946), 318, 320, 324-26.

59. Du Bois, "Negro Education," *Crisis* 15 (Feb. 1918), 177; Woodson to Moton, Mar. 8, 1919, Moton Papers, box 47; Woodson to Moorland, Oct. 6, 1920, Moorland Papers, folder 618.

60. Romero, "Carter G. Woodson," 94-98, 174; interviews with former associates of Woodson; Moorland to Park, Jan. 7, 1921, folder 619, and Moorland to Dr. George C. Hall, Feb. 23, 1917, folder 616, both in Moorland Papers; Lorenzo J. Greene, diary entry for Dec. 6, 1930, copy supplied courtesy of Lorenzo J. Greene.

61. Du Bois to Hope, Mar. 25, 1925, in Aptheker, ed., *Correspondence of Du Bois*, 1:312; Charles H. Wesley, "Retrospect and Prospect," *NHB* 13 (May 1950), 192; Du Bois, "Portrait of Woodson," 22; L. D. Reddick to Du Bois, Aug. 1, 1950, Du Bois Papers, reel 64.

62. Correspondence of Moorland with Woodson, Jackson, and Hall, 1916-17,

in Moorland Papers, folders 615 and 616, passim; Woodson to Graves, May 4, 1922, Rosenwald Papers, reel 4; Woodson to Moorland, July 25, 1917, and Moorland to Hall, July 27, Sept. 15, 1917, folder 616, Moorland to C. B. Purvis, June 15, 1920, folder 684, all in Moorland Papers.

63. Woodson to Moorland, Aug. 24, 1915, Moorland Papers, folder 614; Woodson to Moton, June 6, 1917, Moton Papers, box 7; Woodson to James Rowland Angell, Oct. 12, 1920, Carnegie Corporation Archives; *JNH* 2 (Oct. 1917), 446.

64. Woodson, "The First Third of a Century of the Association for the Study of Negro Life and History," *NHB* 12 (Nov. 1948), 48; Romero, "Carter G. Woodson," 94.

65. Lorenzo J. Greene, "Dr. Woodson Prepares for Negro History Week, 1930," *NHB* 28 (Summer 1965), 175.

66. *AHR* 21 (Apr. 1916), 643; Edward Channing to Woodson, Jan. 31, 1916, Woodson Papers, LC, reel 3; Turner and Du Bois letters printed in *JNH* 1 (Apr. 1916), 227-28.

67. Woodson, "First Third of a Century of ASNLH," 48; A. L. Jackson to Moorland, May 4, 1916, Moorland Papers, folder 615, and untitled comments by Jackson, *NHB* 28 (Summer 1965), 182.

68. Woodson to Abraham Flexner, June 23, 1916, E. C. Sage to Woodson, June 29, 1916, both in GEB, box 205; quote from W. D. Richardson, memorandum, Sept. 14, 1921, LSRM, box 96.

69. Woodson to Moorland, Mar. 14, Apr. 9, 1917, and Moorland to Woodson, Apr. 12, 1917, all in Moorland Papers, folder 616.

70. Du Bois, "Portrait of Woodson," 22; Woodson to Moorland, Apr. 13, June 28, 1917, Moorland Papers, folder 616; Woodson to NAACP, May 8, 1920, NAACP Archives, Group I, Box C-80. For Storey's life membership, see Woodson's obituary for Storey, *JNH* 15 (Jan. 1930), 123.

71. See Moorland to C. E. Morrison, editor of the *Christian Century,* July 20, 1921, copy in Du Bois Papers, reel 9; Moorland to Moton, Nov. 7, 1919, Moton Papers, box 45.

72. Woodson to Moorland, July 25, June 28, 1917, Moorland to Rosenwald, July 30, 1917, Moorland to Woodson, July 30, 1917, all in Moorland Papers, folder 616.

73. Moorland to Moton, July 27, 1917, and Woodson to Moorland, Aug. 15, 1917, Moorland Papers, folder 616.

74. On Hawkins, see especially obituary in *JNH* 24 (Oct. 1939), 489-91. On Jones's career, see Henry Oakes, "The Struggle for Racial Equality in the Methodist Episcopal Church: The Career of Robert E. Jones" (Ph.D. diss., University of Iowa, 1973).

75. For Peabody's career, see Louise Ware, *George Foster Peabody: Banker, Philanthropist, Publicist* (1951). For his role in connection with black YMCA work and Negro philanthropy generally, see R. R. Moton, "One Who Loved His Fellow Men," *Southern Workman* 67 (May 1938); Raymond B. Fosdick, *Adventure in Giving: The Story of the General Education Board* (1962), 4-5, 7, 19-20; Tobias, "Colored YMCA," 33; Moorland to Rosenwald, May 22, 1911, Rosenwald Papers, reel 85.

76. Rosenwald to Woodson, Aug. 27, 1917, Rosenwald Papers, reel 4.

77. Editorial, "Schools," *Crisis* 13 (Jan. 1917), 111-12; Du Bois, "Negro Education," 173, 176, 177.

78. *JNH* 2 (Oct. 1917), 441; Work's review in ibid., 3 (Jan. 1918), 92-93; Anson Phelps Stokes to Moorland, Dec. 15, 1916, Moorland Papers, folder 615.

79. *JNH* 2 (Oct. 1917), 446-47.

80. Ibid., 443.

81. Woodson to Gentlemen, Nov. 23, 1917, GEB, box 205; Woodson to Graves, Nov. 14, 1917, and attached statement, "A Tentative Plan for the Establishment of the Rosenwald Foundation for the Study of the Negro," Rosenwald Papers, reel 4.

82. Abraham Flexner to Woodson, Nov. 26, 1917, Woodson to Peabody, Jan. 11, 1918, and Peabody to Wallace Buttrick, Feb. 15, 1918, all in GEB, box 205; Peabody to Rosenwald, Feb. 15, 1918, Woodson to Graves, Dec. 27, 1917, and Graves to Rosenwald, Jan. 26, 1918, all in Rosenwald Papers, reel 4; Buttrick to Peabody, Feb. 18, 1918, and Dillard to Buttrick, Feb. 21, 1918, both in GEB, box 205.

83. Graves to Woodson, Feb. 14, 1918, and Rosenwald to Peabody, Feb. 19, 1918, both in Rosenwald Papers, reel 4; Buttrick to Woodson, May 28, 1918, GEB, box 205.

84. Moton to Peabody, May 28, 1918, and Moton to Woodson, June 1, 1918, reel 3, Woodson to Col. Charles Young, Mar. 11, 1919, reel 4, all in Woodson Papers, LC.

85. Graves to Woodson, Sept. 19, 1918, Rosenwald Papers, reel 4; *JNH* 4 (Jan. 1919), 110. On Storey, see also Moorland to Graves, Sept. 24, 1918, Rosenwald Papers, reel 4; and Woodson to Gentlemen, Jan. 7, 1919, GEB, box 205. On Dodge's pledges 1919-20, see also Dodge to Woodson, May 12, Dec. 3, 1919, Woodson Papers, LC, reel 3.

86. Woodson to Graves, Nov. 26, 1919, Rosenwald Papers, reel 4; see also William G. Willcox to Woodson, Dec. 26, 1918, Woodson Papers, LC, reel 3.

87. *JNH* 6 (Jan. 1921), 127; Dodge to Woodson, May 12, 1919, Willcox to Woodson, May 16, 1919, both in reel 3, Woodson Papers, LC.

88. Woodson to Emmett J. Scott, June 21, 1919, Scott Papers; report of Second Biennial Convention, *JNH* 4 (Oct. 1919), esp. 478.

89. Michael R. Winston, "Jesse Edward Moorland," in Logan and Winston, eds., *Dictionary of American Negro Biography*, 451, and Moorland to Woodson, Mar. 11, 1920, Moorland Papers, folder 684.

90. Woodson to Sydnor Walker, June 24, 1929, LSRM, box 96, and Woodson to Moorland May 14, 1920, Moorland Papers, folder 684. Logan, *Howard University*, 208. For an account of the course by a student in it, see Arnett G. Lindsay, "Dr. Woodson as a Teacher," *NHB* 13 (May 1950), 183, 191.

91. Alfred A. Moss, Jr., *The American Negro Academy* (1981), 142-46; Woodson, "Negro Life and History in Our Schools," *JNH* 4 (July 1919), 279; Washington *Bee*, Jan. 10, 24, 1920.

92. Washington *Bee*, Jan. 17, 1920; Woodson, press release, "The Capstone of Negro Education Becomes the Capstone of Negro Politics," Apr. 20, 1931, Barnett

Papers; Woodson to Senator _____ [Reed Smoot], Jan. 10, 1920, printed in Washington *Bee*, Jan. 24, 1920; editorial in ibid., Jan. 24, 1920.

93. Raymond Wolters, *New Negro on Campus* (1975), ch. 3; Logan, *Howard University*, ch. 6; Woodson to Moorland, Mar. 10, May 11, 1920, Moorland Papers, folder 684.

94. Correspondence between Moorland and Woodson, March through May 1920, passim, and Woodson to J. Stanley Durkee, May 3, 1920, all in Moorland Papers, folder 684. Regarding Scott's intercession with Durkee, see Woodson to Moorland, May 11, 1920, Moorland Papers, folder 684.

95. Woodson to Moorland, May 22, 1920, Moorland to Woodson, May 29, 1920, Woodson to Moorland, June 5, 1920, enclosing copy of Woodson to Durkee, June 5, 1920, with attached trustees' resolution of June 3, Moorland to C. B. Purvis, June 15, 1920, all in Moorland Papers, folder 684. Depending partly on oral tradition, other scholars have interpreted the action of the trustees as unequivocal support for Durkee rather than a response to the efforts of Woodson's friends to restore the historian to his position. The materials in the Moorland Papers, however, indicate a more complex course of events. See Logan, *Howard University*, 208, and Romero, "Carter G. Woodson," 76-77.

96. Woodson to Buttrick, Mar. 27, 1920, GEB, box 205; Woodson to Scott, June 14, 1920, Scott Papers.

97. See discussions of this matter in the following: Romero, "Carter G. Woodson," 105-12; Du Bois to Woodson, Mar. 19, 1926, Du Bois Papers, reel 18, and Du Bois to Raymond B. Fosdick, Nov. 18, 1927, in Aptheker, ed., *Correspondence of Du Bois*, 1: 365-67.

98. Woodson to NAACP, May 8, 1920, and to Joel E. Spingarn, May 8, 1920, both in NAACP, Group I, box C-80; Woodson to Moorland, May 8, 1920, Moorland Papers, folder 618.

99. Woodson to NAACP, May 8, 1920, NAACP Group I, Box C-80; NAACP Board of Directors' Minutes, May 10, June 14, 1920, LC.

100. John W. Davis telegram to Woodson, June 23, 1920, cited in Romero, "Carter G. Woodson," 79; Woodson to James Angell, Oct. 12, 1920, Carnegie Corporation Archives; Woodson to Moorland, Oct. 6, 1920, Moorland Papers, folder 618.

101. [Woodson], "John Franklin Jameson," *JNH* 23 (Jan. 1938), 133.

102. Jameson to Du Bois, June 22, 1910, in Donnan and Stock, eds., *An Historian's World*, 133.

103. Interview with Francis C. Jameson, July 11, 1983.

104. See especially Jameson to Edward P. Cheyney, Sept. 23, 1921, in Donnan and Stock, eds., *An Historian's World*, 260; Jameson to Ruth Anna Fisher, May 14, 1931, to Allen French, Mar. 5, 1936, ibid., 348, 360; interview with Francis C. Jameson; Fisher to Du Bois, n.d. [1939], reel 51, Fisher to Du Bois, Nov. 18, 1935, reel 44, microfilm of Du Bois Papers. See also her comments in a volume of tributes to Jameson's memory that she herself initiated: Ruth Anna Fisher, "A Tribute," in Fisher and William Lloyd Fox, eds., *J. Franklin Jameson: A Tribute* (1965), 1-8. Biographical material about Fisher was generously furnished by the Oberlin College Archives.

105. Jameson to Graves, Dec. 20, 1917, Jameson Papers, box 126; see also similar views expressed in Jameson to George A. Plimpton, Sept. 24, 1919, to John D. Rockefeller, Jr., Apr. 1, 1930, in Donnan and Stock, eds., *An Historian's World*, 243, 343.

106. Jeffrey R. Brackett, "The Status of the Slave, 1775-1789," in J. Franklin Jameson, ed., *Essays in the Constitutional History of the United States in the Formative Period 1775-1789* (1889); Brackett, *The Negro in Maryland: A Study in the Institution of Slavery* (1889); Brackett, *Notes on the Progress of the Colored People of Maryland Since the War* (1890). See also abstract of Brackett's 1885 AHA convention paper entitled "Report of Certain Studies in the Institution of African Slavery in the United States," in *Papers of the American Historical Association*, 1 (1886), 436-38. On the friendship of Brackett and Jameson, see correspondence between the two men, 1888-90 passim, box 62, and Jameson to Woodson, June 24, 1916, box 25, both in Jameson Papers.

107. Jameson to Carl Russell Fish, Oct. 18, 1913, Jameson Papers, box 83. See the reference to his appearance in the Wisconsin *State Journal*, Mar. 28, 1914.

108. *MVHR 5* (Mar. 1919), 480-81; *American Political Science Review* 12 (Nov. 1918), 722-26.

109. Jameson to Stone, June 28, 1918, Jameson Papers, box 130; and review by Jervey in *AHR* 25 (Oct. 1919), 117-18. On Jervey's interest in blacks and their history, see esp. Jervey to Woodson, Nov. 18, 1932, Woodson Papers, LC, reel 3; and Woodson to Jervey, Oct. 11, Nov. 21, 1932, both in Theodore Jervey Papers.

110. Carnegie Institution of Washington, *Year Book No. 3, 1904*, 59, 146, *Year Book No. 4, 1905*, 41, 48, 238, *Year Book No. 5, 1906*, 160, *Year Book No. 7, 1908*, 79.

111. Carnegie Institution of Washington, *Year Book No. 5, 1906*, 158, *Year Book No. 6, 1907*, 73-75, *Year Book No. 7, 1908*, 82, *Year Book No. 8, 1909*, 80, *Year Book No. 10, 1911*, 76, *Year Book No. 12, 1913*, 95-96.

112. Carnegie Institution of Washington, *Year Book No. 7, 1908*, 84; W. E. B. Du Bois, ed., *Economic Co-Operation among Negro Americans* (1907), 5; Jameson to Graves, Dec. 20, 1917, Jameson Papers, box 126; Alfred H. Stone, "Some Problems of Southern Economic History," *AHR* 13 (July 1908).

113. Jameson to Mrs. R. C. H. (Helen T.) Catterall, Nov. 21, 1918, Jameson Papers, box 69. See also his questioning of the representativeness of the documents Phillips was using in Jameson to Stone, Aug. 5, 1918, Jameson Papers, box 130; and Jameson to Frederick Jackson Turner, Nov. 25, 1927, in Donnan and Stock, eds., *An Historian's World*, 327.

114. Du Bois to Jameson, Jan. 8, 1907, and Jameson to Du Bois, Jan. 14, 1907, Jameson Papers, box 80; Du Bois, "Reconstruction and Its Benefits."

115. Jameson to James H. Dillard, Nov. 22, 1912, in Donnan and Stock, eds., *An Historian's World*, 152; Jameson to Dillard, Oct. 13, 1915, Jameson Papers, box 128; Jameson's report in Carnegie Institution of Washington, *Year Book No. 15, 1916*, 167. Quotation is from Jameson to Catterall, Nov. 21, 1918, Jameson Papers, box 69.

116. Jameson to Woodson, May 17, 1916, Jameson Papers, box 55, and Jameson

to Plimpton, Sept. 24, 1919, in Donnan and Stock, eds., *An Historian's World,* 244; quotation in Jameson to James Rowland Angell, Oct. 9, 1920, copy in LSRM, box 96.

117. Marcus W. Jernegan review of Woodson's *Education of the Negro Prior to 1861* in *AHR* 21 (Apr. 1916), 634-35; Jameson to Woodson, Apr. 8, 1916, Jameson Papers, box 55.

118. [Woodson], "John Franklin Jameson," 132; Woodson to Jameson, May 15, 1916, and Jameson to Woodson, May 17, June 24, 1916, all in Jameson Papers, box 55.

119. Woodson, "A Project for Statistical Study of Free Negro Heads of Families in the United States in 1860" [early 1929], in Rosenwald Fund Papers, box 170; Woodson, *Free Negro Owners of Slaves in the United States in 1830* (1924), and *Free Negro Heads of Families in the United States in 1830* (1925). For Jameson's interest in manuscript census, see Jameson to Plimpton, Sept. 24, 1919, in Donnan and Stock, eds., *An Historian's World,* 243-44.

120. Jameson to Graves, Dec. 20, 1917, Jameson Papers, box 126.

121. Jameson to Angell, Oct. 9, 1920, copy in LSRM, box 96; Woodson to Angell, Oct. 12, 1920, in Carnegie Corporation Archives. On Hart's being placed on ASNLH Council, see *JNH* 6 (Jan. 1921), 128.

122. Angell to Woodson, Oct. 15, 1920, Carnegie Corporation Archives; list of scholars sending supporting letters (based on materials supplied by the Carnegie Corporation) is to be found in W.S.R. [Richardson], "Memorandum, Outline on the Request of the Association for the Study of Negro Life and History to the LSRM," Jan. 28, 1922, LSRM, box 96.

123. For applications from Tuskegee and Urban League, see, respectively, Moton to Angell, Nov. 27, 1920, and Eugene Kinckle Jones to Angell, Dec. 27, 1920, in Carnegie Corporation Archives; see also Angell, "Interview with President Moton of Tuskegee and M. N. Work, Nov. 22, 1920," ibid. For discussions of Park's relationships with Charles S. Johnson, see Raushenbush, *Robert E. Park,* esp. 94-95; Patrick Joseph Gilpin, "Charles S. Johnson: An Intellectual Biography" (Ph.D. diss., Vanderbilt University, 1973), ch. 4; Ralph L. Pearson, "Charles S. Johnson: The Urban League Years" (Ph.D. diss., Johns Hopkins University, 1970), passim.

124. Woodson to Moorland, Dec. 6, 1920, Moorland Papers, folder 618.

125. Moorland to Woodson, Dec. 4, 1920, Moorland Papers, folder 618; Moton to Angell, Nov. 27, 1920, Carnegie Corporation Archives.

126. Angell, "Interview with President Moton of Tuskegee and M. N. Work, Nov. 22, 1920"; Moorland to Woodson, Dec. 4, 1920, folder 618, and esp. Park to Moorland, Feb. 14, June 1, 1921, folder 619, all in Moorland Papers.

127. Woodson to Moorland, Dec. 6, 1920, Moorland Papers, folder 618.

128. Ibid.

129. Angell, "Interview with President Moton of Tuskegee and M. N. Work, Nov. 22, 1920"; Moorland to Woodson, Dec. 4, 1920, Moorland Papers, folder 618.

130. Moorland to Moton, Dec. 21, 1920, Moton Papers, box 65; Moorland to Park, Jan. 7, 1921, Moorland Papers, folder 619. On Woodson's anger over

Moorland's failure to contribute, see Moorland to Woodson, Oct. 1, 1920, and Woodson to Moorland, Oct. 6, 1920, Moorland Papers, folder 618.

131. Woodson to Moton, Dec. 21, 1920, Moton Papers, box 65.

132. Woodson to Moorland, Dec. 6, 1920, folder 618, Moorland to Woodson, Jan. 4, 1921, to Park, Jan. 7, 1921, Woodson to Moorland, Feb. 24, 1921, last three in folder 619, all in Moorland Papers.

133. Moorland to Woodson, Mar. 17, 1921, Moorland Papers, folder 619; Moton to Angell, Mar. 10, 1921, Carnegie Corporation Archives; Angell to Park, Apr. 26, 1921, copy in Moorland Papers, folder 619; Angell to Jameson, Apr. 14, 1921, Carnegie Corporation Archives.

134. Angell to Moton, Mar. 25, 1921, Carnegie Corporation Archives; [Woodson], "John Franklin Jameson," 132; Angell to Jameson, Apr. 14, May 31, 1921, Jameson to Angell, Apr. 15, 1921, and Carnegie Corporation Executive Committee Minutes, May 2, 1921, all in Carnegie Corporation Archives. For Work's bibliography, see McMurry, *Recorder of the Black Experience*, 78-79.

135. Beardsley Ruml to Woodson, June 20, 1921, Carnegie Corporation Archives; Woodson to George Foster Peabody, June 27, 1921, and attached "Budget June 30, 1921–June 30, 1922," Peabody Papers, box 13; Woodson to Scott, Oct. 8, 1921, Scott Papers.

136. Woodson to Angell, June 7, 1921, Carnegie Corporation Archives; Graves to Woodson, July 14, 1921, Rosenwald Papers, reel 4; Woodson to W. S. Richardson, Sept. 9, 1921, and W.S.R. [Richardson], Memorandum, Sept. 14, 1921, both in LSRM, box 96; Woodson to Buttrick, Oct. 14, 1921, GEB, box 205, and W.S.R. [Richardson], "Outline on the Request of the Association for the Study of Negro Life and History to the LSRM," Jan. 28, 1922, LSRM, box 96.

137. Richardson to Woodson, Feb. 16, 1922, LSRM, box 96; Woodson to Buttrick, Apr. 10, 1922, GEB, box 205, and Woodson, *Negro in Our History,* 289-91.

138. [Woodson], "John Franklin Jameson," 133.

139. Woodson to Angell, June 7, 1921, Carnegie Corporation Archives; Woodson to Graves, May 4, 1922, Rosenwald Papers, reel 4; Woodson to Buttrick, Feb. 23, 1921, GEB, box 205. Quotation in Woodson to Graves, May 4, 1922.

140. Woodson to Rosenwald, July 20, 1922, and financial statement, n.d. (ca. July 1922), both in Rosenwald Papers, reel 4; *JNH* 9 (Oct. 1924), 581; 10 (Oct. 1925), 588.

141. For one of Woodson's rare reports on the specifics of the amounts raised among blacks in this way, see *JNH* 8 (Jan. 1923), 119.

142. Park to Woodson, May 2, 1921, quoted in Woodson to Graves, May 4, 1922, Rosenwald Papers, reel 4. On Park's involvement in the Urban League and Tuskegee applications, see correspondence of Park and Moorland, 1921, passim in Moorland Papers, folder 619, and Park to Angell, Apr. 20, 1921, copy in Moton Papers, box 76.

143. Woodson to Graves, May 4, 1922, Moorland to Graves, Apr. 21, 1922, both in Rosenwald Papers, reel 4; Woodson to Moorland, Oct. 12, 1921, Moorland to Woodson, Oct. 21, 1921, Moorland Papers, folder 619.

144. Moorland to Graves, Apr. 21, 1922, Woodson to Graves, May 4, 1922, Scott to Graves, Apr. 25, 1922, all in Rosenwald Papers, reel 4.

145. Du Bois, "Robert Russa Moton," *Crisis* 18 (May 1919), 9.

146. Du Bois, "Thomas Jesse Jones," ibid., 22 (Oct. 1921), 256, 253-54: King, *Pan-Africanism and Education,* 54.

147. King, *Pan-Africanism and Education,* 54; Moton to Moorland, July 19, 1919, Moorland to Moton, Nov. 7, 1919, both in Moton Papers, box 45.

148. Woodson to Graves, May 4, 1922, Rosenwald Papers, reel 4; Woodson press release, printed in New York *Age,* June 4, 1932. Given the reluctance of the black Y workers to air their problems in public and that the relevant files in the YMCA Archives for those years no longer exist, it is difficult to substantiate the accuracy of Woodson's charges. However, in writing to Rosenwald's secretary, Woodson of course knew that he was communicating with an individual who certainly had personal knowledge of what had transpired. Moreover, Channing Tobias, Moorland's successor as the senior black secretary, in reply to Woodson's 1932 press release, issued a statement commending improvement in Y policy, but not denying the specifics of Woodson's accusations. See Tobias, To the Editor, June 10, 1932, copy in Phelps-Stokes Fund Archives.

149. Du Bois, "Thomas Jesse Jones," 254; "Resolutions of Colored Delegates to be presented to the Committee on the International Committee's Report" [1919], Moton Papers, box 65; "Report of the Commission on Colored Work" [Mar. 1920], copies in Moton Papers, box 65, and Rosenwald Papers, reel 85; A. L. Jackson to John R. Mott, Nov. 5, 1920, and C. S. Bishop to W. J. Parker, Jan. 19, 1920, both in Rosenwald Papers, reel 85.

150. On Yergan in Africa during World War I, see Moorland, "The Young Men's Christian Association and the War," *Crisis* 15 (Dec. 1917); Moorland, "The YMCA with Colored Troops," *Southern Workman* 48 (Apr. 1919); Yergan, "A YMCA Secretary in Africa," ibid., 47 (Aug. 1918). On Yergan's magnetism and dedication, see Channing H. Tobias, "A Decade of Student YMCA Work," *Crisis* 24 (Oct. 1922), 265-67, and Tobias, "Max Yergan," ibid., 40 (July 1933), 155, 166. For withdrawal of permission, see Oswin Bull to J. R. Mott, Feb. 18, 1921, copy Du Bois Papers, reel 10. For Yergan's charges, see Yergan to F. DeFrantz, Apr. 21, 1921, copy Du Bois Papers, reel 10.

151. Tuskegee Institute YMCA to John R. Mott, Mar. 31, 1921, Moton Papers, box 55; Kenneth Saunders, "A Forward Move in Africa," *Southern Workman* 49 (Feb. 1920), 83; *Tuskegee Messenger,* Jan. 14-28, 1929; John W. Davis to Yergan, Mar. 31, 1921, copy, Du Bois to Yergan, May 18, 26, Yergan to Du Bois, May 23, 1921, all in Du Bois Papers, reel 10; Du Bois, "Thomas Jesse Jones"; James E. Shepard to Du Bois, Nov. 1, 1921, Du Bois Papers, reel 10; *Southern Workman* 50 (Nov. 1921), 493-94.

152. Woodson to Graves, May 4, 1922, Rosenwald Papers, reel 4; Woodson, *History of the Negro Church* (1921), 309-11.

153. Woodson to editor, Indianapolis *Freeman,* Apr. 12, 1924; L. A. Roy to Woodson, Apr. 18, 1924, Phelps-Stokes Fund Archives; Peabody to Dillard, Apr. 18, 1922, Peabody Papers, box 15; Peabody to Hart, Apr. 18, 1922, and Hart to Rosenwald, Apr. 12, 1922, both in Rosenwald Papers, reel 4; Moton's letter does

not seem to have survived, but is referred to in E. R. Ames (Peabody's secretary) to Moton, May 23, 1922, Moton Papers, box 76.

154. Woodson to Richardson, Apr. 25, 1922, and Richardson to Woodson, May 4, 1922, LSRM, box 96.

155. Thomas Jesse Jones, memorandum re Dr. Carter G. Woodson, attached to Jones to Graves, Apr. 22, 1922, Rosenwald Papers, reel 4.

156. Graves to Scott and to Moorland, both Apr. 19, 1922, Rosenwald Papers, reel 4; Graves to Moton, Apr. 19, 1922, and Moton to Graves, Apr. 29, 1922, both in Moton Papers, box 76. On the mutual admiration between Jones and Moton see, e.g., Moton to Stokes, Oct. 4, 1920, Moton Papers, box 77, and Jones to Peabody, May 24, 1919, GEB, box 262.

157. Moorland to Graves, Apr. 21, 1922, and Scott to Graves, Apr. 25, 1922, both in Rosenwald Papers, reel 4.

158. *JNH* 7 (Apr. 1922), 230-31; Woodson to Rosenwal. Apr. 18, 1922, Woodson to Graves, Apr. 18, May 4, 1922, all in Rosenwald Papers, reel 4. The May 4 letter includes extended verbatim quotations from Woodson's *History of the Negro Church,* 301-3.

159. Winifred Putnam, asst. director, National Information Bureau, to Graves, Oct. 20, 1923, Rosenwald Papers, reel 4.

160. *Southern Workman* 51 (May 1922), 248; and, among others, 53 (May 1924), 227-29; 54 (Oct. 1925), 437; 57 (Dec. 1928), 493-94; 60 (Feb. 1931), 79-81; 62 (Apr. 1933), 188-92; 63 (Jan. 1934), 12-16.

161. *Tuskegee Student,* Dec. 1923; *JNH* 9 (Jan. 1924), 106.

162. Woodson to Du Bois, Jan. 7, 1932, Du Bois Papers, reel 37; Stokes to Woodson, Jan. 8, 1932, Phelps-Stokes Fund Archives.

163. Dykeman and Stokeley, *Seeds of Southern Change,* 131; *Crisis* 21 (Apr. 1921), 247-48; 22 (May 1921), 6-7; 37 (Jan. 1930), 245.

164. Woodson, "Ten Years of Collecting and Publishing the Records of the Negro," *JNH* 10 (Oct. 1925), 598.

165. [Woodson], "Facts about the Association for the Study of Negro Life and History" [1919], LSRM, box 96.

166. *JNH* 7 (July 1922), 347. For Haynes's popularity as a speaker on the subject, see *Southern Workman* 51 (Aug. 1922), 395-96; 53 (Oct. 1924), 473-74.

167. [Woodson], Press release, "Historical Association to Promote Harmony Between the Races by Acquainting the One with the Other" [Oct. 1923], Du Bois Papers, reel 11; *JNH* 9 (Jan. 1924), 105-6; 9 (July 1924), 375; 10 (Jan. 1925), 110, and esp. 107. For sketches of Jackson Davis's career see [Woodson], "Jackson Davis," ibid., 32 (July 1947), and editorial from Richmond *News Leader,* Apr. 21, 1947, clipping in Davis Papers.

168. Alfred K. Stern to Woodson, Nov. 1, 1926, Rosenwald Fund Papers, box 170; Woodson, "Story of the Fund" [1927], Rosenwald Papers, reel 62; Stern to Woodson, Sept. 15, 1927, Woodson to Stern, Sept. 23, 1927, and Woodson to Rosenwald, Sept. 23, 1927, all in Rosenwald Fund Papers, box 170. In regard to the Rockefellers, see Woodson's letters in GEB, box 205, and LSRM, box 96, 1924-26 passim.

169. Interview with Lorenzo J. Greene, Dec. 20, 1983.

170. *JNH* 15 (Jan. 1930), 11; 25 (July 1940), 404-6.

171. Franz Boas to Beardsley Ruml, Mar. 12, 1926, Arthur M. Schlesinger to E. E. Day, May 16, 1929, both in LSRM, box 96; interviews with former students of Schlesinger. On omission of black history from his writings, see Stuart M. Jones, "The Schlesingers on Black History," *Phylon* 33 (Summer 1972).

172. Edward Channing to Gentlemen, Mar. 17, 1926, and letters from others mentioned, Mar. 1926, all in LSRM, box 96; Dodd to Sydnor H. Walker, May 10, 1929, LSRM, box 96; see also A.K.S. [Alfred K. Stern] to Rosenwald, July 11, 1928, Rosenwald Papers, reel 4, regarding conversation with Dodd.

173. Woodson to LSRM, Mar. 22, 1926, LSRM, box 96; Woodson, *Free Negro Owners; Woodson, Free Negro Heads of Families; Woodson, ed., The Mind of the Negro as Reflected in Letters Written during the Crisis, 1800-1860* (1926); Alrutheus A. Taylor, *The Negro in South Carolina during the Reconstruction* (1924); Taylor, *The Negro in the Reconstruction of Virginia* (1926).

174. Woodson to LSRM, Mar. 22, 1926, LSRM, box 96.

175. *JNH* 8 (Oct. 1923), 469; 12 (Apr. 1927), 357; Irene A. Wright, "Dispatches of Spanish Officials Bearing on the Free Negro Settlement of Gracia de Santa Teresa de Mose, Florida," ibid., 9 (Apr. 1924); Ruth Anna Fisher, "Extracts from the Records of the African Companies," ibid., 13 (July 1928).

176. Woodson to Guy Stanton Ford, Jan. 27, 1925, LSRM, box 96.

177. Woodson to Rosenwald, Dec. 3, 1926, and Graves to Woodson, Dec. 11, 1926, in Rosenwald Papers, reel 4; Woodson to Rockefeller, Jr., Mar. 25, 1927, LSRM, box 96; see also, for example, *JNH* 10 (Oct. 1925), 591; 11 (Oct. 1926), 548; 12 (Jan. 1927), 4.

178. Woodson to Keppel, Mar. 31, 1925, and Keppel to Woodson, Apr. 7, 1925, Carnegie Corporation Archives; Ernest Kaiser, "Arthur Alfonso Schomburg," in Winston and Logan, eds., *Dictionary of American Negro Biography*, 547.

179. Waldo Leland to Woodson, Apr. 14, 1925, cited in Logan, "Woodson: Mirror and Molder," 16; Leland to Ruml, Mar. 8, 1926, and attached to it, Charles F. Cochran, "The Association for the Study of Negro Life and History: A Report Made for the American Council of Learned Societies," Dec. 1925, in LSRM, box 96; supporting references from leading scholars are cited in n. 172.

180. *The Laura Spelman Rockefeller Memorial Final Report* (1933), 10, 20-21. See also discussions in [Leonard Outhwaite], "Race Relations" [Autumn 1925], and Outhwaite to Ruml, Mar. 13, Apr. 22, 1925, all in LSRM, box 101; and "Staff Meetings of the Laura Spelman Rockefeller Memorial," Aug. 24-27, 1927, 100-130, LSRM, Series II, box 3.

181. "LSRM Staff Meetings," 103-4; "Proposed Department of Social Science, Fisk University," attached to Thomas E. Jones to Outhwaite, May 3, 1927, LSRM, box 52.

182. For overall discussions, see Fosdick, *Adventure in Giving*, 197-210; Embree and Waxman, *Investment in People*, 85-100, and Appendix D, "Expenditures, 1917-1948," 267-68. For earlier, substantial foundation grants to Fisk, see Fosdick, *Adventure in Giving*, 190, 192. On Johnson and the Fisk social science department, see correspondence of LSRM officials with Thomas E. Jones, 1927-30 passim, and Outhwaite, memorandum of interview with Embree, Feb. 28, 1928, all in

LSRM, box 52; correspondence of GEB officials with Johnson, 1937-42 passim, in GEB, box 419; Gilpin, "Charles S. Johnson," ch. 10.

183. Fosdick, *Adventure in Giving*, 303-6, quote on 303. Embree and Waxman, *Investment in People*, ch. 6.

184. Du Bois, "The General Education Board," *Crisis* 37 (July 1930), 229-30.

185. Jackson Davis memorandum, May 6, 1942, GEB, box 255.

186. Woodson to Guy Stanton Ford, Jan. 27, 1925, LSRM, box 96.

187. Outhwaite to Ruml, Apr. 22, 1925, LSRM, box 101.

188. Outhwaite, memorandum to Ruml, Mar. 13, 1925, 3-5, and Outhwaite, memorandum to Col. Woods and Dr. Ruml, Apr. 22, 1926, 6-7, both in LSRM, box 101; *JNH* 10 (July 1925), 579.

189. *JNH* 10 (Oct. 1925), 597; Woodson to LSRM, Mar. 22, 1926, and Woodson to Sydnor Walker, June 24, 1929, both in LSRM, box 96.

190. Outhwaite, "Memorandum of an Interview with Woodson," June 7, 1926, and Ruml to Woodson, June 10, 1926, both in LSRM, box 96. In regard to revolving fund, see LSRM, "Appropriations, October 18, 1918, through April 30, 1928," 56, Rockefeller Foundation Archives, Record Group III, box 910.

191. See especially Lorenzo J. Greene and Carter G. Woodson, *The Negro Wage Earner* (1930), and Woodson, *The Negro Professional Man and the Community* (1934).

192. Woodson to Outhwaite, Feb. 24, 1928, and Woodson, "The Negro Church in the United States," undated proposal [1928], both in LSRM, box 96.

193. Woodson to Beardsley Ruml, Apr. 30, 1929, and attached "Statement of Receipts and Disbursements from July 1, 1926, to April 30, 1929," LSRM, box 96.

194. Woodson to Rosenwald Fund, Feb. 19, Mar. 4, 1929, Woodson, "A Prospectus for Statistical Study of the Negro Families in the United States in 1860" [1929], and Woodson, "A Prospectus for the Study of the Life Histories of 'Near Great' Negroes" [1929], all in Rosenwald Fund Papers, box 170; Woodson to Rosenwald, Apr. 4, 1929, and Raymond J. Rubinow to Woodson, Dec. 6, 1929, in Rosenwald Papers, reel 4. Embree later stated that Rosenwald had terminated his personal contribution in 1928, but this is in error. See Embree to Woodson, July 16, 1930, Rosenwald Fund Papers, box 170.

195. Outhwaite, memorandum, Oct. 1928, quoted in [no author], "Association for the Study of Negro Life and History," Mar. 13, 1929; Walker to T.B.A. [Trevor Arnett], Sept. 25, 1929. For low sales of books and dissatisfaction over this, see also Outhwaite to Woodson, Jan. 15, Nov. 26, 1927, and Woodson to Outhwaite, Jan. 18, 1927. See also "Statement of Receipts and Disbursements from July 1, 1926, to April 30, 1929," and Woodson to Ruml, Apr. 30, 1929, all in LSRM, box 96.

196. Walker to Woodson, June 18, 1929, Walker to William E. Dodd, to U. B. Phillips, to W. L. Fleming, and to J. G. de Roulhac Hamilton, all May 7, 1929, Phillips to Walker, May [9], 1929, Hamilton to Walker, May 10, 1929, Fleming to Walker, May 9, 1929, Dodd to Walker, May 10, 1929, all in LSRM, box 96.

197. Woodson to Walker, June 24, 1929, LSRM, box 96; Woodson to Evarts Greene, May 11, 1929, Greene Papers; Greene to E. E. Day, May 17, 1929, Carl

Russell Fish to Day, May 14, 1929, Schlesinger to Day, May 16, 1929, and Jameson to Day, May 13, 1929, all in LSRM, box 96.

198. Logan, "Woodson: Mirror and Molder," 16; *JNH* 14 (Oct. 1929), 368-69, and 15 (Oct. 1930), 398-99; Keppel to Woodson, Dec. 26, 1929, Carnegie Corporation Archives; Woodson to Alfred K. Stern, Feb. 28, 1930, and Stern to Woodson, Mar. 4, 1930, in Rosenwald Fund Papers, box 170; Woodson to Jameson, Mar. 20, Mar. 24, 1930, and "Project for the Collection of Manuscript Materials Among Negroes Submitted to Mr. John D. Rockefeller, Jr., by The Association for the Study of Negro Life and History" [1930], all in Jameson Papers, box 115; Jameson to Rockefeller, Apr. 1, 1930, in Donnan and Stock, eds., *An Historian's World*, 343-44.

199. [Sydnor Walker], "Memorandum of Interview with Woodson on June 5," June 7, 1929, Walker to Woodson, June 18, 1929, George E. Vincent to Woodson, June 14, 1929, all in LSRM, box 96.

200. Walker to Woodson, June 18, 1929, LSRM, box 96; Embree to Woodson, Mar. 31, 1930, Rosenwald Fund Papers, box 170; Woodson to Ford, Jan. 27, 1925, and Woodson to Walker, June 24, 1929, both LSRM, box 96.

201. Woodson to Embree, Mar. 18, 1930, Embree to Woodson, Mar. 20, 1930, quotation in Woodson to Walker and Woodson to Embree, both Mar. 22, 1930, Embree to Woodson, Mar. 31, 1930, Secretary (at the Rockefeller boards, signature illegible) to Woodson, May 9, 1930, Walker to Embree, Apr. 24, 1930, all in Rosenwald Fund Papers, box 170. Curiously the relevant documents are not to be found at present in the archives of the Rockefeller Research Center.

202. J.M.P. memorandum [Jan.] 1933, GEB, box 205.

203. Woodson to Embree, May 10, 1930, Rosenwald Fund Papers, box 170; Embree to Rosenwald, July 11, 1930, Rosenwald Papers, reel 4; Embree to Woodson, July 16, 1930, and Woodson to Embree, July 19, 1930, both in Rosenwald Fund Papers, box 170.

204. Embree to Woodson, July 22, 1930, Rosenwald Papers, reel 4; Embree to Woodson, July 23, 1931, and Nov. 9, 1931, Rosenwald Fund Papers, box 170.

205. Woodson to Frederick P. Keppel, May 23, Nov. 25, 1930, and Keppel to Woodson, Dec. 4, 1930, and Jan. 16, 1931, Carnegie Corporation Archives; J.M.P. memorandum [Jan.] 1933, GEB, box 205, and Woodson to Schlesinger, May 31, 1933, Schlesinger Papers.

206. *JNH* 16 (Oct. 1931), 350-51; 17 (Oct. 1932), 391.

207. Woodson, "The Director Speaks," ibid., 16 (July 1931), 344; Du Bois to Woodson, Apr. 6, 1931, Du Bois Papers, reel 36.

208. Horace Mann Bond, review essay, "Dr. Woodson Goes Wool-Gathering," *Journal of Negro Education* 2 (Apr. 1933).

209. Woodson, *The Mis-Education of the Negro* (1933), 31; Woodson, "The Miseducation of the Negro," *Crisis* 38 (Aug. 1931), 266.

210. Woodson, *Mis-Education of the Negro*, 7, 8; "Miseducation of the Negro," 266; "The Director Speaks," 345-46.

211. Referred to in Woodson press release in Chicago *Defender*, Feb. 7, 1931; evidently the text of the press release is printed in "Negro History Week the Fifth Year," *JNH* 16 (Apr. 1931), 127-28.

212. Woodson, "Miseducation of the Negro," 267; "Negro History Week the Tenth Year," *JNH* 20 (Apr. 1935), 125, 124; Woodson press release printed in New York *Amsterdam News,* July 20, 1932.

213. Winston, *Howard University Department of History,* 85.

214. Anson Phelps Stokes to Dear Sir, Oct. 19, 1931; minutes of "Conference on the Advisability of Publishing an Encyclopedia of the Negro, Nov. 7, 1931," and Stokes to Du Bois, Nov. 9, 1931, all in Du Bois Papers, reel 35; Stokes to Woodson, Jan. 8, 1932, Phelps-Stokes Fund Archives. See also Du Bois's account quoted in Associated Negro Press dispatch [Aug. 1932], in Barnett Papers, and Woodson's version of events in "A Duplication of Effort in Producing Two Encyclopedias of the Negro," *JNH* 17 (Jan. 1932), 116-18.

215. Woodson to Du Bois, Jan. 7, 1932, Du Bois Papers, reel 37; Du Bois to Dillard, Nov. 30, 1931, in Aptheker, ed., *Correspondence of Du Bois,* 1:447. See also Woodson to Benjamin Brawley, Jan. 7, 1932, copy in NAACP Archives, Group I, C-80; Du Bois, draft of a "Memorandum to the Conference on the Advisability of Publishing Negro Encyclopedia" [Dec. 1932], Du Bois Papers, reel 35.

216. For Du Bois's earliest effort, see following in the Du Bois Papers, reel 1: Du Bois, circular letter to Edward W. Blyden and others, Apr. 5, 1909, to Charles W. Eliot, Aug. 9, 1909.

217. Du Bois to Dillard, Nov. 30, 1931, and Dillard to Du Bois, Dec. 2, 1931, in Aptheker, ed., *Correspondence of Du Bois,* 1:447, 448; Du Bois to Stokes, Dec. 17, 1931, Du Bois Papers, reel 35.

218. Dillard to Stokes, Dec. 6, 1931, and Stokes to Woodson, Jan. 8, 1932, both in Phelps-Stokes Fund Archives; Woodson to Brawley, Nov. 28, 1931, Dillard Papers.

219. Dillard to Stokes, Dec. 6, 1931, and Stokes to Woodson, Jan. 8, 1932, Phelps-Stokes Fund Archives; Woodson, "Duplication in Producing Two Encyclopedias"; Woodson to Brawley, Jan. 7, 1932, copy in NAACP Archives Group I, Box C-80. Woodson to Ralph J. Bunche, Jan. 9, 1932, Bunche Papers. For the relationship between Woodson and Bunche, see the correspondence in the Bunche Papers, 1932-36 passim.

220. Minutes, "Second Conference on 'Encyclopedia of the Negro,'" Jan. 9, 1932, Phelps-Stokes Fund Archives. On staffing arrangements, see also Stokes to Jackson Davis, Mar. 31, 1932, GEB, box 418; Stokes, introduction to W. E. B. Du Bois and Guy B. Johnson, *Encyclopedia of the Negro: Preparatory Volume with Reference Lists and Reports,* rev. ed. (1946), 12.

221. Du Bois to Woodson, Jan. 29, 1932, Woodson to Du Bois, Feb. 11, 1932, in Aptheker, ed., *Correspondence of Du Bois,* 1:448-49; Woodson press releases in New York *Age,* June 4, 1932, and Pittsburgh *Courier,* Apr. 9, 1932.

222. Woodson to Phelps-Stokes Fund, Oct. 22, 1932, Phelps-Stokes Fund Archives; Woodson to Dillard, Oct. 22, 1932, Dillard Papers.

223. Du Bois to Park, Mar. 3, 1937, in Aptheker, ed., *Correspondence of Du Bois,* 2:141, reviewing earlier events; Du Bois to Woodson, Oct. 26, 1932, and Woodson to Du Bois, Oct. 27, 1932, both in Du Bois Papers, reel 37.

224. Stokes to Woodson, Jan. 20, 1933, and Du Bois to Stokes, Feb. 17, 1933, both in Du Bois Papers, reel 40.

225. J.M.P. memorandum [Jan.] 1933, GEB, box 205.

226. Trevor Arnett to Jackson Davis, Apr. 18, 1932; Woodson to Davis, Apr. 21, 1932; Davis, "Interview: Carter G. Woodson . . . May 13, 1932"; Davis, draft of memorandum to board, Dec. 26, 1933; Davis to John Hope, Nov. 6, 1933; quotation in Davis to Walker, Oct. 30, 1933, all in GEB, box 205.

227. Evarts Greene to Day, June 12, 1933, GEB, box 205; Schlesinger to Walker, June 7, 1933, and Woodson to Schlesinger, May 31, 1933, both in Schlesinger Papers.

228. Woodson to Davis, Jan. 6, 1934; [author's name not clear], memorandum, stamped Jan. 11, 1934, both in GEB, box 205.

229. Woodson to Hope, Feb. 9, 1934, quoted in Stokes to Hope, Feb. 12, 1934, and Hope to Stokes, Mar. 16, 1934, both in Phelps-Stokes Fund Archives; Luther P. Jackson, "The Work of the Association and the People," *JNH* 20 (Oct. 1935), 395.

230. Cochran, "The Association for the Study of Negro Life and History."

231. Woodson to Rosenwald, Mar. 17, 1926, Rosenwald Papers, reel 4.

232. For Woodson's awareness of the importance of the public schoolteacher constituency, see ibid.; for details of the inauguration of the branches, see *JNH* 11 (Oct. 1926), 553-54; 12 (Oct. 1927), 574-75.

233. Woodson to John D. Rockefeller, Jr., Apr. 29, 1935, Woodson to Jameson, Apr. 19, 1935, Jameson to Rockefeller, Jr., Apr. 30, 1935, all in Jameson Papers, box 115.

234. Wesley, "Retrospect and Prospect," 190; for title of the annual drive, see Wesley to Luther P. Jackson, Jan. 27, 1936, Jackson Papers; on inauguration of the campaign, see also *JNH* 21 (July 1936), 246-47.

235. See, for example, the annual reports of director in *JNH* 21 (July 1935), 247; 22 (Oct. 1937), 406-9; 23 (Oct. 1938), 410-11; 25 (Oct. 1940), 408.

236. Jackson to Woodson, Apr. 4, 1935, Jackson Papers; Jackson, "Five Years of Collecting Funds for the Association For The Study Of Negro Life And History" [1940], copy in GEB, box 205; *JNH* 22 (Oct. 1937), 406. See also correspondence between Woodson and Jackson, 1936-45 passim, Jackson Papers. For a good discussion of Jackson's methods, see Jackson to A. A. Taylor, June 14, 1949, in Jackson Papers.

237. Woodson, "An Accounting for Twenty-Five Years," *JNH* 25 (Oct. 1940), 426; Woodson, "The First Third," 48.

238. Woodson to Rosenwald Family Association, May 21, 1935, N. W. Levin to Embree, May 24, 1935, Embree to Levin, Sept. 14, 1935, George Arthur to Levin, Sept. 14, 1935, all in Rosenwald Papers, reel 4.

239. Stokes to Arnett, Apr. 16, 1934, Davis, "The Encyclopedia of the Negro," Apr. 28, 1934, W. W. Brierley to Stokes, June 19, 1934, all in GEB, box 418. Du Bois to Stokes, Feb. 2, 1935, and Stokes to Du Bois, Feb. 6, 1935, both in Du Bois Papers, reel 44.

240. Stokes to Thomas Jesse Jones, Apr. 25, 1935, copy in Du Bois Papers,

reel 44; Hope to Dillard, May 8, 1935, Dillard Papers; Dillard to Stokes, May 20, 1935, Phelps-Stokes Fund Archives.

241. Du Bois, *Black Reconstruction in America* (1935), "To the Reader"; Keppel to Du Bois, Jan. 2, Mar. 16, 1934, Du Bois Papers, reel 41; exchange of letters involving Keppel, Alfred Harcourt, and Du Bois, Nov. and Dec. 1934, in Aptheker, ed., *Correspondence of Du Bois*, 2:17-20.

242. Woodson press release: " 'Race Leaders' Barred from History Conference/ Ablest Scholars Have Been Poor Thinkers" [July 1935], Barnett Papers.

243. Woodson to Gentlemen, Apr. 8, 1936, Rosenwald Papers, reel 4; Woodson to Embree, Apr. 8, 1936, Embree to Woodson, Apr. 16, 1936, Embree to Levin, June 4, 1936, Embree to Woodson, Aug. 5, 1936, Woodson to Embree, Aug. 7, 1936, all in Rosenwald Fund Papers, box 170.

244. Du Bois to Bunche, Sept. 10, 1935, Bunche to Du Bois, Oct. 11, 1935, Woodson to Bunche, Dec. 16, 1936, Bunche to Woodson, Dec. 28, 1936, Du Bois to Bunche, Dec. 2, 1938, Bunche to Du Bois, Feb. 20, 1939, Du Bois to Bunche, Feb. 27, 1939, all in Bunche Papers.

245. Stokes to Du Bois, Oct. 15, 30, Nov. 27, 1935, Du Bois Papers, reel 44; Washington *Afro-American,* May 30, 1936; Woodson, "Open Letter to the Afro-American on the Negro Encyclopedia," June 3, 1936, Taylor Papers, and printed in Baltimore *Afro-American,* June 3, 1936.

246. Brawley to Woodson, Oct. 20, 1932, Woodson to Brawley, Oct. 20, 1932, various correspondence of Brawley with Woodson and authors in the series, 1933, Logan to Brawley, Apr. 18, 1935, all in Brawley Papers, box 1.

247. Brawley to editor, Baltimore *Afro-American,* June 6, 1936; Woodson press release, "Woodson Cites Brawley's Misrepresentations," June 10, 1936, copies in Woodson Papers, Howard University, box 1, and Taylor Papers.

248. Correspondence among Stokes, GEB officials, and Carnegie Institution officers, 1937-38 passim, and Mar. to May 1941 passim, in GEB, box 418; Stokes to Du Bois, Nov. 27, 1935, Du Bois Papers, reel 44; Stokes to Du Bois, Oct. 27, 1937, and correspondence between Stokes and Du Bois in 1942, in Aptheker, ed., *Correspondence of Du Bois*, 2:150-52, 334-36, 340. On endorsement by an initially skeptical Embree, see Du Bois to Embree, Apr. 24, 1935, and Embree to Du Bois, Apr. 30, 1935, in ibid., 64-66.

249. See, e.g., Woodson's annual reports in *JNH* 25 (Oct. 1940), 409-10; 33 (Oct. 1948), 388-89.

250. Ibid., 20 (Oct. 1935), 364. See also Woodson to Schlesinger, Apr. 29, 1935, Schlesinger Papers.

251. Various correspondence of Woodson with the GEB, 1934-41 passim, and unsigned comment on letter from Woodson to Raymond B. Fosdick, Jan. 16, 1937, GEB, box 205.

252. Woodson, "Accounting for Twenty-Five Years," 424, and Woodson to Dorothy Elvidge, Aug. 3, 1942, Rosenwald Fund Papers, box 170; Woodson, review of Embree and Waxman's *Investment in People, JNH* 34 (Apr. 1949), 225.

253. [Woodson], "Robert Ezra Park," *JNH* 29 (Apr. 1944), 248; [Woodson], "Thomas Jesse Jones," ibid., 35 (Jan. 1950), 107, 108; ASNLH press release,

"Remember 1917," June 17, 1936, Taylor Papers; Woodson, "Accounting for Twenty-Five Years," 425.

254. Interviews with former associates of Woodson; Logan, "Carter G. Woodson," *JNH* 35 (July 1950), 346-47, and Logan, "Woodson: Mirror and Molder," 14.

255. Review of T. J. Woofter's *Black Yeomanry: Life on St. Helena Island* (1930), *JNH* 16 (Jan. 1931), 95-96; review of Howard W. Odum's *Race and Rumors of Race* (1943), ibid., 29 (Jan. 1944), 92-94.

256. Ibid., 29 (Apr. 1944), 234-35.

257. Ibid., 9 (July 1924), 377; 10 (Jan. 1925), 109; 13 (Jan. 1928), 3; 23 (July 1938), 377; 29 (Apr. 1944), 235.

258. Ibid., 25 (Oct. 1940), 568-69; 24 (Oct. 1939), 460-63; Du Bois and Johnson, *Encyclopedia of the Negro; JNH* 30 (July 1945), 339-42 (quotations on 342, 341).

259. Du Bois to Stokes, Nov. 1, 1937, in Aptheker, ed., *Correspondence of Du Bois*, 2:152-53; Stokes to Du Bois, Apr. 30, 1935, Du Bois Papers, reel 44; *JNH* 30 (July 1945), 341.

260. Embree and Waxman, *Investment in People*, 273.

261. The best published account of the Durham Conference and the developments that followed is in Raymond Gavins, *The Perils and Prospects of Southern Black Leadership: Gordon Blaine Hancock, 1884-1970* (1977), chs. 5 and 6; for Johnson's role, see Gilpin, "Charles S. Johnson," 345-67. For an excellent statement of the strategy underlying the actions of the southern black leaders, see Luther P. Jackson to Woodson, May 20, 1944, Jackson Papers.

262. Woodson, "Negroes Not United for Democracy," *NHB* 6 (May 1943), 170; Woodson, "The Negro in the Present World Conflict," ibid., 7 (May 1944), 172; Jackson to Woodson, May 20, 1944, Jackson Papers.

263. Du Bois, "Portrait of Woodson," 21-22.

264. Butler A. Jones, "The Tradition of Sociology Teaching in Black Colleges: The Unheralded Professionals," in James E. Blackwell and Morris Janowitz, eds., *Black Sociologists: Historical and Contemporary Perspectives* (1974); August Meier, "Black Sociologists in White America," *Social Forces* 56 (Sept. 1977).

Chapter 2. Generational Change, Part I, 1915-60

1. Charles H. Wesley, "Retrospect and Prospect," *NHB* 13 (May 1950), 192.

2. Biographical data on Taylor, except where otherwise indicated, are from James Woods, "Alrutheus Ambush Taylor, 1893-1954: Segregated Historian of Reconstruction" (M.A. thesis, Louisiana State University, 1969). See also John Hope Franklin, "Alrutheus Ambush Taylor," in *JNH* 39 (July 1954). Important details on his Harvard period are to be found in Patricia Romero, "Carter G. Woodson: A Biography" (Ph.D. diss., Ohio State University, 1971), 139.

3. LSRM, box 98, correspondence 1927-28.

4. Taylor-Woodson correspondence, 1932-46, Taylor Papers; Woodson's description of Taylor in *JNH* 25 (Oct. 1940), 408; Woodson to Taylor, Dec. 23, 1936, and Taylor to Woodson, Jan. 14, 1937, Taylor Papers.

5. Taylor, "Negro Congressmen a Generation After," *JNH* 7 (Apr. 1922).

6. Taylor, *The Negro in South Carolina during the Reconstruction* (1924), 2.

7. See the thinly veiled discussion in the introduction Woodson anonymously wrote for Taylor, *The Negro in the Reconstruction of Virginia* (1926), 3.

8. Carl Russell Fish's review of *The Negro in South Carolina during the Reconstruction*, *AHR* 30 (Apr. 1925), 653; Franklin, "Alrutheus Ambush Taylor," 241; [Woodson], introduction to Taylor's *Negro in the Reconstruction of Virginia*, 3.

9. Unless otherwise indicated, biographical information is from interview data and Michael Winston, *The Howard University Department of History 1913-1973* (1973), 27-30.

10. Wesley, "The Struggle of Haiti and Liberia for Recognition," *JNH* 2 (Oct. 1917); *Catalogue of Howard University, 1913-1914*, 85; Wesley, "Interest in a Neglected Phase of History," *AME Church Review* 32 (Apr. 1916), 268.

11. See also Wesley's two early articles, "Lincoln's Plan for Colonizing the Emancipated Negroes," *JNH* 4 (Jan. 1919), and "The Employment of Negroes as Soldiers in the Confederate Army," ibid., 4 (July 1919).

12. Edward Channing to Wesley, July 26, 1922, text of letter in Janette Harris, "Charles Harris Wesley, Educator and Historian, 1891-1947" (Ph.D. diss., Howard University, 1975), 197-98. For Woodson's statement, see his review of Wesley's *The Collapse of the Confederacy* in New York Age, Feb. 5, 1938.

13. In addition to our own interview material, the foregoing is based largely on the account in Romero, "Carter G. Woodson," 186-88. For a rather different version, see Harris, "Charles Harris Wesley," 134-38. For reports of progress on the project, see *JNH* 12 (Apr. 1927), 357; 13 (Apr. 1928), 213-14; 13 (Oct. 1928), 408. For evidence of reconciliation, see notice regarding Wesley's appearance on the 1929 ASNLH program in ibid., 15 (Jan. 1930), 6.

14. Wesley, "The Neglected Period of Emancipation in Great Britain, 1807-1823," *JNH* 17 (Apr. 1932); "The Emancipation of the Free Colored Population in the British Empire," ibid., 19 (Apr. 1934); "The Participation of Negroes in Anti-Slavery Political Parties," ibid., 29 (Jan. 1944); "The Negroes of New York in the Emancipation Movement," ibid., 24 (Jan. 1939), quotation 103.

15. Wesley, "The Reconstruction of History," ibid., 20 (Oct. 1935), 421, 427; "Racial Historical Societies and the American Heritage," ibid., 37 (Jan. 1952), 14, 33.

16. The foregoing is based chiefly on interview data. See also Lorenzo J. Greene, "Slave-Holding New England and Its Awakening," ibid., 13 (Oct. 1928); foreword to Greene, "Impressions of the Negro Church in 1928," *Midwest Journal* 3 (Summer 1951), 67; *JNH* 13 (Oct. 1928), 546.

17. Greene, "Dr. Woodson Prepares for Negro History Week, 1930," *NHB* 28 (Summer 1965), 174-75, 195.

18. Greene to authors, May 8, 1981.

19. Greene, diary entries for Sept. 5, Dec. 6, 1930, Jan. 11, 1931, and Dec. 18, 1930. Copy of diary supplied courtesy of Lorenzo J. Greene. For advertisement of the book, see, for example, *JNH* 15 (July 1930).

20. Greene, diary entries for Oct. 26, 1930, Feb. 6, Jan. 28, 1931.

21. This paragraph is based mainly on interview data. See also Greene and

Myra Colson-Callis, *The Employment of Negroes in the District of Columbia* (1932); Greene to authors, Aug. 25, 1981 (regarding fellowship supplied by Woodson); Woodson's review in *JNH* 28 (Oct. 1943). On the special GEB grants, see GEB, *Annual Report, 1945,* 86, and *Annual Report, 1946,* 63.

22. Greene, diary entry for Dec. 5, 1930.

23. Greene to Luther Porter Jackson, Feb. 1, 1943, Jackson Papers.

24. For biographical data, see Greene, "W. Sherman Savage," *JNH* 66 (Spring 1981), 80-84; Ray Allen Billington, foreword in Savage, *Blacks in the West* (1976); interview with Mrs. W. Sherman Savage, Mar. 7, 1982.

25. Savage, "Abolitionist Literature in the Mails, 1835-1836," *JNH* 13 (Apr. 1928); "The Negro in the History of the Pacific Northwest," ibid., 13 (July 1928).

26. Savage, *The Controversy over the Distribution of Abolitionist Literature, 1830-1860* (1938), unpaged preface.

27. For a sketch of the school's history, see the pamphlet by Edgar A. Toppin, *A Century of Service at Virginia State University, 1883-1983* (1983).

28. Biographical data are from materials in the James Hugo Johnston Papers, Virginia State College, Petersburg, and information in GEB, *Directory of Fellowship Awards For the Years 1922-1950* [1952], 101.

29. J. Hugo Johnston to V. D. Johnston, May 16, 1932, Johnston Papers.

30. Woodson to J. Johnston, Oct. 21, 1930, correspondence of J. Johnston with Charles S. Johnson and Will W. Alexander, Dec. 1930–Feb. 1931, J. Johnston to Woodson, Mar. 7, 1931, J. Johnston to Johnson, Mar. 10, 1931, Johnson to Woodson, Mar. 12, 1931, all in Johnston Papers.

31. J. Johnston to Woodson, May 10, 1932, Johnston to V. Johnston, May 16, 1932, both in Johnston Papers. J. Johnston, "The Mohammedan Slave Trade," *JNH* 13 (Oct. 1928); "Documentary Evidence of the Relations of Negroes and Indians," ibid., 14 (Jan. 1929); "The Participation of Negroes in the Government of Virginia from 1877 to 1888," ibid., 14 (July 1929); "The Participation of White Men in Virginia Negro Insurrections," ibid., 16 (Apr. 1931).

32. G. Franklin Edwards, "E. Franklin Frazier," in Rayford W. Logan and Michael Winston, eds., *Dictionary of American Negro Biography* (1982), 241; Frazier, "The Pathology of Race Prejudice," *Forum* 70 (June 1927); J. Johnston to Woodson, May 10, 1932, and Woodson to J. Johnston, May 21, 1932, Johnston Papers.

33. See correspondence of J. Johnston and Woodson, Feb. 1933, and Jan. 1938–May 1939 passim, Johnston Papers; Woodson to Luther Porter Jackson, June 27, 1938, Jackson Papers.

34. Winthrop Jordan, foreword to Johnston's *Race Relations in Virginia and Miscegenation in the South, 1776-1860* (1970), 5-6.

35. Biographical data concerning Jackson have been drawn principally from the following sources: J. Hugo Johnston, "Luther Porter Jackson," *JNH* 35 (July 1950); Raymond Gavins, *The Perils and Prospects of Southern Black Leadership: Gordon Blaine Hancock, 1884-1970* (1977), 108-12; interview with Luther Porter Jackson, Jr., July 18, 1981; Petersburg *Progress-Index*, Feb. 26, 1980; Wilhelmina Hamlin, "Luther Porter Jackson: Historian," *NHB* 6 (Nov. 1942); a paper on

Jackson by Lucious Edwards, archivist at Virginia State University, presented at the 1981 convention of the Association for the Study of Afro-American Life and History.

36. Jackson, "Citizenship Training: A Neglected Area in Adult Education," *Journal of Negro Education* 14 (Feb. 1945); *Crisis* 55 (Dec. 1948), 375, 377; Jackson to Woodson, Aug. 16, 1941, Jackson Papers; discussion of formation of Southern Regional Council in ch. 1; quotation from Jackson to Taylor, June 14, 1949, Jackson Papers.

37. Jackson, "The Educational Activities of the Freedmen's Bureau and Freedmen's Aid Societies in South Carolina, 1862-1872," *JNH* 8 (Jan. 1923); "Free Negroes of Petersburg, Virginia," ibid., 12 (Jan. 1927). The most important of his several articles was "Religious Development of the Negro in Virginia from 1760-1860," ibid., 16 (Apr. 1931).

38. Jackson to Avery Craven, Nov. 29, 1942, Jackson Papers; Craven, "Poor Whites and Negroes in the Ante-bellum South," *JNH* 15 (Jan. 1930); Jackson to Woodson, Oct. 14, 1939, Jackson Papers. For the Social Science Research Council grant, see Romero, "Carter G. Woodson," 170-71.

39. Jackson to Craven, Nov. 29, 1942, Jackson Papers.

40. Craven to Jackson, June 10, 1937, May 31, 1939, Jackson to Woodson, Jan. 15, 1942, all in Jackson Papers.

41. Craven to Jackson, Oct. 12, 1939, Jackson Papers. Charles S. Sydnor, *Slavery in Mississippi* (1933), and "The Free Negro in Mississippi before the Civil War," *AHR* 32 (July 1927).

42. John D. Hicks to Jackson, Jan. 22, 1942, Jackson to John Hope Franklin, Oct. 9, 1942, Jackson to Craven, Nov. 29, 1942, all in Jackson Papers.

43. GEB, *Annual Report, 1943,* 60; Jackson to Woodson, Mar. 31, 1946, Jackson Papers. In regard to funding problem, see also Jackson to Taylor, June 14, 1949, Jackson Papers.

44. Jackson to Woodson, May 20, 1944, Woodson to Jackson, Feb. 23, 1946, Jackson to Woodson, Mar. 31, 1946, all in Jackson Papers.

45. Jackson to Woodson, Mar. 31, 1946, to Taylor, June 14, 1949, Jackson Papers.

46. Jackson to Woodson, Jan. 15, 1942, Greene to Jackson, Feb. 1, 1943, Jackson Papers.

47. Biographical data are drawn chiefly from interview material. A useful account is also found in Winston, *Howard University Department of History,* 77-93, and for a list of Logan's publications, 165-71.

48. Interview with Rayford W. Logan, Mar. 3, 1981.

49. On Fauset's role, see Logan, "The Historical Aspects of Pan-Africanism: A Personal Chronicle," *African Forum* 1 (Summer 1965), 95. On the definition of his specialty, see entry on Logan in GEB, *Directory of Fellowship Awards,* 118.

50. Logan, "The Haze in Haiti," *Nation* 124 (Mar. 16, 1927).

51. *JNH* 17 (Oct. 1932), 396.

52. Logan, "Nat Turner: Fiend or Martyr," *Opportunity* 9 (Nov. 1931), 338.

53. Clarence Bacote, "The Negro in Atlanta Politics," *Phylon* 16 (Fourth quarter 1955), 342-43.

54. Logan, review of Du Bois's *Black Reconstruction, JNH* 21 (Jan. 1936).

55. Logan, "Carter G. Woodson," *Phylon* 6 (Fourth quarter 1945), 318; Woodson to Taylor, Dec. 23, 1936, and Logan to Taylor, Dec. 14, 1936, Taylor Papers; Romero, "Carter G. Woodson," 204, and see also 197-200, 205-10; Ludwell Lee Montague, review of Logan's book in *JNH* 26 (July 1941). For Logan's extensive work on the encyclopedia, see esp. Du Bois to Anson Phelps-Stokes, May 19, 1937, May 15, 1942, in Herbert Aptheker, ed., *The Correspondence of W. E. B. Du Bois,* 2 (1976), 145-46, 334.

56. Logan, *The Negro in the United States* (1957).

57. L. D. Reddick, "A New Interpretation of Negro History," *JNH* 22 (Jan. 1937).

58. Wesley, "Retrospect and Prospect," 189-90; Logan, "Carter G. Woodson," 318.

59. ASNLH, "Program of Annual Meeting, Oct. 27-31, 1929," copy in Rosenwald Fund Papers, box 170.

60. J. Fred Rippy, "A Negro Colonization Project in Mexico, 1895," *JNH* 6 (Jan. 1921); Rippy, "The Negro and the Spanish Pioneers in the New World," ibid., 6 (Apr. 1921); Fred A. Shannon, "The Federal Government and the Negro Soldier," ibid., 11 (Oct. 1926); Francis B. Simkins, "The Ku Klux Klan in South Carolina, 1868-1871," ibid., 12 (Oct. 1927); Craven, "Poor Whites and Negroes in the Ante-bellum South"; and Evarts B. Greene, "Perspectives in History," ibid., 17 (Jan. 1932).

61. On Riddell, in addition to his book and his *JNH* articles, 1919-32 passim, see the following biographical sketches: *Macmillan Dictionary of Canadian Biography* (1978), 704; *Who Was Who among North American Authors, 1921-1939* (1976), 1216; E. Fabre Surveyer, "The Honourable William Renwick Riddell," in *Proceedings and Transactions of the Royal Society of Canada,* series 3, 39 (1945). On Landon, in addition to his articles in the *JNH,* 1918-25 passim and 1936, see his M.A. thesis at the University of Western Ontario, "The Relation of Canada to the Anti-Slavery and Abolition Movement in the United States" (1919); his paper, "Ulrich Bonnell Phillips: Historian of the South," *JSH* 5 (Aug. 1939); and the following biographical accounts: Arthur G. Dorland, "Fred Landon 1880-1969," in *Proceedings of the Royal Society of Canada,* series 4, 8 (1970); Fred Armstrong "Fred Landon," *Ontario History* 62 (Mar. 1970); and especially a paper by Patricia G. Skidmore, "Mind and Manuscript: A Profile of Historian Fred Landon" (1979), in the D. B. Weldon Library of the University of Western Ontario, London; interview with Mrs. Fred Landon, July 31, 1982.

62. Klingberg's paper was published as "Carter G. Woodson, Historian, and His Contribution to American Historiography," *JNH* 41 (Jan. 1956). Biographical data on Klingberg are from Samuel McCulloch, "Professor Frank J. Klingberg (1883-1968): Historian of British Humanitarianism," *Historical Magazine of the Protestant Episcopal Church* 38 (June 1969); McCulloch's introduction, in McCulloch, ed., *British Humanitarianism: Essays Honoring Frank J. Klingberg* (1950); and interview with Klingberg's son, Frank W. Klingberg, Mar. 14, 1982.

63. Biographical materials are in Jacob Cooke, *Frederic Bancroft: Historian* (1957); Bancroft's review of Fleming's book in *The Nation* 82 (Apr. 26, 1906), 348-50; Bancroft to Du Bois, Dec. 11, 1918, Du Bois Papers, reel 6.

64. Cooke, *Frederic Bancroft,* 74; Bancroft to Du Bois, Dec. 11, 1918, Du Bois Papers, reel 6. Correspondence between Bancroft and Woodson in Bancroft Papers, Columbia University, New York City, especially Sept. 1928–Feb. 1929, and, regarding prizes, Woodson to Bancroft, Nov. 5, 1931, Sept. 27, 1934, and Oct. 10, 1935; Woodson, "Frederic Bancroft," *JNH* 30 (Apr. 1945), 245-47.

65. Du Bois, review of James C. Ballagh's *A History of Slavery in Virginia* (1902), *AHR* 8 (Jan. 1903), 356-57; Jameson to Woodson, Apr. 26, 1927, Jameson Papers, box 136; and review of *The Negro in Our History, AHR* 33 (Oct. 1927), 192; Woodson, review of Wesley's *Negro Labor,* ibid., 33 (Oct. 1927), 154-56; Wesley, review of Lorenzo Turner's *Antislavery Sentiment in American Literature Prior to 1865* (1929), ibid., 36 (Apr. 1931), 652-53.

66. *AHR* 35 (Apr. 1930), 495; Monroe N. Work, "The Economic Progress of the Negro," Dec. 31, 1929, in Work Papers, box 4.

67. Marion Dargan, Jr., "Clarence Walworth Alvord," in William T. Hutchinson, ed., *The Marcus W. Jernegan Essays in American Historiography* (1937), 324; Samuel M. Alvord, *A Genealogy of the Descendants of Alexander Alvord* (1908), 575-76, 285-87, for sketches of Clarence and J. W. Alvord, respectively.

68. Woodson, review of Phillips's *American Negro Slavery, MVHR* 5 (Mar. 1919), 480-82, quotation, 480. For Woodson's other reviews see ibid., 4 (Mar. 1918), 515-16; 7 (Sept. 1920), 175-76.

69. The following discussion is based on information in William Best Hesseltine and Louis Kaplan, "Negro Doctors of Philosophy in History," *NHB* 6 (Dec. 1942), and Harry W. Greene, *Holders of Doctorates among American Negroes* (1946). The otherwise useful essay by Hesseltine and Kaplan, drawn from their comprehensive study of history Ph.D.s, understates the number of blacks.

70. The following discussion is based on the lists of Rosenwald and GEB fellows in Edwin R. Embree and Julia Waxman, *Investment in People: The Story of the Julius Rosenwald Fund* (1949), and GEB, *Directory of Fellowship Awards, 1922-1950.*

71. Wesley, "Propaganda and Historical Writing: The Emancipation of the Historian," *Opportunity* 13 (Aug. 1935), 245; Taylor, review of *Black Reconstruction* in *New England Quarterly* 8 (Dec. 1935), 608, 610.

72. Mark Naison, *Communists in Harlem during the Depression* (1983), ch. 8.

73. Howard K. Beale, "On Rewriting Reconstruction History," *AHR* 45 (July 1940).

74. Roger Williams, *The Bonds: An American Family* (1971), 97-99, 106-7, 113. This biographical information is confirmed in interview with Mrs. Horace Mann Bond, July 9, 1984.

75. Beale, "On Rewriting Reconstruction History," 810.

76. Horace Mann Bond, "Dr. Woodson Goes Wool-Gathering," *Journal of Negro Education* 2 (Apr. 1933), 212-13.

77. Bond to Gordon J. Laing, editor, University of Chicago Press, Apr. 4, 25,

1938, Woodson to Bond, June 11, July 12, 1938, and Bond to Woodson, July 6, 16, 1938, Bond Papers.

78. See especially effusive letters from Woodson to Bond, Aug. 28, Sept. 26, 1945, Bond Papers, in connection with Bond's appearance as major speaker at 1945 ASNLH convention.

79. Reddick to Bond, postcard, Mar. 30, 1939, and Reddick to Wesley, Apr. 5, 1939, both in Bond Papers.

80. Craven to Jackson, Oct. 12, 1939, Jackson to Craven, Oct. 14, 1939, Jackson to Woodson, Oct. 14, 1939, all in Jackson Papers. The quotation is from Jackson to Woodson, Oct. 14, 1939. The review of Craven's *The Repressible Conflict, 1830-1861,* written by one "E. R. Thomas," appeared in *JNH* 24 (July 1939), 345-48.

81. Interview with Reddick, May 20, 1984; Reddick to Wesley, Apr. 5, 1939, and see also Reddick to Bond, Apr. 7, 1939, both in Bond Papers.

82. Reddick, "New Interpretation of Negro History," 25-28 passim, quotation, 27. For reference to Marxist influence on his thinking, see Reddick to Bond, May 16, 1947, Bond Papers.

83. Biographical data are from the following: Walter G. Daniel, "A Tribute to Marion Thompson Wright," *Journal of Negro Education* 32 (Summer 1963); Clement Price to authors, Dec. 9, 1981; James A. Moss (her son) to authors, Feb. 11, 1982; interviews with James Moss, Jan. 24, 1982, and with Thelma Moss (her daughter), Jan. 10, 1982; interview with Merle Curti, Dec. 6, 1981.

84. Marion M. Thompson Wright, "New Jersey Laws and the Negro," *JNH* 28 (Apr. 1943), and "Negro Suffrage in New Jersey, 1776-1875," ibid., 33 (Apr. 1948).

85. Wright, *The Education of Negroes in New Jersey* (1941), vii; on her debt to Curti, see also Wright to Curti, June 18, Sept. 23, 1939, Curti Papers, box 46.

86. Aptheker, ed., *Correspondence of Du Bois,* 2:266; interview with Curti, Dec. 6, 1981, including information about Walter White.

87. Curti to Du Bois, Dec. 5, 1941, Du Bois Papers, reel 52.

88. Biographical data are from an interview with Mrs. Kenneth Wiggins Porter and Kenneth's brother Russell Porter, July 12, 1981; and introduction to Porter, *The Negro on the American Frontier* (1971).

89. Porter to Curti, Dec. 4, 1948, Curti Papers, box 34; Porter to Du Bois, July 27, 1929, Du Bois Papers, reel 30.

90. Kenneth W. Porter, "Relations between Indians and Negroes within the Present Limits of the United States," *JNH* 17 (July 1932), and "Negroes in the Fur Trade," *Minnesota History* 15 (Dec. 1934).

91. Porter to Curti, Oct. 25, 1963, Curti Papers, box 34.

92. Porter to Curti, Dec. 20, 1950, Nov. 2, 1952, Curti Papers, box 34.

93. Porter, "Negroes and the Seminole War, 1835-1842," *JSH* 30 (Nov. 1964); Porter, *Negro on the Frontier.* See also Porter, "Negro Labor in the Western Cattle Industry, 1866-1900," *Labor History* 10 (Summer 1969).

94. Joseph C. Carroll, *Slave Insurrections in the United States, 1800-1865* (1938), 215. Biographical data on Carroll are from Maggie Jackson, secretary,

Education Center of the Indianapolis Public Schools, in a letter to authors, Mar. 14, 1984.

95. Biographical information on Wish is from the following: Marion C. Siney, "Ups and Downs: The History Department, Western Reserve University–Case Western Reserve University," Harvey Wish Memorial Lectures, series no. 3, n.d.; Louis Filler, "Harvey Wish: Historian of Reform," *Ohioana Quarterly* 19 (Fall 1976); interviews with C. H. Cramer, emeritus professor of Western Reserve University, Mar. 8, 1981, with Wish's daughter, Dorothy Wish Leven, Mar. 10, 1981, and with Wish's former student, Allan Peskin, July 23, 1981.

96. Harvey Wish, "The Administration of Governor John Peter Altgeld of Illinois, 1893-1897" (Ph.D. diss., Northwestern University, 1936); "American Slave Insurrections before 1861," *JNH* 22 (July 1937); "Slave Disloyalty under the Confederacy," ibid., 23 (Oct. 1938). For Wish's indebtedness to Herskovits, see Wish, "Slave Disloyalty under the Confederacy," 435*n*. Wish's *Society and Thought in Early America* (1950) is notable for the extensive treatment he gives to slavery, abolition, and women's rights.

97. Raymond Bauer and Alice Bauer, "Day to Day Resistance to Slavery," *JNH* 27 (Oct. 1942).

98. Wish, "American Slave Insurrections before 1861," 320.

99. Herbert Aptheker, "American Negro Slave Revolts," *Science and Society* 1 (Summer 1937); *Negro Slave Revolts, 1526-1860* (1939); "Maroons within the Present Limits of the United States," *JNH* 24 (Apr. 1939); *The Negro in the Abolitionist Movement* (1941); "Militant Abolitionism," *JNH* 26 (Oct. 1941).

100. See, e.g., Aptheker, "Negro History—A Cause for Optimism," *Opportunity* 19 (Aug. 1941); "Distorting the Negro's History," *New Masses* 40 (Sept. 23, 1941); "Negro History: Arsenal for Liberation," *New Masses* 62 (Feb. 11, 1947).

101. Review by J. G. de Roulhac Hamilton, *AHR* 49 (Apr. 1944), 504-6; Lorenzo J. Greene, "Mutiny on the Slave Ships," *Phylon* 5 (Fourth quarter 1944), 354.

102. Stampp, "Our Historians and Slavery," *Politics* 1 (Mar. 1944), 58.

103. Woodson, review of *Essays in the History of the American Negro, JNH* 31 (July 1946), 360; Franklin, review of *To Be Free, AHR* 53 (July 1948), 897-98.

104. Naison, *Communists in Harlem*, 293-94.

105. Biographical data are chiefly from James Robertson, "Bell I. Wiley," a paper presented at SHA convention, Nov. 1981; John Roper, interview with Bell I. Wiley, Sept. 13, 1974, John Roper Papers, Southern Historical Collection, University of North Carolina, Chapel Hill; and esp. our interview with Wiley's widow, Mrs. Frances Wiley, July 21, 1981.

106. Francis Butler Simkins and Robert H. Woody, *South Carolina during Reconstruction* (1932).

107. Review by Simkins in *MVHR* 25 (Dec. 1938), 425; review by Woodson in *JNH* 23 (July 1938), 370-71; review by Wesley in *AHR* 44 (Apr. 1939), 658.

108. Wiley, review of Brawley's *Negro Builders and Heroes* (1937), in *JSH* 4 (July 1938), 406.

109. August Meier interview with Clarence Bacote, Apr. 15, 1952.

110. Biographical information on Wharton is chiefly from an interview on Feb.

26, 1981, with James Ferguson of the University of North Carolina at Greensboro, Wharton's close friend and long-time colleague at Millsaps College.

111. Warren Ashby, *Frank Porter Graham: A Southern Liberal* (1980), especially chs. 2 and 3 passim.

112. In addition to our interviews, see Roper interviews with Woodward and individuals who knew him during his years in Georgia and Chapel Hill: Bennett H. Wall, J. Carlyle Sitterson, J. Isaac Copeland, and Glenn W. Rainey, Roper Papers.

113. Woodward to Du Bois, Apr. 3, 1938, Du Bois Papers, reel 49.

114. Materials on Beale's life are found in his papers at the State Historical Society of Wisconsin, Madison. We are also indebted to Merle Curti, who shared his recollections about Beale with us.

115. Beale to Du Bois, Dec. 10, 1932, reel 36, and Du Bois to Beale, Jan. 14, 1935, reel 43, Du Bois Papers, regarding *Black Reconstruction;* correspondence 1934 passim, reel 41, Du Bois Papers on both subjects; Beale, *A History of Freedom of Teaching in American Schools* (1941). See also another product of his research on teaching, "The Needs of Negro Education in the United States," *Journal of Negro Education* 3 (Jan. 1934).

116. Beale to Thomas Clark, Feb. 2, 1954, Beale Papers.

117. Beale to Curti, Apr. 7, 1936, Curti Papers, box 3. On Beale at Chapel Hill, see also Roper interview with J. Carlyle Sitterson, Nov. 10, 1978, Roper Papers.

118. Beale, "On Rewriting Reconstruction History." For description of the SHA session, see Roper interviews with J. Isaac Copeland, Nov. 19-20, 1979, Oct. 11, 1982, Roper Papers.

119. Curti to Tom LeDuc, Oct. 18, 1951, Curti Papers, box 26.

120. Franklin to Jackson, Jan. 15, 1941, Jackson Papers; Wright to Curti, Sept. 18, 1941, box 46, Curti to Richard P. McCormick, Jan. 12, 1954, box 12, both in Curti Papers. See also Curti to Du Bois, Dec. 31, 1940, in Aptheker, ed., *Correspondence of Du Bois,* 2:266-67.

121. Howard K. Beale, "The Professional Historian: His Theory and His Practice," *Pacific Historical Review* 22 (Aug. 1953), 235.

122. Du Bois, "A Chronicle of Race Relations," *Phylon* 3 (First quarter 1942), 83, and the following in the SHA Papers, Southern Historical Collection, University of North Carolina: Kendrick to secretary-treasurer James W. Patton, Oct. 25, 1941, Patton to Kendrick, Oct. 26, 1941, minutes of the SHA council meeting Nov. 7, 1941.

123. Beale to Du Bois, Oct. 31, 1941, Du Bois to Beale, Nov. 5, 1941, Du Bois Papers, reel 52; Beale to Du Bois, Nov. 14, Du Bois to Beale, Nov. 18, 1941, in Aptheker, ed., *Correspondence of Du Bois,* 2:307.

124. Du Bois to SHA, Jan. 14, 1942, in Aptheker, ed., *Correspondence of Du Bois,* 2:314; minutes of SHA council meeting, Nov. 7, 1941.

125. Review by Woodson in *AHR* 44 (Jan. 1939), 403-4, and by Wesley in ibid., 44 (Apr. 1939), 657-58; review by Reddick in *JSH* 6 (Feb. 1940), 130-31; reviews by McMillan in *MVHR* 27 (June 1940), 109-11, and 30 (Mar. 1944), 598-99, and by Reid, ibid., 29 (June 1942), 131-32, and 30 (Jan. 1944), 439-40.

126. *JNH* 26 (Oct. 1941), 415.

127. Ibid., 25 (Oct. 1940), 440-49. See also Hesseltine, "Some New Approaches to the Pro-Slavery Argument," ibid., 21 (Jan. 1936).

128. Melville J. Herskovits, ed., *The Interdisciplinary Aspects of Negro Studies,* ACLS Bulletin 32 (1941); Robert L. Harris, Jr., "Segregation and Scholarship: The American Council of Learned Societies' Committee on Negro Studies, 1941-1950," *Journal of Black Studies* 12 (Mar. 1982).

129. For further details on Quarles's career prior to the publication of his *Frederick Douglass* in 1948, see August Meier, "Benjamin Quarles and the Historiography of Black America," *Civil War History* 26 (June 1980), 101-3.

130. *Fellows of the Social Science Research Council, 1925-1951* (1951), 458.

131. In addition to interview materials, for some corroborating information and additional details about Franklin's career, see F. Holton, "John Hope Franklin, Scholar," *University of Chicago Magazine* 73 (Sept. 1980), 14-18.

132. A. A. Taylor to Franklin, Feb. 18, 1937, Taylor Papers.

133. Interview with John Hope Franklin in James Allen Moss, "Utilization of Negro Teachers in the Colleges of New York State" (Ph.D. diss., Columbia University, 1957), 147.

134. *JSH* 4 (Feb. 1938), 61; Roger W. Shugg, "The New Orleans General Strike of 1892," *Louisiana Historical Quarterly* 21 (Apr. 1938).

135. This account is derived chiefly from interviews and conversations with Franklin and Shugg. The quotation is from Roger W. Shugg to Charles S. Johnson, May 24, 1945, in Archives of the Race Relations Department of the United Church Board for Homeland Missions, Amistad Research Center, New Orleans. See also Johnson to Shugg, June 2, 1945, in ibid., suggesting half a dozen possibilities, Franklin among them.

136. Hugh Smythe in *Crisis* 58 (Jan. 1948), 25-26. See also Williston H. Lofton in *JNH* 33 (Apr. 1948), 225.

137. *AHR* 54 (Oct. 1948), 155-56. See also J. G. Randall review in *MVHR* 35 (Sept. 1948), 288-90.

138. Quarles, "The Breach between Douglass and Garrison," *JNH* 23 (Apr. 1938), and "Frederick Douglass and the Woman's Rights Movement," ibid., 25 (Jan. 1940).

139. Ibid., 28 (Jan. 1943), 86-88; 28 (Oct. 1943), 482-85.

140. *AHR* 49 (Jan. 1944), 303-5; Jackson to Franklin, Apr. 9, 1943, Jackson Papers.

141. Franklin, "Slaves Virtually Free in Ante-Bellum North Carolina," *JNH* 28 (July 1943); "The Enslavement of Free Negroes in North Carolina," ibid., 29 (Oct. 1944); "James Boon, Free Negro Artisan," ibid., 30 (Apr. 1945); and "George Washington Williams, Historian," ibid., 31 (Jan. 1946).

142. Franklin, *From Slavery to Freedom* (1947), viii; Quarles, *The Negro in the American Revolution* (1961), xi.

143. Quarles, "Revisionist Negro History," *Social Education* 10 (Mar. 1946).

144. In addition to Quarles's essay on "The Breach between Douglass and Garrison," see the discussion of Robert Gould Shaw in Quarles's *The Negro in the Civil War* (1953), ch. 1; Quarles, *Lincoln and the Negro* (1962); and Quarles, *Allies for Freedom: Blacks and John Brown* (1974).

145. Holton, "John Hope Franklin, Scholar," 17; Franklin, *From Slavery to Freedom*, vii, viii; Franklin, "New Perspectives in American Negro History," *Social Education* 14 (May 1960), 196, 199.

146. See especially E. Horace Fitchett, "The Traditions of the Free Negro in Charleston, South Carolina," *JNH* 25 (Apr. 1940).

147. Franklin to Jackson, Oct. 23, 1946, Jackson Papers.

148. For further discussion of this point, based on communications from Logan, Greene, and Aptheker, see two unpublished manuscripts by Jacqueline Goggin, "Countering White Racist Historiography: Carter G. Woodson and the *Journal of Negro History*, and "Carter Woodson and the Study of Comparative Slavery and Race Relations."

149. Quarles, "Sources of Abolitionist Income," *MVHR* 32 (June 1945).

150. John H. Roper inteviews with John Hope Franklin, Nov. 10, 1978, Isaac Copeland, Nov. 19-20, 1979, and Oct. 11, 1982, Guy and Guion Johnson, Jan. 11, 1980, and J. Carlyle Sitterson, Nov. 10, 1978, all in Roper Papers; Franklin to Curti, Feb. 26, 1948, Curti Papers, box 17.

151. E. Franklin Frazier, "Race: An American Dilemma," *Crisis* 51 (Apr. 1944), 124.

152. Logan's report in *JNH* 35 (Oct. 1950), 365, 366; Wesley, "Racial Historical Societies," 32.

153. See interview with Kenneth Clark in Moss, "Utilization of Negro Teachers," 106-41 passim.

154. List of black faculty at predominantly white colleges in *Phylon* 7 (Fourth quarter 1946), 384; Ivan E. Taylor, "Negro Teachers in White Colleges," *School and Society* 65 (May 24, 1947); Fred G. Wale, "Chosen for Ability," *Atlantic Monthly* 180 (July 1947); James Allan Moss, "Negro Teachers in Predominantly White Colleges," *Journal of Negro Education* 27 (Fall 1958); Gilbert A. Belles, "The College Faculty, the Negro Scholar and the Julius Rosenwald Fund," *JNH* 54 (Oct. 1969). See also Du Bois to Ann Fagan, n.d. [1943], in Aptheker, ed., *Correspondence of Du Bois*, 2:364, re University of Chicago; and correspondence with New York University officials, 1945-50 passim, in GEB, Series 1, box 259. On Reddick, see *Phylon* list and Wale, "Chosen for Ability," 84.

155. Interview with Franklin in Moss, "Utilization of Negro Teachers," 160, 152-53.

156. George H. Colt, "Will the Huggins Approach Save Afro-American Studies?" *Harvard Magazine* 84 (Sept.-Oct. 1981), 44.

157. Beale, "Professional Historian," 245.

158. For sketch of Clarence Bacote's career, see GEB, *Directory of Fellowship Awards*, 10. Mrs. Clarence Bacote shared helpful information in an interview on Oct. 9, 1982. On Elsie Lewis, see Winston, *Howard University Department of History*, 109-11; Lewis, "The Political Mind of the Negro, 1865-1900," *JSH* 21 (May 1955). For her turning to black history, see Lewis to Craven, Nov. 5, 1951, Craven Papers.

159. Vincent Harding, "Lyman Beecher and the Transformation of American Protestantism, 1775-1863" (Ph.D. diss., University of Chicago, 1965).

160. *JSH* 19 (May 1953). The M.A. thesis was entitled "The Civil War and Some Northern Economic Interests in Florida."

161. Logan, *The Negro in American Life and Thought: The Nadir, 1877-1901* (1954), x.

162. Daniel C. Thompson, "Teachers in Negro Colleges (A Sociological Analysis)" (Ph.D. diss., Columbia University, 1956).

163. Earl J. McGrath, *The Predominantly Negro Colleges and Universities in Transition* (1965), 108; Reddick, "Library Facilities for Research in Negro Colleges," *Quarterly Review of Higher Education among Negroes* 8 (July 1940), 127. See also Reddick's remarks in Herskovits, ed., *Interdisciplinary Aspects of Negro Studies*, 27.

164. Jackson to Woodson, Mar. 31, 1946, Taylor to Jackson, June 24, 1949, Jackson Papers; Franklin to Bond, May 24, 1946, Bond to Franklin, June 11, 1946, Bond Papers.

165. Reddick's remarks in Herskovits, ed., *Interdisciplinary Aspects of Negro Studies*, 27. See also Reddick, "Research Barriers in the South," *Social Frontier* 4 (Dec. 1937), 85-86.

166. Jackson to Taylor, June 14, 1949, Jackson Papers; Lewis to Craven, Jan. 15, 1945, Craven Papers; Bond, *Negro Education in Alabama: A Study in Cotton and Steel* (1939), preface; Jackson to Woodson, Sept. 18, 1947, Franklin to Jackson, Sept. 22, 1947, Jackson Papers.

167. Holton, "John Hope Franklin, Scholar," 16.

168. Franklin to Jackson, Apr. 3, 1946, Jackson Papers. In addition to books by Edmonds, Logan, and Franklin cited previously, see Roland C. McConnell, "The Negro in North Carolina Since Reconstruction" (Ph.D. diss., New York University, 1945).

169. See, for example, the discussion of attitudes and policy of many black college presidents, especially Mordecai Johnson of Howard University, in Michael R. Winston, "Through the Back Door: Academic Racism and the Negro Scholar in Historical Perspective," *Daedalus* 100, part 2 (1971), 702-3, 707.

170. See a description of the process in Bond, "The Position of the Negro in the American Social Order . . . ," *Journal of Negro Education* 8 (July 1939), 584-85.

171. Franklin to Jackson, Nov. 8, 1943, and similar sentiment in Franklin to Jackson, Sept. 6, 1948, both in Jackson Papers. Interview with Franklin in Moss, "Utilization of Negro Teachers," 150, 157.

172. *JNH* 28 (Jan. 1943).

173. Stampp, "Our Historians and Slavery," 58-59.

174. *AHR* 57 (Apr. 1952).

175. Woodward, review of Stampp's *The Peculiar Institution*, in New York *Herald Tribune Book Review*, Oct. 21, 1956, 6.

176. Stanley Elkins, *Slavery: A Problem in American Institutional and Intellectual Life* (1959), 21; Eugene D. Genovese, "The Influence of the Black Power Movement on Historical Scholarship: Reflections of a White Historian," *Daedalus* 99 (Spring 1970), 478.

177. Chase C. Mooney, review of Stampp's *The Peculiar Institution*, *JSH* 23

(Feb. 1957), 125-28; David Donald, review of the same book in *Commentary* 22 (Dec. 1956), 583, 584.

178. Richard Hofstadter to Stampp, Dec. 4, 1954, quotation courtesy of Kenneth Stampp in letter to authors, Nov. 29, 1982.

179. See reviews by Margaret Just Butcher, *New Republic* 135 (Dec. 3, 1956), 21; William Brewer, *JNH* 42 (Apr. 1957), 142-44; Hugh H. Smythe, *Crisis* 63 (Dec. 1956), 636-37.

180. David Potter, "A Minority within a Minority," *Yale Review* 46 (Dec. 1956), 260; Aptheker review, *Science and Society* 21 (Summer 1957), 257, 259.

181. Elkins to Bertram Wyatt-Brown, Nov. 24, 1980, copy courtesy of Wyatt-Brown.

182. Stampp, "The Historian and Southern Negro Slavery," *AHR* 57 (Apr. 1952), 617.

183. Interview with Elkins in John A. Garraty, *Interpreting American History: Conversations with Historians* (1970), 1:198.

184. See especially comments by Avery Craven in "The Question of 'Sambo': A Report of the Ninth Newberry Library Conference in American Studies," *Newberry Library Bulletin* 5 (Dec. 1958).

185. David Donald review of Elkins's *Slavery, AHR* 65 (July 1960), 921-22; Franklin, "Slavery and Personality: A Fresh Look," *Massachusetts Review* 2 (Autumn 1960), 183.

186. Carl N. Degler, "The Negro in American History—Where Myrdal Went Wrong," *New York Times Magazine,* Dec. 7, 1969; Degler, "Remaking American History," *JAH* 67 (Jan. 1980); Degler, *Out of Our Past* (1959), xiii-xiv.

187. Degler, "Slavery and the Genesis of American Race Prejudice," *Comparative Studies in Society and History* 2 (Oct. 1959).

188. Larry Gara, "Some Self-Help Plans of Fugitive Slaves," *NHB* 15 (Jan. 1952).

189. See also Litwack, "The Abolitionist Dilemma," *New England Quarterly* 34 (Mar. 1961).

190. LaWanda F. Cox, "The Promise of Land for the Freedmen," *MVHR* 45 (Dec. 1958); see also LaWanda F. Cox and John H. Cox, *Politics, Principle, and Prejudice, 1865-1866* (1963).

191. August Meier, "The Emergence of Negro Nationalism," *Midwest Journal* 4 (Winter 1951-52 and Summer 1952).

192. Francis L. Broderick, *Right Reverend New Dealer: John A. Ryan* (1963), vii.

193. Editorials, *Daily Princetonian,* Sept. 28, 30, 1942.

194. Dudley T. Cornish, "To Be Recognized as Men: The Practical Utility of History," *Military Review* 58 (Feb. 1978), 41-42.

195. See also Leslie H. Fishel, "The Negro in Northern Politics, 1870-1900,"*MVHR* 42 (Dec. 1955), and "The Negro's Welcome to the Western Reserve, 1900-1930," *Midwest Journal* 2 (Winter 1949-50 and Summer 1950).

196. Fishel to [William M. Brewer], Sept. 26, 1956, in *JNH* 41 (Oct. 1956), 372.

197. See also his essay, "The Question of Race in the South Carolina Constitutional Convention of 1895," *NHB* 15 (Jan. 1952).

198. Woodward, *The Strange Career of Jim Crow* (1955), ix.

199. Louis R. Harlan, "Desegregation in New Orleans Public Schools during Reconstruction," *AHR* 67 (Apr. 1962).

200. See also Donald E. Everett, "Emigres and Militiamen: Free Persons of Color in New Orleans, 1803-1815," *JNH* 38 (Oct. 1953); "Demands of the New Orleans Free Colored Population for Political Equality," *Louisiana Historical Quarterly* 38 (Apr. 1955); and "Ben Butler and the Louisiana Native Guards," *JSH* 24 (May 1958).

201. Charles F. Kellogg, "Villard and the NAACP," *Nation* 188 (Feb. 14, 1960); *NAACP: A History of the National Association for the Advancement of Colored People, Volume 1, 1909-1920* (1967). The biographical material on Kellogg is from an interview with his wife, Mary-Margaret Kellogg, June 19, 1981, and from newspaper obituaries and vita that she supplied. For his acquaintance with NAACP officials, see his *NAACP*, ix.

202. Franklin, "The New Negro History," *JNH* 42 (Apr. 1957), 95.

203. Ibid.

204. The following discussion of hotel segregation is based upon interviews, supplemented by documentary materials as indicated.

205. Howard K. Beale to Thomas D. Clark, Feb. 2, 1954, Beale Papers.

206. Roper interviews with Franklin, Nov. 10, 1978, and with Bennett H. Wall, Apr. 11, 1979, Roper Papers; our interview with LeRoy P. Graf, Nov. 28, 1984. Discussion of the 1948 convention at Jackson is based on Meier's personal recollections; the material on the Montgomery meeting is from Bennett H. Wall in an interview on Mar. 10, 1984. On hotel arrangements at Williamsburg, see also Woodward to Franklin, Oct. 6, 1949, in Franklin's possession.

207. This is a well-known event. The fullest documentary information is to be found in Roper's interviews with Franklin, Nov. 10, 1978, with Wall, Apr. 11, 1979, and with Graf (including comments by Wall who was present with Graf), Apr. 12, 1979, Roper Papers. See also the interview with Graf, Nov. 30, 1984, and Graf to authors, Dec. 11, 1984.

208. Beale to Curti, Apr. 16, 1951, Curti Papers, box 3.

209. On Dumond, see Curti to Charles Barker, Apr. 24, 1951, and Curti to Carl Wittke, Apr. 21, 1952, both in Curti Papers, box 26.

210. Quotation in Curti to Barker, Apr. 24, 1951, Curti Papers, box 26.

211. Woodward to Curti, June 25, 1951, Curti Papers, box 46.

212. For published recollections of two individuals who were involved in this long battle at the MVHA, see Thomas D. Clark, "Our Roots Flourished in the Valley," *JAH* 65 (June 1978), 93-97 (which is somewhat misleading), and Ray Allen Billington, "From Association to Organization: The OAH in the Bad Old Days," ibid., 78-80, 82. Our account is based largely on reports of the debates over the issue published in the *MVHR* (see *MVHR* 38 [Sept. 1951], 367-68, 372-73; 39 [Sept. 1952], 398; 41 [Sept. 1954], 390-92, 395); MVHA minutes as follows: executive committee, Apr. 19, 1950, Apr. 18, 19, 1951, Apr. 16, 1952; business meeting, Apr. 18, 1952; executive committee meetings, May 8, Dec. 28, 1953,

Apr. 21, 1954 (copies supplied courtesy of the OAH). Also invaluable was correspondence in the Curti and Beale Papers. See Fred Shannon to Curti, Feb. 10, Apr. 23, 1951, box 26; Beale to Curti, Apr. 16, 1951, box 3; Curti to Charles Barker, Apr. 24, 1951, to Tom LeDuc, Apr. 24, 1951, to Clement Eaton, May 4, 1951, Carl Wittke to Curti, Mar. 13, 1952, Curti to Wittke, Apr. 21, 25, 1952, Clark to Curti, May 5, 1951, Curti to Dwight Dumond, May 14, 1953, all in box 26; Clark to Curti, Nov. 6, 1953, Feb. 16, 1954, box 9, all these in the Curti Papers. Howard K. Beale to Clark, Feb. 2, 1954, Beale Papers. Curti, in interview on Mar. 8, 1983, shared his recollections of the 1952 meetings with us; Robert L. Clarke, a black graduate student of Hesseltine at Wisconsin at the time, in interview on May 2, 1982, confirmed the hotel arrangements at the Lexington meeting, which he attended.

213. Interview with Wall, Mar. 10, 1984; Roper's interview with Wall, Apr. 11, 1979, Roper Papers; Franklin to Bell I. Wiley, Nov. 26, 1954, to James W. Silver, June 14, 1955, both in James Wesley Silver Collection; interview with Franklin, Nov. 28, 1984. See also Silver's recollections in his *Running Scared: Silver in Mississippi* (1984), 59-60.

214. Interview with Wall, Mar. 10, 1984; Roper's interview with Wall, Apr. 11, 1979, Roper Papers.

215. Quarles, "The Colonial Militia and Negro Manpower," *MVHR* 45 (Mar. 1959), and "Lord Dunmore as Liberator," *William and Mary Quarterly*, 3d ser., 15 (Oct. 1958). The other essays by blacks in the *William and Mary Quarterly* were Rayford W. Logan, "Memoirs of a Monticello Slave," 8 (Oct. 1951); Charles H. Nichols, "The Case of William Grimes, the Runaway Slave," 8 (Oct. 1951); and James H. Brewer, "Negro Property Owners in Seventeenth Century Virginia," 12 (Oct. 1955).

216. Franklin, "The Southern Expansionists of 1846," *JSH* 25 (Aug. 1959); Woolfolk, "Taxes and Slavery in the Ante-Bellum South," ibid., 26 (May 1960); Frenise Logan, "India—Britain's Substitute for American Cotton, 1861-1865," ibid., 24 (Nov. 1958), and "India's Loss of the British Cotton Market After 1865," ibid., 31 (Feb. 1965); Lewis, "The Political Mind of the Negro, 1865-1900," ibid., 21 (May 1955); Bacote, "Negro Proscriptions, Protests, and Proposed Solutions in Georgia 1880-1908," ibid., 25 (Nov. 1959).

217. England, "The Free Negro in Ante-Bellum Tennessee," *JSH* 9 (Feb. 1943).

218. Leonard W. Levy and Harlan P. Phillips, "The *Roberts* Case: Source of the 'Separate but Equal' Doctrine," *AHR* 56 (Apr. 1951); Alfred H. Kelly, "The Congressional Controversy over School Segregation, 1867-1875," ibid., 64 (Apr. 1959). Other essays in the *AHR* included Leonard Stavisky, "Negro Craftsmanship in Early America," ibid., 54 (Jan. 1949), and Richard Bardolph, "The Distinguished Negro in America, 1770-1936," ibid., 60 (Apr. 1955).

219. Bennett H. Wall, "Medical Care of Ebenezer Pettigrew's Slaves," *MVHR* 37 (Dec. 1950); Clement Eaton, "Slave Hiring in the Upper South: A Step toward Freedom," ibid., 46 (Mar. 1960); Emma Lou Thornbrough, "The Brownsville Episode and the Negro Vote," ibid., 44 (Dec. 1957); Cox, "Promise of Land for the Freedmen."

220. Interview with Franklin in Moss, "Utilization of Negro Teachers," 153.

On the actions of the AHA in choosing St. Louis, see also AHA executive secretary Boyd C. Shafer to members of the executive committee of the council and President Merle Curti, Jan. 28, 1954, Curti Papers, box 1.

221. Franklin, "New Negro History," 93.

222. Franklin, "New Perspectives in American Negro History," 198.

223. Franklin, "New Negro History," 95.

Chapter 3. Generational Change, Part II, 1960-80

1. Rudolph Lapp, "The Negro in Gold Rush California," *JNH* 49 (Apr. 1964); Lapp, *Blacks in Gold Rush California* (1977). For a discussion of the course Lapp introduced in 1959, see the *San Matean*, Mar. 14, 1969.

2. Herbert G. Gutman, "Reconstruction in Ohio: Negroes in the Hocking Valley Coal Mines in 1873 and 1874," *Labor History* 3 (Fall 1962); Gutman, "Peter Clark: Pioneer Negro Socialist, 1877," *Journal of Negro Education* 34 (Fall 1965); Gutman, "The Negro and the United Mine Workers of America: The Career and Letters of Richard L. Davis and Something of Their Meaning, 1890-1900," in Julius Jacobson, ed., *The Negro and the American Labor Movement* (1968).

3. Eric Foner, "Racial Attitudes of the New York Free Soilers," *New York History* 46 (Oct. 1965); and Foner, "Politics and Prejudice: The Free Soil Party and the Negro, 1849-1852," *JNH* 50 (Oct. 1965).

4. See also Howard Zinn, "A Fate Worse Than Integration," *Harper's Magazine* 219 (Aug. 1959); "Finishing School for Pickets," *Nation* 191 (Aug. 6, 1960); "The Force of Nonviolence," ibid., 194 (Mar. 17, 1962); "Kennedy: The Reluctant Emancipator," ibid., 195 (Dec. 1, 1962); "The Battle-Scarred Youngsters," ibid., 197 (Oct. 5, 1963).

5. See also Gilbert Osofsky, "Progressivism and the Negro: New York, 1900-1915," *American Quarterly* 16 (Summer 1964).

6. See Tuttle, *Race Riot: Chicago in the Red Summer of 1919* (1970), vii-ix.

7. C. Vann Woodward, "The Political Legacy of Reconstruction," *Journal of Negro Education* 26 (Summer 1957); "Equality: The Deferred Commitment," *American Scholar* 27 (Autumn 1958), both reprinted in Woodward, *The Burden of Southern History* (1960). See also his 1965 paper, "Seeds of Failure in Radical Race Policy," in Harold Hyman, ed., *New Frontiers of the American Reconstruction* (1966).

8. See his review essay of these volumes and Dumond's *Antislavery* in "The Antislavery Myth," *American Scholar* 31 (Spring 1962).

9. Willie Lee Rose to Mary Keeler of the Committee on Fellowship Awards, American Association of University Women, Sept. 23, 1958, and "Plan for Study: The Port Royal Experiment" [Sept. 1958], Rose Papers.

10. David Brion Davis, "Abolitionists and the Freedmen: An Essay Review," *JSH* 31 (Feb. 1965), 169.

11. Jane H. and William H. Pease, *Black Utopia: Negro Communal Experiments in America* (1963); "Antislavery Ambivalence: Immediatism, Expediency, Race," *American Quarterly* 17 (Winter 1965).

12. Winthrop Jordan, "The Influence of the West Indies on the Origin of New

England Slavery," *William and Mary Quarterly*, 3d ser., 18 (Apr. 1961); and "American Chiaroscuro: The Status and Definition of Mulattoes in the British Colonies," ibid., 19 (Apr. 1962).

13. Jordan, "Modern Tensions and the Origins of American Slavery," *JSH* 28 (Feb. 1962).

14. Constance Green, *Washington: Village and Capital, 1800-1878* (1962), and *Washington: Capital City, 1879-1950* (1963). Information about Green's intellectual biography was supplied by her daughter, Lois Green Carr.

15. Thomas R. Cripps, "The Lily-White Republicans: The Negro, the Party, and the South in the Progressive Era" (Ph.D. diss., University of Maryland, 1967); "The Reaction of the Negro to the Motion Picture 'Birth of a Nation,' " *The Historian* 25 (May 1963); *Slow Fade to Black: The Negro in American Film, 1900-1942* (1977).

16. Louis R. Harlan, "Desegregation in New Orleans Public Schools during Reconstruction," *AHR* 67 (Apr. 1962), and "Booker T. Washington and the White Man's Burden," ibid., 72 (Jan. 1966).

17. Frenise Logan, "India's Loss of the British Cotton Market after 1865," *JSH* 31 (Jan. 1965).

18. Meier, "Comment on John Hope Franklin's Paper," in Hyman, ed., *New Frontiers of the American Reconstruction*, 86.

19. Quotations from Harlan, *The Negro in American History*, publication no. 61, AHA Service Center for Teachers of History (1965), 5-6; and John Hope Franklin, "The Negro in History Textbooks," *Crisis* 72 (Aug.-Sept. 1965), 427; Stuckey's demonstration was covered in the Black Muslim paper, *Muhammad Speaks*, Aug. 30, 1963.

20. Logan, "India—Britain's Substitute for American Cotton, 1861-1865," *JSH* 24 (Oct. 1958); "India's Loss of the British Cotton Market after 1865"; "The Economic Status of the Town Negro in Post-Reconstruction North Carolina," *North Carolina Historical Review* 35 (Oct. 1958); prize announced in ibid., 37 (Jan. 1960), 146.

21. John W. Blassingame, "Black Studies and the Role of the Historian," in Blassingame, ed., *New Perspectives on Black Studies* (1971), 216-17.

22. Carl N. Degler, "Why Historians Change Their Minds," *Pacific Historical Review* 45 (May 1976).

23. Willard B. Gatewood, Jr., "Theodore Roosevelt and the Indianola Affair," *JNH* 53 (Jan. 1968); "William D. Crum: A Negro in Politics," ibid., 53 (Oct. 1968).

24. David Rankin, "The Origins of Black Leadership in New Orleans during Reconstruction," *JSH* 40 (Aug. 1974); "The Impact of the Civil War on the Free Colored Community of New Orleans," *Perspectives in American History* 11 (1977-78); "The Origins of Negro Leadership in New Orleans during Reconstruction," in Howard Rabinowitz, ed., *Southern Black Leaders of the Reconstruction Era* (1982).

25. Sterling Stuckey to Du Bois, Aug. 6, 1957, in Du Bois Papers, reel 72.

26. Clayborne Carson, *In Struggle: SNCC and the Black Awakening of the 1960s* (1981), 4.

27. Darlene Clark Hine, *Black Victory: The Rise and Fall of the White Primary in Texas* (1978); "Mabel K. Staupers and the Integration of Black Nurses into the Armed Forces," in John Hope Franklin and August Meier, eds., *Black Leaders of the Twentieth Century* (1982).

28. Harvard Sitkoff, *A New Deal for Blacks* (1978), vii.

29. James McPherson et al., *Blacks in America: Bibliographical Essays* (1971).

30. Gary B. Nash, "Slaves and Slaveowners in Colonial Philadelphia," *William and Mary Quarterly*, 3d ser., 30 (Apr. 1973); and "Forging Freedom: The Emancipation Experience in the Northern Seaport Cities, 1775-1820," in Ira Berlin and Ronald Hoffman, eds., *Slavery and Freedom in the Age of the American Revolution* (1983).

31. Linda R. Forcey, "Personality in Politics: The Commitment of a Suicide" (Ph.D. diss., SUNY-Binghamton, 1978); additional information was supplied by Norma Starobin.

32. In addition to interviews with Bracey the following information is based on his paper, "Marxism and Black Nationalism in the Early 1960s: The Origins of Revolutionary Black Nationalism," presented at the OAH annual meeting, Apr. 14, 1979. All quotations are from this paper.

33. Harold Cruse, "Revolutionary Nationalism and the Afro-American," *Studies on the Left* 2, no. 3 (1962); and the following articles in *Liberator*: "The Roots of Black Nationalism" 4 (Mar. and Apr. 1964); "Marxism and the Negro" 4 (May and June 1964), "The Economics of Black Nationalism" 4 (July and Aug. 1964), and "Rebellion or Revolution" 3 (Oct., Nov., Dec. 1963) and 4 (Jan. 1964).

34. In addition to the interview, see also Cruse, "The Origins of *The Crisis of the Negro Intellectual* as a Book," typescript sent by Cruse to authors, Sept. 23, 1982.

35. Cruse, "Revolutionary Nationalism and the Afro-American," 25.

36. John H. Bracey, Jr., August Meier, and Elliott Rudwick, eds., *Black Nationalism in America* (1970), lvi-lvix.

37. *Muhammad Speaks,* Aug. 2, 16, Sept. 27, 1963. See also Stuckey, "Remembering Denmark Vesey," *Negro Digest* 15 (Feb. 1966).

38. Stuckey, "W. E. B. Du Bois as an Inspirer of Negro Youth," *Freedomways* 5 (Winter 1965), 146-47. See also his discussion of Du Bois in "Du Bois, Woodson, and the Spell of Africa," *Negro Digest* 16 (Feb. 1967); and especially, "The Cultural Philosophy of Paul Robeson," *Freedomways* 11 (First quarter, 1971).

39. Stuckey, essay in "Symposium on Black Power," *Negro Digest* 16 (Nov. 1966); Stuckey, ed., *Ideological Origins of Black Nationalism* (1972), introduction, 29; "Through the Prism of Folklore," *Massachusetts Review* 9 (Summer 1968); "Twilight of Our Past," in John A. Williams and Charles F. Harris, eds., *Amistad* 2 (1971), 295; Du Bois, *The Conservation of Races* (1897), reprinted in Bracey, Meier, and Rudwick, eds., *Black Nationalism in America*, 258, 261.

40. Vincent Harding and Staughton Lynd, "Albany, Georgia," *Crisis* 70 (Feb. 1963); Harding, "A Beginning in Birmingham," *Reporter* 28 (June 6, 1963); Harding, "Toward the Other Shore: The Freedom Movement as Seen by a Church Leader," ibid., 29 (Oct. 10, 1963), quotation, 31. See also the views expressed in his *Must Walls Divide?* (1965), a YMCA study pamphlet.

41. Harding, "Where Have All the Lovers Gone?" *New South* 21 (Winter 1966). Quotation from "Black Radicalism: The Road from Montgomery," in Alfred F. Young, ed., *Dissent: Explorations in the History of American Radicalism* (1968), 325.

42. Harding, "Religion and Resistance among Antebellum Negroes, 1800-1860," in Meier and Rudwick, eds., *The Making of Black America* (1969), vol. 1; "You've Taken My Nat and Gone," in John Henrik Clarke, ed., *William Styron's Nat Turner: Ten Black Writers Respond* (1968), 24.

43. Interview with Harding in Henry Abelove et al., eds., *Visions of History* (1984), 227-29 (quotation, 228); Harding, "The Religion of Black Power," in Donald R. Cutler, ed., *The Religious Situation* (1968), 34. See also Harding, "Black Power and the American Christ," *Christian Century* 84 (Jan. 4, 1967).

44. "Black (Studies) Vatican," *Newsweek* 74 (Aug. 11, 1969), 38; interview with Harding in Abelove et al., eds., *Visions of History*, 231.

45. Harding, "The Black Wedge in America: Struggle, Crisis and Hope, 1955-1975," *Black Scholar* 7 (Dec. 1975), quotation, 30; "Black Students and the Impossible Revolution," *Journal of Black Studies* 1 (Sept. 1970), quotation, 97; "Beyond Chaos," in John A. Williams and Charles F. Harris, eds., *Amistad 1* (1970), quotation, 286.

46. Interview with Harding in Abelove et al., eds., *Visions of History*, 234, 233.

47. Harding, "Black Radicalism: The Road from Montgomery"; *The Other American Revolution* (1980); and *There Is a River: The Black Struggle for Freedom in America* (1981).

48. Harding, "The Black Wedge in America"; quotation from Harding, "Black Radicalism: The Road from Montgomery," 324.

49. E. P. Thompson, *The Making of the English Working Class* (1963); Jesse Lemisch, "The American Revolution Seen from the Bottom Up," in Barton Bernstein, ed., *Towards a New Past: Dissenting Essays in American History* (1968). The AHA 1968 convention program included a session on "Writing the History of the Inarticulate," chaired by David Montgomery, with papers by Lemisch and Robert Starobin ("Slavery from the Bottom Up: Privileged Bondsmen and the Process of Accommodation"). See *Annual Report of the American Historical Association for the Year 1968*, 84.

50. August Meier, "Black America as a Research Field: Some Comments," *AHA Newsletter* 6 (Apr. 1968). See also the same idea expressed in Blassingame, "Black Studies and the Role of the Historian," 216.

51. Nancy J. Weiss, "The Negro and the New Freedom: Fighting Wilsonian Segregation," *Political Science Quarterly* 84 (Mar. 1969); Weiss, *The National Urban League 1910-1940* (1974).

52. Alfred Conrad and John Meyer, "The Economics of Slavery in the Ante Bellum South," *Journal of Political Economy* 66 (Apr. 1958), reprinted in their *The Economics of Slavery and Other Studies in Econometric History* (1964).

53. Lavinia Dobler and Edgar A. Toppin, *Pioneers and Patriots: The Lives of Six Negroes of the Revolutionary Era* (1965); Carol Drisko and Toppin, *The*

Unfinished March: The Negro in the United States, Reconstruction to World War I (1967). See also Toppin, *A Biographical History of Blacks in America Since 1528* (1971), and *The Black American in United States History* (1973).

54. Interview with Aida Donald, Apr. 8, 1983, and with Arthur Wang, Dec. 14, 1982; Aida Donald, postscript on letter from David Donald to Wang, July 11, 1960, Hill & Wang Files.

55. Alfred A. Knopf, Jr., to authors, Apr. 24, 1984; interview with Robert J. Zenowich, Mar. 31, 1984; interview with Sheldon Meyer, Apr. 8, 1983, and Richard Wentworth, Apr. 9, 1983.

56. Jimmie L. Franklin, *Journey toward Hope: A History of Blacks in Oklahoma* (1982).

57. *AHR* 74 (Apr. 1969), 1457-58.

58. Edgar A. Toppin, "The Thirty-Seventh Annual Meeting," *JSH* 38 (Feb. 1972), 68, 70. On Franklin's role in this development, see also Bennett Wall's secretary-treasurer's report for 1971 in *JSH* 38 (May 1972), 275.

59. *Annual Report of the American Historical Association for the Year 1972*, 1: 55, 53.

60. Harding, "Beyond Chaos," 269, 271, 272, 279, 274; Stuckey, "Twilight of Our Past," 287, 277-78.

61. Harding, "Beyond Chaos," 286, 278-79, 283, 287, 284; Stuckey, "Twilight of Our Past," 289-90. See also Stuckey's discussion of the antebellum nationalists in his *Ideological Origins of Black Nationalism*.

62. See, for example, C. Vann Woodward, "Clio with Soul," *JAH* 56 (June 1969), 8-9.

63. W. E. B. Du Bois, *Atlanta University Studies* (1897-1914); Carter G. Woodson, *The African Background Outlined* (1936); Melville J. Herskovits, *The Myth of the Negro Past* (1941).

64. Du Bois, *The Philadelphia Negro: A Social Study* (1899); Kenneth Clark, *Prejudice and Your Child* (1963) and *The Dark Ghetto* (1965).

65. Gilbert Osofsky, "The Enduring Ghetto," *JAH* 55 (Sept. 1968); Douglas H. Daniels, *Pioneer Urbanites: A Social and Cultural History of Black San Francisco* (1980), and James Borchert, *Alley Life in Washington: Family, Community, Religion, and Folklife in the City, 1850-1970* (1980).

66. Herskovits, ed., *The Interdisciplinary Aspects of Negro Studies*, ACLS Bulletin 32 (1941), 30; Waldo G. Leland to A. R. Mann, Oct. 16, 1945, Herskovits to Mann, Sept. 17, 1945, and W. W. Brierley to Leland, Oct. 24, 1945, all in GEB, Series 1, box 256; *ACLS Annual Reports for 1946*, 78; *1947*, 57; *1948*, 64; Armistead Scott Pride, "Negro Newspaper Files and Their Microfilming," *Journalism Quarterly* 24 (June 1947); Library of Congress Photoduplication Service, *Negro Newspapers on Microfilm* (1953).

67. E. Franklin Frazier, "The Booker T. Washington Papers," *Library of Congress Quarterly Journal of Current Acquisitions* 2 (Feb. 1945).

68. For survey of the history of the interviewing of ex-slaves, see Norman R. Yetman, "The Background of the Slave Narrative Collection," *American Quarterly* 19 (Feb. 1967).

69. John C. Cade, "Out of the Mouths of Ex-Slaves," *JNH* 20 (July 1935); B. A. Botkin, *Lay My Burden Down: A Folk History of Slavery* (1945); Ophelia Settle Egypt, J. Masuoka, and Charles S. Johnson, *Unwritten History of Slavery: Autobiographical Accounts of Negro Ex-Slaves,* Fisk University Social Science Source Document, no. 1 (1945).

70. On this point see, for example, C. Vann Woodward, "History from Slave Sources," *AHR* 79 (Apr. 1974), 471.

71. See pp. 96-97 herein.

72. See, for example, Woodson, "Annual Report of the Director," *JNH* 10 (July 1925), 597, and regarding Hurston, ibid., 11 (Oct. 1926), 357.

73. Osofsky, ed., *Puttin' On Ole Massa: The Slave Narratives of Henry Bibb, William Wells Brown, and Solomon Northup* (1969), 45.

74. Darlene Clark Hine, *Black Victory: The Rise and Fall of the White Primary in Texas* (1978); Vincent P. Franklin, *The Education of Black Philadelphia: The Social and Educational History of a Minority Community, 1900-1950* (1979).

75. Allison Davis, Burleigh B. Gardner, and Mary R. Gardner, *Deep South: A Social Anthropological Study of Caste and Class* (1941).

76. See especially Harding, *There Is a River.*

77. See especially Thomas Holt, *Black Over White: Negro Political Leadership in South Carolina during Reconstruction* (1977), and Rabinowitz, *Southern Black Leaders of the Reconstruction Era.*

78. Herbert G. Gutman, *The Black Family in Slavery and Freedom, 1750-1925* (1976); Peter Wood, *Black Majority* (1974); Lawrence Levine, *Black Culture and Black Consciousness: Afro-American Folk Thought from Slavery to Freedom* (1977); Ira Berlin, "Time, Space, and the Evolution of Afro-American Society on British Mainland North America," *AHR* 85 (Feb. 1980). See also Berlin and Hoffman, eds., *Slavery and Freedom in the Age of the American Revolution;* and Joel Williamson, *New People: Miscegenation and Mulattoes in the United States* (1980).

Chapter 4. The Historiography of Slavery

1. E.g., Carter G. Woodson to William C. Graves, Oct. 23, 1917, Rosenwald Papers, reel 4.

2. Woodson, review of U.B. Phillips's *American Negro Slavery* (1918), *JNH* 4 (Jan. 1919), 103.

3. Ibid., 7 (Jan. 1922), 123; Charles F. Cochran, "The Association for the Study of Negro Life and History: A Report Made for the American Council of Learned Societies," Dec. 1925, LSRM, box 96.

4. L. D. Reddick, "A New Interpretation for Negro History," *JNH* 22 (Jan. 1937), 20.

5. Raymond and Alice Bauer, "Day to Day Resistance to Slavery," ibid., 27 (Oct. 1942).

6. Susan Stout Baker, "Out of the Engagement. Richard Hofstadter: The Genesis of a Historian" (Ph.D. diss., Case Western Reserve University, 1982). For another

discussion of Hofstadter's background and early radicalism, see Alfred Kazin, *New York Jew* (1978), 14-15.

7. Hofstadter, "U. B. Phillips and the Plantation Legend," *JNH* 29 (Apr. 1944), 124.

8. Arthur M. Schlesinger, Jr., "Richard Hofstadter," in Marcus Cunliffe and Robin Winks, eds., *Pastmasters* (1969), 457n.

9. Kenneth M. Stampp, "The Historian and Southern Negro Slavery," *AHR* 57 (Apr. 1952), 614-18 passim.

10. Stanley Elkins and Eric McKitrick, "Essays in American History," spring 1954, a syllabus consisting of a digest of lectures prepared during the academic year 1952-53. Elkins kindly supplied a copy of this syllabus.

11. David Donald, "Toward a Reconsideration of Abolitionists," in Donald, *Lincoln Reconsidered* (1956); Frank Tannenbaum, *Slave and Citizen* (1947). McKitrick and Elkins knew of Donald's ideas and refer to them in their syllabus.

12. Elkins to Bertram Wyatt-Brown, Nov. 24, 1980, copy supplied courtesy of Wyatt-Brown.

13. Hofstadter to Stampp, n.d. [summer 1954], quoted in Stampp to authors, Nov. 29, 1982. Hofstadter's chapter-by-chapter critiques are contained in letters to Stampp between Mar. 1954 and the spring of 1955.

14. Stampp, *The Peculiar Institution* (1956), 327.

15. David Brion Davis, "Slavery and the Post–World War II Historians," *Daedalus* 103 (Spring 1974), 3.

16. Stampp, *Peculiar Institution*, 364.

17. E. Franklin Frazier, "The Negro Slave Family," *JNH* 15 (Apr. 1930).

18. James M. McPherson et al., *Blacks in America: Bibliographical Essays* (1971), 37. See also Lawrence W. Levine, "Slave Songs and Slave Consciousness: An Exploration in Neglected Sources," in Tamara K. Hareven, ed., *Anonymous Americans* (1971), 100.

19. W. E. B. Du Bois, *Suppression of the African Slave-Trade to the United States of America, 1638-1870* (1896); Lorenzo J. Greene, *The Negro in Colonial New England* (1942); J. Hugo Johnston, *Race Relations in Virginia and Miscegenation in the South, 1776-1860* (1970).

20. Stampp, "Rebels and Sambos: The Search for the Negro's Personality in Slavery," *JSH* 37 (Aug. 1971), 373. See also Davis, "Slavery and the Post–World War II Historians," 4.

21. Sidney Mintz, review of Elkins's *Slavery* in *American Anthropologist* 63 (June 1961), 579-87; Earl E. Thorpe, "Chattel Slavery and Concentration Camps," *NHB* 25 (May 1962). For Genovese's review, see the discussion below.

22. E. Franklin Frazier, *Black Bourgeoisie*, paperback ed. with a new preface by the author (1962), 10. For Franklin's critique, see p. 142 herein.

23. Sterling Stuckey, "Twilight of Our Past: Reflections on the Origins of Black History," *Amistad* 2 (1971), 267-68. The reference to Ellison is to the latter's review of Howard Zinn's *The Southern Mystique* (1964), "If the Twain Shall Meet," *Herald Tribune Book Week*, Nov. 8, 1964, 24.

24. Zinn, *Southern Mystique*, 36.

25. Ibid., 265.

26. Du Bois, ed., *The Negro American Family*, Atlanta University Publications, no. 13 (1908), 26.

27. Eugene D. Genovese, "The Influence of the Black Power Movement on Historical Scholarship: Reflections of a White Historian," *Daedalus* 99 (Spring 1970), 479; Nathan Glazer, review of Elkins's *Slavery* in *Commentary* 29 (Mar. 1960), 454-55.

28. Charles E. Silberman, *Crisis in Black and White* (1964), 75, 77; [Daniel P. Moynihan], *The Negro Family: The Case for National Action* (1965), 15.

29. Elkins, "The Slavery Debate," *Commentary* 60 (Dec. 1975), 42.

30. Ralph Ellison, "An American Dilemma: A Review," 1944, in Ellison, *Shadow and Act* (1964), 316. See also Ellison, "If the Twain Shall Meet"; "A Very Stern Discipline, an Interview with Ralph Ellison," *Harper's Magazine* 234 (Mar. 1967); "Study and Experience: An Interview with Ralph Ellison," *Massachusetts Review* 18 (Autumn 1977).

31. St. Clair Drake, "The Social and Economic Status of the Negro in the United States," *Daedalus* 94 (Fall 1965).

32. Charles A. Valentine, *Culture and Poverty* (1968), 17, referring to a 1966 conference; Robert Blauner, "Black Culture: Lower-Class Result or Ethnic Creation?" drafted in summer 1967, and published in Lee Rainwater, ed., *The Black Experience: Soul* (1970); John Horton, "Time and Cool People," *Transaction* 4 (Apr. 1967); Thomas Kochman, "Toward an Ethnography of Black American Speech Behavior," ibid., 6 (Feb. 1969). Revised versions of the Blauner and Kochman essays also appeared in Norman E. Whitten and John F. Szwed, eds., *Afro-American Anthropology* (1970).

33. George Fredrickson and Christopher Lasch, "Resistance to Slavery," *Civil War History* 13 (Dec. 1967); Genovese, "Rebelliousness and Docility in the Negro Slave: A Critique of the Elkins Thesis," ibid.; Stampp, "Rebels and Sambos," 370, 381.

34. Elkins, "Slavery Debate," 41, 44.

35. This account, obtained from interview materials, is confirmed in Elkins, *Slavery*, acknowledgements, 239; and George P. Rawick to Merle Curti, Feb. 14, 1960, Curti Papers, box 34.

36. Rawick to Curti, Apr. 22, 1961, Curti Papers, box 34.

37. Rawick, "The Historical Roots of Black Liberation," *Radical America* 2 (July-Aug. 1968), 6.

38. Rawick, "The American Negro Movement," *International Socialism* 16 (Spring 1964), 24.

39. Liston Pope, "The Negro and Religion in America," *Review of Religious Research* 5 (Spring 1964), 144-45, 147; Joseph R. Washington, Jr., *Black Religion: The Negro and Christianity in the United States* (1964), esp. 33, 37; Joseph H. Fichter, "American Religion and the Negro," in Talcott Parsons and Kenneth Clark, eds., *The Negro American* (1966), 405-6, 411, 412; Gary T. Marx, "Religion: Opiate or Inspiration of Civil Rights Militancy?" *American Sociological Review* 32 (Feb. 1967).

40. Benjamin Mays, *The Negro's God as Reflected in His Literature* (1938); E. Franklin Frazier, *The Negro Church in America* (1964).

41. Vincent Harding, "Religion and Resistance among Antebellum Negroes, 1800-1860," in August Meier and Elliott Rudwick, eds., *The Making of Black America* (1969), 1:197.

42. Stuckey, "Through the Prism of Folklore: The Black Ethos in Slavery," *Massachusetts Review* 9 (Summer 1968), 418.

43. Ibid., 419, 435, 429, 436, 435, 437.

44. V. Della Chiesa [Genovese], review of Stampp's *The Peculiar Institution* in *Science and Society* 21 (1957), 260, 261-63; Robert W. Fogel, "From the Marxists to the Mormons," *Times Literary Supplement*, June 13, 1975, 668.

45. Genovese, foreword in Louisiana State University Press's reprint of Phillips's *American Negro Slavery* (1966), xv-xvi.

46. Genovese, review essay, "Problems in the Study of Nineteenth-Century American History," *Science and Society* 25 (Winter 1961), 41-47; Genovese, "Rebelliousness and Docility in the Negro Slave," 294, 312.

47. Genovese, foreword to *American Negro Slavery* reprint, evidently based on his 1965 SHA convention paper; and Genovese's 1966 AHA convention paper, "Race and Class in Southern History: An Appraisal of the Work of Ulrich Bonnell Phillips," subsequently published in *Agricultural History* 41 (Oct. 1967).

48. Genovese, foreword to *American Negro Slavery* reprint, vii, viii, xviii.

49. Stampp, "Reconsidering U. B. Phillips: A Comment," *Agricultural History* 41 (Oct. 1967), 365-68, quotation, 366; see also Stampp's review of Genovese's *The World the Slaveholders Made*: "Interpreting the Slaveholders' World: A Review," *Agricultural History* 44 (Oct. 1970), 407-12.

50. David M. Potter, "The Work of Ulrich B. Phillips: A Comment," *Agricultural History* 41 (Oct. 1967), 359-60.

51. Genovese, "The Legacy of Slavery and the Roots of Black Nationalism," *Studies on the Left* 6 (Nov.-Dec. 1966), 4, 8-9.

52. Harding, "Religion and Resistance among Antebellum Negroes," 180; Stuckey, "Through the Prism of Folklore," 431-32; Genovese, "The Nat Turner Case," *New York Review of Books* 11 (Sept. 12, 1968), 34-37. See also Genovese's critique on another issue, "Black Studies: Trouble Ahead," *Atlantic Monthly* 223 (June 1969).

53. Genovese, "Class and Nationality in Black America," paper presented to Boston-Cambridge SDS in 1968, as revised by Christopher Lasch and published in Genovese, *In Red and Black* (1972), 64-65. See also Genovese, "Black Nationalism and American Socialism: A Comment on Harold Cruse's 'Crisis of the Negro Intellectual,'" a paper read at Socialist Scholars Conference in 1968 and published in *In Red and Black*.

54. Genovese, "American Slaves and Their History," *New York Review of Books* 15 (Dec. 3, 1970), 43; see also acknowledgment in Genovese, *Roll, Jordan, Roll* (1974), xx.

55. In addition to interview data, see the acknowledgment to Gutman in Genovese, "American Slaves and Their History," 37*n*. On the mutual interaction at Rochester see, in addition to interviews, Fogel, "From the Marxists to the Mormons," 668.

56. Bobby F. Jones, "The Slave Family: An Instrument of Plantation Discipline," *JSH* 34 (Jan. 1968), based on a paper given at the 1967 SHA convention.

57. Genovese, "American Slaves and Their History," quotations, 41, 35.

58. Herbert G. Gutman and Laurence A. Glasco, "The Buffalo, New York, Negro, 1855-1875: A Study of the Family Structure of Free Negroes and Some of Its Implications," paper, spring 1966, courtesy of Laurence Glasco. See also Gutman and Glasco, "The Negro Family, Household, and Occupational Structure, 1855-1925, with special emphasis on Buffalo, New York, Prepared for the Yale Conference on Nineteenth Century Cities, November 1968" (copy courtesy of Herbert Gutman).

59. John W. Blassingame, *The Slave Community* (1972), vii.

60. Levine, "Slave Songs and Slave Consciousness"; Willie Lee Rose, "Childhood in Bondage," in Rose, *Slavery and Freedom* (1982).

61. Leslie H. Owens, *This Species of Property* (1976), preface.

62. Russell Menard, "The Maryland Slave Population, 1658 to 1730: A Demographic Profile of Blacks in Four Counties," *William and Mary Quarterly*, 3d ser., 32 (Jan. 1975); "From Servants to Slaves: The Transformation of the Chesapeake Labor System," *Southern Studies* 16 (Winter 1977).

63. Allan Kulikoff, "The Origins of Afro-American Society in Tidewater Maryland and Virginia, 1700 to 1790," *William and Mary Quarterly*, 3d ser., 35 (Apr. 1978); "A 'Prolifick' People: Black Population Growth in the Chesapeake Colonies, 1700-1790," *Southern Studies* 16 (Winter 1977); "The Beginnings of the Afro-American Family in Maryland," in Aubrey C. Land et al., eds., *Law, Society, and Politics in Early Maryland* (1977).

64. Gerald (Michael) Mullin, *Flight and Rebellion* (1972), viii-ix, xi.

65. Gilbert Osofsky, *Puttin' On Ole Massa* (1969), 45.

66. Stampp, "Rebels and Sambos," 382, 383, 390.

67. Genovese makes a similar point about the impact of the convergence of black nationalist and working-class history perspectives in his "The Influence of the Black Power Movement on Historical Scholarship," 482-86.

68. New York *Times,* Apr. 13, 1975.

69. Genovese's review of Albert J. Raboteau's *Slave Religion* and Thomas L. Webber's *Deep Like the Rivers* in *New Republic* 180 (Feb. 10, 1979), 30.

70. Ibid., 31-32; Elizabeth Fox-Genovese and Eugene D. Genovese, *Fruits of Merchant Capital* (1983), 179.

71. Ira Berlin, "Time, Space, and the Evolution of Afro-American Society on British Mainland North America," *AHR* 85 (Feb. 1980). See also Ira Berlin and Ronald Hoffman, eds., *Slavery and Freedom in the Age of the American Revolution* (1983).

Chapter 5. On the Dilemmas of Scholarship in Afro-American History

1. John Hope Franklin, "The Dilemma of the American Negro Scholar," in Herbert Hill, ed., *Soon, One Morning: New Writing by American Negroes, 1940-1962* (1963), 64-69 passim, and 73-74.

2. Ibid., 76.

3. Interview with Franklin, in F. Holton, "John Hope Franklin, Scholar," *University of Chicago Magazine* 73 (Sept. 1980).

4. Franklin, "Mirror for Americans: A Century of Reconstruction History," *AHR* 85 (Feb. 1980); "The Great Confrontation: The South and the Problem of Change," *JSH* 38 (Feb. 1972).

5. For initiation of branches, see [Woodson], "Annual Report of the Director," *JNH* 12 (Oct. 1927), 574-75; for the *NHB* see ibid., 23 (Oct. 1938), 413-14; 27 (Oct. 1942), 398.

6. David Potter, "C. Vann Woodward," in Marcus Cunliffe and Robin Winks, eds., *Pastmasters* (1969), 394. See also Woodward's own observations in John A. Garraty, *Interpreting American History: Conversations with Historians* (1970), 2:63.

7. Quoted in Richard Kluger, *Simple Justice: The History of Brown v. Board of Education and Black America's Struggle for Equality* (1976), 623.

8. Herbert Aptheker, *To Be Free: Studies in American Negro History* (1948), 9.

9. Benjamin Quarles, *Black Abolitionists* (1969), vii.

10. Carl N. Degler, "Remaking American History," *JAH* 67 (June 1980), 20.

11. Otey M. Scruggs, "Why Study Afro-American History?" in William Shade and Roy Herrenkohl, eds., *Seven on Black* (1969), 11, 18, 22.

12. Vincent Harding, *There Is a River* (1981), xix; Sterling Stuckey, "Twilight of Our Past," *Amistad* 2 (1971), 277.

13. Nathan Huggins, "Afro-American History: Myths, Heroes, Reality," in Huggins, Martin Kilson, and Daniel Fox, eds., *Key Issues in the Afro-American Experience* (1971), 1:10, 14; John W. Blassingame, "Black Studies and the Role of the Historian," revised version of paper read at Dec. 1969 AHA convention, in Blassingame, ed., *New Perspectives on Black Studies* (1971), 220; see also headnote to this essay, 207.

14. Franklin, *The Future of Negro American History* (pamphlet by New School for Social Research, 1969), 15-16; Blassingame, headnote for "Black Studies and the Role of the Historian," 207; Huggins, "Afro-American History," 19.

15. Robert K. Merton, "Insiders and Outsiders: A Chapter in the Sociology of Knowledge," *American Journal of Sociology* 78 (July 1972); and William J. Wilson, "The New Black Sociology: Reflections on the 'Insiders and Outsiders' Controversy," in James E. Blackwell and Morris Janowitz, eds., *Black Sociologists: Historical and Contemporary Perspectives* (1974).

16. "Black (Studies) Vatican," *Newsweek* 74 (Aug. 11, 1969), 38; quotation from Harding, "Beyond Chaos," *Amistad* 1 (1970), 289.

17. For the debates over the creating, staffing, and content of black studies programs, see esp. Blassingame, ed., *New Perspectives on Black Studies,* and Armstead L. Robinson, Craig C. Foster, and Donald H. Ogilvie, eds., *Black Studies in the University* (1969). For a succinct account of the major confrontations, see Robert H. Brisbane, *Black Activism: Racial Revolution in the United States, 1954-1970* (1974), ch. 10.

18. Woodson, press release printed in New York *Age,* Jan. 18, 1932; Charles

H. Wesley to Woodson, Aug. 8, 1927, text of letter in Janette Harris, "Charles Harris Wesley: Educator and Historian" (Ph.D. diss., Howard University, 1975), 207-10; Franklin, "Reflections on the Evolution of Scholarship in Afro-American History," speech delivered Oct. 6, 1983, at the AHA Conference on the Study and Teaching of Afro-American History, copy supplied courtesy of John Hope Franklin.

19. Washington (D.C.) *Afro-American*, May 30, 1936.

20. Woodson to Benjamin Brawley, Jan. 7, 1932, copy in NAACP Papers, Series I, box C-80; Woodson to the editor, Baltimore *Afro-American*, Jan. 6, 1936.

21. W. E. B. Du Bois, "Memorandum to the Conference on the Advisability of Publishing a Negro Encyclopedia," accompanying draft of letter from Du Bois to Anson Phelps-Stokes, Dec. 9, 1931 (not sent), Du Bois Papers, reel 35; minutes, "Second Conference on 'Encyclopedia of the Negro,'" Jan. 9, 1932, Phelps-Stokes Fund Papers. On the view of black conferees, see also minutes of "Conference on the Advisability of Publishing an Encyclopedia of the Negro," Nov. 7, 1931, copy in Du Bois Papers, reel 35.

22. Du Bois to Jackson Davis, Apr. 16, 1937, and Du Bois, memorandum to Stokes, Feb. 25, 1938, both in GEB, Series I, box 418.

23. Linda Forcey, "Personality in Politics: The Commitment of a Suicide" (Ph.D. diss., SUNY-Binghamton, 1978), 133.

24. Robert H. Wiebe, "The Sixty-Second Annual Meeting of the Organization of American Historians," *JAH* 56 (Dec. 1969), 635-36.

25. C. Vann Woodward, "Clio with Soul," ibid., 56 (June 1969), 8, 9, 15, 16; Blassingame, "Black Studies: An Intellectual Crisis," in Blassingame, ed., *New Perspectives on Black Studies,* 154.

26. Published in *Journal of Social History* 5 (Fall 1971).

27. Julius Lester, "On the Suicide of a Revolutionary," *Liberation* (Spring 1971), reprinted in Lester, *All Is Well* (1976), 280.

28. Lester, *All Is Well,* 279-80.

29. John Henrik Clarke et al., *William Styron's Nat Turner: Ten Black Writers Respond* (1968); Genovese, "William Styron before the People's Court," *New York Review of Books* 11 (Sept. 12, 1968), 34-38; Harding to the editor, ibid., 11 (Nov. 7, 1968), 31-33, and Genovese's reply in same issue, 34-36; Genovese, "Black Studies: Trouble Ahead," *Atlantic Monthly* 223 (June 1969), 39.

30. Stuckey, "Twilight of Our Past," 280, 286-87.

31. Darlene Clark Hine, "The Four Black History Movements: A Case for the Teaching of Black History," *Teaching History: A Journal of Methods* 5 (Fall 1980), 115.

32. Paul Escott, *Slavery Remembered* (1979), xiii.

33. Genovese, "Black Studies: Trouble Ahead," 39.

34. Stuckey, "Twilight of Our Past," 268.

35. Genovese, "Black Studies: Trouble Ahead," 38.

36. Nell Painter, "Who Decides What Is History?" *Nation* 234 (Mar. 6, 1981), 277.

37. Barbara J. Fields, "Ideology and Race in American History," in J. Morgan

Kousser and James M. McPherson, eds., *Region, Race, and Reconstruction: Essays in Honor of C. Vann Woodward* (1982), 150-51.

38. Robinson, "A Concluding Statement," in Robinson, Foster, and Ogilvie, eds., *Black Studies in the University;* Robinson, "Report on the Condition of Black Studies," paper presented at Black Studies Directors' Seminar, Institute of the Black World, Atlanta, Nov. 1969; Robinson, "Beyond the Realm of Social Consensus: New Meanings of Reconstruction for American History," *JAH* 68 (Sept. 1981), 297.

39. Fields to authors, May 4, 1982; Robinson to authors, Oct. 19, 1982.

40. The following discussion about blacks in the American Sociological Association is based on interviews, personal observations, and the discussion in James E. Blackwell, "Role Behavior in a Corporate Structure: Black Sociologists in the ASA," in Blackwell and Morris Janowitz, eds., *Black Sociologists: Historical and Contemporary Perspectives* (1974). For our discussion of the developments among teachers of English, we thank Darwin Turner of the University of Iowa for an illuminating interview, Aug. 2, 1982.

41. Harvard University, *Courses of Instruction, Harvard and Radcliffe, 1968-1969* (1968), 27-28, copy, courtesy of President Derek Bok of Harvard University.

42. On this point see, for example, Franklin, *Future of Negro American History,* 11-12.

43. Franklin, "Reflections on the Evolution of Scholarship in Afro-American History."

44. John E. Fleming, Gerald R. Gill, and David H. Swinton, *The Case for Affirmative Action for Blacks in Higher Education* (1978), 215; the 1983 estimate is in James C. Klotter, "Publishing in State Journals," *OAH Newsletter,* Apr. 1983, 33.

45. The statistics on Ph.D.s in 1970s are supplied by National Research Council, Office of Scientific and Engineering Personnel, Doctorate Records File. For the decrease in the number of blacks undertaking doctoral work, see interviews and "Blacks Decrease but Women Increase on University Faculties," New York *Times,* Jan. 28, 1984.

46. Mary F. Berry, "Blacks in Predominantly White Institutions of Higher Learning," in National Urban League, *The State of Black America 1983* (1983), 307.

47. Berry, "Blacks in Predominantly White Institutions of Higher Learning," 304; see also "For Black Studies, the Fight Goes on," New York *Times,* Jan. 13, 1983; interview with Joseph J. Russell, of the Indiana University black studies department and the National Council of Black Studies, Feb. 10, 1985.

INDEX

Abel, A. H., 96
Abolitionist movement: blacks in, 101, 108; demythologized, 142, 143; historical study of, 78, 83
ACLS. *See* American Council of Learned Societies
Adams, Charles Francis, Jr., 169
Adams, Herbert Baxter, 3
African Background Outlined, or Handbook for the Study of the Negro (Woodson, 1936), 91
African cultural survivals, 56, 108n, 230-31, 237, 246, 274-75
Africanisms in the Gullah Dialect (Turner, 1949), 275
African Mandate question, 92
Afro-American history, 7, 13, 71; at Columbia University, 127-28, 307-8; as a fashionable subject, 161, 215; Logan's survey of, 92; in Roosevelt era, 100-101; white interest in, 123. *See also* Black history; Negro history
Afro-American Woman: Struggles and Images (Harley and Terborg-Penn, 1978), 193
After Slavery: The Negro in South Carolina during Reconstruction (Williamson, 1965), 168, 230
AHA. *See* American Historical Association
Ahmad, Akbar Muhammad, 204
AHR. See American Historical Review
Alexander, Will W., 17, 43, 111
Alley Life in Washington (Borchert, 1980), 236
Altgeld, John Peter, 107
Alvord, Clarence W., 4, 28, 98
American Council of Learned Societies (ACLS): Committee on Negro Studies, 115; Conference on Negro Studies (1940), 233; funding from, 87
American Dilemma (Myrdal, 1944), 115, 122, 136n, 251

American Diplomacy and the Narcotics Traffic, 1900-1939 (Taylor, 1969), 220
American Historical Association (AHA): Beveridge Award, 87, 153, 306n; black historians in, 97-98, 152-54, 158, 173-74, 223, 225, 293, 300-301, 302; Carnegie Revolving Fund, 87; rise of, 3
American Historical Review (*AHR*), 29n, 114n, 121, 157, 173, 226
American Negro Academy, 24
American Negro Academy: Voice of the Talented Tenth (Moss, 1981), 192
American Negro Historical Society (Philadelphia): establishment of (1897), 3
American Negro Slave Revolts (Aptheker, 1943), 108-9, 138, 205, 242, 298
American Negro Slavery (Phillips, 1918), 4, 28, 98, 233, 240
American Political Tradition (Hofstadter, 1948), 241
American Revolution Considered as a Social Movement (Jameson, 1926), 28
American Sociological Association (ASA), 301
America's Black Past (Foner, 1970), 203
Amistad Research Center, 233
Amistad Society, 176, 204, 206
Anderson, Eric (b. 1949), 182
Andrews, Charles M., 46
And the War Came (Stampp, 1950), 138, 242
Angell, James Rowland, 31-33
Angelo Herndon Case and Southern Justice (Martin, 1976), 180
Anna T. Jeanes Fund, 16
Annales School, 178, 212, 214
Anti-Slavery Movement in England: A Study in English Humanitarianism (Klingberg, 1926), 95
Appraisal of the Negro in Colonial South Carolina (Klingberg, 1941), 96

BOOKS IN THE SERIES BLACKS IN THE NEW WORLD

Before the Ghetto: Black Detroit in the Nineteenth Century
David M. Katzman

Black Business in the New South: A Social History of the North Carolina
Mutual Life Insurance Company   *Walter B. Weare*

The Search for a Black Nationality: Black Colonization and Emigration,
1787-1863   *Floyd J. Miller*

Black Americans and the White Man's Burden, 1898-1903
Willard B. Gatewood, Jr.

Slavery and the Numbers Game: A Critique of *Time on the Cross*
Herbert G. Gutman

A Ghetto Takes Shape: Black Cleveland, 1870-1930
Kenneth L. Kusmer

Freedmen, Philanthropy, and Fraud: A History of the Freedman's Savings
Bank   *Carl R. Osthaus*

The Democratic Party and the Negro: Northern and National Politics,
1868-92   *Lawrence Grossman*

Black Ohio and the Color Line, 1860-1915   *David A. Gerber*

Along the Color Line: Explorations in the Black Experience
August Meier and Elliott Rudwick

Black over White: Negro Political Leadership in South Carolina during
Reconstruction   *Thomas Holt*

Keeping the Faith: A. Philip Randolph, Milton P. Webster, and the
Brotherhood of Sleeping Car Porters, 1925-37   *William H. Harris*

Abolitionism: The Brazilian Antislavery Struggle
Joaquim Nabuco, translated and edited by Robert Conrad

Black Georgia in the Progressive Era, 1900-1920
John Dittmer

Medicine and Slavery: Health Care of Blacks in Antebellum
Virginia   *Todd L. Savitt*

Alley Life in Washington: Family, Community, Religion, and Folklife in
the City, 1850-1970   *James Borchert*

Human Cargoes: The British Slave Trade to Spanish America,
1700-1739   *Colin A. Palmer*

Southern Black Leaders of the Reconstruction Era
Edited by Howard N. Rabinowitz

Black Leaders of the Twentieth Century
Edited by John Hope Franklin and August Meier

Slaves and Missionaries: The Disintegration of Jamaican Slave Society,
1787-1834   *Mary Turner*

Father Divine and the Struggle for Racial Equality
Robert Weisbrot

Communists in Harlem during the Depression
Mark Naison

Down from Equality: Black Chicagoans and the Public Schools,
1920-41   *Michael W. Homel*

Race and Kinship in a Midwestern Town: The Black Experience in
Monroe, Michigan, 1900-1915   *James E. DeVries*

Down by the Riverside: A South Carolina Slave Community
Charles Joyner

Black Milwaukee: The Making of an Industrial Proletariat, 1915-45
Joe William Trotter, Jr.

Religious Philanthropy and Colonial Slavery: The American
Correspondence of the Associates of Dr. Bray, 1717-1777
John C. Van Horne

Black History and the Historical Profession, 1915-1980
August Meier and Elliott Rudwick

Rise to Be a People: A Biography of Paul Cuffe
Lamont D. Thomas

Reprint Editions

King: A Biography
David Levering Lewis   Second edition

The Death and Life of Malcolm X
Peter Goldman   Second edition

Race Relations in the Urban South, 1865-1890
Howard N. Rabinowitz, with a Foreword by C. Vann Woodward

Race Riot at East St. Louis, July 2, 1917
Elliott Rudwick

W. E. B. Du Bois: Voice of the Black Protest Movement
Elliott Rudwick

The Negro's Civil War: How American Negroes Felt and Acted during
the War for the Union   *James M. McPherson*

Lincoln and Black Freedom: A Study in Presidential Leadership
LaWanda Cox